P9-CDZ-247

[Hiking Ohio]

Gary S. Williams

Human Kinetics

917.71
W1L

Library of Congress Cataloging-in-Publication Data

Williams, Gary S.
    Hiking Ohio / Gary S. Williams.
        pages cm
    1. Hiking--Ohio--Guidebooks. 2. Trails--Ohio--Guidebooks. 3. Ohio--Guidebooks. I. Title.
    GV199.42.O32W55 2014
    796.5109771--dc23
                        2013013511

ISBN-10: 1-4504-1253-X (print)
ISBN-13: 978-1-4504-1253-7 (print)

Copyright © 2014 by Gary S. Williams

All rights reserved. Except for use in a review, the reproduction or utilization of this work in any form or by any electronic, mechanical, or other means, now known or hereafter invented, including xerography, photocopying, and recording, and in any information storage and retrieval system, is forbidden without the written permission of the publisher.

The maps in this book were created with reference to multiple sources. Primary reference information for maps on the following pages was provided by the Ohio Department of Natural Resources: 4, 5, 24, 25, 27, 28, 30, 31, 33, 34, 39, 40, 42, 44, 57, 58, 59, 66, 67, 71, 73, 75, 76, 82, 83, 85, 86, 95, 97, 99, 101, 102, 104, 105, 108, 109, 110, 112, 113, 114, 116, 117, 120, 121, 123, 145, 146, 150, 151, 162, 163, 198, 199, 201, 203, 214, 215, 217, 218, 225, 226, 228, 230, 233, 234, 236, 237, 239, 240, 243, 245, 247, 248, 251, 252, 258, 259. Primary reference information for other maps was gathered from the following sources: Maps on pages 8, 10, 11, 13 Cleveland Metroparks; 15, 16, 19, 20, 21, 22 National Park Service, USDOT; 36, 37 Lake Metroparks; 46, 47 Muskingum Watershed Conservancy District; 49, 50 Norma Johnson Center; 52, 54 Ohio & Erie Canalway Association; 62, 64 Stark County Park District; 78, 79 Broughton Nature and Wildlife Education Area; 89, 90 Ohio University; 92, 93, 181, 183, 185, 186, 193, 196, 221, 222 Ohio Historical Society; 125, 126, 129, 131, 132, 133, 134,135, 137, 138 USDA Forest Service; 141, 143 The Wilds (The International Center for the Preservation of Wild Animals, Inc.); 154, 156, 158, 160 Columbus and Franklin County Metropolitan Park District; 165, 166 Cincinnati Parks; 169, 171, 172 The Nature Conservancy; 175, 176, 177, 179 Five Rivers Metroparks; 188, 189 Antioch College; 191, 192 Great Parks of Hamilton County; 206, 207 Miami County Park District; 209, 211 Ohio Historical Society and City of Piqua, Ohio; 254, 255 Ohio Department of Natural Resources and Miami and Erie Canal Corridor Association; 262, 263, 269, 271 Metroparks of the Toledo Area; 265, 267 Sandusky County Park District.

The web addresses cited in this text were current as of December 2013, unless otherwise noted.

Acquisitions Editor: Tom Heine; **Developmental Editor:** Anne Hall; **Assistant Editor:** Tyler M. Wolpert; **Copyeditor:** Pat Connolly; **Graphic Designer:** Nancy Rasmus; **Graphic Artist:** Julie L. Denzer; **Cover Designer:** Keith Blomberg; **Photograph (cover):** Gary S. Williams; **Photographs (interior):** Gary S. Williams; **Photo Asset Manager:** Laura Fitch; **Visual Production Assistant:** Joyce Brumfield; **Photo Production Manager:** Jason Allen; **Art Manager:** Kelly Hendren; **Associate Art Manager:** Alan L. Wilborn; **Illustrations:** © Human Kinetics; **Printer:** Sheridan Books

Printed in the United States of America   10 9 8 7 6 5 4 3 2 1

The paper in this book is certified under a sustainable forestry program.

Human Kinetics
Website: www.HumanKinetics.com

United States: Human Kinetics
P.O. Box 5076
Champaign, IL 61825-5076
800-747-4457
e-mail: humank@hkusa.com

Canada: Human Kinetics
475 Devonshire Road Unit 100
Windsor, ON N8Y 2L5
800-465-7301 (in Canada only)
e-mail: info@hkcanada.com

Europe: Human Kinetics
107 Bradford Road
Stanningley
Leeds LS28 6AT, United Kingdom
+44 (0) 113 255 5665
e-mail: hk@hkeurope.com

Australia: Human Kinetics
57A Price Avenue
Lower Mitcham, South Australia 5062
08 8372 0999
e-mail: info@hkaustralia.com

New Zealand: Human Kinetics
P.O. Box 80
Torrens Park, South Australia 5062
0800 222 062
e-mail: info@hknewzealand.com

E5486

Hiking Ohio

Contents

Southwest

Northwest

Trail Finder

#	Park	Trails	Miles	Difficulty	Hills	Prairie/grass	Forest	Lake	Wetlands	Overlook	River/stream	Rock formations	Page #
Northeast													
1	Beaver Creek State Park	Beaver Creek State Park Trail	2.8	3 boots			X			X	X	X	5
2	Cleveland Metroparks	Hinckley Reservation: Whipps Ledges and Hinckley Lake	4.3	3 boots	X			X	X		X	X	9
		Bedford Reservation: Tinker's Creek Gorge and Buckeye Trail	3.8	3 boots	X		X			X	X		12
3	Cuyahoga Valley National Park	Three Waterfalls Hike	5.0	4 boots	X		X			X	X		17
		Towpath and Deep Lock Quarry Trails	2.8	1 boot			X			X	X	X	20
		Ledges Trail	2.2	3 boots	X		X			X		X	21
		Towpath Trail, Botzum to Ira and Back	3.4	2 boots			X		X		X		22
4	Eagle Creek State Nature Preserve	Clubmoss Trail	2.0	2 boots		X	X	X	X				25
5	Fernwood State Forest	Fernwood State Forest Trail	3.5	3 boots	X		X	X			X		28
6	Findley State Park	Findley State Park, Buckeye Trail	1.2	2 boots			X	X	X				31

RV camping   Canoeing   Picnicking

Tent camping   Fishing   Biking

Swimming   Boating

#	Park	Trails	Miles	Difficulty	Hills	Prairie/grass	Forest	Lake	Wetlands	Overlook	River/stream	Rock formations	Page #
Northeast > *continued*													
16	West Branch State Park	West Branch State Park, Buckeye Trail	9.0	🥾🥾🥾🥾			X	X					67
Southeast													
17	Blackhand Gorge State Nature Preserve	Blackhand and Quarry Rim Trails	2.5	🥾🥾	X		X		X		X	X	72
18	Boord State Nature Preserve	Boord State Nature Preserve	0.7	🥾	X		X			X			76
19	Broughton Nature and Wildlife Education Area	Southwest Overlook, Western Ridge and Valley Trails	2.0	🥾🥾🥾	X		X						79
20	Burr Oak State Park	Buckeye Loop, Tanager and Chipmunk Trails	2.6	🥾🥾🥾	X		X	X					83
21	Conkle's Hollow State Nature Preserve	Rim and Gorge Trails	3.0	🥾🥾🥾	X		X			X		X	86
22	Dysart Woods Outdoor Laboratory	Dysart Woods Red and Blue Trails	1.5	🥾🥾🥾	X		X						90
23	Flint Ridge State Memorial	Quarry and Creek Trails	2.0	🥾🥾	X		X					X	93
24	Hocking Hills State Park	Grandma Gatewood and Rim Trails	6.0	🥾🥾🥾	X		X			X	X	X	96
		Ash Cave to Cedar Falls	5.5	🥾🥾🥾	X		X			X			98
		Rock House	0.5	🥾🥾	X		X					X	100
		Cantwell Cliffs	1.0	🥾🥾🥾	X		X					X	102
25	Hocking State Forest	Hocking State Forest, Buckeye Trail	7.5	🥾🥾🥾🥾	X		X			X		X	105

(continued) ix

#	Park	Trails	Miles	Difficulty	Hills	Prairie/grass	Forest	Lake	Wetlands	Overlook	River/stream	Rock formations	Page #
Southwest													
35	Caesar Creek State Park	Spillway Trail	1.6	🥾🥾	X		X	X			X		151
36	Columbus Metro Parks	Highbanks Metro Park Trail	3.4	🥾🥾		X	X	X	X	X	X		157
		Blendon Woods Metro Park Trail	2.4	🥾🥾	X		X	X	X				159
37	East Fork State Park	Backpack Trail and Backcountry Trail Loop	5.0	🥾🥾🥾	X		X	X					163
38	Eden Park, Cincinnati Park District	Eden Park Trail	2.0	🥾🥾	X			X		X			166
39	Edge of Appalachia Preserve	Buzzardroost Rock Trail	3.5	🥾🥾🥾	X					X		X	170
		Lynx Prairie Trail	1.5	🥾		X	X						172
40	Five Rivers Metroparks	Taylorsville Dam to Tadmor	2.6	🥾🥾							X		177
		Englewood Metropark, White and Green Trails	2.4	🥾🥾	X		X				X		178
41	Fort Ancient State Memorial	Earthworks Terrace and Connector Trails	1.5	🥾🥾	X	X	X			X	X	X	182
42	Fort Hill State Memorial	Fort Trail	2.3	🥾🥾🥾	X		X			X		X	186
43	Glen Helen Nature Preserve	Glen Helen Natural Area	1.5	🥾🥾	X		X				X	X	189

(continued)

					Landscape								
#	Park	Trails	Miles	Difficulty	Hills	Prairie/grass	Forest	Lake	Wetlands	Overlook	River/stream	Rock formations	Page #
Northwest													
55	Delaware State Park	Lakeview Trail	1.6	🥾🥾			X	X					234
56	Goll Woods State Nature Preserve	Toadshade Trail	1.6	🥾🥾		X	X				X		237
57	Independence Dam State Park	Towpath and Buckeye Trail	4.8	🥾🥾🥾							X		240
58	Kelley's Island State Park	Kelley's Island North Shore Loop Trail	4.6	🥾🥾🥾				X	X	X		X	244
59	Magee Marsh Wildlife Area	Magee Marsh Walking Trail	1.0	🥾					X	X	X		248
60	Maumee Bay State Park	Boardwalk Trail	2.2	🥾🥾			X	X	X	X			252
61	Miami and Erie Canal Corridor	Miami and Erie Towpath Trail, Deep Cut to Bloody Bridge	5.3	🥾🥾🥾		X					X		255
62	Mt. Gilead State Park	Lakeside Trail	1.7	🥾🥾🥾	X		X	X					259
63	Oak Openings Preserve Metropark	Sand Dunes Trail	1.9	🥾🥾		X	X						262
64	Sandusky County Parks	Wolf Creek Park, Buckeye Trail	3.0	🥾🥾			X				X		265
65	Toledo Metroparks	Farnsworth to Bend View Metroparks	6.8	🥾🥾🥾					X	X	X	X	270

Acknowledgments

I would like to thank Human Kinetics—and editor Anne Hall and acquisitions editor Tom Heine in particular—for giving me the opportunity to write *Hiking Ohio*. The excellent maps are the work of Joe LeMonnier. I would also like to thank Bob Pond for recommending me for this project.

Thanks should also go to all of the employees and volunteers throughout the state who work to build and maintain trails. Particular gratitude is extended to the Buckeye Trail Association, an all-volunteer group that builds and maintains a 1,440-mile loop trail that loops around Ohio. Approximately half of the hikes in this book are either on, or connect with, the Buckeye Trail.

Among the truest friends of this book are the friends who did the hikes with me. Solitary hiking can be wonderful and beneficial, and many of the hikes in this book were done solo. But being out in the woods with kindred spirits is one of the best things a person can do, and I would like to thank all of those who hiked with me, including the following: Steve Cooper, Mark Hagloch, Paul Hagloch, Ed Haglock, Travis Haglock, Bill Hanner, Bob Hirche, Al Klammer, Dave Lentz, Bob McGregor, Alan Marcosson, Kevin Moore, Nancy Piunno, Bob and Connie Pond, Tim Straub, Ron Swegheimer, Steve Tristano, Brian Williams, Lee Ann Williams, Meryl Williams, Luke Williams, Owen Williams, and Larry Zachrich. All of these folks came along on hikes, and many of them also offered their homes for overnight stays all over the state.

And finally, none of this would have been possible without the support and inspiration of my new bride, Lee Ann. In thanks for the reawakening that she brought to my life, I would like to dedicate this book to her.

How to Use This Book

Whether done alone, with kindred spirits, or in a large group, hiking is one of the most beneficial activities that a person can engage in. Hiking is great for both body and mind, and it requires little more than legs, spaces, and a desire to stretch and explore. Every state in the country has plenty of good places to hike, but Ohio has surprisingly varied options. Ohio is a great state for hiking because it is a microcosm of what the entire country contains. The state may not have snow-capped mountains, but the rugged hills of southern Ohio can involve an unbroken series of invigorating climbs. And Ohio may not have a seacoast, but the rocky shores of Lake Erie sure make for a good approximation. The routes of the trails in this book will take you past sand dunes, Indian mounds, cliffs and gorges, canals and rivers, flat farmland, hills both rolling and steep, swamps and marshes, and 500-year-old trees. Hikers in Ohio can be treated to a wide variety of both natural and human history.

All of the hikes in this book are meant to be completed in a single day. Some may take all day or lead to backpacking areas that offer multiple-day trips, while others may be less than a half-mile stroll. The majority of these hikes could easily be completed by a family, and I did almost all of them without a daypack while wearing tennis shoes. When hiking boots or walking sticks are recommended for a particular hike, this is noted in the text. All the hikes are located on land that is open to the public.

The hikes are broken down by what quadrant of the state they are in. This method of quartering the state is somewhat arbitrary, because the geological regions of the state tend to blend together. But each section of the book includes an introduction that discusses this and puts these distinctions in perspective. Another connector between the various regions is the Buckeye Trail. At 1,440 miles in length, this is the longest single-state loop hiking trail in the country. The Buckeye Trail passes through over half of Ohio's 88 counties as it loops around Ohio. Built and maintained by the all-volunteer Buckeye Trail Association, the Buckeye Trail is divided into 26 sections of about 50 miles each. Because of difficulties in finding public lands, it's not currently practical for people to through-hike the Buckeye Trail as they do the Appalachian Trail; however, the Buckeye Trail does pass through the best hiking and camping portions of the state. And the Buckeye Trail is also part of a national trails network. The southern portion of the Buckeye Trail is concurrent with the American Discovery Trail, which runs from Delaware to California. Also, much of the western and southern portions of the Buckeye Trail are shared with the North Country Trail, which goes from North Dakota to New York. Approximately half of the hikes in this guide are either on or connect with the Buckeye Trail.

Within each of the four regions of the state, the hikes are arranged geographically by owning agency. Many of them are within Ohio State Parks. Despite recent budget cuts, the 72 state parks in the Ohio system still offer a variety of hiking and camping options. Many state parks have nature centers, and a handful also offer lodges. Other trails are found in less developed state forests, which offer more isolated trails with fewer amenities. And even more primitive trails are located in state nature preserves that are intended to protect unique features and may require permission for access. State parks, forests, and preserves with the same name are often found adjacent to each other, because it wasn't until 1949 that the state of Ohio separated public land by intended usage. There is not much federal land in Ohio, except for two fortunate exceptions. In southeastern Ohio, the Wayne National Forest contains 238,000 acres that are administered in three separate regions. This forest land offers some of the most rugged and isolated hikes in the state. In northeastern Ohio, the Cuyahoga Valley National Park offers a multitude of spectacular day trips found in the most populated part of the state. This text also includes several hikes in various urban metropolitan park systems, a selected number of county park systems, and a few privately owned preserves that are open to the public.

This guide contains separate chapters for 64 parks, and the same categories of information are supplied in each chapter. Each chapter begins with a brief description of the highlights of the park; then, area information is provided in detail. For each chapter, the following information is also provided: directions to the park, hours open, facilities offered, rules and permits, other hiking trails (when applicable),

contact information, and other areas of interest nearby. Many of the chapters cover only a single hike, while a few contain information for several hikes. Many of the hikes in the book follow more than one named trail. Standard information is provided for each of the 83 hikes in this book. This information includes distance, estimated hiking time, and a difficulty rating of 1 (easiest) to 5 (most difficult) boots. Directions to the trail head are provided, as well as text that guides you through the hike and explains major junctions and highlights. And, of course, excellent maps of all hikes and parks are provided. Cautions are given where applicable, and the information is as current as possible, although scouting ahead is always recommended.

These are not necessarily the 83 best hikes in Ohio. The hikes here were selected in part for their variety, and there are plenty of other great hikes located near the ones described here. The particular trails chosen here within a park are merely a suggested route, and hikers are encouraged to customize their path. The important thing is to get out and enjoy Ohio's outdoors.

[Ohio]

Northeast

The northeast quadrant of Ohio roughly corresponds with what is called the Western Reserve. This region is part of the Western Glaciated Allegheny Plateau, and the glacier that passed through left behind rounded hills among ponds, bogs, and wetlands. These lands were claimed by colonial Connecticut when that colony claimed all land coast to coast between its northern and southern borders. Connecticut forfeited its claims after the American Revolution on the condition that first crack at purchasing land in this area be reserved for veterans from that state. The result is that this region has a sort of New England feel to it with quaint village greens in towns named for their English founders. This is enhanced by the fact that Geauga County gets 5 times as much annual snowfall as the rest of the state because of lake effect squalls.

The main river here is the Cuyahoga, a crooked river that runs south before turning north around Akron and meeting Lake Erie at Cleveland. This stretch is home to the splendors of Cuyahoga Valley National Park. It seems odd to think of a national park between Akron and Cleveland, but beneath the interstates that cross the area is a park that features 125 miles of trail. Much of this trail also follows the route of the Ohio and Erie Canal Towpath Trail that runs from Cleveland to Zoar. Side trails from that multi-purpose trail through the rocky hills lead to attractions such as the 65-foot Brandywine Falls, the most impressive waterfall in Ohio.

Below Akron, the canal route passes into the south-flowing Tuscarawas, which is part of the Muskingum watershed that drains one-fifth of the state. The Muskingum Watershed Conservancy District has constructed a series of recreational lakes that all have hiking trails. To the east, Beaver Creek State Park follows a feeder canal along a rocky stream on the Pennsylvania border. To the west, Malabar Farm State Park offers a literary-themed hike to a hill that offers a view of the entire route.

This part of the state contains a variety of wildflowers and trees that are present throughout the state. Not only are the usual white-tailed deer found here, but recently, bald eagles and black bear have been seen moving west from Pennsylvania.

> Hike along a rocky stream reminiscent of the Appalachians.
> View the remains of Ohio's canal era.
> Tour an old-fashioned restored pioneer village.
> See an area with connections to many villains from Ohio's past.

Area Information

Established as an Ohio State Park in 1949, Beaver Creek offers over 2,700 acres of land and water located near where Ohio, Pennsylvania, and West Virginia meet. The Little Beaver Creek valley is the only known stream in the country containing evidence of all four major glaciers to have once been present on the continent. Today the stream is bordered by steep sandstone cliffs in several places. Among the trees found in the park are some that are normally found in more northern climates. In addition to common wildlife such as raccoon, deer, wild turkey, and various waterfowl, increasing numbers of black bears are seen in the area. These bears are usually yearlings from western Pennsylvania in search of mates.

In terms of human history, evidence of native life has been found near Beaver Creek that goes back nearly 10,000 years. By the time white men appeared in the area in the 1700s, Beaver Creek was a part of an Indian trail that connected Fort Pitt to Detroit. In the 1840s, this same route was used for the Sandy and Beaver Canal, which ran for 73 miles from the Ohio River to the Ohio and Erie Canal. Construction of the 90 locks and 30 dams required for the thoroughfare took several years, and by the time it was completed in 1851, railroads were already starting to make canals obsolete. Several of the old canal locks are on the trails that line the creek, and many of them have tales that go along with them.

Another historical theme of the area is the presence of some of the bad guys of history. One of the abandoned locks has been named Simon Girty's Lock, in dishonor of the notorious renegade who skulked in the area during the American Revolution while leading Indian raids on his former neighbors near Pittsburgh. In the park on Sprucevale Road is the spot where bank robber Pretty Boy Floyd was gunned down in 1934. And just a few miles away, near West Point, is the spot where Confederate cavalry general John Hunt Morgan surrendered at the end of his famous raid in 1863.

In the park today is a Pioneer Village and Gaston's Mill, several concentrated buildings that show how life was lived there in the 1830s. The turbulent nature of the rocky stream bed makes for ideal canoeing but also contributes to an abundance of mill grinding. Gaston's Mill still grinds meal today, and the abandoned Hambleton's Mill stands a few miles downstream. Also near Pioneer Village is the Beaver Creek Wildlife Education Center.

Directions: Beaver Creek State Park is 2 miles east of SR 170, just north of East Liverpool.

Hours open: The park is open year round.

Facilities: Three picnic areas provide restrooms, tables, and grills. Camping includes 6 electric and 44 nonelectric sites and 59 equestrian sites. There is also a group camping area and two teepees that can be rented seasonally. Also available are fishing, hunting and sledding areas, a horseshoe pit, playground equipment, and an archery range.

Rules and permits: Licenses must be obtained for hunting and fishing.

Contact information: Beaver Creek State Park, 12021 Echo Dell Road, East Liverpool, Ohio 43920. The park phone number is 330-385-3091.

Park Trails

There are six hiking-only trails:

Fitness Trail, 0.5 mile

Logan's Loop, 0.5 mile

Nature Center Trail, 0.2 mile

Overlook Trail, 0.3 mile

Oak Hill Trail, 1 mile

Upper Vondergreen Trail, 1 mile

▌ The Pioneer Village in Beaver Creek State Park is located near the covered bridge trailhead.

There are three biking trails that permit hiking:

Pine Ridge Trail, 0.5 mile

Fisherman's Trail, 0.5 mile

Lower Vondergreen Trail, 3.35 miles

In addition, there are 23 miles of bridle trails. Much of the hiking trail mileage is a part of the North Country Trail, a 3,000-plus-mile trail that runs from North Dakota to New York.

Other Areas of Interest

Guilford Lake State Park, near Lisbon, has a 10-horsepower limit.

Jefferson Lake State Park, near Richmond, allows only boats with electric motors.

Highlandtown Wildlife Area, off SR 39, offers 2,000 acres for hunting and fishing on a 170-acre lake that permits boats with electric motors only.

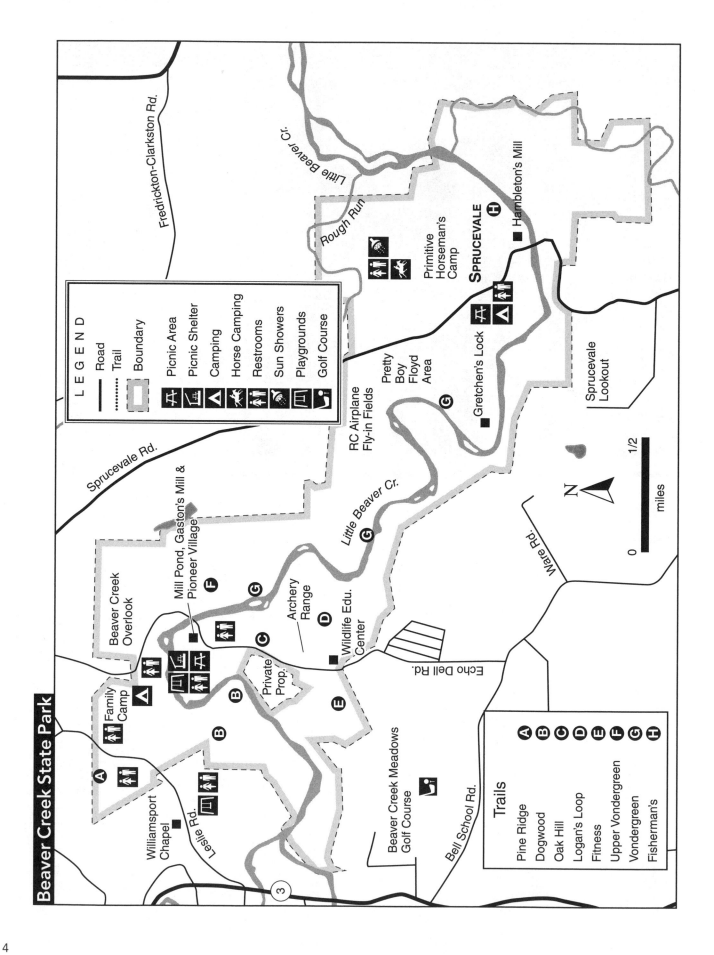

Beaver Creek State Park Trail

Hiking distance: 2.8 miles one way

Estimated hiking time: 2 hours

Enjoy a rugged hike alongside a weathered stream.

Caution: Trail along the riverbed is rough, rocky, and hilly with many roots and rocks sticking out to trip you up.

Trail directions: Leave SR7 north of East Liverpool at Bell School Road. Go about a mile past Echo Dell Road, which is the main entrance to the park. Go another 1.5 miles to Cannon's Mill Road and take it for a half mile. Take the first left onto CR428 and go for a mile down a steep hill, but on the way stop and admire the view of the stream valley at the Sprucevale Overlook. At the bottom of the hill, cross Little Beaver Creek and turn left at the abandoned Hambleton's Mill. Follow the road to the end of the paved parking area at N 40° 42.294, W 80° 35.144 (1).

Enter into the forest here, but stay to the left and keep on the trail closest to Little Beaver Creek. This stream has a rocky bed that is reminiscent of New England or the Appalachians and in fact is the only canoeable stream in Ohio that has anything as challenging as class II rapids. But it is also the site of the Sandy and Beaver Canal, a 73-mile corridor that connected the Ohio River to the Tuscarawas River at Bolivar. Despite the immense work involved in the construction, the canal was used for only a few years in the 1850s.

Following the stream's bank is not as easy as it sounds. The trail has some pretty steep hills; after a 0.8-mile walk to the tallest one, it becomes necessary to climb down a wooden ladder placed along a rock face at 40 42 671/80 35 669 (2). Once you drop down about 40 feet, the trail along the bank is still rocky, wet, and slippery. At 1.2 miles you will come to Gretchen's Lock at 40 42 841/80 35 755 (3), which is the first of a series of canal locks you will encounter. Gretchen was the daughter of the canal's chief engineer. When she died of malaria during construction, her father had her entombed in the lock until he could take her body with him on his return to Europe. The boat sank on this voyage, and the bodies of father and daughter were lost at sea. Her ghost is said to haunt the lock today.

Continue along the stream bank, noting the sandstone cliffs and hemlock trees in abundance. The area is also popular with horse riders, and you may see them crossing the

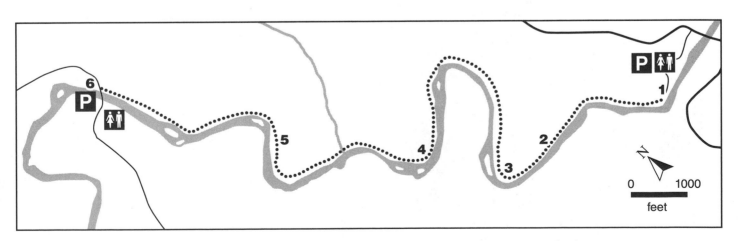

1. Lot
2. Wooden ladder
3. Gretchen's Lock
4. Vondergreen's Lock
5. Gray's Lock
6. Covered bridge

stream at various fords. In another 0.2 mile, you will arrive at Vondergreen's Lock at 40 42 770/80 35 964 (4). Here the riverside trail rejoins the main trail, which is now called the Vondergreen Trail. Less than a mile from here, back on Sprucevale Road, is where notorious bank robber Pretty Boy Floyd was killed in a shootout with G-Men on October 22, 1934. Also just a few miles away is the spot where Confederate cavalry General John Hunt Morgan surrendered at the end of his ill-fated 1863 raid into Ohio.

Continue on for another 0.6 mile until you get to Gray's Lock at 40 43 111/80 36 379 (5). A plaque explains more about the canal locks. In another 0.2 mile, the trail splits into Upper and Lower Vondergreen Trails. Stick to the white blazed lower trail that follows the stream. Proceed along the banks for another 2/3 mile until you get to the bridge at Pioneer Village at N 40° 42.657, W 80° 35.688 (6). Here you can cross over to a large parking lot and Pioneer Village.

Pioneer Village features a restored canal lock, log cabins, chapel, covered bridge, schoolhouse, blacksmith shop, trading post, and the 1830 Gaston Mill, which still operates for tourists today. It can also be approached from Echo Dell Road if you want to spot a car for a one-way trip, or you can return the way you came.

> Tour the Emerald Necklace of public land that rings the Cleveland metro area.
> Take advantage of hundreds of miles of trails in 16 reservations.
> View a variety of wildflowers and rock formations over a wide area.

Area Information

The most famous Cleveland Metropark may be the highly regarded zoo in the city, but the system actually comprises 16 separate parks, or reservations, that encircle the land around the metropolitan area. Known as the Emerald Necklace, the Metroparks system covers 21,000 acres and includes hundreds of miles of trails. There are 60 miles of paved trail for multiple uses and many more for specialized uses such as cycling, riding, and hiking. The park system also contains several nature centers, eight golf courses, and the aforementioned Cleveland Zoo.

The various reservations that form the Emerald Necklace tend to follow the rivers and creeks that flow through the region. This has resulted in a system that expands beyond one city or even one single county; parts of the Metroparks system are also in Lake, Summit, Lorain, Medina, and Cuyahoga counties. Some of the reservations are Other Areas of Interest included in Cuyahoga Valley National Park but are administered under the Metroparks system.

This is the oldest metro park system in Ohio. The man with the vision was city engineer William Stinchcomb, whose tireless efforts accounted for the purchase of most of the park land in the 1920s. Stinchcomb was able to set up taxing authority so that public land would be available to all. And that is certainly true today, because the Metroparks hosted nearly 17 million recreational visits in 2010. Many of these visits were to the zoo or various public golf courses, but the parks also hosted many outdoor lovers eager to sample the natural diversity of the region.

Directions: The Metroparks form a ring around the Cleveland metropolitan area, although it is not contiguous; there is a breach on the east side and on the southwest.

Hours open: Admission is free and basically unlimited during daylight hours year-round. Special programs at specialized locations will have more specific hours.

Facilities: Numerous trails, shelters, picnic areas, fishing spots, and nature and education centers exist through the system. There are also 8 municipal golf courses and the Cleveland Zoo. Each of the 16 reservations that make up the system has its own special offerings.

Rules and permits: Camping is not allowed because most visitors from the nearby metro area are day users. Pets must be on leashes, and cyclists and horseback riders must stay on designated trails.

Contact information: The park office is at 4101 Fulton Parkway, Cleveland, Ohio 44144. The phone number is 216-635-3200.

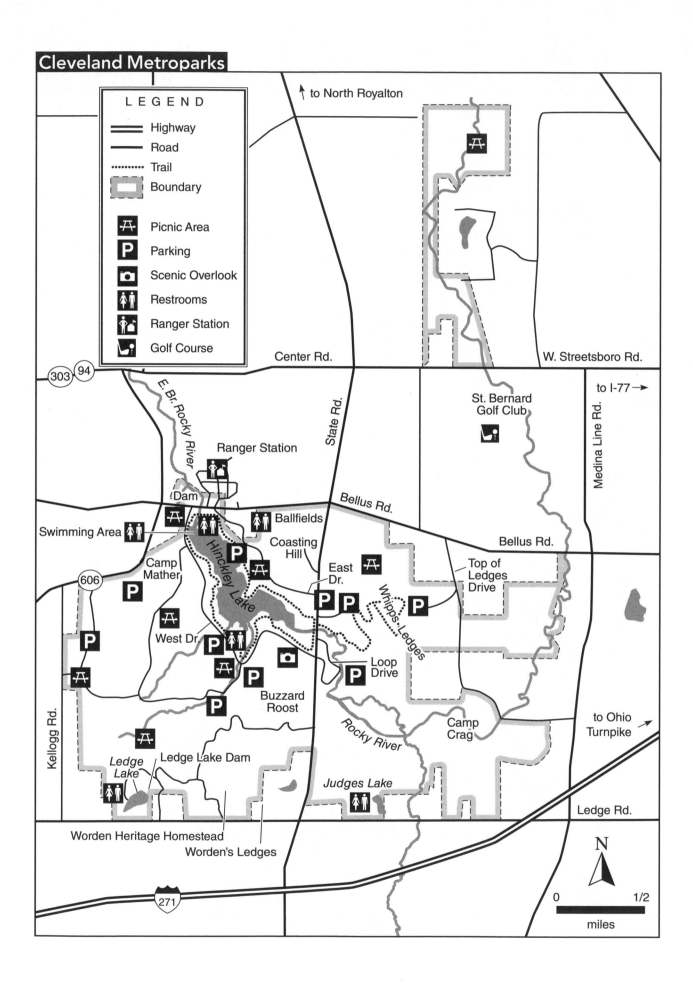

Cleveland Metroparks

LEGEND

- ═══ Highway
- ─── Road
- ···· Trail
- ▢ Boundary
- 🏕 Picnic Area
- P Parking
- 📷 Scenic Overlook
- 🚻 Restrooms
- 👤 Ranger Station
- 🏌 Golf Course

to North Royalton

Center Rd.

W. Streetsboro Rd.

303 94

E. Br. Rocky River

State Rd.

to I-77 →

St. Bernard Golf Club

Medina Line Rd.

Ranger Station

Dam

Bellus Rd.

Swimming Area

Ballfields

Coasting Hill

Bellus Rd.

Hinckley Lake

East Dr.

Top of Ledges Drive

Camp Mather

606

Whipps Ledges

P

West Dr.

Loop Drive

Buzzard Roost

Rocky River

Camp Crag

to Ohio Turnpike

Kellogg Rd.

Ledge Lake

Ledge Lake Dam

Judges Lake

Ledge Rd.

Worden Heritage Homestead

Worden's Ledges

N

271

0   1/2

miles

Hinckley Reservation: Whipps Ledges and Hinckley Lake

Hiking distance: 4.3 miles

Estimated hiking time: 2.5 hours

Hike among some impressive Sharon Conglomerate formations and look for buzzards.

Caution: Stay off of dangerous cliffs except in designated areas.

Trail directions: Take State Route 303 between the Richfield exit off Interstate 77 and the Brunswick exit off Interstate 71. Three miles east of Hinckley, go south on State Road, cross Bellus Road, and turn left at the Whipps Ledges Picnic Area and Trailhead. Park near the restrooms at N 41° 13.135, W 81° 42.214 (1). Enter the woods and begin climbing into an area with impressive rock formations. These Sharon Conglomerate ledges are unique because they are composed of rounded quartz embedded into sandstone. They are also an impressive 50 feet high and over 350 million years old and rise some 350 feet above the elevation of nearby Hinckley Lake.

❚ It's easy to get lost among the rocks at Whipps Ledges.

After about 0.3 mile the Whipps Ledges trail meets the Buckeye Trail at N 41° 13.226, W 81° 42.079 (2). One option is to continue on to the Top O' Ledges Picnic Area, but for now, turn right and follow the Buckeye Trail back toward point 1. The Buckeye Trail soon meets the east branch of the Rocky River at N 41° 13.008, W 81.42 204 (3) and follows it toward Hinckley Lake. Follow this stream through a marshy area for about 0.2 mile and cross State Road. At N 41° 13.116, W 81° 42.395 (4), the Buckeye Trail turns off south here, but you should go straight on the Hinckley Lake Loop Trail for another 0.1 mile until reaching the shores of the lake at N 41° 13.150, W 81° 42.543 (5).

The beautiful 90-acre Hinckley Lake was formed when the east branch was dammed in 1926. Walking along the shore past several scenic fishing spots offers abundant opportunities to observe various waterfowl. But these aren't the birds that Hinckley is most famous for. As Capistrano has its swallows, Hinckley has its buzzards. Every year on March 15, crowds gather to watch for the return of the buzzards (who are actually turkey vultures) from their southern migration, one of the few occasions when these ugly carrion eaters are welcomed by enthusiastic crowds.

Follow the scenic lakeshore for 0.8 mile to where it crosses East Drive at N 41° 13.495, W 81° 42.858 (6). Restrooms are here at the Indian Point Picnic Area. Continue on for another 0.3 mile, where the trail recrosses East Road at the junction with Bellus Road at N 41° 13.667, W 81.43 056 (7). Here is the main parking lot for Hinckley Lake that is used for the public swimming area. Continue along Bellus Road past the Spillway Picnic Area across the road from the park office. Restrooms are available here.

In about 0.2 mile, the trail turns south at the junction with West Drive at N 41° 13.689,

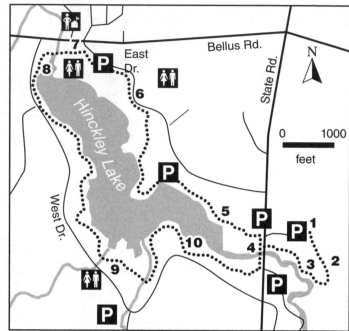

1. Lot
2. Meet Buckeye Trail
3. Meet East Branch of Rocky River
4. Cross road
5. Lake shore
6. Cross road
7. Left at Bellus Road
8. Left on West Drive
9. Boathouse Road
10. Rejoin Buckeye Trail

W 81° 43.231 (8). Follow the shoreline past the turnoff for the Redwing Picnic Area and continue for 0.8 mile to the junction with Boathouse Road at N 41° 13.089, W 81° 43.096 (9). Veer left here and follow the route past the Boathouse Trailhead to Johnson's Picnic Area, both of which have restrooms. At the end of the paved road at the picnic area, the Buckeye Trail rejoins the trail at N 41° 13.015, W 81° 42.825 (10). Continue to follow the Buckeye Trail around the rest of the lake until returning to point 4. From here, it is shorter to cross State Road and walk along the Whipps Ledges Picnic Area road to return to point 1.

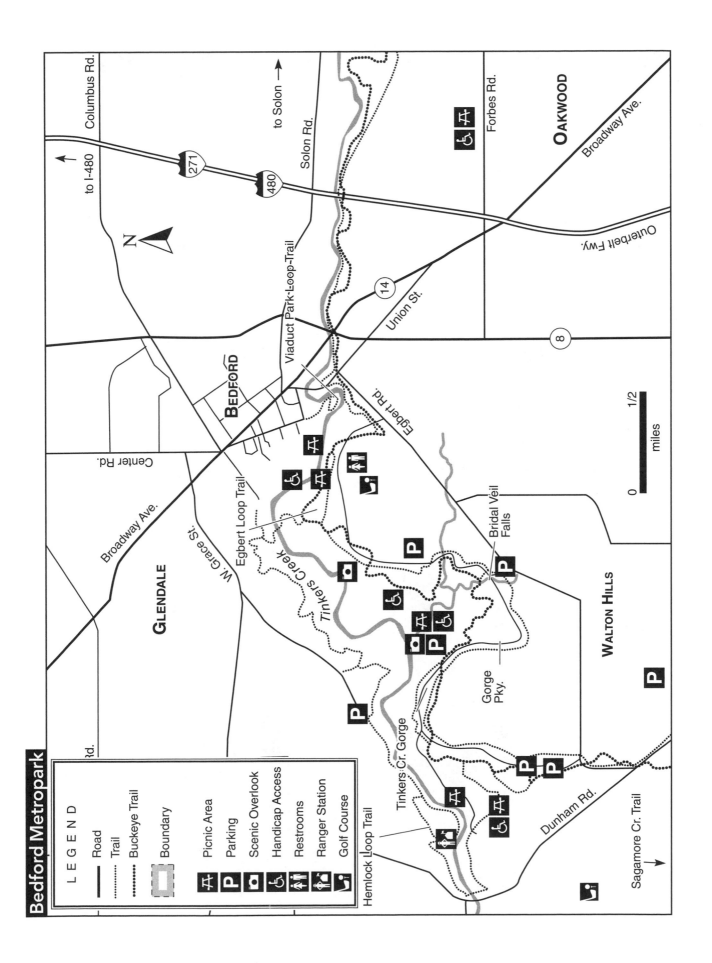

Bedford Metropark

L E G E N D

——	Road
⋯⋯	Trail
∙∙∙∙∙	Buckeye Trail
▢	Boundary

Picnic Area
Parking
Scenic Overlook
Handicap Access
Restrooms
Ranger Station
Golf Course

Columbus Rd.

to I-480

to Solon →

271

480

Solon Rd.

N

Viaduct Park Loop Trail

BEDFORD

14

Union St.

8

Center Rd.

Broadway Ave.

GLENDALE

W. Grace St.

Egbert Loop Trail

Egbert Rd.

Tinkers Creek

P

P

P

Bridal Veil Falls

P

Forbes Rd.

OAKWOOD

Broadway Ave.

Outerbelt Fwy.

WALTON HILLS

Gorge Pky.

Tinkers Cr. Gorge

P

P

P

Hemlock Loop Trail

Dunham Rd.

Sagamore Cr. Trail

0   1/2
miles

11

Bedford Reservation: Tinker's Creek Gorge and Buckeye Trail

Hiking distance: 3.8 miles

Estimated hiking time: 2 hours

Take a rugged hike through a national natural landmark and view a scenic waterfall.

Caution: This trail is steep in spots.

Trail directions: Bordered by Interstates 77, 80, 271, and 480, Tinker's Creek can best be accessed by exiting 480 at State Route 14 and heading south. At the junction with State Route 17 (Granger Road) is a turnoff for Dunham Road. Take Dunham south to where it meets Tinker's Creek at the Gorge Parkway. Turn left and follow the Gorge Parkway to the Gorge Scenic Overlook lot at N 41° 22.637, W 81° 33.532 (1). Park here near the restrooms and check out the view.

This route is on the Buckeye Trail, which crosses the parkway and enters the woods in 0.1 mile at N 41° 22.581, W 81° 33.461 (2).

❙ Tinker's Creek Gorge is known for spectacular views.

The Bedford Reservation contains 2,154 acres centered on the scenic gorge of Tinker's Creek as it approaches confluence with the Cuyahoga River. The area lies within the boundaries of the Cuyahoga Valley National Park but is administered by the Cleveland Metroparks system. The steep gorge has been designated a national natural landmark.

Begin descending immediately through a mixed-hardwood forest that offers an array of wildflowers in spring and a variety of ferns most of the year. It is about 0.6 mile to Bridal Veil Falls at N 41° 22.416, W 81° 32.973 (3). A deck has been built here overlooking the gentle cascade of the falls. After a bridge at the head of the falls is a set of stairs at N 41° 22.370, W 81° 32.968 (4) that leads up to a parking lot at 0.3 mile away for those who prefer driving to the falls.

Continue for another 0.3 mile to where the trail rises up alongside the Gorge Parkway at N 41° 22.550, W 81° 32.745 (5). The parkway is a busy thoroughfare but is more likely to be filled with bicyclists and slow-moving drivers out enjoying the scenery. The trail parallels the parkway briefly before dropping off steeply into the woods again. In about 0.3 mile, the trail crosses a road at N 41° 22.635, W 81° 33.027 (6). This is the road to Lost Meadows Picnic Area, and a left turn and short walk lead to restrooms.

Continue through the forest, and in another 0.3 mile the trail ascends onto the parkway at N 41° 22.845, W 81° 32.872 (7). The trail now crosses the parkway and the Buckeye Trail goes back into the woods on the other side, but you can stay alongside the trail for another 0.2 mile to get to an overlook parking lot at N 41° 22.974, W 81° 32.775 (8). Enjoy the view of the gorge from here; then, unless you have a second car waiting here, return via the same route.

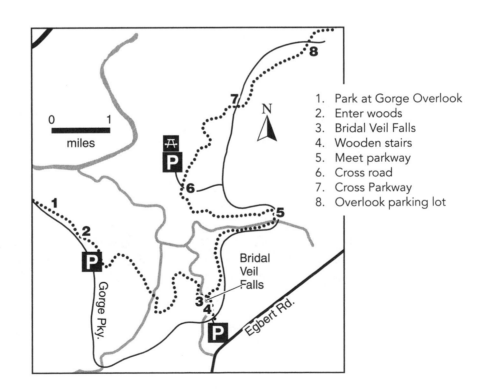

1. Park at Gorge Overlook
2. Enter woods
3. Bridal Veil Falls
4. Wooden stairs
5. Meet parkway
6. Cross road
7. Cross Parkway
8. Overlook parking lot

③ Cuyahoga Valley National Park

> Take advantage of a lesser known national park found near major urban areas.

> Explore the scenic Cuyahoga—Ohio's "Crooked River."

> See unique rock formations in a hilly area suitable for downhill skiing.

Area Information

Some people might not believe that there is a national park located between Cleveland and Akron, but Cuyahoga Valley National Park is one of the six most visited national parks, with over 2 million annual visitors. The park is located on a 22-mile stretch of the Cuyahoga River. The Indians used their word for "crooked" to name the 90-mile-long river that flows south before bending sharply to the north and Lake Erie. More recently, the Cuyahoga was best known as the polluted river that caught fire in 1969 in the industrial portion of Cleveland; however, just a few miles downstream, the river is an oasis in a region crisscrossed by interstates.

The park's 33,000 acres (51 square miles) are about more than just the river, although the 20-mile stretch of towpath trail that follows the route of the old Ohio and Erie Canal is a major attraction. The park also has diverse landscapes that feature sandstone ledges, 70 waterfalls, and 186 miles of trails. Most activities in the park are free, and adjacent areas offer opportunities such as downhill skiing at two resorts, live music at Blossom Music Center, and tourism spots such as Hale Farm and Stan Hywet Hall. And the Cuyahoga Valley Scenic Railroad runs right through the heart of the valley.

The canal helped bring prosperity to the region in the 19th century. In the 1920's, businessman Hayward Kendall donated 430 acres around a series of ledges to the state. In the 1930s, the Civilian Conservation Corps built the first lodges and shelters in what is now the park. By 1974, some Ohio leaders obtained the federal designation of the Cuyahoga Valley National Recreation Area for this territory, and in 2000, the Cuyahoga was elevated to national park status.

Directions: Cuyahoga Valley National Park is located north of Akron; the park is south of Interstate 480, east of Interstate 77, and west of State Route 8. Interstate 80 passes through the center, and Interstate 271 cuts through at an angle. The park can be accessed through any of these roads.

Hours open: The park is open year-round during daylight hours.

Facilities: Public restrooms and informational kiosks are found all along the park's 186 miles of interconnected trails. Some places of special interest include the Canal Way Center in Cuyahoga Heights, the Canal Visitor Center in Valley View, the 1826 Frazee House, the Boston Store, Hale Farm and Village, various canal locks, and the entire village of Peninsula.

Rules and permits: Very little camping takes place in the park, and it must be done with advance permission. Most park visits are for day use, but several state parks in the area have campgrounds.

Contact information: The park office is at 15610 Vaughn Road, Brecksville, Ohio 44141. The phone number is 216-524-1497.

Other Areas of Interest

Just north of the park are the Bedford and Chagrin Reservations of the Cleveland Metroparks, which offer a continuation of the same terrain. To the south, visitors will find Akron Metroparks such as the O'Neil Woods and the F.A. Seiberling Nature Realm.

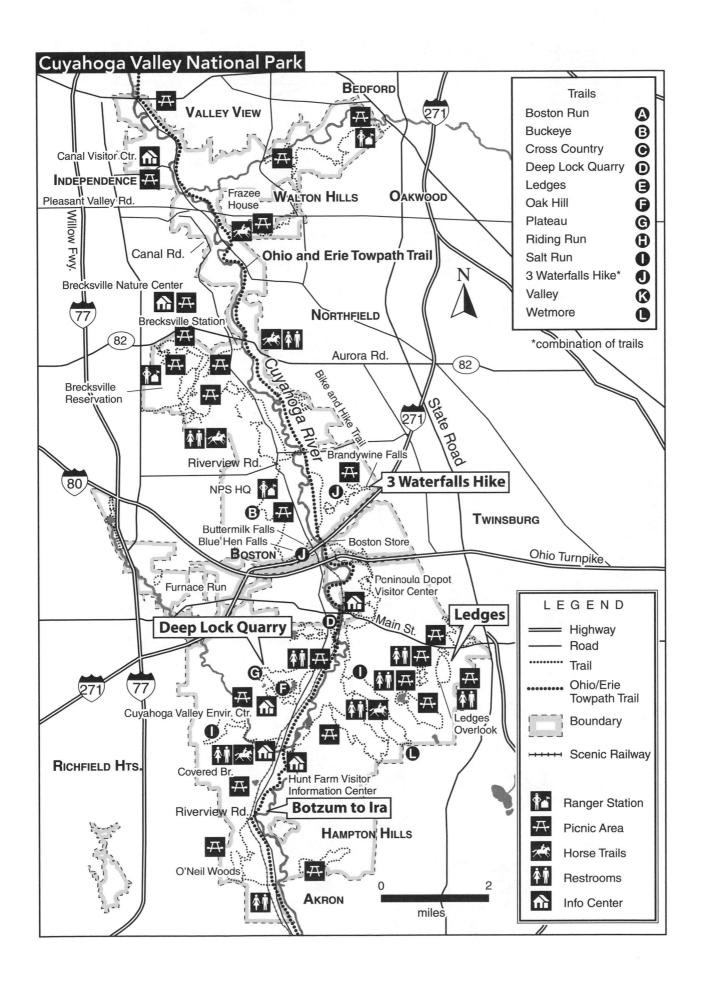

Cuyahoga Valley National Park

BEDFORD

271

VALLEY VIEW

Canal Visitor Ctr.

INDEPENDENCE

Pleasant Valley Rd.

Frazee House

WALTON HILLS

OAKWOOD

Canal Rd.

Ohio and Erie Towpath Trail

Willow Fwy.

Brecksville Nature Center

77

NORTHFIELD

Aurora Rd.

82

82

Brecksville Station

Brecksville Reservation

Cuyahoga River

Bike and Hike Trail

271

State Road

Riverview Rd.

Brandywine Falls

3 Waterfalls Hike

NPS HQ

B

J

TWINSBURG

80

Buttermilk Falls

Blue Hen Falls

BOSTON

J

Boston Store

Ohio Turnpike

Furnace Run

Peninsula Depot Visitor Center

Deep Lock Quarry

D

Main St.

Ledges

271

77

Cuyahoga Valley Envir. Ctr.

G

F

I

L

Ledges Overlook

RICHFIELD HTS.

I

Covered Br.

Hunt Farm Visitor Information Center

Riverview Rd.

Botzum to Ira

HAMPTON HILLS

O'Neil Woods

AKRON

0   2
miles

Trails

Boston Run	Ⓐ
Buckeye	Ⓑ
Cross Country	Ⓒ
Deep Lock Quarry	Ⓓ
Ledges	Ⓔ
Oak Hill	Ⓕ
Plateau	Ⓖ
Riding Run	Ⓗ
Salt Run	Ⓘ
3 Waterfalls Hike*	Ⓙ
Valley	Ⓚ
Wetmore	Ⓛ

N

*combination of trails

LEGEND

Highway
Road
Trail
Ohio/Erie Towpath Trail
Boundary
Scenic Railway

Ranger Station
Picnic Area
Horse Trails
Restrooms
Info Center

Cuyahoga Hikes Detail

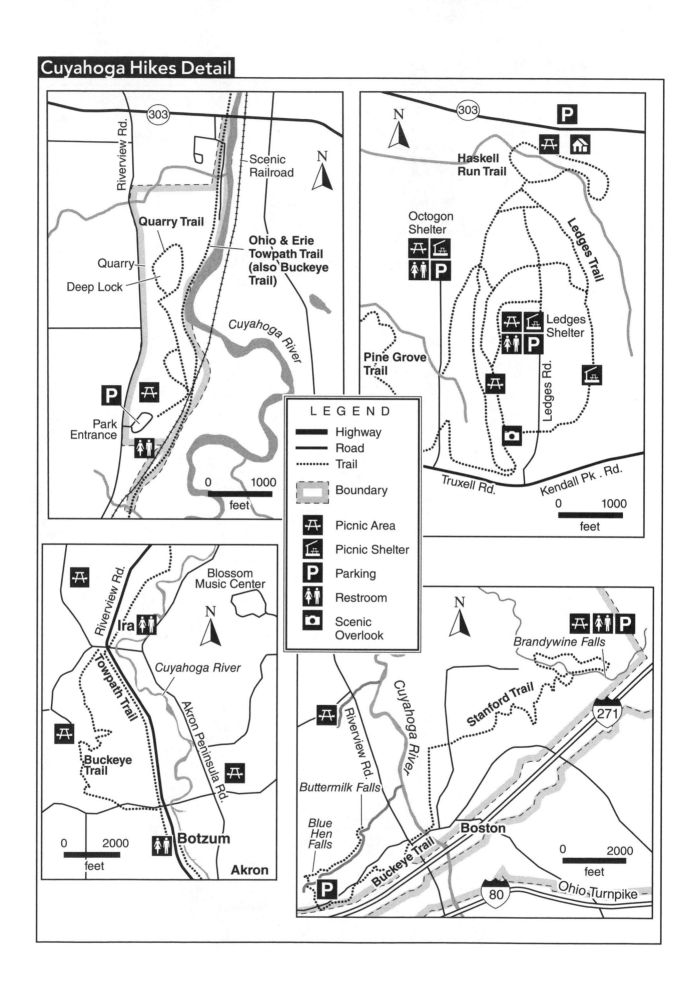

Quarry Trail

Quarry

Deep Lock

Riverview Rd.

Scenic Railroad

Ohio & Erie Towpath Trail (also Buckeye Trail)

Cuyahoga River

Park Entrance

LEGEND

▬▬▬	Highway
────	Road
········	Trail
▦	Boundary
🄰	Picnic Area
🄿	Picnic Shelter
P	Parking
👫	Restroom
📷	Scenic Overlook

Haskell Run Trail

Octogon Shelter

Ledges Trail

Pine Grove Trail

Ledges Shelter

Ledges Rd.

Truxell Rd.

Kendall Pk . Rd.

0   1000
feet

0   1000
feet

Riverview Rd.

Blossom Music Center

Ira

Cuyahoga River

Towpath Trail

Akron Peninsula Rd.

Buckeye Trail

Botzum

Akron

0   2000
feet

Brandywine Falls

Stanford Trail

271

Cuyahoga River

Riverview Rd.

Buttermilk Falls

Blue Hen Falls

Boston

Buckeye Trail

80

Ohio Turnpike

0   2000
feet

Three Waterfalls Hike

Hiking distance: 5 miles one way

Estimated hiking time: 3 hours

Take a long hike that features three unique waterfalls, including the most spectacular one in the state.

Caution: This is a difficult hike with several muddy spots, but it is worth the effort.

Trail directions: To get to the trail, from the small former village of Boston, cross the Cuyahoga and Riverview Road and begin climbing up Boston Mills Road. After about a mile, you will see a sign that points to a turnoff for the Blue Hen Falls parking lot. Park in the small dirt lot at N 41° 15.425, W 81° 34.356 (1). Begin the hike by descending. Cross the wooden bridge where the Buckeye Trail branches off to the left; in less than 0.2 mile,

❚ Buttermilk Falls is at one end of the Waterfalls Hike in the Cuyahoga Valley National Park.

you'll arrive at a bench at the top of Blue Hen Falls at N 41° 15.521, W 81° 34.363 (2). This pretty 15-foot-high waterfall flows over Bedford shale that lies below the Berea sandstone. You can walk down to the pool below this falls or move on to the next one.

To proceed, you will head downstream on a rugged hillside trail that is barely discernible. On your left, when the leaves are off, you can see the lifts for the Boston Mills ski resort; thus, the terrain here is steep enough for downhill skiers. The trail also crosses the stream several times on flagstones that are useless in high water, so be prepared for wet feet. After about 0.4 mile, the trail ends at Buttermilk Falls at N 41° 15.772, W 81° 34.051 (3). This sparkling 20-foot cascade is impressive when viewed from the top or bottom, and the difficulty in getting there guarantees that you will enjoy it in solitude.

From here, retrace your steps back to point 1 and proceed out to Boston Mills Road. Cross the road and follow the blue blazes of the Buckeye Trail into the woods again, near the edge of Interstate 271. Follow the trail downhill

for about a mile, recross Riverview Road and the Cuyahoga, and enter the village of Boston, where the National Park Service has restored the Boston Store at N 41° 15.815, W 81° 33.474 (4). A trailhead parking lot is located here, as well as restrooms and exhibits about life in the heyday of the canal. The Ohio and Erie Canal Towpath passes by here, and the intermingling in the park of the Towpath and Buckeye Trails offers the serious hiker multiple opportunities to customize loop hikes.

From the Boston Store, you should turn left (north) on the Towpath Trail. Follow this route for about 0.5 mile until you see a sign and side trail that direct you toward the Stanford House. Take this route for 0.1 mile, cross Stanford Road, and arrive at the Stanford House at N 41° 16.231, W 81° 33.416 (5). This 1843 farmhouse has been remodeled by the park service and converted into a youth hostel. The trail goes beside the house and reenters the woods behind the barns.

For the next 1.5 miles, the trail goes through a forest of oak and hickory; bridges provide passage over most of the wet spots. The route

While 65-foot high Brandywine Falls is at the other end.

then comes to the Brandywine Gorge Loop Trail and a steep set of stairs at N 41° 16.575, W 81° 32.581 (6). Turn right after climbing, and soon the trail follows the abandoned roadbed of Stanford Road. After about 0.2 mile, a parking lot with restrooms can be seen on the right at N 41° 16.608, W 81° 32.414 (7). To the left, a boardwalk leads down toward Brandywine Falls, the best waterfall in Ohio. Explore the top of this spectacular site before climbing 0.2 mile down to get a closer view.

Although Cedar Falls in Hocking Hills may be the more famous, Brandywine Falls can't be beat in terms of size and volume. The 65-foot-high falls is always running strong and makes so much noise that you can't even hear Interstate 271 just a few hundred yards away. Stay here a while, or better yet, stay next door at the Inn at Brandywine Falls, built in 1814. You may want to have someone meet you here to provide transportation, unless you would prefer to make the 5-mile return trip.

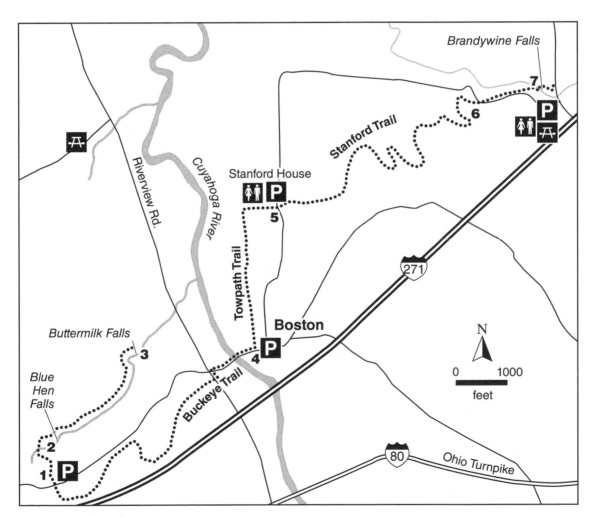

1. Blue Hen lot
2. Blue Hen Falls
3. Buttermilk Falls
4. Boston Store
5. Stanford House
6. Stairs to falls loop trail
7. Stairs to Brandywine Falls

Towpath and Deep Lock Quarry Trails

Hiking distance: 2.8 miles
Estimated hiking time: 1 hour

Tour the past with a river hike that features train tracks, canal locks, and an abandoned quarry.

Caution: Anything off trail is apt to be muddy, and on the canal trail, hikers must share the path with cyclists and crowds.

Trail directions: To get to the starting location for this hike, take State Route 303 into the village of Peninsula. Turn north just east of where 303 crosses the Cuyahoga in this charming town. Two blocks north, you will find the Lock 29 Trailhead at N 41° 14.572, W 81° 33.022 (1). At this spot, a large lot is located at a scenic curve in the river where a dam creates a roaring waterfall, and the train station for the Cuyahoga Scenic Railroad is right across the street. To leave this scene of activity and begin the hike, cross the river and proceed south along the Ohio and Erie Towpath Trail, which is also a part of the Buckeye Trail at this point.

In just 0.1 mile, the trail crosses under Route 303 in downtown Peninsula at N 41° 14.481, W 81° 33.009 (2). The paved surface on this popular trail accommodates cyclists, joggers, and families with strollers. The Cuyahoga remains on the left and is particularly active and attractive in this section. Proceed for another 0.6 mile to where the quarry trail branches off on the right at N 41° 13.945, W 81° 33.097 (3).

Turn up off the towpath here and enter Deep Lock Quarry Metropark, which is administered by the Summit County Park System, although it is within the boundaries of the national park. This trail leads to Deep Lock Quarry, a Berea sandstone quarry that was opened in 1829. Among the stones fashioned here were millstones used to grind oats for the Quaker Oats Company in nearby Akron. Some abandoned millstones are still visible as the trail passes through the heart of the original quarry.

After about a mile, the quarry trail rejoins the towpath trail at N 41° 13.802, W 81° 33.124 (4). From here, it is just 0.1 mile farther to the

Deep Lock Quarry parking lot at N 41° 13.794, W 81° 33.225 (5). This lot is off of River Road and offers primitive restrooms, information kiosks, and a picnic area. Take a break here before returning on the towpath trail.

On the return trip, the towpath trail almost immediately comes to the remains of Lock 28 at a spot where the tracks of the Cuyahoga Scenic Railroad cross the river. The walls to this lock are 17 feet deep—this is about 5 feet deeper than the rest of the locks in the area, which explains why this is called Deep Lock. From here, it is less than a mile back upstream to point 1.

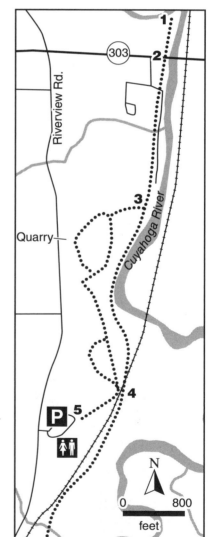

1. Lock 29 Trailhead
2. Cross under SR 303
3. Quarry Trail junction
4. Quarry Trail rejoins Towpath
5. Deep Lock parking lot

Ledges Trail

Hiking distance: 2.2 miles

Estimated hiking time: 1.5 hours

Hike among some unique rock formations and see some great views.

Caution: Rocks are slippery when wet, and the trail can be muddy.

Trail directions: Park in the lot at the Happy Days Visitor Center on State Route 303 just 2 miles east of Peninsula and just west of the junction with Route 8. The parking lot is on the north side of the road, but a tunnel takes you under the highway to the center. The Happy Days Visitor Center was built in the 1930s by the Civilian Conservation Corps and offers exhibits and classes. Behind the center, a kiosk offers trail information at N 41° 13.795, W 81° 30.502 (1).

Head into the woods here; the first stretch is a part of the Haskell Run Nature Trail, a 0.5-mile loop that features several interpretative signs at designated points. Cross a bridge and begin a gradual climb. At about 0.2 mile, you'll encounter a short connector to the Ledges Trail at N 41° 13.724, W 81° 30.642 (2). At the Ledges Trail junction, take the left fork and begin skirting some large rock formations. In another 0.2 mile, Ice Box Cave appears on the right at N 41° 13.571, W 81° 30.505 (3). More of a slit in the rock than a cave, this formation gets its name because of the year-round low temperatures found here. In this area, a side trail branches off that leads to the Ledges Shelter, which has a parking lot and restrooms.

Continue on, crossing a big bridge at N 41° 13.394, W 81° 31.466 (4) and then a road that leads to the Ledges Shelter at N 41° 13.255, W

81° 30.616 (5). The trail is still skirting the edge of Sharon conglomerate ledges that give the trail its name. At about the 1-mile mark, the trail comes to an overlook that covers a broad view at N 41° 13.222, W 81° 30.726 (6). This is a great spot for photos or a lunch break, and picnic tables are located here.

After soaking up the view at the Ledges Overlook, continue down the trail toward Kendall Park Road and admire the steep cliffs that are now on your right. After about 0.1 mile, a side trail on the right leads off toward the Pine Grove Trail at N 41° 13.165, W 81° 30.700 (7). Stay on the route for another 0.5 mile to the other connection that leads to the Pine Grove loop and the Octagon Trail at N 41° 13.536, W 81° 30.797 (8). From here, it is just 0.3 mile to point 2. On the return trip, bear left at point 2 to complete the Haskell Run Nature Trail and return to the Happy Days Visitor Center.

1. Kiosk at Happy Days Visitor Center
2. Connector to Ledges Trail
3. Ice Box Cave
4. Bridge
5. Road
6. Overlook
7. Side trail
8. Side trail

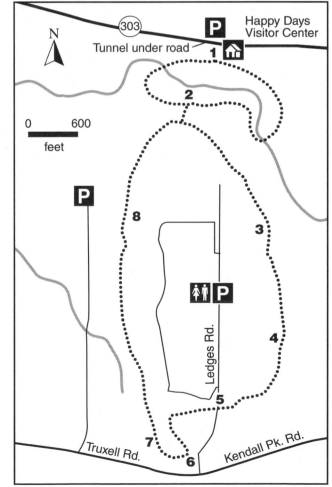

Towpath Trail, Botzum to Ira and Back

Hiking distance: 3.4 miles round trip

Estimated hiking time: 1.5 hours

Take an easy hike on a paved trail on the fringes of a national park.

Caution: This is a flat paved trail with no dangers other than traffic.

Trail directions: Park in the Indian Mound lot and get on the trail at N 41° 09.727, W 81° 34.539 (1). Soon you will cross Bath Road, where you can turn right and cross the Cuyahoga to find one of the largest great blue heron rookeries in the state. In March, the treetops here are filled with hundreds of blue herons building treetop nests where their eggs will hatch. Follow the paved path north for 0.3 mile to the remains of Lock 24 at N 41° 10.322, W 81° 34.675 (2). Plaques here tell the story of

the canal that ran by this location. Continue on the route, which is right next to the road, for another 0.6 mile; at that point, you will cross the road to the Conrad Botzum Farmstead at N 41° 09.457, W 81° 34.735 (3). In another 0.2 mile, you will come to the remains of Lock 25 at N 41° 09.533, W 81° 34.722 (4). Just past this (another 0.1 mile) is Ira Road, the road that leads to the restored 1830s Hale Farm and Village. Here the Buckeye Trail joins the route at N 41° 09.898, W 81° 35.050 (5).

Cross the road here as the route continues along the other side, where the Cuyahoga River is located. In another 0.5 mile, you will come to the Ira Trailhead lot at N 41° 11.024, W 81° 34.925 (6). The trail follows along the river, and pursuing this is worthwhile for the views alone. Then turn around and follow the same route back (unless you have a second car to park at the Ira Trailhead).

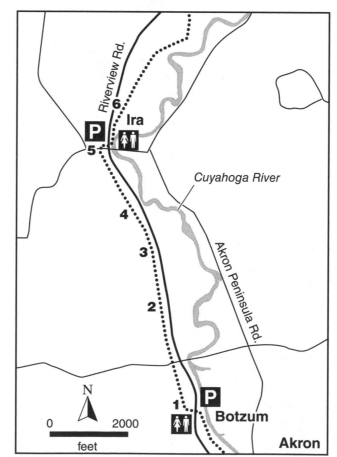

1. Indian Mound lot
2. Lock 24
3. Botzum Farmstead Road
4. Lock 25
5. Ira Road
6. Ira Trailhead lot

> See a variety of plant and animal life typical of northeastern Ohio.

> Visit a sphagnum bog, a relic of the Pleistocene epoch.

> Savor the isolation of a secluded preserve.

Area Information

This 440-acre preserve is a great place to spend a solitary afternoon. The 5 miles of trail here wind through forests and past ponds that offer encounters with a wide variety of wildlife. The preserve is host to over 100 species of trees, including such rarities as the cucumber magnolia and yellow birch. The forests—which are predominantly made up of beech, maple, and white oak—also feature over 70 species of wildflowers. Over 20 kinds of ferns alone are found here, as well as two carnivorous plants—the round-leaved sundew and the pitcher plant. In terms of fauna, the area has an abundance of deer, beaver, fox, and various waterfowl that may be viewed from a bird observation blind. Spotted turtles and four-toed salamanders, both classified as rare and endangered species, can also be found in the preserve.

Eagle Creek became a state nature preserve in 1974. The park is drained by the stream that gives the park its name. Eagle Creek flows into the Mahoning River, which is part of the Ohio River watershed. But just a few miles away is the Cuyahoga River, which eventually flows north to Lake Erie. The preserve positioned on this moraine, as well as the abundance of bogs and marshes, helps contribute to the diversity of wildlife.

Eagle Creek is located in the middle of the Western Reserve, a northeastern quadrant of Ohio that was originally set aside for purchase by New England veterans of the Revolutionary War. The northern and southern boundaries of the Western Reserve correspond to the same boundaries as Connecticut, which originally claimed the area as part of its coast-to-coast colonial charter. Connecticut relinquished these claims as part of the compromise that made all westward expansion possible, but it stipulated that Connecticut veterans must have first chance at purchasing the land. The New England background of the original settlers is seen in the layout of towns such as the nearby village of Nelson, which includes a quaint village green surrounded by white church steeples. A weather pattern known as the lake effect also contributes to the New England–like atmosphere by providing annual snowfalls that are two to five times higher than the rest of the state.

Park Trails

In addition to the trail used for the hike described here, Eagle Creek Nature Preserve also contains the following trails:

Beech Ridge Trail, 0.8 mile

Beaver Run Trail, 2.5 miles

Directions: From State Route 88 in the Portage County village of Garrettsville, turn right on State Route 82, go two blocks, and turn right on Center Road. Go north for 2 to 3 miles, then turn right on Hopkins Road and go south for 1 mile to the parking lot.

Hours open: The preserve is open year-round during daylight hours.

Facilities: None. A kiosk with a trail map is located in the parking lot, but the nature preserve has no drinking water or restrooms.

Rules and permits: Removing any plants from the preserve is forbidden. Camping, fires, and pets are not allowed.

Contact information: The address for the preserve is 11027 Hopkins Road, Garrettsville, Ohio 44231; however, to actually contact someone, you will have to call the Ohio Department of Natural Resources at 614-265-6561.

Other Areas of Interest

The popular Nelson-Kennedy Ledges State Park is located less than 5 miles from Eagle Creek. This large deposit of Sharon conglomerate provides hikers with an abundance of large rock to hike on or around. Also, Punderson State Park, which also has a lodge on the grounds, is located in nearby Geauga County.

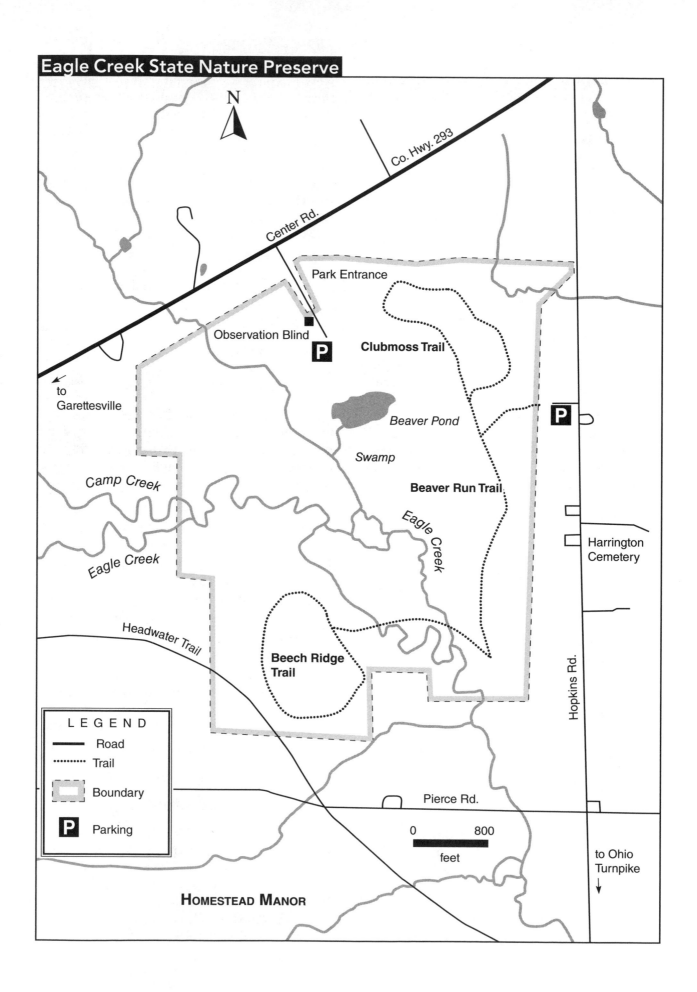

Eagle Creek State Nature Preserve

Co. Hwy. 293

Center Rd.

Park Entrance

Observation Blind

Clubmoss Trail

to Garettesville

Beaver Pond

Swamp

Camp Creek

Eagle Creek

Beaver Run Trail

Eagle Creek

P

Harrington Cemetery

Headwater Trail

Beech Ridge Trail

LEGEND
— Road
.... Trail
Boundary
P Parking

Hopkins Rd.

Pierce Rd.

0   800
feet

to Ohio Turnpike

HOMESTEAD MANOR

Clubmoss Trail

Hiking distance: 2 miles

Estimated hiking time: 1.5 hours

Enjoy a quiet walk through some pretty and diverse wetlands.

Caution: The marshes and bogs here make this location an active breeding ground for mosquitoes, which can be a real nuisance in summer months.

Trail directions: Park in the small lot off Hopkins Road and proceed to the kiosk at N 41° 17.369, W 81° 03.448 (1). Follow the mowed path through a meadow for 0.1 mile to where it enters the woods at N 41° 17.345, W 81° 03.589 (2). Proceed another 0.1 mile to N 41° 17.307, W 81° 83.750 (3). At this point, a fork appears in the path, and the Beaver Ridge Trail goes off to the left. Take the right fork on the Clubmoss Trail and proceed 0.3 mile past the first of several bogs and another junction at N 41° 17.501, W 81° 03.778 (4).

Take the right fork, and you will almost immediately come to an ancient sphagnum bog at N 41° 17.492, W 81° 03.709 (5). A board-walk leads to the center of the pond and offers a good view of cranberry bushes and visiting waterfowl. Continue on through a woods filled with maples, oaks, black walnuts, and cotton-woods. After 0.6 mile, you'll come to a long boardwalk at N 41° 17.617, W 81° 03.875 (6). Shortly afterward, the trail reaches its northern apex and begins to loop back.

Follow this loop back until you arrive at a large beaver pond at N 41° 17.547, W 81° 03.800 (7). At this location, an observation blind offers a great vantage point for observing the flora and fauna of the pond. Also present here is the club moss that gives the trail its name. Take the time to savor this view before continuing on to where the loop is completed at point 4, then return via the same route to the parking lot.

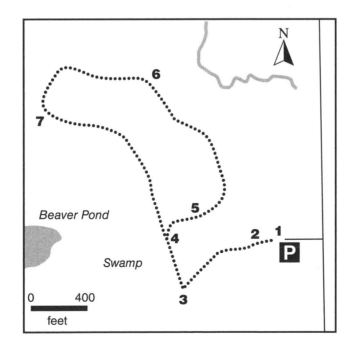

Beaver Pond

Swamp

0   400

feet

1. Kiosk
2. Enter woods
3. Fork right
4. Fork right
5. Bog
6. Boardwalk
7. Pond

> Hike in strip-mined land that has been reclaimed and restored.

> Stop to enjoy the numerous fishing ponds that are located throughout the forest.

> Check out the view of the Cross Creek Valley, some 350 feet below.

Area Information

Fernwood State Forest is a 3,023-acre tract in the rugged Ohio Valley hills not far from Steubenville. The site was purchased in 1961 after the land had been strip-mined for coal. However, area limestone deposits minimized damage, and, thanks to active reclamation, a healthy forest has been restored here. This has resulted in a playground for hikers, hunters, and particularly fishermen, because the forest's many ponds have been stocked with smallmouth bass, bluegill, and channel catfish. These numerous fishing holes are quite popular, and judging from the tracks, not everyone obeys the restrictions against motor vehicles off of designated roadways.

Fernwood also has Hidden Hollow Campground, with 22 sites that offer picnic tables, fire rings, and latrines, but no water. Hunters are free to pursue game anywhere in the forest except for campgrounds and roadways. In addition, three shooting ranges are located southwest of the campground—one each for pistols, rifles, and trap shooting. These ranges are open during daylight hours.

The road that skirts the northern edge of the forest offers some spectacular views of Cross Creek Valley some 300 feet below. Picnic tables and pull-off areas are provided at several locations so that visitors can soak up the views.

Directions: From the west, get off U.S. Route 22 at the Reeds Mill/Wintersville exit. Go left (east) on County Road 22A for a mile and turn right on Bantam Ridge Road. You will see a sign for the forest. Proceed 3.5 miles and turn right, crossing a set of railroad tracks and Cross Creek. Then go straight uphill for about 1 mile to the park entrance and a small parking lot.

Hours open: The forest is open year-round from 6 a.m. to 11 p.m.

Facilities: Restrooms are available only at the campground. Picnic tables are found in the campground and at scenic spots along the road. No water is available.

Rules and permits: Camping is only allowed in the designated area. Permits can be obtained from a forest officer. Operation of motor vehicles is not permitted off designated roadways. Attended fires are permissible only at the campground. Pets are permitted.

Contact information: For further information, contact Fernwood State Forest, 11 Township Road 181, Bloomingdale, Ohio 43910; the phone number is 740-266-6021.

Other Areas of Interest

Several of the lakes in the Muskingum Watershed Conservancy District are located in nearby Harrison County. These man-made lakes provide an abundance of recreational opportunities. Lakes Piedmont, Clendening, Tappan, and Leesville all have facilities in the area.

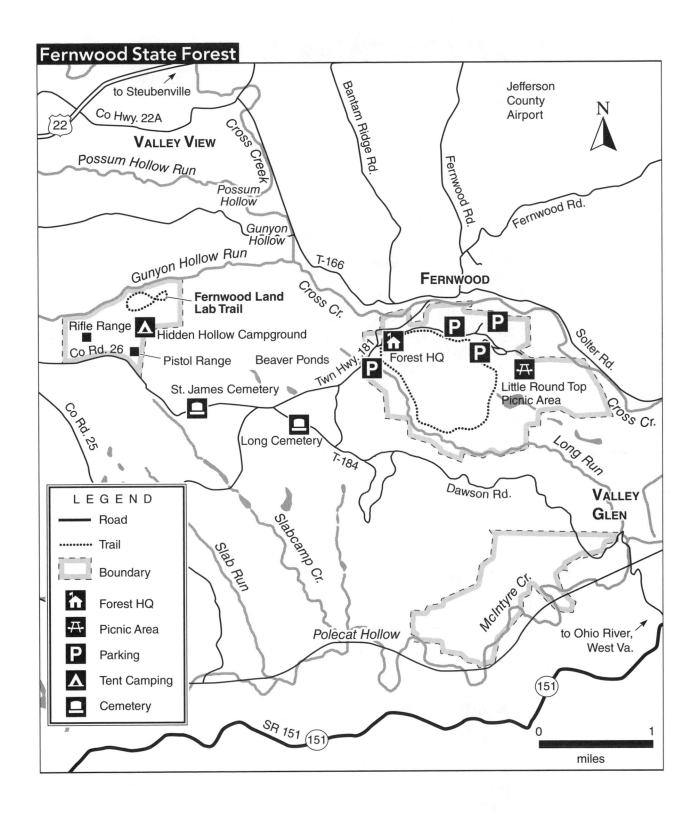

Fernwood State Forest

to Steubenville
Co Hwy. 22A
22
VALLEY VIEW
Possum Hollow Run
Possum Hollow
Gunyon Hollow
Gunyon Hollow Run
Cross Creek
Bantam Ridge Rd.
Jefferson County Airport
Fernwood Rd.
Fernwood Rd.
N
T-166
Cross Cr.
FERNWOOD
Fernwood Land Lab Trail
Rifle Range
Hidden Hollow Campground
Co Rd. 26
Pistol Range
Beaver Ponds
Twn Hwy. 181
Forest HQ
Solter Rd.
Cross Cr.
Little Round Top Picnic Area
St. James Cemetery
Co Rd. 25
Long Cemetery
T-184
Long Run
Dawson Rd.
VALLEY GLEN
LEGEND
Road
Trail
Boundary
Forest HQ
Picnic Area
Parking
Tent Camping
Cemetery
Slab Run
Slabcamp Cr.
McIntyre Cr.
Polecat Hollow
to Ohio River, West Va.
151
SR 151 151
0   1
miles

Fernwood State Forest Trail

Hiking distance: 3.5 miles
Estimated hiking time: 2 hours

Take a hike in hilly eastern Ohio, where beaver dams and fishing ponds abound.

Caution: This steep trail does not drain well and is always wet. Mosquitoes are also abundant.

Trail directions: Park in the small lot marked for trail parking at the top of the hill near the main entrance. This spot is at N 40° 19.680, W 80° 43.579 (1) and is right next to where the trail enters the woods. Proceed into the mixed hardwood forest and begin descending. At 0.3 mile, you will come to a pond at the bottom of a hill at N 40° 19.541, W 80° 43.337 (2). Continue on, moving past several smaller ponds that may not be visible from the trail in full foliage. At 0.8 mile, a side trail appears at N 40° 19.175, W 80° 43.174 (3), but it only goes a short distance to a well-used fishing spot at a pond just off the trail.

Continue on for another 0.6 mile of up-and-down trail. The trail is not blazed but is marked by frequent carsonite signs. However, the path seems to be mainly used by ATV users searching for fishing spots, and the poor drainage reflects this; standing water is often present on the path, especially in low-lying areas near ponds. At 1.4 miles, the trail turns sharply to the left just after a culvert at N 40° 19.042, W 82° 42.561 (4). Just to the left is yet another pond with a beaver dam and with a side path leading to it.

Stay on the main route for another 0.4 mile until a large pond appears on the left at N 40° 19.373, W 80° 42.476 (5). This is another popular fishing spot, and it is not unusual to catch 4-pound bass here. In another 0.3 mile, the trail is joined by an even more well-worn ATV path at N 40° 19.519, W 80° 42.371 (6). Bear left and follow the route uphill for 0.4 mile. The trail ends on a paved township road with a hiker's parking lot at N 40° 19.803, W 80° 42.604 (7). If you have two cars, you could leave one here and have a 2.5-mile hike through the woods.

If not, turn left and follow the township road back to the main entrance. In 0.5 mile, you'll come to a parking lot with a vista view at N 40° 19.873, W 80° 43.100 (8), but the ridge road offers multiple opportunities to glimpse the Cross Creek Valley some 350 feet below. Follow the road for another 0.5 mile and return to the main entrance lot.

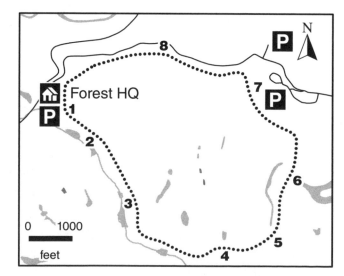

Forest HQ

0   1000

feet

1. Lot
2. Pond
3. Side trail
4. Left turn at pond
5. Large pond
6. ATV path
7. Lot at paved road
8. Lot with overlook

> Enjoy the unique ambience of Lorain County, which is not typical of the Midwest.

> Hike along the lake in one of the best state parks for miles around.

> See a variety of woodland, aquatic, and bird life.

Area Information

Findley State Park is located in a part of Ohio that doesn't have a lot of state parks or other public land. The park's roots can be traced back to 1936 when the land was purchased by Lorain County judge Guy Findley. He later donated the property to the state, and it became Findley State Forest. In 1950, the forest became a state park, and 6 years later the dam that formed Findley Lake was completed.

The geologic underpinning of the area is 300-million-year-old Bedford shale and Berea sandstone. Although most sandstone layers in Ohio are only 10 to 40 feet thick, those in nearby South Amherst are the deepest in the world, with a thickness of more than 200 feet. The forest in the park is secondary growth containing a variety of hardwoods such as maple, oak, wild cherry, white ash, and beech. Deer, fox, beaver, and raccoon are found here, and a variety of reptiles and amphibians can be found along the shoreline. Among the wildflowers commonly found here are Dutchman's breeches, hepatica, bloodroot, and trillium.

The park hosts a large campground with 90 electric sites and 180 nonelectric sites. The campground has showers, flush toilets, and laundry facilities. The park also has a nature center, amphitheater, and recreation area that offers volleyball, basketball, and horseshoes. In addition, a group camp area and three camper cabins are available. The 93-acre Findley Lake is stocked with bass, bluegill, and crappie; and it contains two boat ramps, although electric motors are the only ones permitted. Canoes, kayaks, and rowboats can be rented at the marina, and there is a 435-foot beach with a concession stand. The park also has eight picnic areas and an 18-hole disc golf course. In winter, the park offers opportunities for skating, ice fishing, and cross-country skiing. The park contains 16 miles of hiking and biking trails, including a 1.6-mile stretch of the Buckeye Trail.

Lorain County is known for its crop and dairy farms and progressive people. In 1858, just miles from the park in nearby Wellington, an angry mob broke in the jail, seized a black prisoner, and freed him. This reverse lynch mob was composed of abolitionists from nearby Oberlin whose purpose was to free a recaptured runaway slave, and the ensuing court proceedings caused national controversy just before the Civil War. Wellington was also the home of Archibald Willard, the artist who did the famous painting *Spirit of '76.*

Directions: The park is located off State Route 58 just 2 miles south of Wellington. The main entrance on park road 1 is on the east side of the road.

Hours open: The park is open year-round in daylight hours.

Facilities: The campground offers a full range of amenities. In addition, eight picnic areas and one picnic shelter with electricity are located elsewhere in the park.

Rules and permits: Pets are permitted in campgrounds. Hunting is permitted only for migratory waterfowl and only in designated areas during the hunting season.

Contact information: The park office is at 25381 State Route 58, Wellington, Ohio 44090; the phone number for this office is 440-647-5749. The camp office phone number is 440-647-4490.

Other Areas of Interest

Wellington State Wildlife Area is adjacent to the park; this 200-acre plot is reserved for public hunting. Other nearby attractions include Fowler Woods State Nature Preserve near Ashland and Old Woman Creek State Nature Preserve along Lake Erie near Huron.

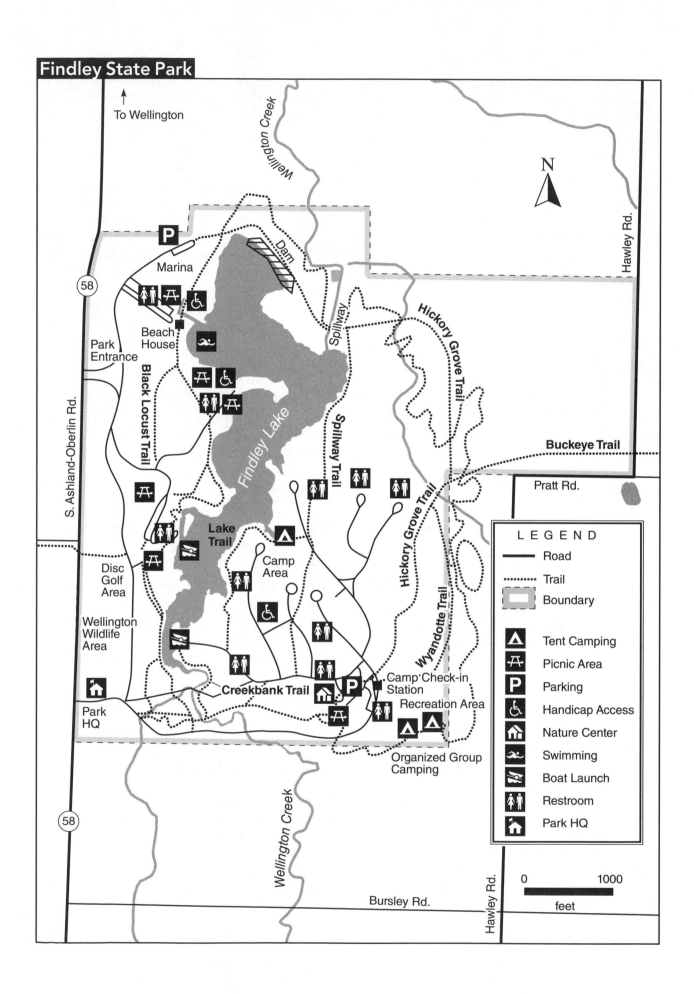

Findley State Park

To Wellington

Wellington Creek

N

Hawley Rd.

P

Marina

58

Park Entrance

S. Ashland-Oberlin Rd.

Beach House

Black Locust Trail

Findley Lake

Dam

Spillway

Hickory Grove Trail

Buckeye Trail

Pratt Rd.

Spillway Trail

Lake Trail

Disc Golf Area

Camp Area

Hickory Grove Trail

Wyandotte Trail

Wellington Wildlife Area

Creekbank Trail

Camp Check-in Station

Recreation Area

Park HQ

Organized Group Camping

LEGEND

— Road
····· Trail
▢ Boundary

▲ Tent Camping
⊼ Picnic Area
P Parking
♿ Handicap Access
⌂ Nature Center
🏊 Swimming
🚣 Boat Launch
🚻 Restroom
⌂ Park HQ

Wellington Creek

58

Bursley Rd.

Hawley Rd.

0   1000
feet

Findley State Park, Buckeye Trail

Hiking distance: 1.2 miles round trip

Estimated hiking time: 45 minutes

A short walk between the campground and the disc golf course offers views of the lake and a walk in the woods.

Caution: Much of this trail is shared with mountain bikers, who tend to leave the trail muddy.

Trail directions: From the main park entrance off State Route 58, go left on park road 3 for 0.5 mile until the disc golf parking lot appears on the left. Park here and enter the woods at the Buckeye Trail sign at N 41° 07.660, W 82° 12.907 (1). This trail is marked with the familiar blue blazes of the Buckeye Trail, but the numerous side trails that crisscross the area are not as well marked, so you must be sure to follow the blue blazes.

In 0.1 mile, Findley Lake appears on the left at N 41° 07.595, W 82° 12.916 (2). Continue to skirt the headwaters at the southern edge of the lake for another 0.2 mile until you come to a bridge over Wellington Creek—a feeder tributary—at N 41° 07.400, W 82° 12.854 (3). The main trail now goes inland a bit, but an abundance of wildlife is visible throughout. On the afternoon that I took this brief walk, I flushed both blue herons and deer. Unfortunately, an abundance of insect life, particularly mosquitoes, is in the area.

Continue through the hardwood forest for another 0.2 mile until the park amphitheater appears on the left at N 41° 07.354, W 82° 12.508 (4). Then climb a slight hill to a clearing that comes out at the edge of the park's 200-plus-site campground. The Buckeye Trail continues all the way around the lake. But this small stretch is a good short walk, especially for campers who want to walk to the disc golf course. After viewing the campground, turn around and return the way you came. Restrooms are nearby at both ends of the hike.

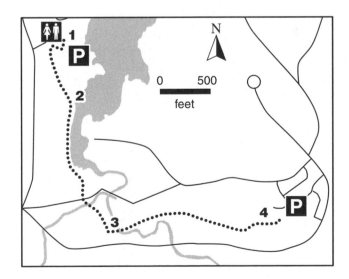

1. Lot
2. Lake in view
3. Bridge
4. Amphitheater

> Visit a smaller, out-of-the-way state park that is less crowded.
> Enjoy a hike with a secluded beach and a horsepower limit for boats.

Area Information

Nestled near the corner of the state where Ohio, West Virginia, and Pennsylvania meet, Jefferson Lake State Park is a quiet and secluded getaway. The 962-acre park is centered around the 17-acre, man-made Jefferson Lake. A small campground and a 4-horsepower limit for boats on the lake complete the intimate scenario.

The park is located on top of the sandstone bedrock that contains the layers of coal that were made millions of years ago. Today, this hilly region is covered by second-growth oak and hickory forests, and it also contains a variety of beeches, maples, tulips, walnuts, elms, and ashes. Among the wildflowers found here are geranium, hepatica, and bloodroot. A variety of smaller songbirds are present, as well as larger fowl such as wild turkey and ruffed grouse.

This land in the Yellow Creek watershed was inhabited by the Mingo tribe when white men arrived in the late 18th century. The family of the Mingo chief, Logan, was murdered opposite where Yellow Creek enters into the Ohio River in a barbarous incident that set off a year of raids and warfare in 1774.

In 1928, land was purchased along Town Fork of Yellow Creek, and a dam and other facilities were later constructed as a Civilian Conservation Corps project. Although the dam was completed in 1934, the lake was not filled until 1946, and the area was turned over to the state's park division 4 years later.

Directions: Jefferson Lake State Park is located off of State Route 43 about 0.2 mile north of its junction with U.S. Route 22. From the town of Richmond, go north on State Route 43 for 1 mile and turn right on County Road 54. Proceed almost 2 miles to the park entrance at the dam and go left 0.3 mile to the beach parking lot.

Hours open: The park is open year-round in daylight hours.

Facilities: Nearly 100 campsites are available at the park campground, although only 5 are electric. In addition, 30 equestrian sites are located at the Trillium Trailhead. Picnic tables, vault latrines, and water fountains are located at the camp and beach; hot showers are also available at the 200-foot beach. There is a boat launch on the lake. The park has basketball and volleyball courts and a horseshoe pit for summer recreation. In winter, the park offers skating, ice fishing, and cross-country skiing. The park contains 20 miles of hiking and riding trails.

Rules and permits: Pets are permitted at all sites. All campsites are first come, first served.

Contact information: Jefferson Lake State Park is located at 501 Township Road 261A, Richmond, Ohio 43944. The phone number for the park office is 740-765-4459.

Other Areas of Interest

Guilford Lake State Park, which is coadministered with Jefferson Lake, is in Columbiana County near Lisbon. Other nearby attractions include the Brush Creek and Highlandtown Wildlife Areas (which are popular for hunting) and Yellow Creek State Forest near Salineville.

In addition to the trail used for the hike described here, Jefferson Lake State Park also contains the following trails:

Campground Hikers Trail, 2 miles	🥾🥾
Fernview Trail, 2 miles	🥾
Beaver Dam Trail, 2 miles	🥾🥾
Lakeside Loop Trail, 2.5 miles	🥾🥾
Trillium Trail, 1.3 miles	🥾🥾🥾
Logan Trail, 4.5 miles	🥾🥾🥾

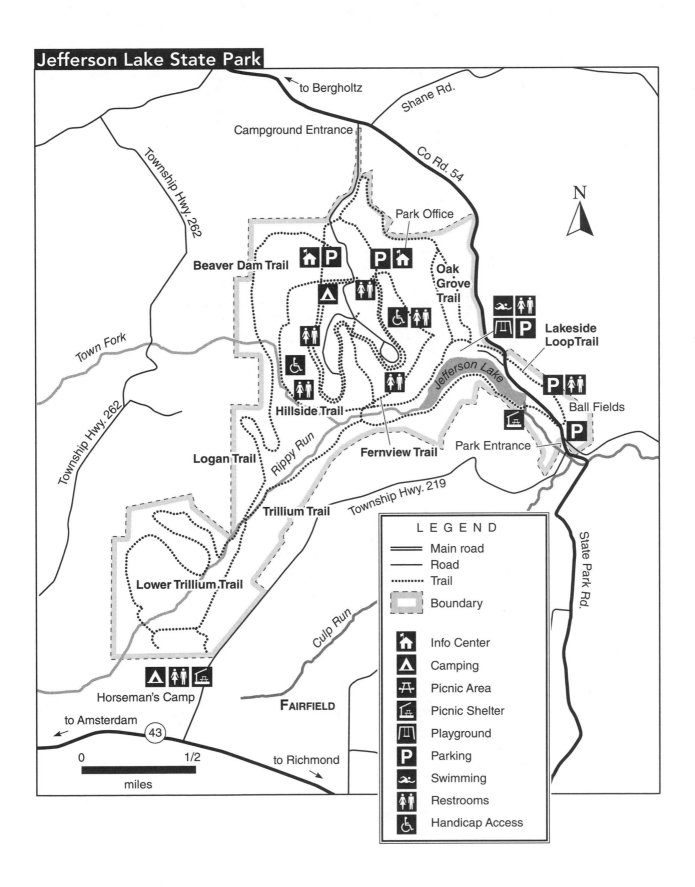

Jefferson Lake State Park

Oak Grove Trail

Hiking distance: 1 mile
Estimated hiking time: 30 minutes

Enjoy walking a quiet trail in a secluded park.

Caution: This trail is shared with horses, so it can get quite muddy. Mosquitoes can also be a problem in summer.

Trail directions: Park in the northern part of the beach parking lot near the restrooms at N 40° 27.900, W 80° 47.870 (1). Enter the woods at the sign for the Oak Grove Trail. This is also an equestrian trail, so beware of horse tracks that can bog a hiker down in wet weather. Go uphill for 0.2 mile to a junction at N 40° 27.917, W 80° 47.910 (2). Turn left here and proceed parallel to the lakes through a mixed hardwood forest.

In another 0.3 mile, you'll come to the junction with the Fernview Trail at N 40° 27.937, W 80° 48.110 (3). Turn left here and head back toward the lake. In another 0.2 mile, you will reach the beach shower house right on the lake at N 40° 27.804, W 80° 48.025 (4). Pit toilets and a water fountain are also located here. This is also a junction for several other trail options. Ambitious hikers can go around the lake on the Lakeside Loop Trail or hike uphill to the campgrounds (Campground Hikers Trail) or to a beaver dam (Beaver Dam Trail).

The easiest option is to turn left again and follow along the lakeshore. But first, you should stop to enjoy the view of the small serene lake and the waterfowl that inhabit it. In about 0.1 mile, you will come to a wooden bridge at N 40° 27.840, W 80° 47.985 (5). Cross the bridge and proceed alongside the lake for less than 0.2 mile to return to point 1.

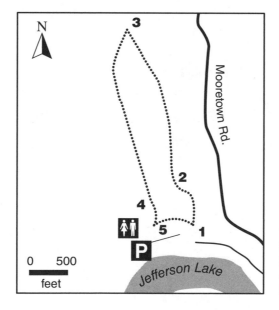

1. Lot
2. Junction
3. Junction
4. Shower house
5. Bridge

> Hike (or ski) in the one part of Ohio that gets real winters.
> Climb surprisingly high hills with excellent views.
> Explore the shores of Lake Erie, Ohio's northern coast.

Area Information

Lake County may be one of the newest and smallest of Ohio's 88 counties, but this area has a lot to offer. The area east of Cleveland gets annual snowfalls of up to 80 inches a year, making Lake and Geauga Counties a wintertime playground. And being on the shores of Lake Erie makes the area a summertime playground as well. The surprisingly steep hills and rock formations make the area an outdoor fun spot anytime of the year.

The Lake County Metroparks system takes advantage of all this. Established in 1958, this system now includes 30 parks that total 7,500 acres. These parks contain 43 miles of trails. One of the best spots in the Metroparks system is Chapin Forest Reservation, a 390-acre preserve that boasts both hiking trails and a cross-country skiing center.

Chapin Forest became public land in 1949, when Frederic Chapin purchased the land to protect it from logging and then donated it to the state. The Ohio Department of Natural Resources still owns the land, but under a lease agreement, the land is managed by Lake Metroparks. The park features a mature forest filled with beech, maple, oak, tulip, and hemlock trees; a former sandstone quarry; and rocky outcroppings of Sharon conglomerate. From the top of one of these ledges, viewers can see Lake Erie and the downtown Cleveland skyline 18 miles away.

The preserve has 5.3 miles of trails, including a stretch of the Buckeye Trail. In winter, these hiking trails become groomed cross-country ski trails. Winter sport enthusiasts can rent skis or snowshoes at the Pine Lodge and ski the local hills on lighted and groomed trails. The lodge offers ski lessons, concessions, and a warm fireplace. The park also features four picnic areas and shelters with grills.

Directions: Take the Route 306 exit off Interstate 90 and go south for 3 miles. The entrance will be on the right.

Facilities: Chapin Forest has four picnic areas, all of which have shelters, restrooms, and drinking water. The preserve also has playgrounds, volleyball courts, and opportunities for cycling, sledding, and fishing, as well as a lodge for cross-country ski rentals.

Hours open: The park is open daily from sunrise to one-half hour after sunset.

Rules and permits: Visitors are asked to stay on trails and to refrain from picking wildflowers.

Contact information: The Lake County Metroparks office is at 11211 Spear Road, Concord Township, Ohio 44077; the phone number is 440-639-7275. The trailhead parking lot is at 9938 Chillicothe Road, Kirtland, Ohio 44094. The Pine Lodge Center is at 10381 Hobart Road, Kirtland, Ohio 44097; the phone number is 440-256-3810.

Other Areas of Interest

The North Chagrin Reservation of the Cleveland Metroparks is just a few miles to the west, and Hatch-Otis Sanctuary is in the same neighborhood. Just to the north, you will find Mentor Marsh and Headlands Beach State Park, which is the northern terminus of the Buckeye Trail. Holden Arboretum is just to the east (and also on the Buckeye Trail).

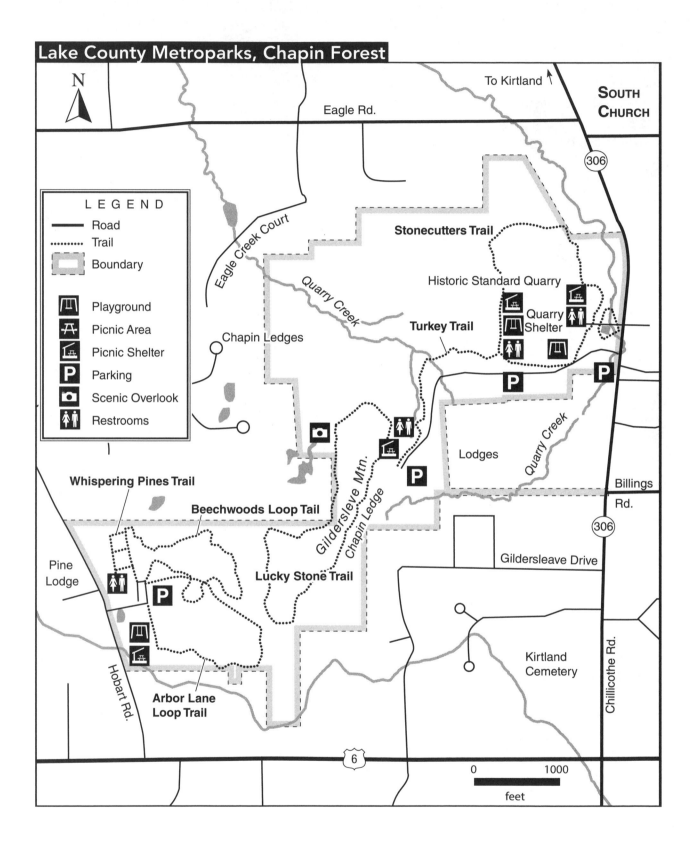

Lake County Metroparks, Chapin Forest

N

To Kirtland ↑

SOUTH CHURCH

Eagle Rd.

306

LEGEND

— Road

···· Trail

Boundary

🛝 Playground

🪑 Picnic Area

🏠 Picnic Shelter

P Parking

📷 Scenic Overlook

🚻 Restrooms

Eagle Creek Court

Quarry Creek

Chapin Ledges

Stonecutters Trail

Historic Standard Quarry

Quarry Shelter

Turkey Trail

P   P

Lodges

Quarry Creek

Billings Rd.

306

Gildersleave Drive

Whispering Pines Trail

Beechwoods Loop Tail

Gildersleve Mtn.

Chapin Ledge

Pine Lodge

P

Lucky Stone Trail

Kirtland Cemetery

Chillicothe Rd.

Hobart Rd.

Arbor Lane Loop Trail

6

0   1000

feet

Chapin Forest, Buckeye Trail

 Hiking distance: 4.5 miles round trip

Estimated hiking time: 3 hours

Hike the Buckeye Trail to Gildersleeve Knob and enjoy the view.

Caution: Stay on the trails while on the steep ledges.

Trail directions: Park in the lot just off of State Route 306 at N 41° 35.855, W 81° 20.938 (1). This location has restrooms, a shelter, and an informational kiosk. Head north past Quarry Pond. Sandstone was taken here for several buildings, including Joseph Smith's 1836 Mormon temple in Kirtland (which you would have driven by on your way to the trail). The Buckeye Trail soon comes in from the right, and after about 0.7 mile, you will come to a four-way intersection at N 41° 35.835, W 81° 21.221 (2). Stay on the blue blazes and go past the shelter here; in another 0.4 mile, you'll come to the Ledges Picnic Shelter at N 41° 35.649, W 80° 21.443 (3).

At this point, the trail turns uphill and soon meets a junction with the Lucky Stone Loop Trail at N 41° 35.652, W 81° 21.525 (4). Stay to the right and keep climbing. In about 0.2 mile, you will arrive at Gildersleeve Knob at N 41° 35.696, W 81° 21.644 (5). The altitude here is 1,160 feet, which doesn't seem that high; however, Lake Erie, just 8 miles away, is about 600 feet, so it's not surprising that you can see the lake from here on a clear day. On a really clear day, you can also see the Cleveland skyline 18 miles away. The ledges here are made of Sharon conglomerate and were formed over 300 million years ago. Just below is an abandoned stone quarry where they used to separate the conglomerate into sand and quartz pebbles.

Stay on the Buckeye Trail–Lucky Stone Loop through a beech and maple forest and begin a gradual descent. Bypass the link to Morning Cloak Trail in 0.3 mile and complete the Lucky Stone Loop in another 0.3 mile at N 41° 35.307, W 81° 21.811 (6). Stay on the Arbor Lane Trail for another 0.3 mile to the junction with the Ash Grove Trail link at N 41° 35.249, W 81° 22.038 (7). From here, it is less than 0.2 mile to the Pine Lodge and Hobart Road parking lot at N 41° 35.344, W 81° 22.155 (8). This is a good place to park a second car if you want a shorter hike. Or you could return via the same, or a slightly different, route.

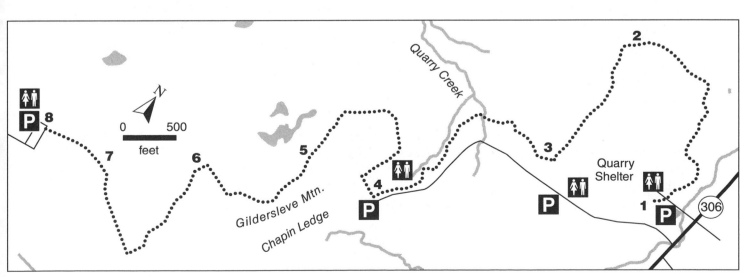

1. State Route 306 lot
2. Four-way intersection
3. Ledges shelter
4. Junction
5. Gildersleeve Knob
6. Junction
7. Junction
8. Hobart Road lot

> Tour a working farm that is a laboratory for modern efficient farming practices.

> Hike to the top of a hill that offers an oath-inspiring view.

> Visit the house where Bogart and Bacall were married.

Area Information

There was a time when people moved to Ohio to seek fame and fortune, but it lasted only until the state was settled. Afterward, Ohioans tended to move away to seek these things, and they rarely returned if successful. Louis Bromfield was a welcome exception to this trend. After leaving his native Mansfield, Bromfield found renown as a screenwriter and Pulitzer Prize–winning novelist. He had Hollywood friends and a home in the south of France, but in 1939, he returned home and bought a farm in Richland County. Bromfield codesigned a 32-room farmhouse called the Big House and devoted the rest of his life to running his farm. Although his early books were novels, such as *The Green Bay Tree* and *Early Autumn,* after his return to his native state, he wrote nonfiction works—including *Pleasant Valley* and *Malabar Farm*—that stressed simplicity, self-reliance, and good farming practices.

Bromfield still hosted some of his celebrity friends, most notably in 1945, when Humphrey Bogart and Lauren Bacall were married at the Big House in an effort to avoid the paparazzi. But until his death in 1956, Bromfield was more likely to play host to conservationists and agricultural leaders, and his last books were devoted to sound farming practices. In 1972, the State of Ohio acquired the 914-acre farm, and it became a state park 4 years later. Today, the rolling hills of Malabar Farm are a tourist attraction as well as a tribute to sustainable farming practices. A new visitor center showcases the farm, and activities include a year-round tour of the Big House and a seasonal tour of the farm. The park includes a small campground containing 15 nonelectric sites with fire rings, picnic tables, water, and latrines; equestrian camping is also available, as are picnic areas. A 19-bed youth hostel is also located on the grounds. Bluegill and catfish can be caught in the farm pond. The park has an 11-mile bridle trail and three short hiking trails. Hikers can also hike to the top of Mt. Jeez, which gets its name from the oath that visitors would involuntarily utter when they first saw the view from the top.

Every effort is made to preserve the spirit of Bromfield's work. Nature programs are offered year-round at the visitor center, and the Pugh Cabin is a day use facility that can host up to 50 people. The Malabar Farm Market offers local produce from Memorial Day through October harvest. The Malabar Farm Restaurant, located in a restored 1820 stage coach inn at the foot of Mt. Jeez, supports the locavore movement by offering products straight from the farm.

Directions: Malabar Farm is located off of State Route 603 just north of the junction with State Route 95. Turn onto Pleasant Valley Road and follow the signs.

Facilities: The visitor center has restrooms and a gift shop.

Hours open: The hours vary by season and year, so you should check in advance.

Rules and permits: Pets are permitted, but no hunting or swimming is allowed.

Contact information: The park address is 4050 Bromfield Road, Lucas, Ohio 44843; the phone number is 419-892-2784.

Other Areas of Interest

Pleasant Hill Lake (a lake in the Muskingum Watershed Conservancy District) is practically next door. Fowler Woods State Nature Preserve is north on State Route 13.

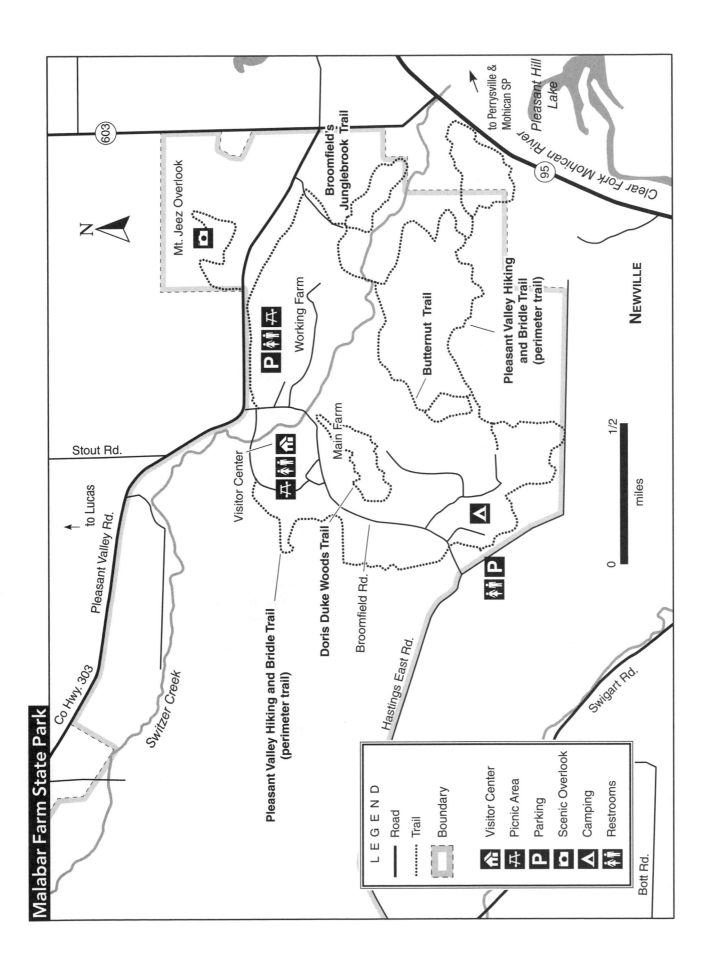

Malabar Farm State Park

LEGEND

——	Road
....	Trail
▭	Boundary
🏠	Visitor Center
⛱	Picnic Area
P	Parking
◉	Scenic Overlook
▲	Camping
🚻	Restrooms

Co Hwy. 303

Pleasant Valley Rd.

to Lucas

Switzer Creek

Stout Rd.

(603)

Mt. Jeez Overlook

Working Farm

Broomfield's Junglebrook Trail

Visitor Center

Main Farm

Pleasant Valley Hiking and Bridle Trail (perimeter trail)

Doris Duke Woods Trail

Broomfield Rd.

Hastings East Rd.

Butternut Trail

Pleasant Valley Hiking and Bridle Trail (perimeter trail)

NEWVILLE

to Perrysville & Mohican SP

(95)

Clear Fork Mohican River

Pleasant Hill Lake

N

Bott Rd.

Swigart Rd.

0   1/2

miles

Bridle and Ski Trails

Hiking distance: 3.6 miles
Estimated hiking time: 1.5 hours

Tour a scenic working farm with a literary background, ending your hike at a location with a great view.

Caution: The trail is not well marked and may be difficult to follow in certain seasons.

Trail directions: Take State Route 95 to State Route 603 and turn left on Pleasant Valley Road. Enter the park right away, but rather than proceed to the visitor center, make a left on Bromfield Road, just after entering the park. Park in the farm parking lot next to the barn at N 40° 39.085, W 82° 23.570 (1). An active youth hostel is located across the road from this lot. Bromfield lived in this building while he was having the Big House built, but he dismissed his quarters here as a "mail order house." Restrooms are located near the barn.

Take the path near the barn, which is a one-way road at this point. In about 0.2 mile, you will come to the family cemetery at N 40° 39.002, W 82° 23.363 (2). Louis Bromfield, a World War I veteran, is buried here on the farm that meant so much to him. Continue on, going past a junction where the Bridle Trail joins the route; in another 0.4 mile, you'll reach a junction with the Jungle Brook Trail at N 40° 38.907, W 82° 22.984 (3). This 1-mile loop trail is one of three hiking trails on the grounds; feel free to take it and add 1 mile to your total hike.

After you complete this loop, or if you bypass it, you should continue on by turning left, keeping the farm field on your left. In another 0.2 mile, a mowed path veers left and almost immediately crosses Pleasant Valley Road at N 40° 39.075, W 82° 22.849 (4). Just down the road on the right is the Malabar Farm Restaurant, an 1820 building where the specialty is local produce. Cross the road and turn left back toward the park entrance. A sometimes soggy path runs parallel to the road for about 0.3 mile until meeting the road to Mt. Jeez at N 40° 39.198, W 82° 23.191 (5). The fact that there is a road to the top of 1,300-foot Mt. Jeez does diminish the feeling of accomplishment somewhat, but it's still worthwhile to walk up the route. Follow the road, and in another 0.6 mile, you will be at N 40° 39.275, W 82° 23.012 (6), enjoying a wonderful view of the farm below.

This is the only hike in this book where you can view every step of the route from a single vantage point. From the top of Mt. Jeez, you can retrace your route and see every landmark. You can see five counties from this spot, and the view of the rolling farmland is spectacular in any season. Soak up the view for a while before returning to point 1, either by retracing your route or by following alongside Pleasant Valley and Bromfield Roads.

1. Park
2. Bromfield's Grave
3. Junction with Jungle Brook Trail
4. Cross Pleasant Valley Road
5. Meet gravel road
6. Mt. Jeez

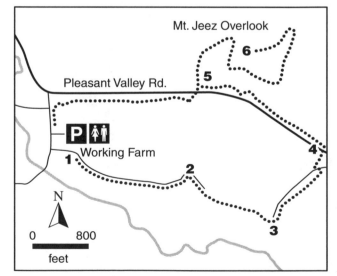

> See the spectacular 300-foot Clear Fork Gorge from above and below.

> Take advantage of opportunities for hiking, mountain biking, horseback riding, canoeing, and snowmobiling.

Area Information

The Clear Fork of the Mohican River is a popular destination for outdoor recreation lovers. The 1,100-acre Mohican State Park and the 5,000-acre Mohican State Forest (which surrounds the park) are popular destinations for hikers, horseback riders, and mountain bikers. In addition, the canoeing here is among the best in the state. At the end of the stream, Pleasant Hill Reservoir—a lake in the Muskingum Watershed Conservancy District—offers excellent boating and fishing opportunities. And two downhill ski resorts are located nearby.

The reason for all of this goes back to glacier activity. The last glaciers to visit Ohio some 12,000 years ago stopped less than a mile from here, and the melt waters helped create steep cliff walls. The gorge is over 1,000 feet wide at the top and 300 feet deep. It contains all kinds of trees—most notably hemlock and white pine—and has earned the designation as a Registered National Natural Landmark. Other trees here include oaks and maples at the top of the gorge; beech, birch, ash, and tulip along the hillsides; and sycamore, willows, buckeye, hawthorn, and dogwood along the stream bottom. In this area, visitors will find 15 species of fern as well as a wide variety of birds. Larger birds such as wild turkey and even eagles can be found here, and 15 species of nesting warblers may be seen in the area. The river contains smallmouth bass and has become a popular place for fly-fishing for trout.

In 1949, a portion of the Mohican State Forest was separated off and designated as a state park. The park contains six hiking trails, three bridle trails, and three biking trails, one of which was noted the best mountain bike trail in Ohio by biking enthusiasts. A snowmobile trail is located in the adjacent Mohican State Forest, and the area includes several canoe liveries that work on the Clear Fork. The park contains 12 picnic areas with latrines and drinking water, as well as 3 shelter houses that can be reserved.

For overnight guests, the park campground contains nearly 200 sites, most of which have electric hookups. In addition, 25 two-bedroom cottages (which can be rented) are located along the river. And, for those seeking maximum comfort, there is the 96-room Mohican State Lodge, where each room has a private balcony. The lodge also has meeting and banquet rooms, a restaurant, a lounge, a gift shop, a sauna, and indoor and outdoor pools. Pool access is also available to campground and cottage guests.

Directions: Mohican State Park is located off of State Route 97 between Butler and Loudonville.

Facilities: The campground includes restrooms, showers, and a commissary, but such amenities are lacking in much of the hiking area.

Hours open: The park is open year-round during daylight hours.

Rules and permits: Visitors are asked to stay on marked trails, and pets must be leashed.

Contact information: The park office is at 3116 State Route 3, Loudonville, Ohio 44842; the phone number is 419-994-5125.

Other Areas of Interest

Pleasant Hill Lake is at the edge of the park, and Charles Mill Lake is north of that. These two Muskingum Watershed Conservancy lakes offer abundant recreational and boating activities.

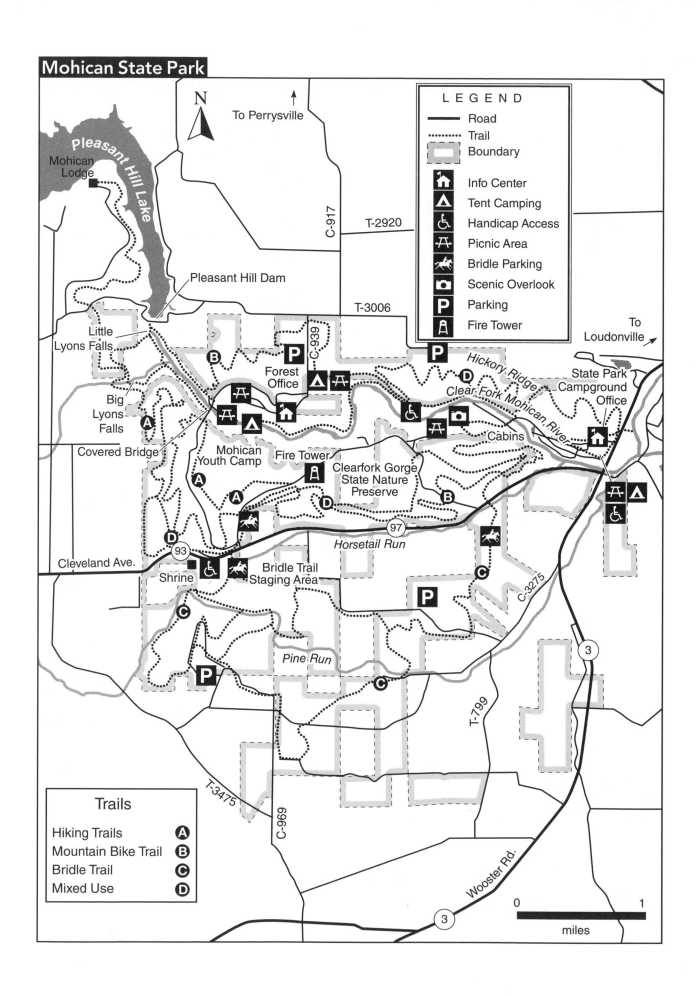

Mohican State Park

N
To Perrysville

LEGEND
— Road
····· Trail
▭ Boundary
🏠 Info Center
⛺ Tent Camping
♿ Handicap Access
🪑 Picnic Area
🐎 Bridle Parking
📷 Scenic Overlook
P Parking
🗼 Fire Tower

Pleasant Hill Lake

Mohican Lodge

C-917

T-2920

T-3006

C-939

To Loudonville

Pleasant Hill Dam

Little Lyons Falls

Big Lyons Falls

Covered Bridge

B

P

Forest Office

Hickory Ridge

Clear Fork Mohican River

State Park Campground Office

Cabins

Mohican Youth Camp

A

A

Fire Tower

Clearfork Gorge State Nature Preserve

D

B

D

Cleveland Ave.

93

D

Shrine

Bridle Trail Staging Area

Horsetail Run

97

C-3275

C

P

3

C

Pine Run

P

C

T-799

C-969

T-3475

Wooster Rd.

3

3

Trails

Hiking Trails Ⓐ
Mountain Bike Trail Ⓑ
Bridle Trail Ⓒ
Mixed Use Ⓓ

0   1
miles

Lyons Falls and Pleasant Hill Trails

Hiking distance: 2.4 miles

Estimated hiking time: 1.5 hours

Hike through an impressive gorge to see two waterfalls and a large lake.

Caution: The trails can be steep and muddy, so you must be careful around waterfall precipices.

Trail directions: From State Route 97, just 3 miles west of its terminus at State Route 3, turn north on Park Road 8. Drive down 1.5 miles to the covered bridge across the Clear Fork of the Mohican River. This landmark bridge, built in 1969, is located at N 40° 36.784, W 82° 19.012 (1). Please note that there are no restrooms here. Park in the lot and enter the woods on the south shore of Clear Fork. The white blazed trail follows along the stream, and there are several spots where you can walk right down to this shallow branch that is ideal for canoeists.

After about 0.4 mile, a side trail appears on the left that leads to Lyons Falls; this trail is located at N 40° 37.073, W 82° 19.365 (2). Leave the river trail and take the left fork. Head uphill through woods filled with hemlock, beech, oak, maple, and hickory trees. Pass by a turnoff that goes directly to Little Lyons Falls and continue until you arrive at Lyons Falls at N 40° 36.990, W 82° 19.717 (3). Among the early visitors to this recessed-cave falls was pioneer folk hero Johnny Appleseed, who had orchards in the area. He carved his name

The covered bridge at the trailhead of the Lyons Falls hike in Mohican State Park.

in the sandstone cliffs here, but the signature has worn away.

After skirting the base of these larger falls, continue on, passing a junction with the former stagecoach trail. Keep an eye out for birds—15 kinds of warblers alone stay here during the summer. In about 0.5 mile, the trail crosses over the top of Little Lyons Falls at N 40° 37.165, W 82° 19.763 (4). This smaller overhang is at a steep spot in the trail, so watch your step. Follow along the ridge top and make a sharp left turn; the trail leaves the woods at the Pleasant Hill Dam at N 40° 36.372, W 82° 19.540 (5).

Pleasant Hill Reservoir is one of the lakes in the Muskingum Watershed Conservancy District that was built for flood control as well as recreation. The dam here drains a 199-square-mile area. There is no spillway over the top of the dam, which is 775 feet long and 113 feet high. At the parking lot, you will find informational kiosks and a good view of the lake. Take the steps down the front of the dam and follow the Clear Fork along the north shore where the trail reenters the woods at N 40° 36.291, W 82° 19.447 (6). This is the Pleasant Hill Trail, which follows the north shore back to the covered bridge at point 1.

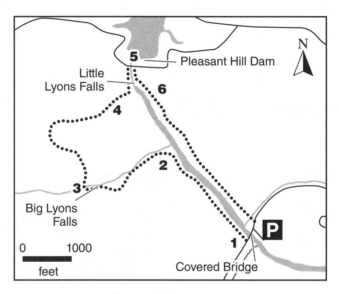

1. Covered bridge
2. Trail turnoff
3. Lyons Falls
4. Little Lyons Falls
5. Pleasant Hill dam
6. Pleasant Hill Trail

> Take advantage of any of several lakes offering boating, fishing, swimming, camping, or hiking.

> Walk scenic shores anywhere in the Muskingum River drainage basin.

> Follow the Buckeye Trail through the rolling hills of eastern Ohio.

Area Information

The Muskingum Watershed Conservancy District (MWCD) is sort of like Ohio's version of the Tennessee Valley Authority. Originally implemented for flood control, the MWCD now also promotes water conservation and recreational opportunities via a series of man-made lakes spread over a wide region. In fact, the Muskingum River watershed drains more than 8,000 square miles, which represents about 20 percent of the entire state, the largest such watershed in Ohio. The district was created during the Depression, and between 1933 and 1938, a series of 14 dams were constructed to regulate water flow, resulting in a series of man-made lakes.

Today, the MWCD is a political subdivision of state government charged with managing these dams and the lakes they created. At several of these reservoirs—Atwood, Leesville, Tappan, Clendening, Piedmont, and Seneca— the district maintains a park that serves the same functions as Ohio's 72 state parks. Recreational opportunities here include boating, fishing, swimming, camping, and hiking. The Buckeye Trail passes by all of these lakes, and it lingers on the shores of some impressive scenery. The MWCD manages 54,000 acres of land and water but has limited the development along the shores to better facilitate maximum enjoyment.

Tappan Lake is at the center of this skein of recreational havens. At 2,350 acres, Tappan is only half the size of its neighbor, Clendening Lake. But, while Clendening has a 10-horsepower limit on motorboats, boats with up to 400 horsepower can race about on Tappan. Launch ramps are located at the marina, at a rest area, and inside Tappan Lake Park. At the park campground on the south shore of the lake, visitors will find food, restrooms, and water; however, these are not found anywhere else, except for the marina. Despite the high horsepower limit, Tappan Lake Park includes quiet, secluded coves, and six different trails, including the Buckeye, lead to them.

Directions: Tappan Lake is located along U.S. Route 250 between Dennison and Cadiz. To get to the campground, cross the lake on Deersville Road and go 2 miles to the sign for the park entrance.

Facilities: Camp sites, picnic areas, and cabins are available at the campground; and boaters can find service at the marina on U.S. Route 250, but there is little else.

Hours open: The lake is open year-round.

Rules and permits: All state boating and fishing regulations are enforced.

Contact information: The mailing address for MWCD headquarters is P.O. Box 349, New Philadelphia, Ohio 44683. The phone number is 330-343-6647.

Other Areas of Interest

Also in Harrison County, sister MWCD lakes Piedmont and Clendening are located to the south. To the east, hiking trails are also found at Harrison State Forest.

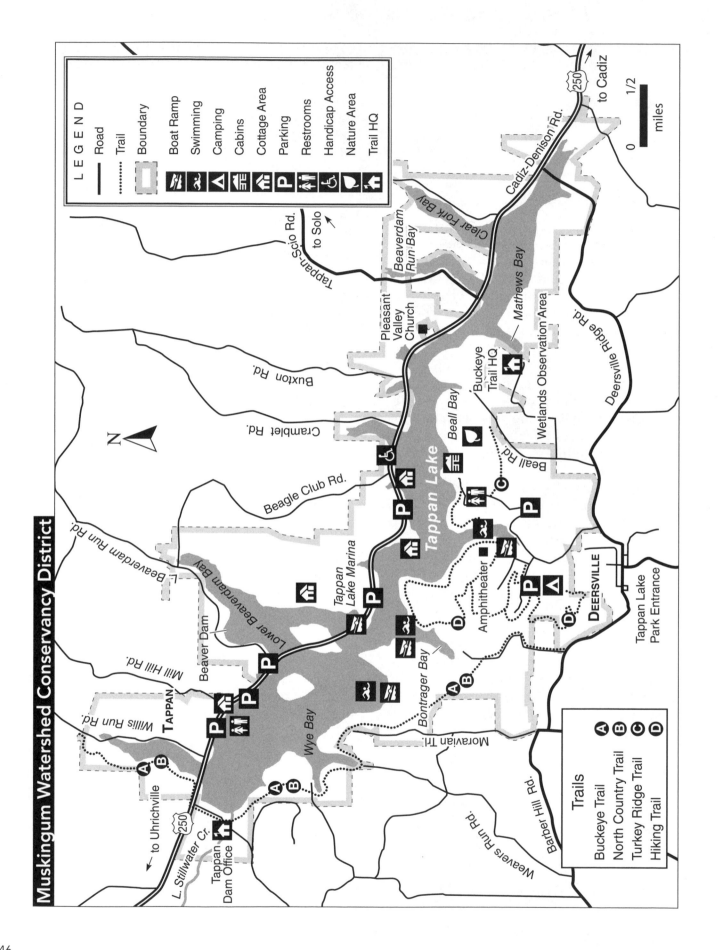

Muskingum Watershed Conservancy District

LEGEND

— Road
····· Trail
□ Boundary

🏊 Boat Ramp
🏃 Swimming
⛺ Camping
🏕 Cabins
🏘 Cottage Area
P Parking
🚻 Restrooms
♿ Handicap Access
🍃 Nature Area
⛺ Trail HQ

to Cadiz

1/2

0   miles

to Solo

Tappan-Scio Rd.

Pleasant Valley Church

Beaverdam Run Bay

Clear Fork Bay

Buxton Rd.

Mathews Bay

Cramblet Rd.

Beall Bay

Buckeye Trail HQ

Wetlands Observation Area

Deersville Ridge Rd.

Beagle Club Rd.

Tappan Lake

Beall Rd.

C

Tappan Lake Marina

P

P

P

Beaverdam Run Rd.

Lower Beaverdam Bay

Amphitheater

D

DEERSVILLE

Mill Hill Rd.

Beaver Dam

P

P

Bontrager Bay

D

Tappan Lake Park Entrance

Willis Run Rd.

TAPPAN

P

P

Wye Bay

Moravian Trl.

A B

Barber Hill Rd.

to Uhrichville

250

L. Stillwater Cr.

Tappan Dam Office

A B

A B

Weavers Run Rd.

N

250

Trails

Ⓐ Buckeye Trail
Ⓑ North Country Trail
Ⓒ Turkey Ridge Trail
Ⓓ Hiking Trail

Tappan Lake, Buckeye Trail

 **Hiking distance:** 3.5 miles round trip

Estimated hiking time: 2 hours

Hike the Buckeye Trail along the scenic shores of a large, yet quiet, lake.

Caution: Watch out for wet spots.

Trail directions: Take U.S. Route 250 south of State Route 151 near the Harrison and Tuscarawas County lines. Signs mark the turnoff for Tappan Dam just above a rest room and boat launch area. Cross the dam and park in the small lot at N 40° 21.443, W 81° 13.661 (1). The familiar blue blazes of the Buckeye Trail go past the dam building and follow along the shore through a fishing area.

In about 0.2 mile, the trail enters the woods at N 40° 21.280, W 81° 13.558 (2). The trail sometimes co-mingles with an ATV and bridle path, but keeping an eye out for the blue blazes will keep you on course. In another 0.2 mile, the trail meets a road near a private boat dock at N 40° 21.159, W 81° 13.397 (3). Near here, you will cross a small inlet stream and begin a steady climb into a mixed hardwood forest.

This climb ends a quarter mile later and nearly 200 feet higher at a crest at N 40° 20.934, W 81° 13.365 (4). The trail now turns away from the lake and goes deeper into the woods. It crosses the bridle path, passes through a grove of pines, and begins to descend again. In about 0.3 mile, the route crosses a wooden bridge over a large inlet stream at N 40° 20.734, W 81° 13.450 (5). Now the trail returns to the lakeshore and continues to follow its winding path. From the secluded coves on the less developed side of the lake, hikers can get a great view of the lake and the rolling hills beyond.

After following the shore for about 0.5 mile, the trail encounters one last cove and has to travel inland to cross a large feeder stream. This part of the route is more overgrown and gets wet easily. At N 40° 20.406, W 81° 13.134 (6), the trail meets a road. Turn left here, and in less than 0.2 mile, the road ends at a lakeside boat dock at N 40° 20.513, W 81° 13.084 (7). The Buckeye Trail goes back into the woods here, but you can quit here if you have parked a second car at this location; otherwise, you can return on the route back to the dam for a 3.5-mile hike.

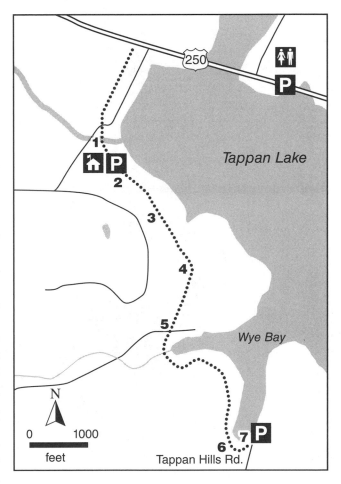

1. Dam lot
2. Enter woods
3. Road
4. Hilltop
5. Bridge
6. Road
7. Boat dock

> Take a walk on rolling farmland on the fringes of Ohio's Amish country.

> Learn about the environment in a preserve that makes education a priority.

Area Information

Norma Johnson was an independent-thinking Tuscarawas County farmer who has left a legacy. Since 2001, a 303-acre portion of her farm has been dedicated as a preserve to promote the conservation of natural resources though education, community outreach, and personal experience. The land is now under the auspices of the Tuscarawas County commissioners and Soil and Water Conservation District and is the site of many activities.

The Norma Johnson Center hosts several classes and activities for everyone. There are crafts and classes for the young and lectures on a variety of specialized topics for older enthusiasts. The center also has three separate hiking trails that put as much emphasis on education and conservation as on recreation:

Conservation Loop: 1.2 miles

Preservation Loop: 1.2 miles

Johnson Loop: 1.3 miles

All three hikes have separate parking lots, but the Preservation and Conservation Loops are connected by a side trail. Also on the grounds is the 1861 Christian Pershing barn, which is on the National Historic Registry.

Directions: The Norma Johnson Center is on State Route 39 just 4 miles west of the Dover interchange of Interstate 77. Parking lots for all three hikes are clustered around the intersections of State Road 39, County Road 139, and Gasser Road.

Hours open: The center is open year-round in daylight hours.

Facilities: Restrooms are at the Conservation Road exit off of County Road 139.

Rules and permits: Pets are permitted on leashes, but there are no trails for horsemen, bikes, or ATVs. Please stay on trails and refrain from picking plants.

Contact information: The center's business office is at 2201-B Progress Street, Dover, Ohio 44622. The phone number is 330-339-7976.

![Photo of a tree trunk with an interpretive sign labeled "AMERICAN BEECH / Fagus grandifolia" describing the tree species]

AMERICAN BEECH
Fagus grandifolia

is one of the best known of eastern trees. The ghostlike, smooth, silvery-gray bark is characteristic. Beechnuts, produced in pairs in spiny pods, are quite tasty and an important wildlife food. Older beeches are very susceptible to interior decay and the larger trees tend to be hollow, with their higher branches broken out by wind, making excellent den trees. The beech, along with the sugar maple, is a successional climax plant species in this area.

❚ Labels for trees help make the Norma Johnson Center an educational experience.

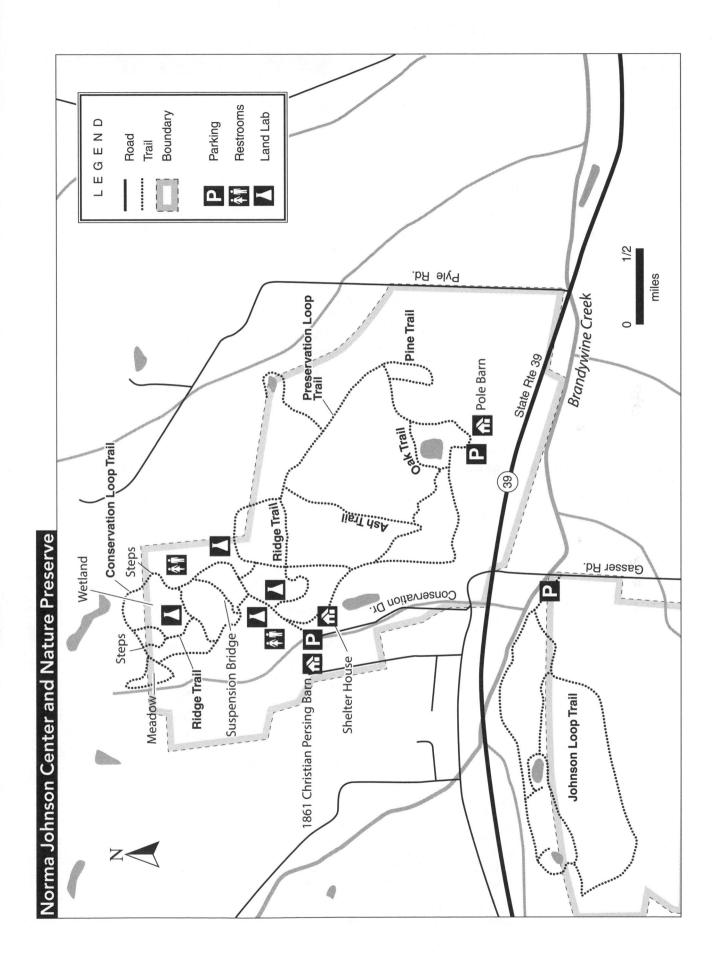

Norma Johnson Center and Nature Preserve

L E G E N D

Road
Trail
Boundary

P Parking
Restrooms
Land Lab

N

Meadow
Steps
Wetland
Steps
Conservation Loop Trail
Steps
Ridge Trail
Suspension Bridge
Ridge Trail
1861 Christian Persing Barn
Shelter House
Conservation Dr.
Gasser Rd.

Preservation Loop Trail
Pine Trail
Oak Trail
Ash Trail
Pole Barn
Pyle Rd.
State Rte 39
39
Brandywine Creek

Johnson Loop Trail

0   1/2
miles

Preservation and Conservation Loops

Hiking distance: 2.5 miles

Estimated hiking time: 1.5 hours

Take a meadow and woods hike on some rolling hillside farmland.

Caution: Trail can be muddy and side trails can be confusing

Trail directions: Turn right off of State Route 39 right before it becomes a divided highway. A sign marks the spot, and the Preservation Loop parking lot and kiosk are at N 40° 30.464, W 81° 32.197 (1). Head uphill on the right side of a large pond on a mowed path through a meadow. After about 0.2 mile, a side trail branches right at a leveling spot at N 40° 30.519, W 81° 32.124 (2). The main trail turns left here and heads uphill. In another 0.2 mile is a side trail to the right at N 40° 30.578, W 81° 32.185 (3) and heads down to another pond. Stay on the main trail until it levels out and a sign marks a side trail to the Conservation Loop at N 40° 31.051, N 81° 32.334 (4).

Turn right here and enter the woods on a trail that leads downhill via switchbacks. At the bottom of a short hill is a sign marking the Conservation Loop at N 40° 31.065, W 81° 32.355 (5). Turn right and follow the route up into the woods. In keeping with the center's educational goals, trees are often labeled with signs that also illustrate leaf shapes. Among the trees found here are several types of oak and maple, aspen, black cherry, sassafras, white ash, shagbark hickory, elm, black walnut, yellow poplar, beech, and white pine. After passing by a side trail that leads to a suspension bridge, the trail leads up to a wetland pond at N 40° 31.098, W 81° 32.398 (6). This pond has an observation deck and a side trail around it. Bear right on the main trail and pass an observation blind that overlooks the pond, and come to a set of stairs at N 40° 31.132, N 81° 32.354 (7). Bear left at the top of the steps and skirt the outer edges of the center for over

0.5 mile. You can see strip-mined ponds from unreclaimed mining areas on the right.

Eventually the trail winds back, and a meadow at N 40° 31.145, W 81° 32.414 (8) meets a side trail that leads back to the wetland pond. Continue through the edge of the meadow until it meets a junction at N 40° 31.051, W 81° 32.372 (9). A right turn leads to restrooms and the Conservation Road parking lot, while veering left completes the Conservation Loop at point 5. Retrace your steps back to point 4, but this time turn right to complete the Preservation Loop.

As you head downhill, be sure to appreciate the views of neighboring rolling farms. After about 0.2 mile is a junction at N 41° 30.553, W 81° 32.342 (10). A right turn here leads to the Conservation Loop lot, so stay on the main trail as it descends toward Route 39 and then runs parallel to it as it heads back to the large pond and point 1.

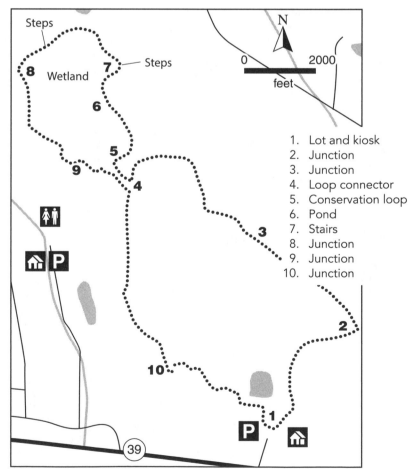

1. Lot and kiosk
2. Junction
3. Junction
4. Loop connector
5. Conservation loop
6. Pond
7. Stairs
8. Junction
9. Junction
10. Junction

> Follow an 80-mile stretch of the towpath of the old Ohio Erie Canal.

> Hike or bicycle past abandoned locks and other historical relics.

> View a variety of land- and water-based wildlife from a well-maintained and popular vantage point.

Area Information

The Ohio Erie Canal was a tremendous undertaking. Built between 1825 and 1832, the 309-mile canal route was built by mainly Irish and German immigrants who were paid 30 cents per day. Once finished, the canal revolutionized frontier conditions because goods could now be moved at the rapid pace of 4 miles per hour. The towpath alongside the waterway was used by mules hauling the boats along, and the many locks along the route helped spawn and nurture the growth of many communities. From completion until 1913, the Ohio Erie Canal was a boon to Ohio.

Now the canal's towpath is making a comeback as a recreational entity. Through cooperation between agencies across county lines, an 81-mile stretch of the towpath between Cleveland and Dover will be open to the public. Not to be confused with the 110-mile Ohio Erie Scenic Canal Byway, which is a driving route along nearby highways, the Towpath Trail is a walking or cycling path that follows the original route. And, like the original canal, the success of the endeavor depends on cooperation. Various sections of the route are maintained with the help of the Cleveland Metroparks, Valley National Park, Metro Parks Serving Summit County, Stark Parks, and the Tuscarawas County Parks Department. Some hikes along the route are included in chapters devoted to some of these agencies. In addition, the ever-present Buckeye Trail follows much of this 81-mile route. The Ohio and Erie Canalway Coalition oversees these efforts.

There are 48 trailheads along the route, so hikers are free to fashion their own routes to suit their tastes. And the route through a heavily populated region is quite popular, with over two million visits per year. The trail surface varies from the pavement in Cuyahoga County to crushed limestone to hard-packed earth, but the surface and flat terrain are always ideal for walking or bicycling. In addition to opportunities to view birds, amphibians, and wildflowers, there are numerous canal remains and signs discussing items of historical significance.

Directions: The Towpath Trail can be accessed at 48 trailheads along the Cuyahoga and Tuscarawas Rivers between Cleveland and Zoar.

Facilities: Many of the trailheads have restrooms, and some are connected with very nice parks, but there is great diversity.

Hours open: The Towpath Trail is open year-round during daylight hours.

Rules and permits: No permits are needed for the trail. Various county agencies are responsible for enforcement in different parts of the trail, so rules may vary.

Contact information: The Ohio and Erie Canalway Coalition office is located at 47 West Exchange Street, Akron, Ohio 44308. Their phone number is 330-374-5657.

Other Areas of Interest

The Towpath Trail passes through several parks and other hikes mentioned in this book. Among some of the other attractions found on or near the trail are the Helena III, a working canal boat in Canal Fulton, Portage Lakes State Park, Stan Hywet Hall, and Hale Farm and Western Reserve Village.

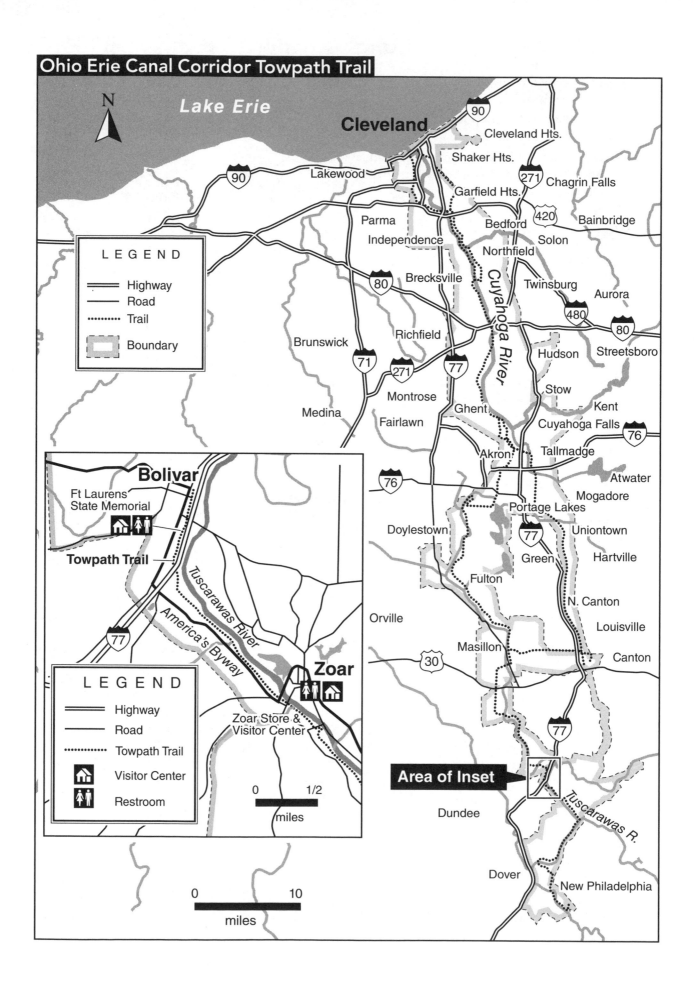

Ohio Erie Canal Corridor Towpath Trail

Lake Erie

Cleveland

Cleveland Hts.

Shaker Hts.

Lakewood

271 Chagrin Falls

Garfield Hts.

420 Bainbridge

Parma Bedford

Independence Solon

Northfield

Brecksville

Twinsburg Aurora

Richfield Hudson

Brunswick Streetsboro

Stow

Montrose Kent

Medina Ghent Cuyahoga Falls

Fairlawn

Akron Tallmadge

Atwater

Mogadore

Portage Lakes

Doylestown Uniontown

Green Hartville

Fulton

N. Canton

Orville Louisville

Masillon

Dundee Canton

Dover New Philadelphia

Cuyahoga River

Tuscarawas R.

Area of Inset

LEGEND

━━━ Highway
─── Road
••••• Trail
▨ Boundary

Inset map

Bolivar

Ft Laurens
State Memorial

Towpath Trail

Zoar

Zoar Store &
Visitor Center

Tuscarawas River

America's Byway

LEGEND

━━━ Highway
─── Road
••••• Towpath Trail
🏠 Visitor Center
🚻 Restroom

0   1/2
miles

0   10
miles

52

Zoar to Bolivar, Buckeye Trail

Hiking distance: 6 miles

Estimated hiking time: 2.5 hours

Hike a scenic stretch along the Tuscarawas River that is full of history.

Caution: Trails close to waterways are likely to get muddy.

Trail directions: From the Bolivar exit off Interstate 77, take State Route 212 east through the historic village of Zoar, then turn right on County Road 82, which crosses the levy at the edge of town. Immediately after crossing the Tuscarawas River, turn left at the trailhead parking lot at N 40° 36.418, W 81° 25.601 (1). A kiosk here has maps and information, but there are no restrooms. At the corner of the parking lot, a trail leads down to the river. Take this path and turn to head upstream. The route is again on the Buckeye Trail, so follow the blue blazes.

In about 0.3 mile, the trail crosses under an abandoned bridge at N 40° 36.508, W 81° 25.709 (2). This bridge leads to Zoar, a community founded by German separatists in 1817. This religious group essentially pooled their resources and worked as a commune until 1895. By serving as canal builders, they were able to pay off their mortgage, and they continued to thrive for years afterward. The Zoarites did not live as families but in communal buildings as they developed their self-sufficient community. Today, the Ohio Historical Society owns some of the original buildings and gardens and hosts many special activities in town.

Continue on the towpath route for another 0.2 mile, where a side trail comes in on the

▌A picnic shelter at the site of Fort Laurens, Ohio's only Revolutionary War fort.

right at N 40° 36.622, W 81° 25.629 (3). This trail leads to Zoar Dam on the Tuscarawas River, and the peaceful spot is worthy of a side trip. Afterward, continue on and soon come to the remains of lock 10 of the canal, along with some signage explaining how the locks worked. Follow alongside the river, and in another 1.1 miles is the remains of lock 9 at N 40° 37.412, W 81° 26.801 (4). There are two more abandoned canal locks spaced over the next half mile. You can walk on all the lock walls, and they all have informational signs.

After about 2.5 miles of riverside walking, the trail crosses Interstate 77 at N 40° 38.001, W 81° 27.332 (5). The bridge here is a modern sturdy structure built just to accommodate hikers and horseback riders. Former Congressman Ralph Regula of Canton, a longtime friend of hikers, had a lot to do with getting the bridge built. After crossing the interstate, turn to the right. Walk between a road and the highway past a few picnic shelters, and in 0.5 mile, arrive at the location of Fort Laurens at N 40° 38.357, W 81° 27.303 (6).

Built in 1778, Fort Laurens was the only Revolutionary War fort built in what is now Ohio. At that time, the Americans based in Pittsburgh and the British at Detroit were fighting over Ohio and the loyalty of the Native Americans who lived here. The Americans built the fort in hope of launching an attack on Detroit from here the following spring. But the isolated and poorly supplied outpost was besieged by Indians serving with the notorious renegade Simon Girty in February 1779. During the siege, the Americans were reduced to eating roots and boiling their own moccasins to survive. The fort held out but was abandoned the following summer. In 1972, an archaeological excavation of the Ohio Histor-

ical Society found the outlines of the original fort, and artifacts from that expedition are on display at the museum now standing here.

Tour the museum or at least walk around the outlines of the fort, and be thankful that you didn't have to spend a hungry winter inside such confines. Then, unless you have a second car here, turn around and retrace your route back to point 1.

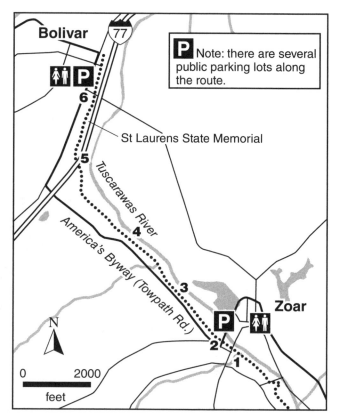

1. Lot and kiosk
2. Cross under bridge
3. Zoar Dam turnoff
4. Lock 9
5. Cross over I-77
6. Fort Laurens

> Enjoy a park that is easy to get to for many people.
> Sample the bogs that are examples of Ohio's only natural lakes.
> Visit a park that has its own mansion.

Area Information

Quail Hollow is a gift from the Stewart family, who sold the property to the state for half of its appraised value. The Stewarts were railroad magnates who bought the 700-acre property from the original pioneer family in 1914. They used the existing farmhouse as a vacation and weekend cottage until they completely renovated and made the new manor their main home in 1937.

But well before that, it was the glacier that made more of an impact on the property. Some 12,000 years ago, advancing glaciers covered the region and altered the topography. At the end of this ice age, pieces of the glacier broke off and melted in depressions, leaving behind small kettle lakes. Natural lakes are rare in Ohio, and the ones here are more like bogs or marshes. Marshland seems kind of unusual here, since the base elevation is around 1,000 feet, which is fairly high for Ohio. The area is higher because it is near the divide that separates the Great Lakes watershed from the Ohio Valley watershed.

This condition makes for a diversity of plants and wildlife. There are both prairie grasses and woodland swamps that host their respective plant life and forests that provide homes to fox, raccoon, deer, and wild turkey.

Most state parks don't have mansions on site, and Quail Hollow takes full advantage

Boardwalk through a soggy marsh at Quail Hollow State Park.

of this unique feature. The former Stewart manor now hosts a visitors' center and also serves as a meeting center. Next door, the former carriage house has been turned into a nature center that features live animals and hosts educational and other special activities. Nearby is a 9,000-square-foot herb garden and a 2,000-foot interpretive trail that is handicap accessible.

Also on the grounds is a primitive group camp that can host up to 25 people. Fishing is available at the two-acre Shady Lane Pond. In the picnic nearby are a playground, volley-ball court, and basketball hoop. For the long Northeast Ohio winters, Quail Hollow offers sledding, ice skating, and cross-country ski rentals. There are 5 miles of a bridle mountain bike trail and 8 separate hiking trails.

Directions: Quail Hollow is near Hartville on the border between Stark and Portage counties. From the junction of State Routes 43 and 619 in Hartville, go north on Congress Lake Road for less than a mile to the park entrance on the right.

Hours: The park is open year-round, but manor and nature center hours vary.

Facilities: Restrooms are at the campground at four picnic areas and at the nature center and manor.

Rules and permits: All state park and fishing regulations apply.

Contact information: The park address is 13480 Congress Lake Road, Hartville, Ohio 44632; phone number is 330-877-6652. It is administered through Portage Lakes State Park, 5031 Manchester Road, Akron, Ohio 44319; phone number is 330-644-2220.

Park Trails

Coniferous Forest, 1.2 miles

Deciduous Forest, 1.2 miles

Woodland Swamp, 1.5 miles

Peatland, 0.7 mile

Meadowlands, 1.5 miles

Beaver Lodge, 1.5 miles

Tall Grass Prairie, 0.3 mile

Nature for All, 0.5 mile (paved)

These trails intersect and are sometimes concurrent. Consult a park map to construct your own route.

Other Areas of Interest

West Branch and Portage Lake State Parks are nearby and offer swimming, boating, and fishing. Two nearby state nature preserves, Triangle Lake and Kent Bog, offer good examples of bog vegetation.

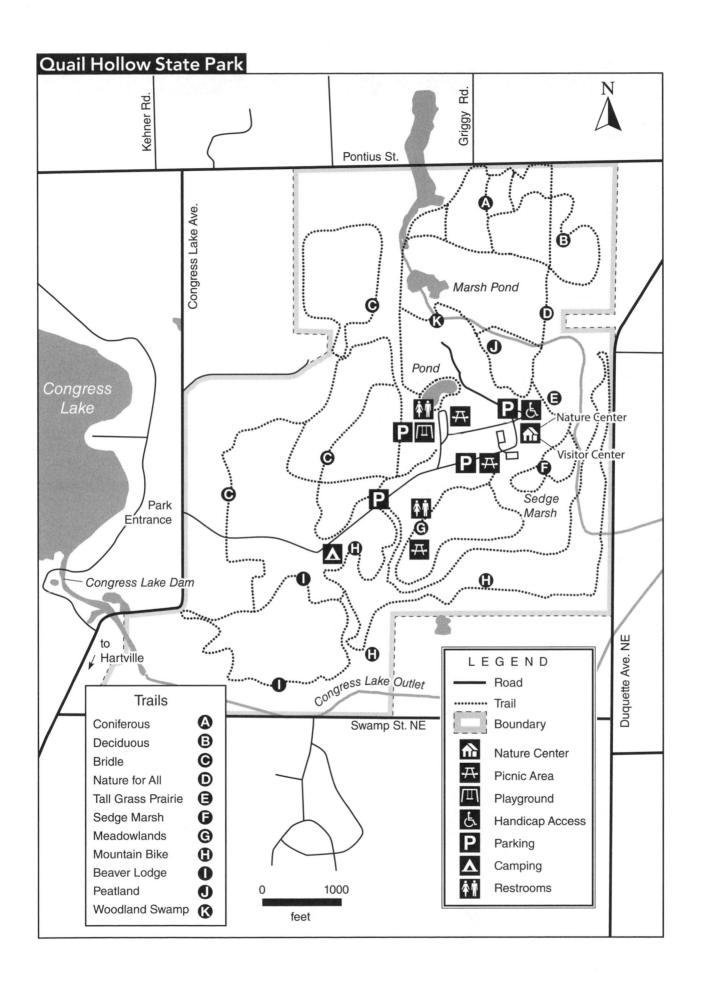

Quail Hollow State Park

Kehner Rd.

Pontius St.

Griggy Rd.

N

Congress Lake Ave.

Marsh Pond

Ⓐ

Ⓑ

Ⓒ

Ⓓ

Ⓚ

Ⓙ

Congress Lake

Pond

Ⓔ

Nature Center

Visitor Center

Ⓒ

Ⓕ

Sedge Marsh

Ⓒ

Ⓒ

Ⓖ

Park Entrance

Ⓗ

Ⓗ

Congress Lake Dam

Ⓘ

to Hartville

Ⓗ

Ⓘ

Congress Lake Outlet

Swamp St. NE

Duquette Ave. NE

Trails

Coniferous	Ⓐ
Deciduous	Ⓑ
Bridle	Ⓒ
Nature for All	Ⓓ
Tall Grass Prairie	Ⓔ
Sedge Marsh	Ⓕ
Meadowlands	Ⓖ
Mountain Bike	Ⓗ
Beaver Lodge	Ⓘ
Peatland	Ⓙ
Woodland Swamp	Ⓚ

LEGEND

——	Road
········	Trail
▢	Boundary
🏠	Nature Center
⛩	Picnic Area
🎏	Playground
♿	Handicap Access
P	Parking
▲	Camping
🚻	Restrooms

0   1000

feet

57

Sedge Marsh and Tall Grass Trails

Hiking distance: 1.4 miles
Estimated hiking time: 1 hour

Take a walk in a marsh at one of Northeast Ohio's most secluded parks.

Caution: Although the trail is mowed, it is not blazed and it can be very soggy during wet weather.

Trail directions: Park in the lot right before the main lot for the house, it is located at N 40° 58.690, W 81° 18.349 (1). Go right into the woods and bear right. At just under 0.4 mile is a turnoff for the Beaver Lodge Trail at N 40° 58.481, W 81° 18.614 (2). Here the Buckeye Trail joins the route and remains concurrent for a while. At about 0.7 mile, you will come to a bridge at the edge of a pine forest at N 40° 58.569, W 81° 18.301 (3).

In another 0.1 mile is a turnoff for the Sedge Marsh Trail at N 40° 58.660, W 81° 18.302 (4). Stay on the Buckeye Trail and proceed another 0.1 mile to the Tallgrass Trail turnoff at N 40° 58.721, W 81° 18.185 (5). Continue for another 0.2 mile to a log where the Sedge Marsh Trail branches off at N 40° 58.663, W 81° 18.174 (6). Continue back this way through moist terrain for another 0.1 mile. At N 40° 58.640, W 81° 18.248 (7) is a boardwalk that crosses over the marsh and offers a good vantage point for observing the waterfowl that frequent the area. After crossing the marsh, return to the main trail in less than 0.1 mile and turn right to return to the parking lot.

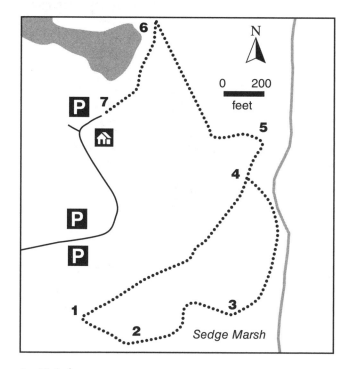

1. Main lot
2. Junction
3. Bridge
4. Junction
5. Junction
6. Junction
7. Boardwalk

Beaver Lodge Trail

Hiking distance: 2 miles

Estimated hiking time: 1 hour

Take a soggy walk in beaver country.

Caution: This trail is not well marked and can get very muddy, so boot up accordingly.

Trail directions: Park at the small lot for mountain bikes near the main entrance at N 40° 58.368, W 81° 18.371 (1). There are primitive restrooms and an information kiosk here. Ignore the mountain bike trail on the left and follow the hiking path on the right. In about 0.1 mile is an old family cemetery at N 40° 58.327, W 81° 18.380 (2), which soon afterward merges with the bike trail.

Continue on the windy route for 0.3 mile to a four-way junction at N 40° 58.252, W 81° 18.436 (3). Turn right and follow the sign marked Beaver Lodge Trail, which is also part of the Buckeye Trail here. Just beyond this, the trail splits at a meadow. It also starts to get muddy. Take the right fork and go about 0.2 mile, where the Buckeye Trail leaves on the right at N 40° 58.236, W 81° 19.043 (4). Continue left on the Beaver Lodge Trail.

From here, the trail winds around for a mile before returning to point 3, where you can retrace your route. But when hiking in beaver neighborhoods, you need to watch for wet spots. And if you get off the trail, it can be confusing. Generally, the Buckeye Trail portion of this trail is well marked and maintained, but the park trails are soggy and hard to follow.

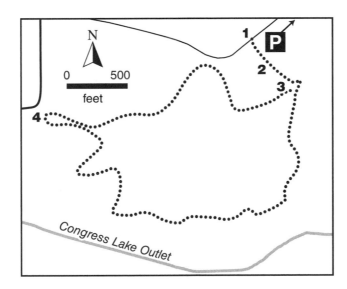

1. Mountain bike lot
2. Cemetery
3. Four-way intersection
4. Buckeye Trail splits off

> Enjoy a diversity of sylvan experiences in an urban area.

> Follow a river and canal route with a historical overview.

> Take advantage of the opportunities offered by man-made lakes.

Area Information

The Stark County Park District's mission is "to acquire, preserve, and develop natural areas accessible to all residents of Stark County for purposes of passive recreation, conservation, education, and outdoor nature appreciation." From the park administrator's offices (located at 5300 Tyner Street Northwest, Canton, Ohio 44708), the park district oversees a dozen parks, 15 trails, and a variety of year-round outdoor activities.

One of the unique aspects of the Stark County Park District is its participation in the Ohio and Erie National Heritage Canalway, a 110-mile corridor that runs from Cleveland to Zoar. The Stark County portion of this route is the Congressman Ralph Regula Towpath Trail, named for the recently retired official who has always been a strong supporter of trails. This trail and bordering land follow the route of the historical canal that was the life-blood of the community in the 19th century. The trail parallels the Tuscarawas River and passes through the towns of Canal Fulton, Massillon, and Navarre. In Canal Fulton, a replica canal flatboat takes tourists for a trip, and the Canalway Visitor Center and Museum are also nearby. Fourteen parking lots offer access to the 25 miles of towpath trail; the stretch from John Glenn Grove to Craig Pittman Park near Navarre is noted for being particularly scenic.

Stark County Parks also offer several man-made lakes, such as Walborn Reservoir in the northeastern part of the county. Named for former Alliance mayor Dale Walborn, this lake came under the jurisdiction of the park district in 1998. The reservoir park covers 1,850 acres and offers ample opportunities for hikers, bikers, horseback riders, boaters, and fishermen. The mostly flat terrain offers woods of pine, hickory, and oak, as well as seasonal wildflowers such as mayapple and trillium. The fauna in the area includes a variety of birds such as wild turkey, osprey, waterfowl, and even bald eagles.

Directions: The towpath trail has multiple parking lots available at locations just off U.S. Route 21, which is parallel to the trail. To get to Walborn Reservoir, take U.S. Route 62 east from Canton to State Route 44 north. Turn east on Pontius Street and continue to follow it after it becomes Price Street. The reservoir is on the right.

Hours open: All parks along the towpath are open year-round during daylight hours.

Facilities: The Congressman Ralph Regula Towpath Trail has restrooms at most parking lots. Picnic tables and shelters are also available, and restrooms are located at the visitor center.

Rules and permits: At all Stark County Parks, pets must be kept on a leash. Camping, fires, ATVs, alcohol, and swimming are prohibited. The speed limit is 15 mph on all park roads.

Contact information: The John Glenn Grove Trailhead is at 8000 Warmington Road Southwest, Massillon, Ohio 44646. The Craig Pittman Trailhead of the Towpath Trail is at 8200 Harding Drive Southwest, Navarre, Ohio 44662. Walborn Reservoir is located at 11324 Price Street, Alliance, Ohio 44601.

Other Areas of Interest

The Stark County Park system also includes the following 10 parks:

Sippo Lake, 5712 12th Street Northwest, Canton, Ohio 44708

Molly Stark, 7900 Columbus Road, Louisville, Ohio 44641

Deer Creek Reservoir, 14514 Price Street Northeast, Alliance, Ohio 44601

Devonshire, 4400 South Boulevard, Canton, Ohio 44718

Whitacre Greer Equestrian Park, 4290 Irish Road Northwest, Waynesburg, Ohio 44688

Petros Lake, 5100 block of Perry Drive Southwest, Canton, Ohio 44706

Frank Esmont, 200 block of Mill Street Southeast, Canton, Ohio 44707

Cook's Lagoon, 1800 block of Mahoning Road Northeast, Canton, Ohio 44705

Magnolia Flouring Mills, 216 Main Street, Magnolia, Ohio 44643

David Fichtner Outdoor Education Center, 12833 Market Avenue North, Hartville, Ohio 44632

Ohio and Erie Canal Corridor

As mentioned before, this portion of the Stark County system is also another part of the Ohio and Erie National Heritage Canalway. Within this section of the corridor, there are other parks worth traversing.

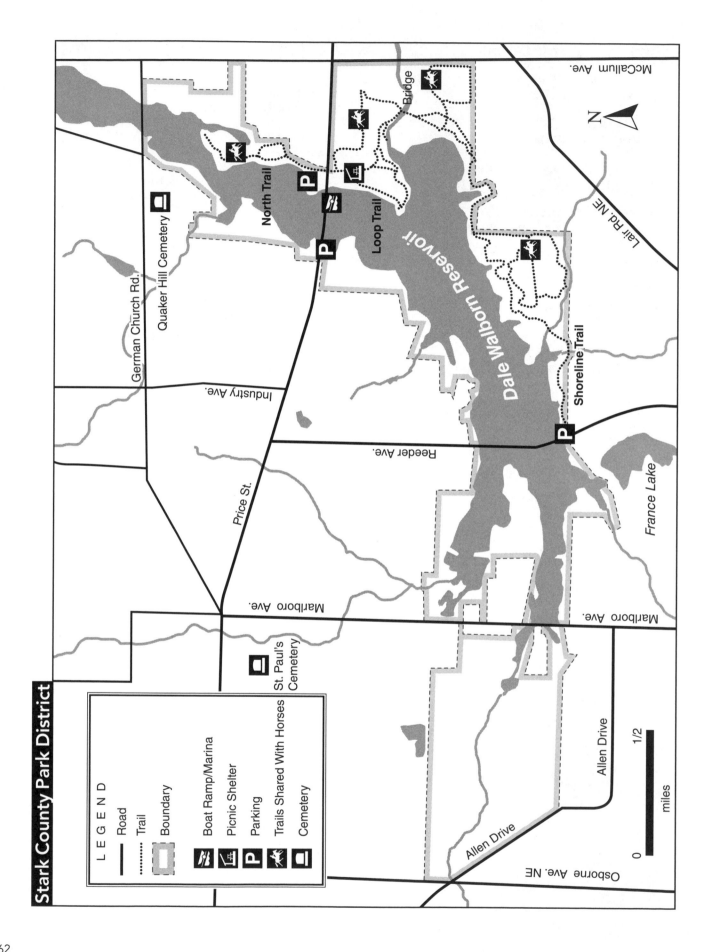

Stark County Park District

LEGEND

——	Road
··········	Trail
	Boundary
	Boat Ramp/Marina
	Picnic Shelter
P	Parking
	Trails Shared With Horses
	Cemetery

Dale Walborn Reservoir

North Trail

Loop Trail

Shoreline Trail

Bridge

Quaker Hill Cemetery

St. Paul's Cemetery

France Lake

German Church Rd.

Industry Ave.

Price St.

Reeder Ave.

Marlboro Ave.

Marlboro Ave.

McCallum Ave.

Lair Rd. NE

Allen Drive

Allen Drive

Osborne Ave. NE

N

0   1/2
miles

Warmington Road to Craig Pittman Park

Hiking distance: 7 miles round trip
Estimated hiking time: 3 hours

Caution: This trail is paved and perfectly flat, but keep an eye out for the bicyclists who share the route.

Trail directions: The trail parking lot is on Warmington Road less than 1 mile west of Route 21 at N 40° 45.103, W 81° 31.675 (1). Park in the John Glenn Grove lot and follow the signs to the Canal Corridor Trail. The paved path follows the route of the old canal towpath; the Tuscarawas River is on one side, and the remains of the canal is on the other. The route is also frequented by joggers and bicyclists, so you should be prepared to share. A clear view of the canal bed is available, and you will be able to spot frogs trying to hide themselves on floating logs.

Continue south 1.8 miles until you come into the town of Navarre at the town water plant at N 40° 43.588, W 81° 31.733 (2). Go on past the building and follow the route another 0.3 mile until you come to a railroad bridge at N 40° 43.355, W 81° 31.856 (3). The railroad tracks will remain on your left as you proceed about another 0.3 mile. Here the tracks cross U.S. Route 62 at the western edge of town at N 40° 43.164, W 81° 31.787 (4). Continue to skirt the edge of downtown Navarre for another 0.4 mile until this trail crosses U.S. Route 21 at the southern end of town at N 40° 43.071, W 81° 31.367 (5). Follow the route and the river east for another 0.8 mile until you get to Craig Pittman Park at N 40° 43.227, W 81° 30.692 (6). This location contains a large parking area where one-way hikers can park a car; restrooms are also available for those who need them before making the return trip.

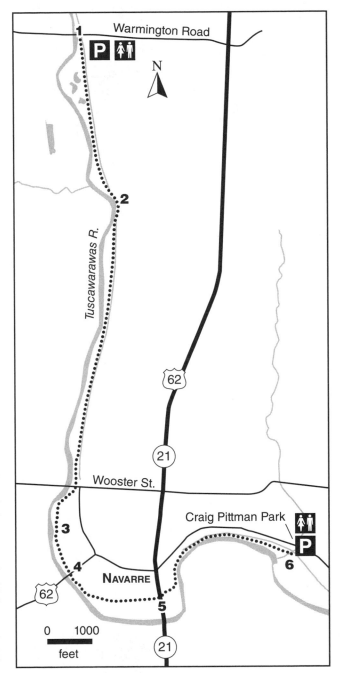

1. John Glenn Grove lot
2. Water plant
3. Railroad bridge
4. Cross Route 62
5. Cross Route 21
6. Craig Pittman Park lot

Walborn Reservoir, Shoreline Trail

 Hiking distance: 5.2 miles round trip

Estimated hiking time: 3 hours

Caution: The trails are not well marked, and the intermingling of horse and hiking trails can cause confusion.

Trail directions: From the junction of U.S. 62 and State Route 183 in downtown Alliance, take 183 north to the village of Limaville and turn left on Main Street. Go 2 miles (the road name changes to Price Street) and turn left at the sign for the reservoir. The marina parking lot can be found immediately at N 40° 58.607, W 81° 10.867 (1). The Shoreline Trail begins just at the rear of the marina.

The park consists of 1,235 acres; water covers 472 of these acres. The Shoreline Trail is marked only by sporadic signs that say "Shoreline Trail." In addition, the hiking and horse trails are both called Shoreline Trail, and the two frequently cross each other between areas where they are concurrent. Your best bet is to always take the trail option that is closest to the lake shore.

After going about a quarter mile, you will come to a short side trail at N 40° 58.435, W 81° 10.985 (2); this side trail leads to a bench overlooking the lake at a promontory. Enjoy the view here, which includes an island that is supposed to be the site of an eagle's nest, and then proceed another 0.2 mile until you come to the dam at N 40° 58.465, W 81° 10.798 (3). Follow the stream banks near the dam past several crossings with the horse trail for 0.3 mile until you come to a bridge over the feeder stream at N 40° 58.393, W 81° 10.553 (4). Cross the bridge and proceed another 0.15 mile to where you cross a road at N 40° 58.303, W 81° 10.639 (5). Now you will find a levee on your right that blocks your view of the lake.

Soon afterward, you will go back into the woods as the Shoreline Trail goes north out of sight of the shoreline for the next 1.25 miles. But while the lake is out of sight, you will be in a diverse hardwood forest that features a mix of oak, maple, hickory, poplar, beech, and black cherry trees.

The trail still frequently crosses the horse trail. At 2.2 miles into the hike, you will come to a causeway over wetlands at N 40° 57.888, W 81° 11.582 (6). An abundance of waterfowl is visible in this marshy area as well as on the lake and shore.

After crossing the causeway, proceed another 0.3 mile to a small parking area off Reeder Avenue (7). If you have two cars, you can leave one here for a 2.6-mile hike, or you can reverse your route for a 5.2-mile hike. Walborn Reservoir is an outdoor recreation haven in any season. On the winter day that I hiked it with three friends, we saw a group setting up an ice fishing tent in the middle of the lake.

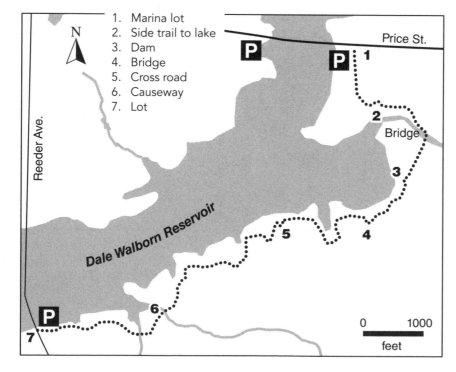

1. Marina lot
2. Side trail to lake
3. Dam
4. Bridge
5. Cross road
6. Causeway
7. Lot

N

Price St.

Bridge

Reeder Ave.

Dale Walborn Reservoir

0   1000
feet

> Hike around a portion of one of Ohio's largest man-made lakes.
> Observe the wildlife found in glaciated northeastern Ohio.

Area Information

West Branch State Park may be centered around a man-made reservoir, but the current attractions of the area are all natural. The park is located on the glaciated plateau of northeastern Ohio, which has resulted in the gentle rolling farmland of the area. The glacier is also responsible for marshy areas and small kettle lakes that were formed when ice blocks broke off and melted in hollowed-out pockets. These bog areas are filled with plants such as buttonbush, adder, and skunk cabbage.

The woodlands of the region are predominantly beech and maple, but tulip poplar, hickory, pine, and red oak are also plentiful. Common woodland wildflowers found here include Dutchman's breeches, bloodroot, and trillium. The area also has an abundance of fauna, such as deer, fox, skunk, opossum, and raccoon. Various fowl can be found near the lake, and flocks of wild turkey frequent the area.

The West Branch in the park name refers to the west branch of the Mahoning River that runs through this portion of Portage County. The first settlement here was Campbellsport, named for pioneer surveyor and land agent Captain John Campbell. But the topography of this farmland changed in 1965, when the U.S. Army Corps of Engineers completed construction of Michael J. Kirwan Reservoir. The 2,650-acre lake was developed for flood control, water supply, and recreation. Because of the many possibilities for the latter, West Branch was designated a state park in 1966.

Kirwan Reservoir is clearly the centerpiece of the park. For anglers, the lake is stocked with bass, walleye, catfish, and muskellunge. Fishing can be done from shore at multiple spots, including a wheelchair accessible pier near the marina. For boaters, six launch ramps are available, and there is no horsepower limit. This makes the large lake a natural haven for boating enthusiasts. The marina also features boat rentals, gasoline, and other supplies. Among the dock rentals available is one that is wheelchair accessible. The park also has a 700-foot swimming beach composed of sand.

Directions: Take State Route 5 east past the junction with State Route 59, just east of Ravenna. Proceed a few miles to Rock Spring Road and turn right. Just before the causeway that crosses the reservoir, you will find the main parking lot on the shoreline on the right (west).

Facilities: On the left off of Rock Spring Road, you will see Esworthy Road, which leads to the main campground. This area features 155 sites with electric hookups. The area also includes 29 full-service sites, 14 nonelectric sites, and some lakeside sites that offer boating access. Each site has a picnic table and fire ring, and water and latrines are readily available. A separate equestrian camp is also located in the park. The park includes 20 miles of bridle trails, 12 miles of mountain biking trails, and 14 miles of hiking trails.

Rules and permits: The park is open year-round. Hunting, fishing, and no-wake zones are clearly marked. Pets are permitted in the campgrounds. Target shooting is prohibited.

Contact information: The park office is located at 5708 Esworthy Road, Ravenna, Ohio 44266. The phone number is 330-296-3239.

Other Areas of Interest

Portage County also contains Tinker's Creek State Park, which is located near Streetsboro in the northwest corner of the county. Just to the southeast are Lake Milton State Park and Berlin Lake Wildlife Area.

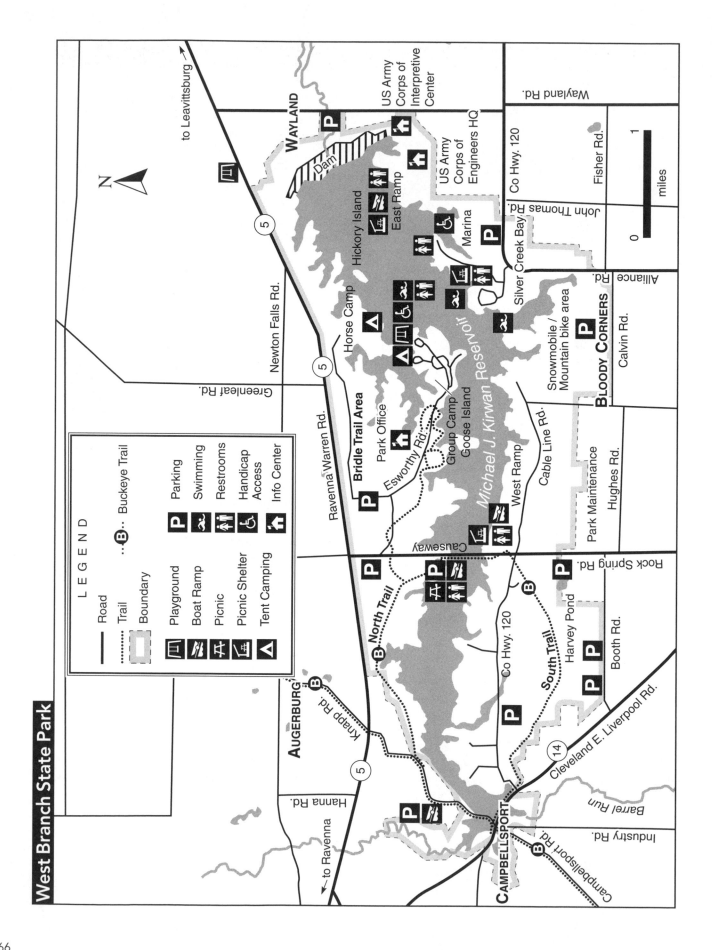

West Branch State Park

LEGEND

— Road
······ Trail
▢ Boundary
···**B**··· Buckeye Trail

P Parking
🏊 Swimming
🚻 Restrooms
♿ Handicap Access
🏠 Info Center

▥ Playground
🚤 Boat Ramp
⛱ Picnic
🏕 Picnic Shelter
⛺ Tent Camping

N

Michael J. Kirwan Reservoir

WAYLAND

US Army Corps of Interpretive Center
US Army Corps of Engineers HQ

Dam

East Ramp
Hickory Island

Marina

Horse Camp

Bridle Trail Area

Park Office

Esworthy Rd.

Group Camp
Goose Island

West Ramp

Causeway

North Trail

South Trail

Harvey Pond

CAMPBELLSPORT

AUGERBURG

BLOODY CORNERS

Snowmobile / Mountain bike area

Park Maintenance

to Leavittsburg

to Ravenna

Newton Falls Rd.

Greenleaf Rd.

Ravenna Warren Rd.

Hanna Rd.

Knapp Rd.

Industry Rd.

Campbellsport Rd.

Barrel Run

Cleveland E. Liverpool Rd.

Booth Rd.

Rock Spring Rd.

Hughes Rd.

Cable Line Rd.

Calvin Rd.

Alliance Rd.

John Thomas Rd.

Silver Creek Bay

Co Hwy. 120

Fisher Rd.

Wayland Rd.

Co Hwy. 120

5

5

5

14

0   1
miles

66

West Branch State Park, Buckeye Trail

Hiking distance: 9-mile loop

Estimated hiking time: 5 hours

A long, but level, hike around the eastern third of Kirwan Reservoir offers a great opportunity to view lakeshore wildlife.

Caution: As with any lakeshore walk, the trail gets muddy pretty easily.

Trail directions: Park in the small lot for the boat ramp on Rock Spring Road on the northern end of the reservoir at N 41° 08.472, W 81° 08.887 (1). Follow the sign that directs you into the woods here and then head west for a counterclockwise loop. Hike along the northern shore of the reservoir in a forest of hickory, pine, and oak. This is also part of the blue-blazed Buckeye Trail, as is most of this hike. Follow this stretch for over 3 miles through marshy areas with nearby power lines and a railroad track.

Eventually, the trail emerges to intersect with Knapp Road at N 41° 08.670, W 81° 10.915 (2). Here the Buckeye Trail splits off to the right (north), but you should turn left instead and follow Knapp Road for another 0.8

mile. Just before the road crosses the western tip of the reservoir, you will come to a small parking lot at N 41° 08.206, W 81° 11.476 (3). Cross the reservoir and rejoin the Buckeye Trail where Knapp Road meets State Route 14 at N 41° 08.038, W 81° 11.505 (4). At this corner of the reservoir was the original town of Campbellsport, as named for Captain John Campbell, an officer in the War of 1812 and early Portage County sheriff.

Turn left here and follow along State Route 14 for about 0.3 mile to the junction with Cable Line Road at N 41° 07.904, W 81° 11.226 (5). Just after this junction, the trail reenters the woods on the left and follows the hills that ring the southern shore of the lake. This portion is well off the lake, goes through public hunting ground, and is less traveled. But you are more likely to see wildlife such as deer, coyote, and wild turkey here. Follow this trail for over 3 miles, moving through field and forest and across small streams until the trail crosses Cable Line Road at N 41° 07.937, W 81° 08.944 (6). The trail then reenters the woods briefly before coming out on Rock Spring Road. Turn left here and travel 0.7 mile back across the causeway to return to point 1.

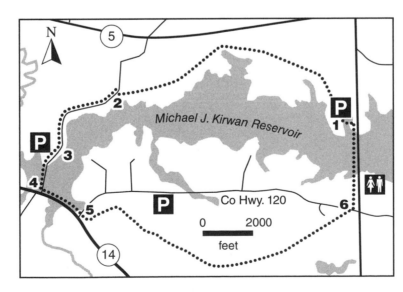

1. Lot
2. Knapp road
3. Parking lot
4. State Route 14
5. Cable Line road
6. Cross road

Southeast

When demographers were marking the borders for the War on Poverty in the 1960s, they found that Ohio's 29 unglaciated counties had the lowest per capita income of all 88 counties. The southeastern quadrant of Ohio is mostly filled with these Appalachian counties. Technically considered part of the Western Unglaciated Allegheny Plateau, this rugged and isolated region is known for producing oil, coal, gas, and, more recently, shale. But this region also contains some of the best hiking and backpacking in the state.

The main rivers that flow south to the Ohio here are the Muskingum, the Hocking, and the Scioto. Upstream on the Hocking is Hocking Hills State Park, which contains five separate rock-based features that form the most popular natural region in the state. In Belmont County, Dysart Woods Preserve is a last stand of original growth featuring 500-year-old poplars. Spread across southeastern Ohio is the Wayne National Forest, the only national forest in Ohio. A patchwork forest that is administered from three separate locations, "the Wayne" offers many rugged trails that can be hiked in solitude. Near Zanesville, the Wilds offers hiking in an area used by zoos for breeding and research involving wild animals. For backpackers, multiday hiking options can be found at Archer's Fork and Lake Vesuvius in the Wayne National Forest, as well as at Burr Oak State Park and Zaleski State Forest.

Vegetation in this region features oaks and hickories on the ridges and maples and beeches in the lowlands. In addition to the ubiquitous white-tailed deer, recently spotted animals also include black bear and bobcat.

> Pass through a narrow sandstone gorge on a scenic river.

> View a wide variety of trees, rock formations, and seasonal wildflowers.

> Explore an area used for a variety of transportation methods.

Area Information

It seems that the Blackhand Gorge on the Licking River has always been a major transportation route. The ancient Indians of prehistoric times used the river route to canoe toward the rich deposits at nearby Flint Ridge. They were the ones who emblazoned a large black hand on a cliff wall that gives the gorge its name. Their reason was unknown, but some people speculate that the hand marked a neutral territory where no one could raise a hand against another.

Unfortunately, the black hand was dynamited by the builders of the Ohio and Erie Canal in 1828, although the name Blackhand was ironically preserved to describe the type of sandstone that the canal was made of. The canal was soon replaced by the railroad, and in 1850 the Central Ohio Railroad blasted a deep cut through the bedrock conglomerate along the river. In the early 20th century, the interurban electric railroad system blasted a tunnel through the gorge in building a route between Newark and Zanesville.

Now that State Route 16 passes peacefully by, mankind is through blasting this scenic area, and in 1975, this 950-acre area was designated a state nature preserve. A paved walking and bicycling trail runs along the river for 4 miles along the old railroad bed, and five other trails combine for a total of 10 miles of trail. These trails go past the steep sandstone cliffs and abandoned quarries, and they offer views of abundant wildlife.

On the hilltops, hikers will find oak and hickory trees, along with mountain laurel. Birch and hemlock can be found on northern exposures, while the floodplain contains sycamore, cottonwood, and box elder. Springtime wildflowers include trillium, wild geranium, phlox, and Dutchman's breeches. In summer, hikers can view wingstem, Sweet William, and oxeye daisy. Three parking lots are located around the narrow east-west gorge cut out by the river, and unlike some state nature preserves, Blackhand Gorge has restroom facilities.

Directions: The main parking lot is near the junction of State Routes 16 and 146. Take 146 south from 16 for 0.1 mile and turn west on County Road 273. Cross the Licking River in 1.7 miles and turn right into the lot.

Facilities: The main parking lot has pit toilets, informational kiosks, and canoe access near the road.

Hours open: The preserve is open daily from one-half hour before sunrise to one-half hour after sunset.

Rules and permits: Picking wildflowers, collecting rocks, picnicking, camping, and fires are prohibited. Pets must be on a leash. No horses are allowed, and bicycles and skates are permitted only on the paved Blackhand Trail.

Contact information: The preserve is located at 2200 Gratiot Road Southeast, Newark, Ohio 43056; however, to contact anyone, you should write to the Division of Natural Areas and Preserves, 2045 Morse Road, Building F-1, Columbus, Ohio 43229. The phone number is 614-265-6453.

Other Areas of Interest

Just downstream on the Licking River is Dillon State Park, a reservoir made by damming the river.

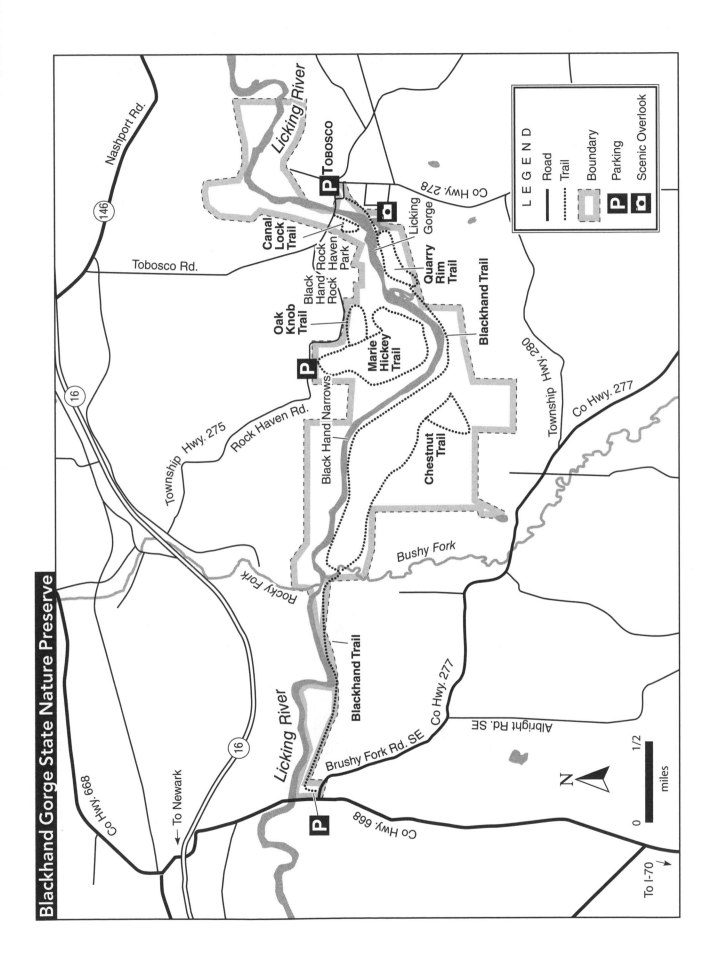

Blackhand Gorge State Nature Preserve

LEGEND
Road
Trail
Boundary
Parking
Scenic Overlook

Nashport Rd.
146
Tobosco Rd.
Licking River
Tobosco
Co Hwy. 278
Canal Lock Trail
Black Hand Rock
Rock Haven Park
Licking Gorge
Quarry Rim Trail
Oak Knob Trail
Blackhand Trail
Marie Hickey Trail
Township Hwy. 280
Co Hwy. 277
16
Township Hwy. 275
Rock Haven Rd.
Black Hand Narrows
Chestnut Trail
Bushy Fork
Rocky Fork
Co Hwy. 668
To Newark
16
Licking River
Blackhand Trail
Brushy Fork Rd. SE
Co Hwy. 277
Albright Rd. SE
Co Hwy. 668
To I-70
N
0   1/2
miles

Blackhand and Quarry Rim Trails

Hiking distance: 2.5 miles

Estimated hiking time: 1 hour

Take a walk along a scenic river and an abandoned stone quarry.

Caution: Don't get too close to the edge of the steep cliffs in the quarry.

Trail directions: Park in the east, or main, parking lot on County Road 273 near the village of Toboso. This location has restrooms and an informational kiosk at N 40° 03.366, W 82° 13.090 (1). Also, a pioneer log cabin has been moved here to be used for special programs. Follow the paved Blackhand Trail along the scenic banks of the Licking River, but watch out for joggers and bicyclists who share this path.

In about 0.4 mile, a sign notes that the Quarry Rim Trail is on the left at N 40° 03.216, W 82° 13.419 (2). Bypass this for now and continue along the riverbank.

In another 0.4 mile, another sign notes the spot of the original black hand carving at N 40° 03.142, W 82° 13.739 (3). No one knows for sure why the natives adorned the steep cliff wall along the river with a large black hand, but because of this petroglyph, the name Blackhand is used to classify the type of sandstone found all over this part of Ohio. A short side trail leads down to the riverbank overlooking the place where the hand was located before it was blown up by workers building the Ohio and Erie Canal. This part of the Licking River is also good for canoeing.

▌ A pioneer log cabin in the parking lot at Blackhand Gorge.

Returning to the Blackhand Trail, the next sign of man's destructive capabilities is just ahead. The trail now passes through Deep Cut, a narrow path through sandstone cliffs that was made when railroad builders dynamited a path through here in 1850. Deep Cut is 330 feet long, 65 feet deep, and 30 feet wide. This path is no longer used by the Central Ohio Railroad; the current tracks cross the river a short distance ahead. Not long after passing through Deep Cut, the trail is joined on the left by the Quarry Rim Trail at N 40° 03.016, W 82° 13.872 (4).

Take this trail, leaving the paved route behind, and climb a set of stairs to a ridge overlooking a former sandstone quarry. This ridge top trail winds around through abandoned ponds and pits, and it provides some good views. These hills are also a good place to spot white-tailed deer. After about a mile, this trail passes by a buttonbush swamp before descending to reconnect with the Blackhand Trail at point 2. From here, you can return to your car at point 1.

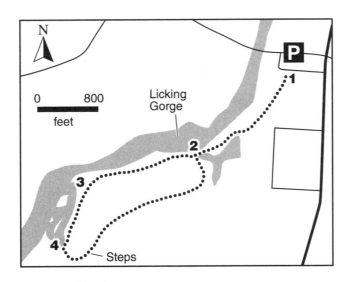

1. Lot and kiosk
2. Quarry Trail turnoff
3. Blackhand sign
4. Quarry Rim Trail

> Enjoy a short walk in the woods that leads to a scenic waterfall.

> Savor the solitude of a little-known reserve off the beaten path.

Area Information

The Boord State Nature Preserve is easy to miss but worth the trouble to find. This little 127-acre parcel features a short trail through pines and a hemlock ravine that leads to a sandstone gorge with a quaint waterfall. The park is named for Elza and Cora Boord, whose family made a partial gift of the preserve to the state in 1986.

State nature Preserves are specifically designated for preservation and therefore stress only low-impact contact. So there are no facilities here, but that doesn't mean there are no attractions. For one thing, the lack of amenities and the obscure location guarantee a peaceful visit to a park that is almost always devoid of visitors. Another attraction is the flora. In addition to a white pine plantation and hemlock grove, the preserve features such wildflowers as rock skullcap, narrow-leaved toothwart, and golden knees. But the most spectacular feature is the waterfall on Falls Run. This stream cuts through the sandstone and makes many small cliffs and overhangs along the way. A platform has been built overlooking the falls.

Directions: Take SR 550 west from Marietta 6 miles to Washington County Road 6. Go south for 0.7 mile to the junction with Township Road 69. Veer right for 0.2 mile to arrive at the small parking lot.

Hours open: The preserve is open year round in daylight hours.

Facilities: None. The only improvements the state has made on the property are a kiosk in the parking lot, a wooden platform overlooking the falls, and the trail itself. There are no restrooms, picnic tables, or other amenities.

Rules and permits: Pets are prohibited. And since the purpose of the preserve is to protect all wildlife, picking wildflowers or otherwise disturbing the natural habitat is forbidden.

Contact information: The address of the preserve is 254 Falls Run Road, Cutler, Ohio 45724, but the preserve has no staff members present. Contact the Ohio Department of Natural Resources, 2045 Morse Road, Building C-3, Columbus, Ohio 43229; the phone number is 614-265-6453.

Other Areas of Interest

Two other state nature preserves are in the area. Arcadia Cliffs on the Washington and Athens County line features some spectacular rock formations. In Athens County off U.S. Route 50 is Marie J. Desonier Preserve, which offers an abundance of wildflowers and birds. For further information, contact ODNR at the location and number listed previously.

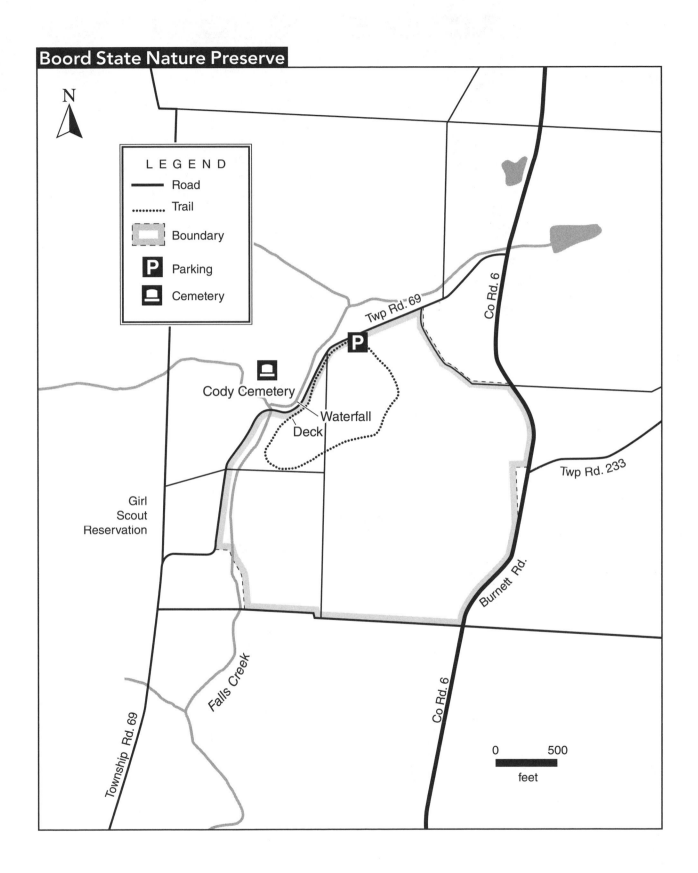

Boord State Nature Preserve

N

LEGEND
- Road
- Trail
- Boundary
- P Parking
- Cemetery

Twp Rd. 69

Co Rd. 6

P

Cody Cemetery

Waterfall
Deck

Twp Rd. 233

Girl
Scout
Reservation

Burnett Rd.

Falls Creek

Township Rd. 69

Co Rd. 6

0   500
feet

Boord State Nature Preserve

Hiking distance: 0.7 mile

Estimated hiking time: 30 minutes

A short stroll to a secluded waterfall.

Caution: An absence of road signage makes the location hard to find. No pets are allowed.

Trail directions: Park in the small parking lot at N 39° 23.697, W 81° 44.809 (1). Take the left entrance into the woods and follow a path that is mowed at first but later marked by white triangles. The trees are mainly white pine at first but blend into hardwoods.

After 0.2 mile, come to a hollow at N 39° 23.531, W 81° 44.811 (2), and the trail starts to climb uphill. After crossing a few short wooden bridges, at about 0.5 mile is a deck overlooking a 10-foot waterfall in the creek. This spot, located at N 39° 23.562, W 81° 44.942 (3), offers a view that makes the hike worth the trip. Just a little farther down the trail is a path that leads to the stream near the top of the falls. The trail now parallels the stream, and in another 0.1 mile the township road comes into view at N 39° 23,647, W 81° 44.896 (4). Continue another 0.1 mile back to the parking lot.

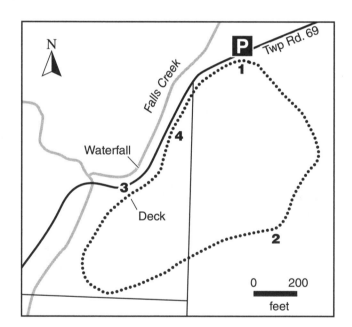

1. Lot and kiosk
2. Hollow
3. Falls
4. Road in sight

> Enjoy a hike that is easy to get to yet offers solitude.

> Climb hills where cross country teams train.

> Sample a diverse collection of spring wildflowers.

Area Information

This 500-acre area is brought to you by the nonprofit Broughton Foundation for recreational and environmental use for groups and individuals. Local businesspeople Carl and Elizabeth Broughton established their foundation in 1991, and the area has been undergoing improvements ever since. There are currently six trails, two ponds, and a stream on site as well as a Frisbee golf course and a cross country course used by local schools.

The area is located near where State Route 821 ends at State Route 60 at the northern end of the city of Marietta. There are three separate parking lots, but the one near the junction of SR 821 and Interstate 77 and the one off of State Route 60 both lack facilities and clear signage. The main lot along 821 is easier to see and get to and also has restrooms, a kiosk with maps and regulations, and a shelter that can be rented.

The terrain is quite hilly, with up to 300 feet of vertical relief. The trails also drain poorly, so any trail can be muddy at any time of the year. But there are good views. It is a fine example of a mixed hardwood forest and plenty of wildflowers in spring. There is also a surprising amount of solitude for any area so close to highways and a city.

Directions: The main parking lot is off State Route 821, about 2.5 miles below exit 6 of Interstate 77 and almost 0.5 mile above where 821 ends at the Muskingum River and State Route 60. A sign is visible near the business complex there.

Hours open: The area is open daily from 6:30 a.m. to 8:30 p.m.

Facilities: The main parking lot has porta-johns, information kiosks, and a shelter that can be rented for events. There is also a Frisbee golf course and a cross country course used by local teams.

Rules and permits: No fires, firearms, or alcohol are permitted on the grounds. Camping for youth groups is available with permission.

Contact information: Broughton Nature and Wildlife Recreation Area, 619 State Route 821, Marietta, Ohio 45750. The phone number is 740-376-0831.

Other Areas of Interest

Just a mile or so away is Devola Lock and Dam, the first in a series of 10 hand-operated canal locks on the Muskingum River between Marietta and Zanesville. These locks were built in 1841 and are still used today as an extended state park. Fishermen and recreational boaters can use these to navigate on the largest river within state borders.

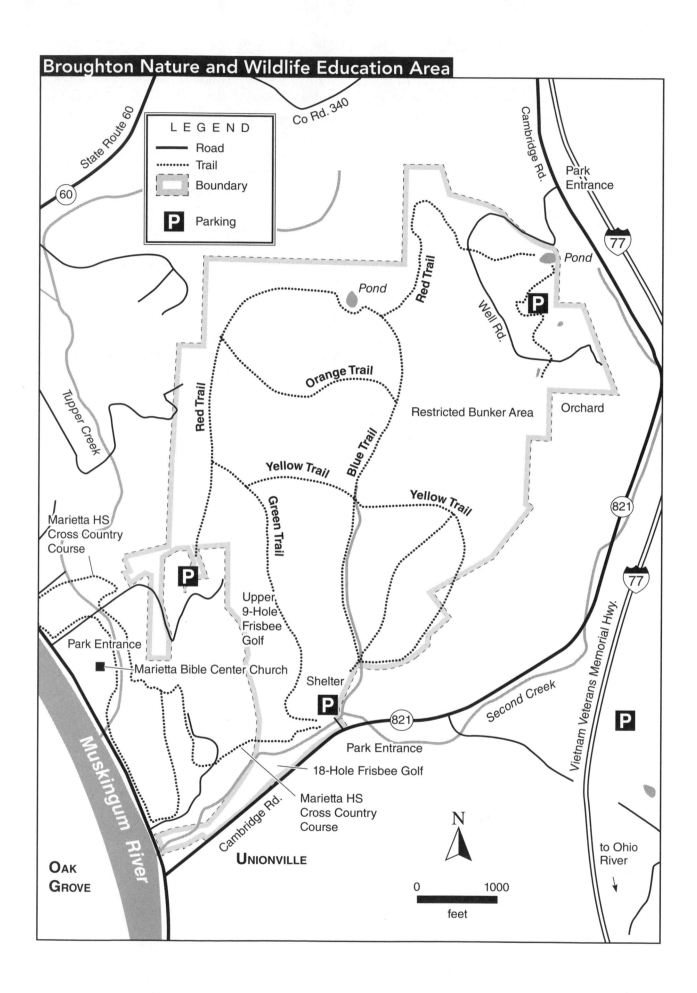

Broughton Nature and Wildlife Education Area

LEGEND
- —— Road
- ······ Trail
- Boundary
- **P** Parking

State Route 60

Co Rd. 340

Cambridge Rd.

Park Entrance

60

77

Pond

Red Trail

Pond

Well Rd.

Orange Trail

P

Restricted Bunker Area

Orchard

Tupper Creek

Red Trail

Blue Trail

Yellow Trail

Yellow Trail

Marietta HS Cross Country Course

821

77

Green Trail

P

Upper 9-Hole Frisbee Golf

Park Entrance

Marietta Bible Center Church

Shelter

P

821

Second Creek

P

Vietnam Veterans Memorial Hwy.

Park Entrance

18-Hole Frisbee Golf

Marietta HS Cross Country Course

Muskingum River

Cambridge Rd.

UNIONVILLE

OAK GROVE

N

to Ohio River

0   1000
feet

Southwest Overlook, Western Ridge and Valley Trails

Hiking distance: 2.0 miles

Estimated hiking time: 1 hour

Enjoy a brisk hike in a secluded yet accessible area.

Caution: Trails can be extremely muddy.

Trail directions: Park in the main lot at N 39° 27.264, W 81° 27.038 (1). A kiosk has a map and park rules, and a shelter and restrooms are there. Follow a gravel path that soon turns uphill at the Frisbee golf course. After about 0.3 mile, the gravel ends in an open field that has a shelter at N 39° 27.298, W 81° 27.097 (2). A green sign marks the beginning of the Southwest Overlook Trail. Follow the green blazed signs farther up the hill and reenter the woods on a dirt trail.

Pass a side trail on the right in about 0.3 mile at N 39° 27.486, W 81° 27.116 (3). Bear left and continue uphill, staying on the marked trail. In another 0.3 mile is the junction with the Western Ridge Trail at N 39° 27.579, W 81° 27.253 (4). A left turn leads to the parking lot along State Route 60, but to continue the hike, turn right and proceed through the oak-dominated forest. This point is about 250 feet higher in elevation than point 1. Follow the red blazes past a brief conjunction with an oil well trail and turn back into the woods.

Continue on a ridge top that is really wet for 0.6 mile to N 39° 28.173, W 81° 27.050 (5). Here the Valley Trail with blue blazes becomes concurrent briefly with the Northern Ridge Trail. At the bottom of a short hill is a pond with a viewing bench. At N 39° 28.146, W 81° 26.552 (6), the Valley Trail forks off to the right. A side trail comes in on the right in 0.3 mile at N 39° 28.065, W 81° 26.585 (7). Proceed through a forest of elm, oak, maple, poplar, and sycamore. Go another 0.3 mile alongside a stream bed that may be drier than the trail. A side trail now branches off to the right at

N 39° 27.520, W 81° 27.064 (8). From here, go past the left turn off to the Powerline Trail and go about 0.3 mile by way of a commercial parking lot to point 1.

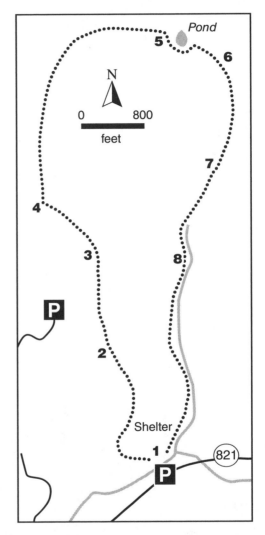

1. Lot and kiosk
2. Shelter
3. Junction
4. Junction; turn right
5. Junction
6. Junction; start to head back
7. Junction
8. Junction

20 Burr Oak State Park

> Visit a state park that is beautiful all year, particularly in fall.

> Hike along a hilly lakeside that features views, wildlife, and caves.

> Take short scenic hikes or a 30-mile backpack loop around Burr Oak Lake.

Area Information

Tucked in where Morgan, Athens, and Perry counties meet, Burr Oak State Park is a quiet little gem in the state park system. Although State Route 78 that leads to the park doesn't quite live up to its grandiose title, "The Rim of the World," it is still one of the most scenic drives in the state. The winding highway here is only 1,100 feet above sea level, but from the narrow ridge, you can see for miles in all directions, and it feels as if you are on the rim of something. The hills around Burr Oak are visually impressive all year long, but especially in autumn, when the hills are ablaze with color.

The centerpiece of the park is 664-acre Burr Oak Lake, which was created in 1950 when the Army Corps of Engineers built Tom Jenkins Dam on the east branch of Sunday Creek. Burr Oak was dedicated as a state park 2 years later. The lake is a haven for fishermen. It is also a quiet spot because all boats must have motors of 10 horsepower or less or they must not create a wake. The rugged hills that surround the lake are ideal for hiking, and the park contains seven hiking trails and three bridle trails. A backpack loop encircles the park and connects to another 15-mile backpack loop in the adjacent Wayne National Forest.

Although the lodge overlooking the lake has recently closed, there are still places to stay here. The park offers 30 family cottages that sleep six people and are fully furnished. Camping is available at two of the lake's four boat docks. Boats can also be rented and fueled at the marina. The campsites have 17 electrical and 78 nonelectric sites, and they offer

Scenic view along the shore at Burr Oak Lake.

showers and flush toilets. Pets are permitted at some campsites and cottages. The park also has a 500-foot public beach for swimmers. The backpack trail includes primitive campground sites that offer drinking water.

Burr Oak gets its name from the stately trees that dominated the area before 1850. Most of these trees were felled to make railroad ties or sturdy timbers to shore up the walls of coal mines, but the forest cover today is still mainly oak and hickory based. Among the wildflowers seen here are Dutchman's breeches, trillium, hepatica, and bloodroot.

Unfortunately, the isolation that is part of the charm of Burr Oak did not generate enough activity to maintain the lodge overlooking the lake. The Burr Oak lodge and restaurant closed in 2011, and recent plans may result in an influx of ATV trails. So if you want to visit pristine Burr Oak, you may want to hurry.

Directions: The park office is located off of State Route 78 between McConnelsville and Glouster. Highway signs point to all major park attractions.

Facilities: In addition to camping sites and cottages, the park includes several picnic areas with tables and grills, as well as one reservable shelter with electrical hookups. Restrooms are provided at the boat launch docks and the dam.

Hours open: The park is open year-round in daylight hours.

Rules and permits: Pets are permitted in designated areas. The lake is a no-wake zone for boaters.

Contact information: The address of the park office is 10220 Burr Oak Lodge Road, Glouster, Ohio 45732; the phone number is 740-767-3570.

Other Areas of Interest

The park is bordered by the Wayne National Forest, which maintains a campground and the Wildcat Hollow Backpack Trail nearby. The Sunday Creek Wildlife Area also borders the park. Strouds Run State Park is located nearby in Athens County.

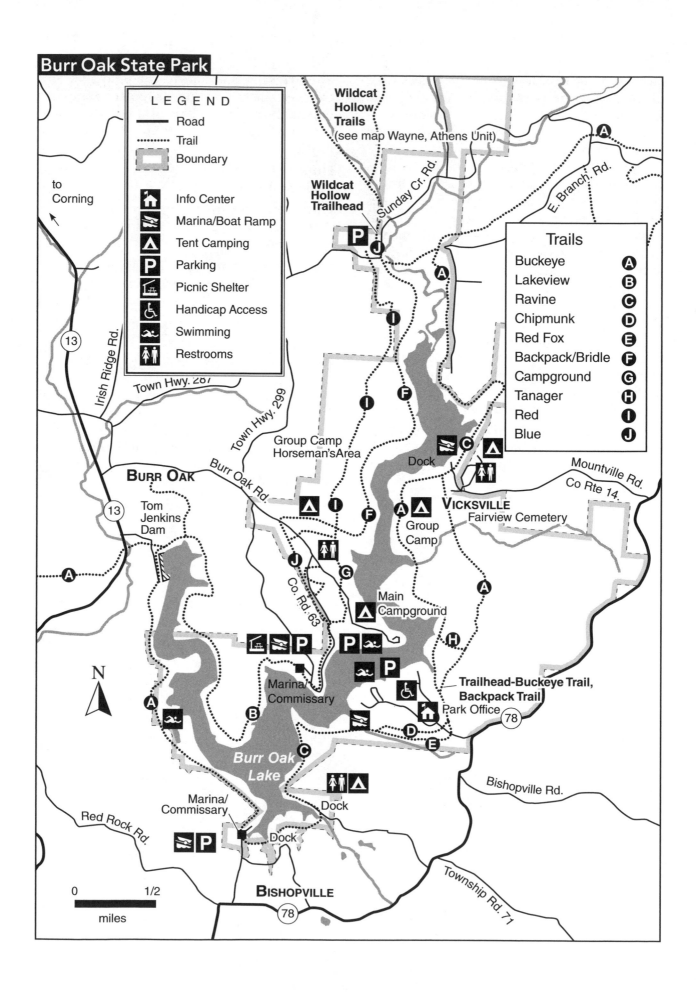

Burr Oak State Park

LEGEND

——	Road
····	Trail
▢	Boundary
🏠	Info Center
🚤	Marina/Boat Ramp
⛺	Tent Camping
P	Parking
⛱	Picnic Shelter
♿	Handicap Access
🏊	Swimming
🚻	Restrooms

to Corning

Trails

Buckeye	Ⓐ
Lakeview	Ⓑ
Ravine	Ⓒ
Chipmunk	Ⓓ
Red Fox	Ⓔ
Backpack/Bridle	Ⓕ
Campground	Ⓖ
Tanager	Ⓗ
Red	Ⓘ
Blue	Ⓙ

Wildcat Hollow Trails
(see map Wayne, Athens Unit)

Wildcat Hollow Trailhead

Sunday Cr. Rd.

E. Branch Rd.

Irish Ridge Rd.

Town Hwy. 287

Town Hwy. 299

BURR OAK

Burr Oak Rd.

Tom Jenkins Dam

Group Camp Horseman's Area

Dock

VICKSVILLE
Fairview Cemetery

Mountville Rd.
Co Rte 14

Group Camp

Main Campground

Co. Rd. 63

Marina/Commissary

Trailhead-Buckeye Trail, Backpack Trail
Park Office

N

Burr Oak Lake

Marina/Commissary

Red Rock Rd.

Dock

Dock

Bishopville Rd.

Township Rd. 71

BISHOPVILLE

0   1/2
miles

Buckeye Loop, Tanager and Chipmunk Trails

Hiking distance: 2.6 miles

Estimated hiking time: 1.5 hours

Hike in the woods, meadows, and lakeshore of a particularly scenic area.

Caution: This trail is steep and rugged, and it can be muddy in spots.

Trail directions: Take State Route 78—also called the "Rim of the World" highway—between McConnelsville and Glouster. South of the village of Ringgold, the road straddles a scenic ridge, and signs mark the turnoff for the lodge and park headquarters. Turn in here at the main park entrance and park in the lot next to the office at N 39° 31.753, W 81° 01.583 (1). This spot is also the trailhead for the 30-mile Burr Oak Backpack Trail that encircles the lake. The eastern half of this loop is also concurrent with the Buckeye, North Country, and American Discovery Trails.

Follow the blue blazes north and enter the woods at a sign that dedicates this section to Buckeye Trail pioneers Bob and Mary Lou Paton. Descend into the woods for about 0.3 mile to a junction with the Buckeye Loop Trail at N 39° 31.934, W 81° 01.419 (2). Signs posted here point out that the Buckeye Trail continues on the left, so take this route and follow the lakeshore. The lake is not always visible in full foliage, but in another 0.3 mile—at N 39° 32.148, W 81° 01.622 (3)—you will come to a turnoff for a short side trail that leads to a rock with a good view of the lake below.

A common misconception about lakeside trails is that they are level, beachfront paths. Trails alongside man-made Appalachian lakes are more likely to be steep and winding routes that have to go upland and inland in order to ford feeder streams. In another 0.4 mile, the trail meets up with the red-blazed Tanager Trail

at N 39° 32.171, W 81° 01.464 (4). A couple of ledge overhang caves are located ahead on the Buckeye Trail, but to make a shorter loop, you should turn right here and ascend into a broad meadow.

The Tanager Trail is only 0.5 mile long, and it ends at the edge of a meadow at N 39° 32.148, W 81° 01.094 (5). Here it meets the Buckeye Trail, so turn right, reenter the woods, and follow the white blazes back to point 2 and then to point 1. To prolong your adventure, continue on the Buckeye Trail in the other direction past the park office; cross the main road and reenter the woods on the Chipmunk Trail. This 0.4-mile trail drops down through the woods and meets the lakeshore at a scenic cove and boat launch at N 39° 31.702, W 81° 02.020 (6). It's well worth a side trip, especially in fall, to see the lake close up before concluding the hike.

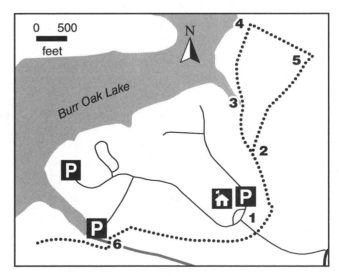

1. Lot
2. Junction
3. Lake view
4. Junction
5. Junction
6. Lakeshore

> Enjoy spectacular views from one of the most photographed spots in the state.

> Explore a classic box canyon from top to bottom.

> See a waterfall, steep cliffs, and long-range vistas from a single trail.

Area Information

The Hocking Hills area is Ohio's best known natural highlight. The area of Hocking County west of Logan contains a variety of rock formations, waterfalls, and sylvan vistas that attract visitors from all over. Many of these sites are a part of Hocking Hills State Park, and Conkle's Hollow is generally thought to be a part of this. Conkle's Hollow contains two trails. The Rim Trail encircles the rim of the gorge for over 2 miles and includes the best views. The Gorge Trail, a path that is so flat and short that it has become sort of a complement to the Rim Trail, goes a half mile into the heart of the gorge to the waterfall at the end. This trail is paved for most of the way and offers a chance to view wildflowers, ferns, and rock formations (even for people who otherwise may not be able to access these things). But Conkle's Hollow has been administered separately as a state nature preserve since 1977, though it is only a few miles away from the region's other stellar attractions, Old Man's Cave and Cedar Falls.

Regardless of which state agency owns it, Conkle's Hollow ranks right up there with these other attractions as a premier destination for nature-loving Ohioans. The hollow is actually a box canyon that is as narrow as 100 feet in places. But the canyon walls are 200-foot cliffs of Blackhand sandstone that offer some of the best views found anywhere in Ohio.

The origin of this canyon goes back 350 million years to when Ohio was under the waters of an inland sea. Sedimentary deposits compressed into sandy rock remained as the sea receded, and the eroded remains evolved into their current configuration. Today, the gorge contains many species of plants and ferns that are usually found in more northern locales. These plants include Canada yew and teaberry. The area also has an abundance of hemlock, tulip poplar, and other hardwoods. Deer, grouse, and wild turkey are commonly seen, and bobcats are now making a reappearance. In more recent years, Native Americans inhabited the area, but the current name comes from one of the first white residents, W.H. Conkle, who carved his name on a gorge wall in 1797.

Directions: From the junction of U.S. Route 33 and State Route 664 in Logan, go 12 miles south on 664 past the parking lot for Old Man's Cave. Turn right on State Route 374 and go downhill for 1 mile. Turn right on Big Pine Road; the parking lot is 0.25 mile down the road and is marked by signage.

Hours open: The preserve is open year-round during daylight hours, but the rocky and potentially dangerous Rim Trail is sometimes closed in icy weather.

Facilities: Restrooms and picnic tables are available in the parking area.

Rules and permits: No permits are necessary, but pets, fires, camping, and rock climbing are prohibited.

Contact information: The park address is Conkle's Hollow, 24858 Big Pine Road, Rockbridge, Ohio 43149. The phone number for the Columbus office of the Ohio Department of Natural Resources is 614-265-6453.

Other Areas of Interest

Other areas of interest include the Hocking State Forest (located at 19275 State Route 374, Rockbridge, Ohio 43149; phone number 740-383-4402). This state forest contains 9,700 acres and includes bridle trails, an equestrian camp, and a unique area set aside for rock climbing and rappelling. The rappelling area is just across Big Pine Road near Conkle's Hollow and also includes a part of the Buckeye Trail that leads to Old Man's Cave just 3 miles away.

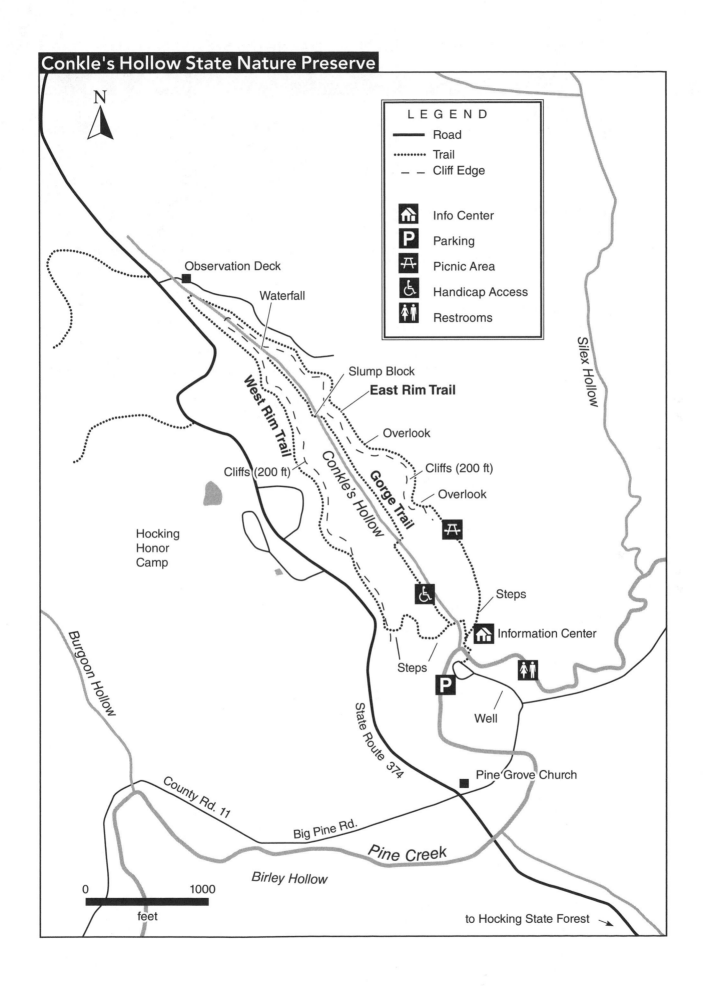

Conkle's Hollow State Nature Preserve

N

LEGEND
— Road
.... Trail
– – Cliff Edge

🏠 Info Center
🅿 Parking
🛆 Picnic Area
♿ Handicap Access
🚻 Restrooms

Observation Deck

Waterfall

Slump Block

East Rim Trail

Overlook

West Rim Trail

Cliffs (200 ft)

Cliffs (200 ft)

Overlook

Hocking
Honor
Camp

🛆

♿

Steps

🏠 Information Center

Steps

🚻

🅿

Well

Conkle's Hollow

Gorge Trail

Silex Hollow

Burgoon Hollow

State Route 374

Pine Grove Church

County Rd. 11

Big Pine Rd.

Pine Creek

Birley Hollow

0   1000

feet

to Hocking State Forest →

Rim and Gorge Trails

Hiking distance: 3 miles round trip

Estimated hiking time: 2 hours

The view from the top of this canyon may be the best in the state, and it is certainly one of the most photographed. Conkle's Hollow at the peak of the fall foliage is about as spectacular a sight you will see anywhere in Ohio.

Caution: The abundant warning signs are to be taken seriously. Every year hikers are hurt or killed on the 200-foot cliffs. Stay on the marked trail and watch out for roots and stumps.

Trail directions: This 87-acre area was made a state nature preserve in 1977, but it has been an object of marvel ever since German immigrant W.H. Conkle carved his name on the rocks here in 1797. The parking lot and restrooms are located just off Big Pine Creek Road, which intersects with State Route 374 just a mile down the hill from the junction with State Route 664. Park in the lot at N 39° 37.185, W 82° 34.325 (1) and proceed over the bridge across Big Pine Creek.

Immediately after entering the preserve, you will find kiosks with displays explaining the geology and natural history of this region. Just past this on the right—at N 39° 27.256, W 82° 34.325 (2)—you will see steps that go up a steep ridge. This is a steep climb of over 250 feet to the top, but it will be the only climb needed all day, and the view will be well worth it.

After the climb, the trail levels out and follows the rim of the gorge. At 0.3 mile in, you will come to the first of a series of spectacular overlooks at N 39° 27.389, W 82° 34.424 (3). The box canyon has a wider outside face

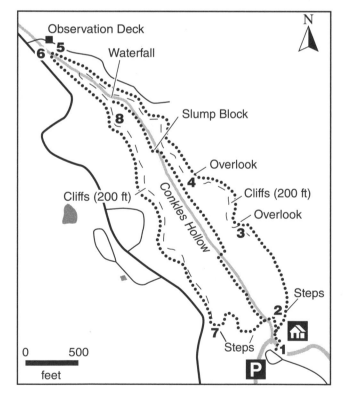

1. Lot
2. Steps
3. First overlook
4. Walls narrow
5. Deck
6. Cross creek
7. Begin descent
8. Falls

that offers views of far distant ridges, and it is particularly pretty in autumn. Proceed along the rim for another quarter mile to where the canyon walls narrow at N 39° 27.495, W 82° 34.580 (4). From here, you can look back out at the canyon as well as view the steep walls in the inner portion. The sheer rock face visible from here is one of the most photographed in the state.

Continue on the trail, stopping to compare vistas. At about 0.9 mile, you will come to a wooden platform at N 39° 27.683, W 82° 34.808 (5). This deck overlooks the 95-foot waterfall at the head of the canyon. In less than 0.1 mile, you will cross the stream that feeds the waterfall. After crossing the bridge at N 39° 27.707, W 82° 34.870 (6), you should begin your return on the opposite canyon wall. Some of the best views on the return trip will be of the wall that you came in on.

Follow the trail for nearly a mile until it starts to descend at N 39° 37.245, W 82° 34.541 (7). The 200-foot descent is partly over steps and partly just steep hillside. At the bottom, you return to point 2 where the trails meet up. But this time, you should take a left and follow the Gorge Trail into the canyon. The Gorge Trail is perfectly flat and paved most of the way, so this is an excellent stroll for those not able or willing to climb the canyon walls. This trail also offers ample opportunity to survey the 50 or more varieties of plants that grow in this preserve. Several side trails lead to caves and other attractions along the way. Proceed to the falls at the head of the gorge, which is about a half mile farther and culminates at N 39° 27.578, W 82° 34.682 (8). After viewing the falls, return on the Gorge Trail to point 2 and then return to the parking lot from there.

> Take advantage of your only opportunity to see what Ohio looked like before European settlers arrived.

> Climb scenic hills in solitude in an isolated corner of the state.

> View some of the largest and oldest trees found anywhere in Ohio.

Area Information

It has been said that at one time the Ohio forest was so thick that squirrels could travel from Lake Erie to the Ohio River without ever touching the ground. Today, an estimated 99.996 percent of that original old-growth forest is gone, but at Dysart Woods you can still see what the area looked like before European settlers arrived. This 50-acre preserve not only has several trees that are close to 400 years old, but it also has many that are nearly 5 feet in diameter and up to 140 feet tall.

This last patch of virgin timber was originally part of the 455-acre farm of the Dysart family. The family never timbered or cultivated the area until 1967. In that year, the parcel was named a National Natural Landmark, and the Dysarts sold the property to Ohio University (with help from the Nature Conservatory) for use as an outdoor laboratory that would allow biology students to get field experience.

The area is regularly used by classes from Ohio University, which also has a branch campus in nearby St. Clairsville. The old family farmhouse near the entrance serves as a headquarters, but there are no regular hours or personnel on duty. The grounds can be explored anytime; two separate trails are on opposite sides of Township Road 194, which runs through the center. The forest features a variety of hardwoods, including beech, oak, hickory, maple, tulip poplar, and ash. But you may want to hurry to visit this area. Within the past few years, a local mining operation has gotten permission to begin longwall mining near Dysart Woods. Despite considerable opposition, this proposal passed muster in the courts, and it may turn out that man will be able to undo what 400 years of nature created. If the mining draws groundwater away from the woods, this could seriously damage the forest.

Directions: Go to the village of Belmont, which is on State Route 149 just south of Interstate 70. From Belmont, go south on State Route 147 for 3 miles and turn right at the sign for Township Road 194.

Hours open: Dysart Woods is open year-round in daylight hours.

Facilities: Primitive restrooms are located at the farmhouse near the entrance, but no water, picnic, or camping options are available.

Rules and permits: No dogs are permitted.

Contact information: Contact the Belmont County Tourism Council at 740-695-4359. To make a donation to the Ohio Union Fund—Dysart Woods Laboratory, contact the Ohio Union Fund, P.O. Box 869, Ohio University, Athens, Ohio 45701.

Other Areas of Interest

Barkcamp State Park, just outside of Belmont, has a large man-made lake and hiking trails. (The phone number for this park is 740-484-9064.)

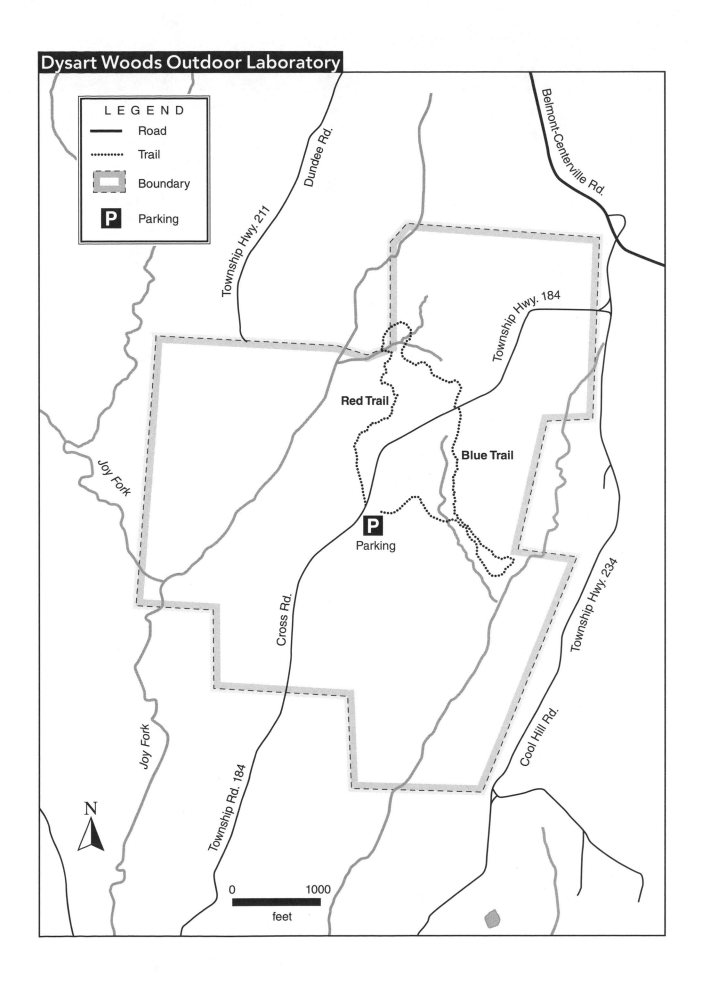

Dysart Woods Outdoor Laboratory

LEGEND
—— Road
········· Trail
▨ Boundary
P Parking

Dundee Rd.

Belmont-Centerville Rd.

Township Hwy. 211

Township Hwy. 184

Red Trail

Blue Trail

Joy Fork

P Parking

Joy Fork

Cross Rd.

Township Hwy. 234

Cool Hill Rd.

Township Rd. 184

N

0   1000
feet

Dysart Woods Red and Blue Trails

 **Hiking distance:** 1.5 miles round trip

Estimated hiking time: 1.5 hours

The best place to experience what Ohio looked like 500 years ago, this site is the only remaining example of the state's original-growth forest and contains many of the largest trees you can see here today.

Caution: The trail is hilly and steep and can be slippery when wet. The area also has many roots, downed trees, and some relatively unstable bridges.

Trail directions: The grass parking area is on Dysart Ault Road (Township Road 194). This road separates the red trail to the west from the blue trail on the east. From the lot at N 39° 58.939, W 80° 59.942 (1), cross the road and proceed down the red trail. You will enter the woods immediately and descend 200 feet in altitude over the next 0.4 mile before coming to a bridge at N 39° 59.212, W 80° 59.914 (2). You will already be among some old-growth trees of impressive size. Not only are some of them 5 feet in diameter, but many are ramrod straight with no branches for the first 20 feet or so. This 50-acre tract has never been logged or homesteaded, so it is truly virgin forest. Many trees, however, have fallen naturally, and this available timber makes a good habitat for woodpeckers.

Proceed for another 0.15 mile until you come to a rickety bridge and crude handrail at N 39° 59.229, W 80° 59.855 (3). Cross the ravine and begin a slight ascent. Previously, the hardwood forest featured beeches, maples, and oaks, but this section features some spectacular tulip trees. Although commonly referred to as tulip poplars, these trees are technically not part of the poplar family. But whatever they are called, they are truly impressive. In this section, you will find the remains of a champion poplar tree that was felled in a storm in 1995. This tree, 58 inches in diameter, was a

recent casualty, but there are many other trees here that are still going strong after 400 years.

Continue on the trail, now going steadily uphill until it reaches the road at N 39° 59.120, W 80° 59.749 (4) at about 0.8 mile into the hike. The altitude at road level is about 1,350 feet, which is about 200 feet less than the highest point in the state, so this road is fairly high on a ridge. You should continue across the road, but the paint markings on the trees are now blue rather than red.

Proceed through the woods about 0.3 mile until you come to a junction with a sign at N 39° 58.931, W 80° 59.743 (5). You may return to the parking lot by turning right here, but first you can take a loop that explores the outer regions of the outdoor laboratory. This outer loop goes on for about 0.3 mile before returning to this spot. From here, you can travel less than 0.2 mile of a steep hill to return to the parking area.

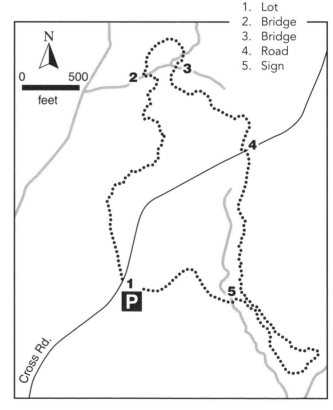

> Visit the economic center of an ancient trading network.

> Hike a secluded, wooded ridge that contains some of the best flint outcroppings anywhere.

> Tour a museum devoted to flint knapping, and hike a rare handicap accessible trail.

Area Information

The members of the ancient Hopewell culture who inhabited Ohio 2,000 years ago were at the center of a prosperous commercial empire. For any culture to thrive, it usually needs to have control of a valuable natural resource, such as oil or coal. For the primitive Hopewell culture, that essential resource was the flint needed to fashion spear points, arrowheads, and tools. On a desolate, windswept ridge just a few miles north of Interstate 70, an 8-mile vein of flint protrudes through the ground.

Flint Ridge is currently owned by the Ohio Historical Society, which maintains a museum on the grounds. The 525-acre site contains hundreds of quarry pits that range from 12 to 80 feet in diameter and from 3 to 20 feet in depth. The Hopewell people, who thrived between 100 BC and 500 AD, quarried the flint from exposed pits and fashioned it into crude tools. Some of the more colorful flint was also valued for its beauty. No evidence indicates that the Hopewell lived on the site, but the flint mined here was clearly the basis of trade all over North America. In various burial mounds elsewhere in Ohio, the teeth of grizzly bear and sharks are found that were probably acquired in trade for flint tools.

On the grounds today, visitors can walk on three separate nature trails and see all the flint outcroppings. This location even has a paved handicap access trail with a rope guide and signs in braille. A museum on the site is built around a stone quarry, and it includes a gift shop that sells jewelry made with the flint that has been named Ohio's official gemstone.

Directions: Flint Ridge is 3 miles north of the Licking County village of Brownsville at the junction of County Roads 668 and 312.

Facilities: In addition to the museum, gift shop, and trails, Flint Ridge also has picnic tables, grills, restrooms, and drinking water.

Hours open: The grounds are open year-round in daylight hours, but the museum is open on weekends only from May through October.

Rules and permits: Removing flint from the grounds is expressly forbidden. Pets are permitted.

Contact information: Flint Ridge is located at 15300 Flint Ridge Road, Glenford, Ohio 43739; but the mailing address is 3800 Pleasant Chapel Road Southeast, Newark, Ohio 43056. The phone number is 740-787-2476.

Other Areas of Interest

Dillon State Park is just to the east, and Dawes Arboretum is a few miles west off State Route 13.

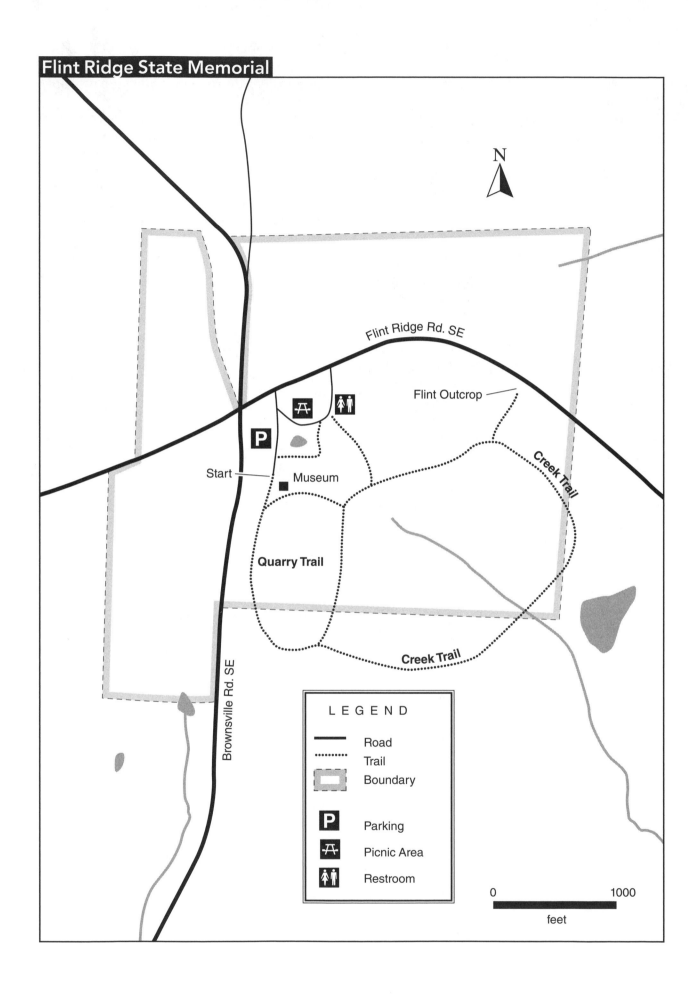

Flint Ridge State Memorial

N

Flint Ridge Rd. SE

Flint Outcrop

Creek Trail

Start

Museum

Quarry Trail

Creek Trail

Brownsville Rd. SE

LEGEND

Road
Trail
Boundary

P   Parking
⊼   Picnic Area
👫   Restroom

0   1000
feet

Quarry and Creek Trails

Hiking distance: 2 miles

Estimated hiking time: 1 hour

Hike in the middle of one of the best outcroppings of flint found in the eastern United States.

Caution: The trails can get really muddy in wet weather.

Trail directions: Park in the main lot near the museum, which is at N 39° 59.241, W 82° 15.745 (1). A bulletin board near the museum has maps and hike information. Enter the woods here and go 0.1 mile to a junction near a flint pit at N 39° 59.183, W 82° 15.758 (2). Turn left and follow along on what is also called the wagon shortcut trail. In another 0.1 mile, the Creek Trail appears on the right at N 39° 59.204, W 82° 15.661 (3). Take this trail and proceed through the forest of beech, maple, oak, and hickory. Among the wildflowers that can be seen here in spring are trillium, phlox, bloodroot, and mayapple.

The Creek Trail descends slightly and eventually follows the outer perimeter of the park. In about 0.3 mile, at N 39° 59.140, W 82° 15.402 (4), you will come to the first of three bridges over a small stream. These bridges are about 0.1 mile apart, and a couple of them are sturdy Eagle Scout projects built by local youths. About 0.2 mile after the last bridge, you'll find a marked turnoff for a flint outcropping at N 39° 59.244, W 82° 15.543 (5). Turn right here and follow the side trail up a steep hill.

Flint outcroppings are found all over the trail, but they are particularly impressive on this hill. They contain several variations of colors, and it is easy to see how the well-defined flint could be chipped away to fashion

tools. This unblazed side trail ends in an open meadow, so after exploring the flint, you should retrace your route back to point 5 and turn right to continue along the Creek Trail. Almost immediately, the trail comes to a junction at N 39° 59.233, W 82° 15.604 (6).

The blue blazes of the Creek Trail are sporadic at best, but you will see signs at the major trail junctions that point the way. At this spot, a sign notes that a right turn leads to a secondary parking area that also has picnic tables and restrooms. But to continue, you should turn left here and follow the trail back to point 3; you can then return to the museum from there.

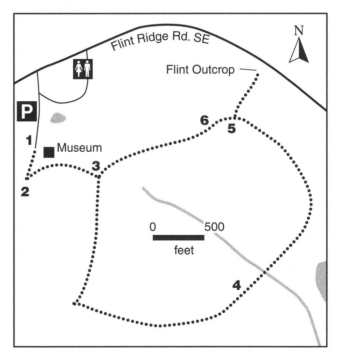

1. Lot
2. Junction
3. Junction
4. Bridge
5. Outcrop on hill
6. Junction

> Visit the most popular natural attraction in the state.

> Hike among a series of spectacular cliffs, caves, and waterfalls.

> Take advantage of abundant tourist accommodations to take a real Ohio vacation.

Area Information

With possible apologies to the Lake Erie Islands, Amish Country, and the theme parks at Cedar Point and King's Island, the Hocking Hills region may be Ohio's most popular tourist destination. Centrally located just an hour from Columbus, the area is easily accessible and packed with natural attractions. Hocking Hills State Park is at the center of this getaway location.

The spectacular rock formations that define the area are carved in erosion-resistant Blackhand sandstone that was deposited some 350 million years ago when Ohio was covered by a shallow sea. The glacier never reached the area, but the ice age did affect the climate, which resulted in some plants being here that normally prefer a cooler climate. When the glacier receded, these plants remained behind in the cooler gorges of the Hocking region, which explains why trees such as eastern hemlocks, the bigleaf magnolia, Canada yew, and yellow and black birches thrive here outside of their more regular range.

The Adena culture inhabited this region nearly 2,000 years ago, and by the late 1700s, the Wyandot, Delaware, and Shawnee tribes lived in the area. White settlers began moving in around 1800, and the caves found here were an attraction right away. The first public purchase of any land came in 1924, when the state acquired Old Man's Cave. By 1949, Hocking Hills became one of Ohio's first state parks, and a lodge was built in 1972. Today, Hocking Hills State Park is a noncontiguous region within the area of Hocking State Forest. The park consists of four separate sections—Old Man's Cave to Cedar Falls, Ash Cave, Cantwell Cliffs, and Rock House. Conkle's Hollow, another nearby natural attraction, is a separate state nature preserve.

The hiking trail that goes the 6 miles between Old Man's Cave and Ash Cave is part of the Buckeye, North Country, and American Discovery Trails. This section has been designated the Grandma Gatewood Trail in honor of the Ohio farmwife who became the first woman to through-hike the Appalachian Trail, a feat she accomplished three times while in her 60s and 70s. Every January, the park hosts thousands of hikers for an annual winter hike over this route, but for this book, that section has been broken into two hikes.

The campground at Hocking Hills has 156 sites with electrical hookups and paved pads. It includes heated showers, flush toilets, laundry facilities, and a camp store. The campground also has a pool, playground, and volleyball court. In addition, 40 family cottages are available for rental. Other accommodations are available throughout the region, including many cabins and cottages that are equipped with hot tubs. Some finer restaurants are also located here to serve the tourist clientele. A zipline canopy tour has recently been added.

Directions: The park office is near Old Man's Cave and the junction of State Routes 374 and 664. Take Route 33 to the 664 exit in Logan and then go southwest for about 10 miles.

Facilities: A visitor center is located at Old Man's Cave, and most park attractions also have restrooms. The park has five picnic areas (with grills, latrines, and water) and five shelters.

Hours open: The park is open year-round in daylight hours.

Rules and permits: Visitors must remain on marked trails.

Contact information: The park office is at 19852 State Route 664, Logan, Ohio 43138. The phone number is 740-385-6842.

Other Areas of Interest

Hocking Hills State Park is contained within the area of Hocking State Forest, which offers a rock climbing and rappelling area near Conkle's Hollow. Lake Logan State Park is at the junction of Routes 33 and 664.

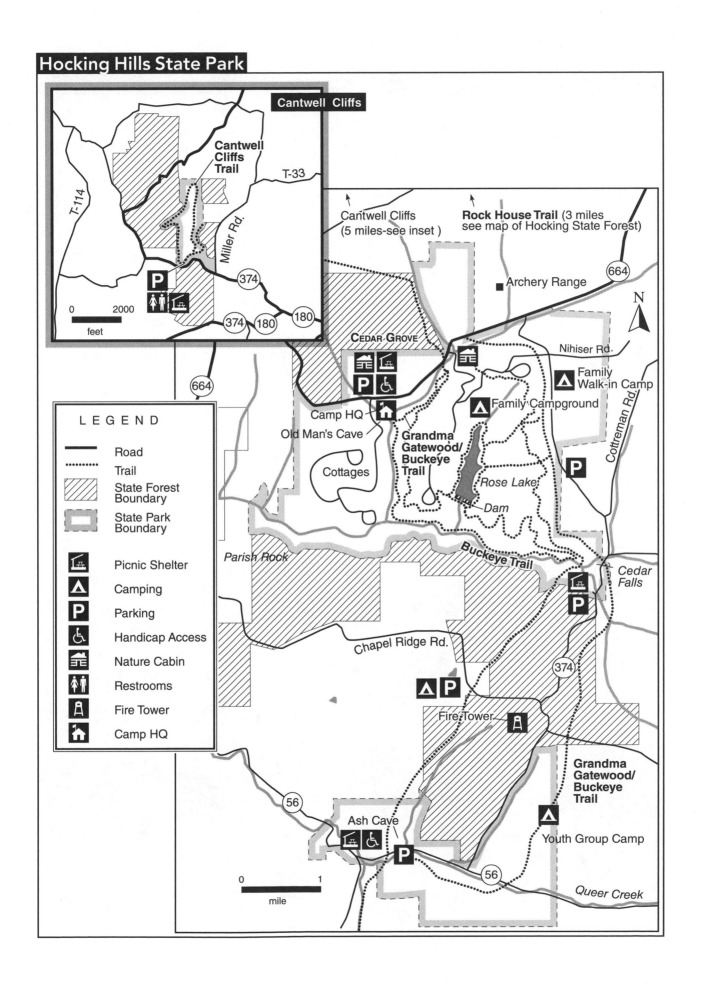

Hocking Hills State Park

Cantwell Cliffs

Cantwell Cliffs Trail

T-114

T-33

Miller Rd.

374

374 180 180

0   2000
feet

664

Cantwell Cliffs
(5 miles-see inset)

Rock House Trail (3 miles
see map of Hocking State Forest)

664

■ Archery Range

N

Nihiser Rd.

CEDAR GROVE

Family
Walk-in Camp

Cottreman Rd.

Camp HQ

Old Man's Cave

**Grandma
Gatewood/
Buckeye
Trail**

Family Campground

P

Cottages

Rose Lake

Dam

Parish Rock

Buckeye Trail

Cedar
Falls

P

Chapel Ridge Rd.

374

LEGEND

———	Road
·········	Trail
▨	State Forest Boundary
▢	State Park Boundary
🏕	Picnic Shelter
⛺	Camping
P	Parking
♿	Handicap Access
🏠	Nature Cabin
🚻	Restrooms
🗼	Fire Tower
🏠	Camp HQ

Fire Tower

**Grandma
Gatewood/
Buckeye
Trail**

56

Ash Cave

P

Youth Group Camp

56

Queer Creek

0   1
mile

Grandma Gatewood and Rim Trails

Hiking distance: 6 miles

Estimated hiking time: 3 hours

Enjoy one of the best and most popular hikes that Ohio has to offer.

Caution: Trails can be muddy, and rocks may be slippery. Also, both ends of the hike can get crowded on sunny summer weekends.

Trail directions: Park in the large lot at Old Man's Cave and cross the road to the visitor center at N 39° 26.081, W 82° 32.484 (1). The building here has exhibits, a book and nature store, restrooms, and a concession stand. A stone stairway leads to the gorge, but instead of descending here, follow the trail that goes along the rim of the gorge. This route goes for 0.1 mile near the road before crossing the Upper Falls on a stone bridge at N 39° 26.177, W 82° 32.342 (2). Check out the view below before proceeding on the opposite side to a set of stairs that leads to the bottom of this scenic waterfall at N 39° 26.163, W 82° 32.360 (3).

Now follow the gorge trail along the stream past a whirlpool known as the Devil's Bathtub, just one of the many natural items left over from one of Satan's garage sales. In about 0.3 mile, after going through a tunnel, you will come to a bridge at the base of Old Man's Cave at N 39° 25.986, W 82° 32.609 (4). Across the creek here is a large overhang ledge cave that gets its name from a hermit who used to live here around 1800. At this spot, a set of stairs leads back to the visitor center, but after exploring the cave, you should recross the bridge and continue on for another 0.1 mile to the Lower Falls at N 39° 25.961, W 82° 32.702 (5). After

❙ Cedar Falls in Hocking Hills State Park is one of the most photographed spots in the state.

you descend a steep hill, the ledge overhang of the Lower Falls offers another spot to soak up a scenic view.

A side trail leads from here back to the visitor center, but to proceed to Cedar Falls, continue on the main trail and gradually leave the crowds behind. Follow the stream for almost a mile to a bench that is located at a curve in the trail at N 39° 25.420, W 82° 32.755 (6). A sign here marks this as halfway to Cedar Falls. You will later note that the Lower Falls and Cedar Falls seem to be facing each other, which is physically impossible even in a magical place like this. The mystery is explained here, because the separate streams below the falls meet here just off the trail and then flow away from the trail.

So the trail now follows a different creek upstream past more benches and another overhang ledge. Continue on this route for over a mile, cross the stream, and come to a junction at N 39° 25.150, W 82° 31.664 (7). Here the Buckeye Trail branches off and heads toward Ash Cave, completing the Grandma Gatewood Trail. To continue to Cedar Falls, bear left and

stay along stream level. Recross the stream twice more, and in another 0.2 mile, you will come to Cedar Falls at N 39° 26.130, W 82° 31.514 (8). This scenic falls is one of the most photographed spots in the state, so stay a while and enjoy the view.

To return via the Rim Trail, turn left and climb a long flight of stairs that overlooks the falls. Once you climb out of the gorge, bear left and follow the trail to a large suspension bridge at N 39° 26.173, W 82° 31.448 (9). Cross the bridge and follow the well-maintained route back. After going nearly 1.5 miles, climb the steep hill that ends at the dam overlooking Rose Lake at N 39° 25.477, W 82° 32.236 (10). This well-stocked, man-made lake marks the halfway point, and benches make this a good spot for a break.

Continue on back into the woods and proceed for almost a mile until a bridge over the gorge appears on the left at N 39° 26.009, W 82° 32.457 (11). Cross this bridge and turn right to return to point 1, or continue on to return to point 2.

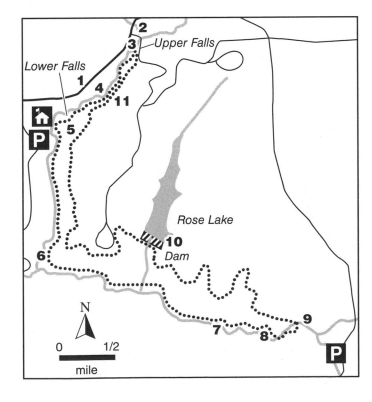

1. Lot
2. Stone bridge
3. Upper Falls
4. Old Man's Cave
5. Lower Falls
6. Turn left
7. Junction
8. Cedar Falls
9. Suspension bridge
10. Rose Lake
11. Bridge

Ash Cave to Cedar Falls

 **Hiking distance:** 5.5 miles round trip

Estimated hiking time: 4 hours

This is half of one of the most famous hiking stretches in Ohio, and it is in the heart of one of the prettiest areas in the state. This recently rerouted trail offers views of an abundance of wildflowers scattered over hilly terrain.

Caution: This trail follows streams much of the way and can become quite muddy in rainy weather.

Trail directions: The parking lot for the Ash Cave Trailhead is less than a half mile west of the junction of State Route 374 and State Route 56. Park your car at N 39° 23.764, W 82° 32.741 (1) and proceed on a paved path past a kiosk and restrooms. This first section of trail to Ash Cave is paved and level and is accessible for all. In less than 0.3 mile, you will come to Ash Cave at N 39° 23.976, W 82° 32.666 (2). This recess cave is 700 feet long and 100 feet deep with a 90-foot waterfall; these dimensions make this the largest recess cave and highest waterfall in Ohio. The name comes from the large amounts of ashes found here, presumably from the many fires made by ancient peoples over the years.

After marveling at the splendor of the panorama for a suitable period of time, proceed under the falls and up the hill on a set of steps. Continue along the ledge at the top; at 0.5 mile, you will arrive at the top of the falls at N 39° 23.981, W 82° 32.647 (3). Don't get too close to the slippery edge; people are injured every year from falls on these rocks. From the ledge, follow the blue-blazed trail along the creek

that feeds the falls. These blazes indicate that you are on the Buckeye Trail, and the 6-mile stretch between Ash Cave and Old Man's Cave is named the Grandma Gatewood Trail in honor of a Buckeye Trail founder and the first woman to through-hike the Appalachian Trail.

Follow along the creek for 0.2 mile; at that point, the trail turns away from the stream at N 39° 24.192, W 82° 32.478 (4). Here the Buckeye Trail Association has recently fashioned a new route, so if you haven't hiked this popular stretch of trail recently, it will be something new for you. The new trail begins a steady ascent through a pine woods for 0.3 mile. At N 39° 24.137, W 82° 32.190 (5), the trail meets a gravel path and follows it to the left. Over the next 0.3 mile, the trail follows the gravel, leaves it to go into the woods, and rejoins it again before leaving for good at N 39° 24.292, W 82° 31.917 (6). Just 0.1 mile after this, you will come to a fire tower at N 39° 24.351, W 82° 31.841 (7). Ignore the temptation to climb the tower, and proceed on to Wesley Chapel Road right at the point where it joins State Route 374 at N 39° 24.461, W 82° 31.862 (8). You have now come 1.5 miles.

Cross the road, reenter the woods, and begin a steady descent. After a little over 0.3 mile, the trail meets a stream at N 39° 24.655, W 82° 32.053 (9). Follow the stream for about 0.3 mile, until the trail meets a Hocking State Forest road at N 39° 24.924, W 82° 31.887 (10). Stay on the lower portion of the trail (on the right, closer to the stream) and follow the forest route for another 0.3 mile. At N 39° 25.050, W 82° 31.597 (11), the trail arrives at the Cedar Falls parking lot. Bear left and follow the edge of the lot past the restrooms to where the trail enters the woods.

Follow the path down a steep set of stairs built into the hillside for about 0.2 mile. At the bottom of the hill, the trail meets the Old Man's Cave Trail at N 39° 25.144, W 82° 31.663 (12). The Grandma Gatewood Trail goes left, but you will want to turn right, cross the stream, and go another 0.1 mile to Cedar Falls at N 39° 23.126, W 82° 31.512 (13). The cedar trees that give the falls its name are actually hemlocks.

But everything else about the scene is perfect. Cedar Falls is one of the most photographed spots in the state, and you should allow sufficient time to soak up the sublime splendor. After doing so, you want to continue on the Grandma Gatewood Trail to Old Man's Cave, or you may return to Ash Cave via the same route that you took to get here.

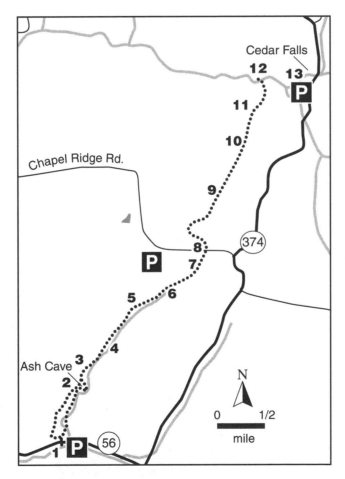

1. Lot
2. Ash Cave
3. Top of falls
4. Turn
5. Gravel road
6. Leave gravel
7. Fire tower
8. Cross road
9. Stream
10. Road
11. Cedar Falls lot
12. Junction
13. Cedar Falls

Rock House

Hiking distance: 0.5 mile

Estimated hiking time: 30 minutes

Explore a real above-ground cave with some impressive rock formations.

Caution: The Rock House is dark inside with uneven surfaces that are slippery when wet—and they are always wet.

Trail directions: Take State Route 33 to State Route 180, which is just 3 miles north of Logan. Take State Route 180 west for 9 miles, then turn left on State Route 374 toward Conkle's Hollow. Go 1 mile and turn into the Rock House parking lot. Park near the shelter at N 39° 29.466, W 82° 36.536 (1). The Rock House Trail enters the woods near the latrine here.

After a short descent, the red-blazed rim trail appears on the right at N 39° 29.499, W 82° 36.531 (2). Bear left and continue to descend through a mixed hardwood and pine forest. At the bottom of the hill, the trail crosses a wooden bridge and then climbs a steep stone staircase that leads to the entrance of the Rock House at N 39° 29.520, W 82° 36.512 (3).

Unlike the ledge overhangs at Old Man's Cave and Ash Cave, Rock House really is a cave. The tunnel-like corridor is located halfway up a 150-foot cliff of Blackhand sandstone with a 25-foot-high ceiling. The main corridor is 200 feet long with a width of between 20 and 30 feet; seven giant arched windows look over the valley and are positioned between the sandstone columns of the cave. Native Americans built fires and baked here, and later the

View of the forest from Rock House in Hocking Hills State Park.

spot was used as a hideout by criminals. After the spot became a popular attraction, a hotel was built near the site, but today this remote location is one of the most secluded of the Hocking Hills attractions. Enjoy exploring the cave, but watch your step on the wet surface and be advised that rock climbing and throwing are prohibited.

After exploring Rock House, go back out the main entry and turn right to resume the hike. Continue on through a forest filled with ferns and cliffs. After you climb another stone staircase, the rim trail forks off to the right at N 39° 29.530, W 82° 36.449 (4). Turn here and follow the rocky precipice from the top until returning to point 2.

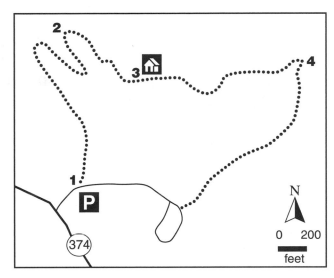

1. Lot
2. Junction
3. Rock House
4. Turn

Cantwell Cliffs

Hiking distance: 1 mile

Estimated hiking time: 1 hour

Explore the tops and bottoms of some steep, sheer cliffs.

Caution: Stay on the trail and away from cliff faces.

Trail directions: Take State Route 33 to State Route 180 just north of Logan. Go west on State Route 180 for 5 miles and then turn north on State Route 374. The Cantwell Cliffs lot is 2 miles ahead on the right at a sharp bend in the road. The lot here has a small log building and pit latrines, but no water. Park near the trailhead kiosk at N 39° 32.244, W 82° 34.332 (1) and check the map here. The trail goes around a picnic shelter and down a short set of stone steps; the trail then stops at a junction at N 39° 32.297, W 82° 34.308 (2). A steep stone stairway descends on the left, but for now, you should turn right on the red-blazed rim trail.

Follow along the top of a steep ledge past a side trail that leads directly down. After crossing a stone bridge, the trail climbs slightly and comes to a small log shelter at N 39° 32.358, W 82° 34.251 (3). A short distance past this, the trail descends a flight of stone stairs and begins to double back. The return route is on the yellow-blazed gorge trail, but trails are not well blazed. The gorge trail splits off in both directions at a spectacular gorge at N 39° 32.344, W 82° 34.244 (4). From here, you can look straight up and see the cliff top and the stone bridge that you recently crossed. Bear left here and continue to follow along the base of the cliffs. Be careful—the terrain is steep, and the trail surfaces are not level. Follow the worn path past some stunning views of the reddish brown Blackhand sandstone as it makes a horseshoe bend. Some of these sheer cliffs are 150 feet high.

Continue to follow along the base of the cliffs until arriving at a short wooden staircase on the left at N 39° 32.299, W 82° 34.310 (5). These steps lead to "Fat Woman's Squeeze," a narrow break between two boulders. Just on the other side is the steep stone staircase that leads back up to point 2.

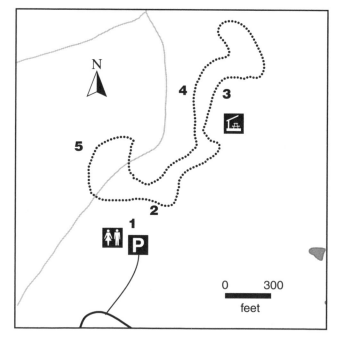

1. Lot and kiosk
2. Junction at top of stairs
3. Log shelter
4. Gorge
5. Fat Woman's Squeeze

0 300
feet

> Visit a quiet stretch of trail in the middle of the state's most popular hiking area.

> View one of Ohio's few public rappelling areas.

> Enjoy spectacular views and a lush forest environment.

Area Information

The five sites included in Hocking Hills State Park make it the most popular hiking location in Ohio, and the trails here can get crowded at peak times of the year. But in between these separate locations lies the Hocking State Forest, which contains the same kind of scenery but without the crowds. This 9,000-acre state forest also offers several unique features, such as a bridle trail, an equestrian campground, and a rappelling area.

The state began purchasing land in the Hocking Hills region in 1924, but it wasn't until a major reorganization in 1949 that the state park and state forest were separated. While the state parks tend to be mainly for recreational use, Ohio's state forests are multipurpose and involve timber harvesting and habitat protection. Older birch and hemlock trees—some as old as 500 years—can be found in Hocking State Forest. Modern growth includes pine, sassafras, and oaks on the dry ridges; beech, poplar, maples, ash, and hickory can be found in the cooler gorges and on slopes. Many varieties of plants and ferns are found here, as well as a unique mix of northern and southern species. And the forest also features the same 300-million-year-old sandstone cliffs found throughout the region.

Hocking State Forest also offers a variety of recreational opportunities. In addition to hunting, fishing, and hiking, the forest contains a bridle trail that has a free camping area with 23 sites for horses and riders. A 99-acre section of the forest has been set aside for rock climbing and rappelling. This section contains a sandstone cliff that is nearly a mile long and 100 feet high; this cliff has enough slump blocks, cracks, chimneys, and overhangs to challenge any climber. And the Buckeye Trail passes through this area, with side trails that lead to Conkle's Hollow and Old Man's Cave, two of the most popular hikes in the state.

Directions: The parking area for rock climbers and hikers is on Big Pine Road, a mile east of State Route 374 and a mile north of State Route 664.

Facilities: A staging and parking area is located next to the equestrian camp to facilitate use of the bridle trail.

Hours open: The forest is open daily year-round during daylight hours.

Rules and permits: Fires and camping are permitted in designated areas only. Horses are permitted only on designated bridle trails, and there are no provisions for all-terrain vehicles or mountain bikes. Hunting and fishing are permitted.

Contact information: The mailing address is 19275 State Route 374, Rockbridge, Ohio 43149; the phone number is 740-385-4402.

Other Areas of Interest

Two nature preserves—Sheick Hollow and Little Rocky Hollow—are located within the borders of Hocking State Forest. These both contain fragile ecosystems and are dedicated as interpretative and scientific preserves. Admission is by permit only.

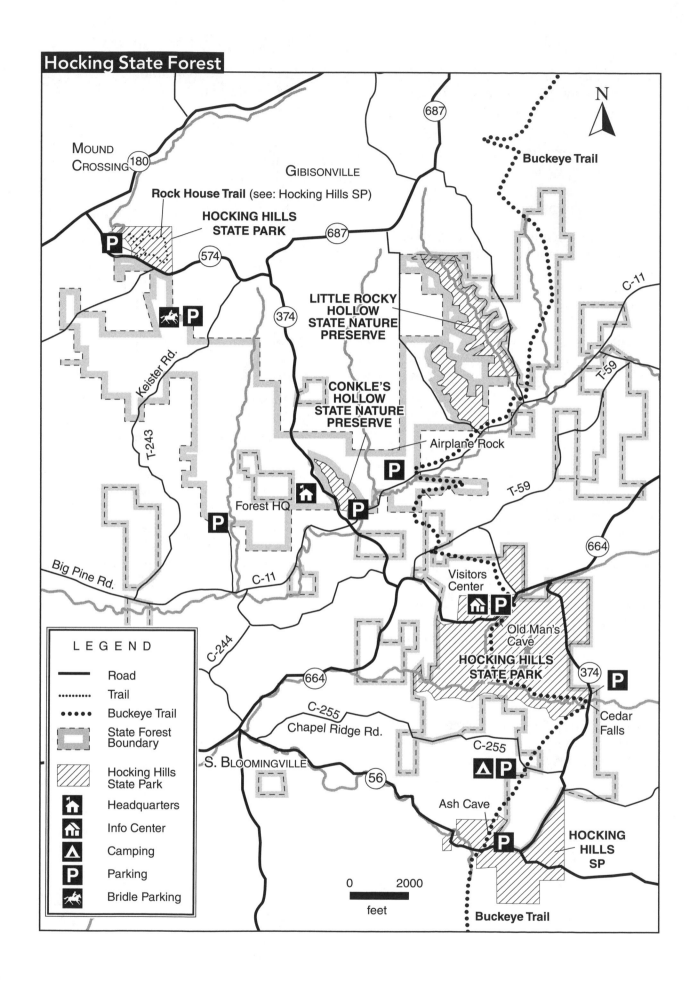

Hocking State Forest

MOUND
CROSSING (180)

Buckeye Trail

GIBISONVILLE

Rock House Trail (see: Hocking Hills SP)

**HOCKING HILLS
STATE PARK**

687

574

C-11

374

Keister Rd.

**LITTLE ROCKY
HOLLOW
STATE NATURE
PRESERVE**

T-59

T-243

**CONKLE'S
HOLLOW
STATE NATURE
PRESERVE**

Airplane Rock

T-59

Forest HQ

664

Big Pine Rd.

C-11

Visitors
Center

Old Man's
Cave

**HOCKING HILLS
STATE PARK**

374

C-244

LEGEND

— Road

···· Trail

•••• Buckeye Trail

State Forest
Boundary

Hocking Hills
State Park

Headquarters

Info Center

Camping

Parking

Bridle Parking

664

C-255

Chapel Ridge Rd.

C-255

S. BLOOMINGVILLE

56

Cedar
Falls

Ash Cave

**HOCKING
HILLS
SP**

0   2000

feet

Buckeye Trail

Hocking State Forest, Buckeye Trail

Hiking distance: 7.5 miles

Estimated hiking time: 5 hours

Take a rugged and scenic hike between two of the state's most popular trails.

Caution: Beware of dangerous cliffs. Also, portions of the trail that are concurrent with bridle trails can be extremely muddy.

Trail directions: From the junction of State Routes 374 and 664, just west of Old Man's Cave, take 374 north for 1 mile downhill. Turn right on Big Pine Road, go past the lot for Conkle's Hollow, and go about 1 mile. The parking lot is on the left side. Park and cross Big Pine Road, then proceed to the explanatory kiosk at N 39° 27.533, W 92° 33.510 (1). Veer left to cross a bridge, and in 0.1 mile, you will come to a T intersection at N 39° 27.492, W 82° 33.417 (2). Turn left and follow the familiar blue blazes of the Buckeye Trail, which you will remain on for the entire hike.

After a straight stretch, the trail begins climbing sharply toward the base of a steep rock wall. In about 0.4 mile, the trail cuts through this rock face at N 39° 27.435, W 82° 33.314 (3). After emerging through a sort of tunnel, you should veer right and follow the blazes with the rock face now on the right. In about 0.1 mile, you will come to the unusual Balanced Rock formation at N 39° 27.433, W 82° 33.134 (4). Beyond this pillar, Big Pine Road can be seen below.

Turn right here and follow some switchbacks that stay on top of the cliff face. In the next half mile, you will pass by several spots used by rock climbers and rappellers. This part of the trail is also used by horseback riders, but the bridle trail veers off and up on the left at N 39° 27.344, W 82° 33.433 (5). Continue to follow along the cliff face for another 0.4 mile until you arrive at a clearing at N 39° 27.162, W 82° 33.617 (6). This location provides the most spectacular view and is a favored spot for climbers; in addition, other local trails converge near this location.

Here the trail breaks left, away from the cliff face, and is immediately reunited with the bridle trail. The trail continues to climb uphill through a pine forest for about a mile until it crosses Unger Road at N 39° 28.723, W 82° 33.366 (7). The altitude here is about 350 feet higher than at the parking lot, so serious ascending is involved. But by now you have left the crowds behind and should have the forest to yourself. This stretch of trail runs right between two of the most popular outdoor attractions in the state, but when we were hiking on a gorgeous day in mid-October, we never saw another soul.

Cross Unger Road and head back into the mixed hardwood forest. The trail veers left and begins to descend, and in almost a mile, it drops down to Culp Road at N 39° 26.578, W 82° 32.510 (8). Turn right and follow the road for 0.5 mile until you arrive at State Route 374 and the parking lot for Old Man's Cave at N 38° 26.251, W 82° 32.350 (9). The Upper Falls at Old Man's Cave is just a quarter mile away from here. Hikers can go on to this site and proceed 3 miles farther to Cedar Falls, or they may have a second car parked here. Another option is to return via the same route for a 7.5-mile hike.

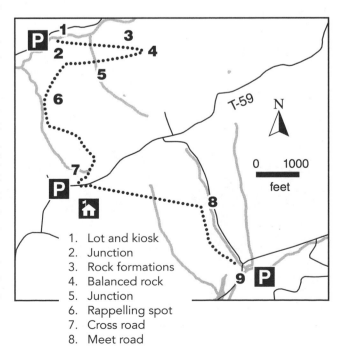

1. Lot and kiosk
2. Junction
3. Rock formations
4. Balanced rock
5. Junction
6. Rappelling spot
7. Cross road
8. Meet road
9. Old Man's Cave lot

> Stay in one of the more than 60 cabins near a pristine man-made lake.

> Enjoy a secluded hike in a remote area off the beaten path.

> Take advantage of a system of nearby backpack trails for a multiday adventure.

> View the remains of Ohio's original iron industry that helped win the Civil War.

Area Information

Despite its location so near to the popular Hocking Hills region of southeast Ohio, Lake Hope State Park is a largely undiscovered treasure. The prime feature is a 120-acre horseshoe-shaped lake nestled in the rugged hills. Lake Hope contains bluegill, catfish, crappie, and bass for the anglers; it also offers a 600-foot swimming beach near the dam.

On the hilly peninsula adjacent to the lake, visitors will find 66 smaller cottages and the Laurel Lodge, which sleeps up to 22 people.

But there is more to the park area than the lake. At the headwaters, visitors can see the chimney and foundation remains of Hope Furnace, a symbol of Ohio's early iron ore industry. It seems that this portion of the state, known as the Hanging Rock region, contained the right combination of iron ore from sandstone bedrock and charcoal to fire the furnaces. From the 1850s to the 1870s, the area enjoyed an economic heyday. In particular, the furnaces were burning local hardwood 24 hours a day to produce ammunition and cannon for the Union Army in the Civil War. It is also believed that the Hope Furnace may have supplied plating for the *Monitor*, the first ironclad ship in the U.S. Navy.

Hope Furnace in Lake Hope State Park played a major role in Ohio's early iron ore industry.

When other iron ore deposits were discovered, the local furnaces were closed down, and a second-growth forest grew to replace the original burned-out trees. Oak and hickory are now the dominant trees, and the area also boasts an abundance of wildflowers, such as bloodroot, wild geranium, and the rare yellow lady's slipper. Deer, wild turkey, and especially beaver are abundant within the park. Zaleski State Forest, which includes over 20 miles of backpacking trails, is adjacent to the park.

Directions: Lake Hope State Park is on State Route 278, 10 miles south of its junction with Route 33 in Nelsonville.

Hours open: The park is open year-round.

Facilities: In addition to full-service cottages, Lake Hope has a campsite featuring 46 electric and 141 nonelectric sites as well as 9 picnic areas. The beach area has concessions and restrooms; in addition, canoes, kayaks, and rowboats can be rented. In winter, sledding, cross-country skiing, ice skating, and ice fishing are options. The park contains eight biking trails, including one that was voted the best in the state by *Mountain Bike Magazine,* as well as 33 miles of bridle trails.

Rules and permits: Pets are permitted in the campground and in some cottages. Only electric motors are permitted on boats.

Contact information: The address for Lake Hope State Park is 27331 State Route 278, McArthur, Ohio 45651. The phone number for the park office is 740-596-4938; the phone number for cottage check-in is 740-596-5253.

Other Park Trails

In addition to the trail used for the hikes described here, Lake Hope State Park also contains the following trails:

Habron Hollow Trail, 1.5 miles

Hope Furnace Trail, 3.2 miles

Other Areas of Interest

Zaleski State Forest surrounds the park and provides hiking, backpacking, and bridle trails. Lake Alma State Park is located 15 miles to the southeast; this park offers fishing, swimming, camping, and picnicking.

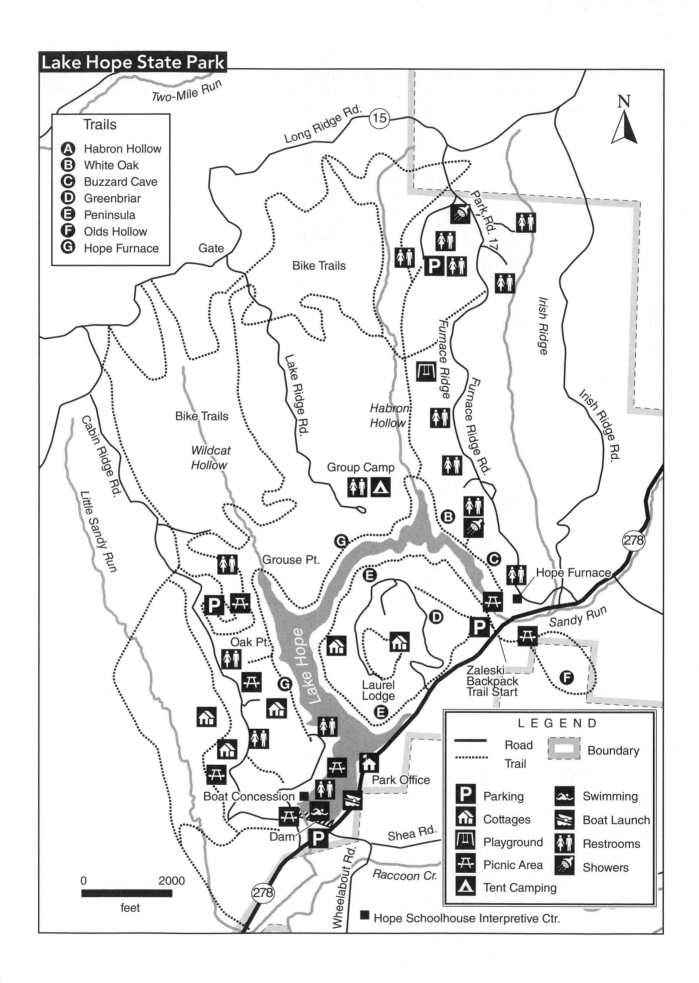

Lake Hope State Park

Trails

- **A** Habron Hollow
- **B** White Oak
- **C** Buzzard Cave
- **D** Greenbriar
- **E** Peninsula
- **F** Olds Hollow
- **G** Hope Furnace

LEGEND

—— Road	Boundary		
···· Trail			
P Parking		Swimming	
Cottages		Boat Launch	
Playground		Restrooms	
Picnic Area		Showers	
Tent Camping			

■ Hope Schoolhouse Interpretive Ctr.

0   2000

feet

Two-Mile Run

Long Ridge Rd. 15

Gate

Bike Trails

Park Rd. 17

Furnace Ridge

Irish Ridge

Furnace Ridge Rd.

Irish Ridge Rd.

278

Bike Trails

Lake Ridge Rd.

Habron Hollow

Wildcat Hollow

Cabin Ridge Rd.

Little Sandy Run

Group Camp

B

C

Hope Furnace

Grouse Pt.

G

E

D

Sandy Run

Oak Pt.

Zaleski Backpack Trail Start

F

G

Lake Hope

Laurel Lodge

E

Park Office

Boat Concession

Dam

Shea Rd.

Wheelabout Rd.

Raccoon Cr.

278

Lake Hope Peninsula Trail

 Hiking distance: 2.9 miles round trip

Estimated hiking time: 1.5 hours

Hike along a newer man-made lake located at the site of a historic nature-based industry.

Caution: Although this trail is generally easy to follow, there is no blazing. Also, the trail can be uneven and slippery even though it follows the shoreline.

Trail directions: Park in the lot at Hope Furnace, which gives its name to the lake. Cross Sandy Run along State Route 278 and immediately enter the woods at N 39° 19.898, W 82° 20.424 (1). The Peninsula Trail follows the inside loop of Lake Hope (which is a C-shaped lake) along the shoreline. Just 0.2 mile after this trail enters the woods, the Lodge Road Trail veers off to the left at N 39° 19.892, W 82° 20.984 (2). Stay on the main trail, which follows the backwaters of Sandy Run as the stream gradually widens and runs into Lake Hope.

At about 0.5 mile, the trail starts veering left at N 39° 20.134, W 82° 20.710 (3). The Peninsula Trail is not blazed, but it is easy to follow because it hugs the shoreline. But because Lake Hope is a man-made lake created by flooding the valley, the trail is located on what was originally steep hillside, so it is not level. Follow the shoreline down the back end of the lake for another 0.8 mile until the trail starts to turn back toward the highway at N 39° 19.310, W 82° 21.330 (4). Continue to follow the shoreline past where you can see cabins on the opposite shore.

After 0.5 mile, you will come to State Route 278 at N 39° 19.482, W 82° 21.008 (5). Follow alongside the road and the backwaters of the lake for about 0.3 mile until you get to the park road at N 39° 19.638, W 82° 20.803 (6). This is the main entrance to the park, and the road goes into the peninsula and past the hill to where several cabins can be rented. After crossing the park road, continue to follow along State Route 278 for another 0.3 mile to where the trail crosses a small stream and moves away from the road at N 39° 19.802, W 82° 20.740 (7).

As the trail goes into the woods, you will begin a gradual ascent. After climbing for 0.2 mile, you will be out of earshot of the road and will intersect with the Greenbrier Trail at N 39° 19.879, W 82° 20.699 (8). Veer right here and continue on, going back downhill for another 0.2 mile until you return to point 2. Follow the trail out of the woods and return to the Hope Furnace parking lot.

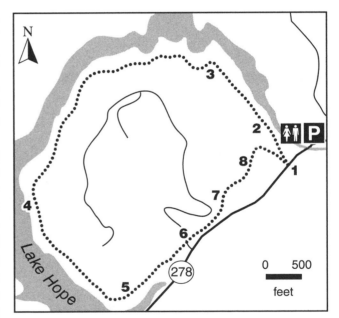

1. Enter woods
2. Junction
3. Veer left
4. Veer left
5. Meet SR 278
6. Cross park road
7. Cross stream
8. Junction

Olds Hollow

Hiking distance: 1 mile

Estimated hiking time: 1 hour

Enjoy a short hike on a route that connects to a much longer backpacking trail.

Caution: The trail is steep and can be slippery when wet.

Trail directions: Park in the Hope Furnace lot and cross the road and the creek. Cross a footbridge at a sign marked Point A at N 39° 19.857, W 82° 20.464 (1). Bear left and go into the woods; proceed about 0.2 mile to where the trail splits at N 39° 19.782, W 82° 20.246 (2). Take the right fork up a hill, and at 0.4 mile, you will arrive at the Pioneer Cemetery at N 39° 19.837, W 80° 20.122 (3). The cemetery dates back to the 1850s, before the economic boom of the furnace era.

Proceed another 0.1 mile along a ridge until you come to wooden stairs at N 39° 19.832, W 82° 20.016 (4). Descend the stairs to encounter a waterfall in the creek below. The trail continues to descend and follow the creek past some recess caves for 0.5 mile until you meet the junction with the King Hollow Trail at N 39° 19.851, W 81° 20.047 (5). This is a beginning point for the 24-mile Zaleski Backpack loop. Unless you want to take a hike of several days, proceed on the Olds Hollow Trail as it moves along some wetlands near the creek for another 0.4 mile until returning to point A. In another 0.1 mile, you will be back at the parking lot.

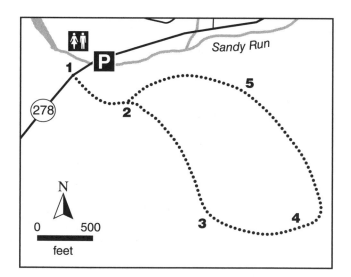

1. Enter woods
2. Junction
3. Pioneer Cemetery
4. Wooden stairs
5. Backpack trailhead

> Sample a variety of plants and ferns and some rare trees usually not found this far north.

> Hike along sandstone cliffs and cool creeks and a lake.

> Enjoy it all in solitude in a little-used park in a remote area.

Area Information

Lake Katherine State Nature Preserve really is a gem. Although there are many well-known state parks nearby, Lake Katherine is just as impressive and has the advantage of anonymity, which keeps the crowds down. The lake itself is the least accessible part of the preserve, and is not the main attraction, although it is the reason the preserve exists.

Lake Katherine came into being when local businessman Edwin Jones and James McKittereck built a dam on their property along Rock Run to create a lake. They donated their property to the state in 1977, and the preserve was later expanded to include over 1,800 acres. The lake today is accessible only by permit and only to nonmotorized boats that must be carried 110 yards to the shore.

The 6 miles of hiking trails offer the most to the visitor. The Appalachian forest is cut here by steep ravines and sandstone cliffs that feature diverse plant life. The preserve is the northernmost home of the bigleaf and umbrella magnolia trees and is the only known Ohio location of the former. Other native trees include oak, hemlock, sweet gum, birch, and beech. The preserve also features many ferns such as the Christmas fern and common polypody. Among the common wildflowers are calico bush (mountain laurel), mountain watercress, starflowers, puttyroot, and stemless lady's slipper. Deer and wild turkey are abundant, and you may even spot an elusive bobcat.

Directions: From U.S. Route 32, take State Route 93 north into downtown Jackson. Just north of the courthouse, go left on Bridge Street where 93 branches off to the right. Go 2 miles, veering right onto State Street, which turns into County Road 76. After crossing a set of railroad tracks, turn right on County Road 85. It is 1.5 miles to the entrance to the preserve and another 0.6 mile to the parking lot.

Hours open: The preserve is open year-round in daylight hours.

Facilities: No facilities are available, not even a restroom or picnic table in the entire preserve. Near the administration building that is closed to the public is a parking lot with a kiosk. All trails meet at this lot.

Rules and permits: Pets are not allowed. Do not pick wildflowers. No fires, camping, or rock climbing. No swimming is allowed in the lake, and boating permits are tightly regulated.

Contact information: The preserve address is 1703 Lake Katherine Road, Jackson, Ohio 45640. To inquire about a boating permit, write to 784 Rock Run Road, Jackson, Ohio 45640, or call 740-286-2487.

Park Trails

Three trails are in the preserve with a combined total of just over 6 miles.

Other Areas of Interest

Nearby Jackson Lake State Park near Oak Hill to the south and Lake Alma State Park near Wellston to the north offer many of the amenities that are not found in state nature preserves. For those who prefer the primitive and pristine, Richland Furnace State Forest and Wellston Wildlife Area are just to the north on the Jackson County and Vinton County border.

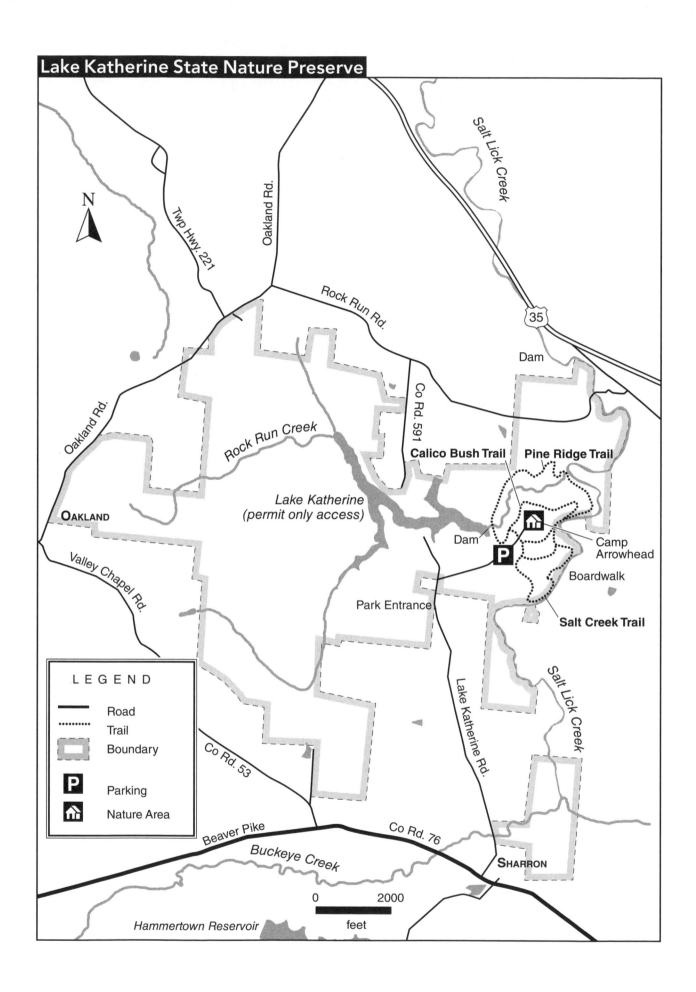

Lake Katherine State Nature Preserve

N

Twp Hwy. 221

Oakland Rd.

Salt Lick Creek

Rock Run Rd.

35

Dam

Co Rd. 591

Oakland Rd.

Rock Run Creek

Calico Bush Trail   **Pine Ridge Trail**

Lake Katherine
(permit only access)

Dam

P

Camp
Arrowhead

OAKLAND

Boardwalk

Valley Chapel Rd.

Park Entrance

Salt Creek Trail

LEGEND

————— Road

············· Trail

Boundary

P   Parking

Nature Area

Co Rd. 53

Lake Katherine Rd.

Salt Lick Creek

Beaver Pike

Co Rd. 76

Buckeye Creek

SHARRON

0   2000

feet

Hammertown Reservoir

Pine Ridge and Calico Bush Trail

Hiking distance: 2.5 miles

Estimated hiking time: 1 hour 45 minutes

A rugged hike that has a lake, a waterfall, creeks, hills, and spectacular rock formations.

Caution: Trail is steep and can be slippery when wet.

Trail directions: From the kiosk at N 39° 05.169, W 82° 40.179 (1), head into the woods on the mowed path at the southwest edge of the parking lot. After just 0.1 mile is the turnoff for the Calico Bush Trail at N 39° 05.123, W 82° 40.253 (2). As you veer left, you may hear the sound of a waterfall below. After descending for 0.2 mile, the trail arrives at Lake Katherine at N 39° 05.110, W 82° 40.377 (3). The manmade lake is off limits without special permission, but it is a scenic spot.

Immediately afterward is a bridge across Rock Run, a feeder stream. A gentle waterfall cascades below the bridge. The trail then begins to climb sharply, and in another 0.2 mile is an overlook as the trail turns left at N 39° 05.262, W 82° 40.291 (4). Remain in the woods at this higher altitude, and there is another cliff overlook turnoff in 0.6 mile at N 39° 05.404, W 82° 39.953 (5). Stay on the ridge line for another 0.2 mile until a road is visible off to the left at N 39° 05,522, W 82° 39.806 (6). Here the trail begins to descend sharply and eventually comes alongside Salt Creek. The valley floor here is strewn with ferns as the stream flows on the left and high sandstone cliffs are on the right where the trail behind it lies.

In 0.6 mile, the trail leaves the creek and crosses a wooden bridge at N 39° 05.267, W 82° 39.939 (7). Then it climbs a hill for 0.1 mile to the junction with the Calico Bush Trail at N 39° 05.184, W 82° 40.898 (8). This trail winds around just below the rim of the hill where the parking lot is and offers an abundance of wildflowers. Follow this trail for almost 0.5 mile until it returns to the Pine Ridge Trail at point 2. Then follow that trail back another 0.1 mile to the parking lot.

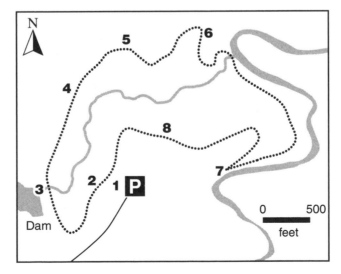

1. Lot and kiosk
2. Junction
3. Lake Katherine
4. Overlook
5. Overlook
6. Descend to creek
7. Wooden bridge
8. Junction

Salt Creek Trail

Hiking distance: 1.7 miles

Estimated hiking time: 1 hour 15 minutes

A well-built trail that features steep cliffs along a stream.

Caution: Trail can be wet; be careful on stairs built along the trail.

Trail directions: From the kiosk at the paved parking lot at N 39° 05.151, W 82° 40.168 (1), enter the woods at the marked mowed path at the northwest corner of the lot. This part of the trail is concurrent with the Calico Bush Trail for almost 0.3 mile until they separate at N 39° 05.169, W 82° 39.933 (2). Take the right fork and follow along a ridge line until you descend a flight of stairs to overlook Salt Creek.

Continue on a path between the creek and some tall sandstone cliffs past where a shorter Salt Creek loop turns off to the right at about 0.5 mile at N 39° 05.038, W 82° 40.042 (3). Here the trail gets bogged down and uses boardwalks. In about 0.3 mile is a long wooden bridge at N 39° 04.915, W 82° 40.103 (4). Not long afterward is a side trail that leads to a pretty spot along Salt Creek, but the main trail also soon becomes creekside. After another 0.3 mile, the trail turns away from the creek and begins to climb uphill at N 39° 04.792, W 82° 40.206 (5).

After climbing through a hardwood forest for 0.4 mile, the trail meets with the other end of the shorter loop at N 39° 04.955, W 82° 40.134 (6). From here it is just 0.2 mile back to the kiosk at the parking lot.

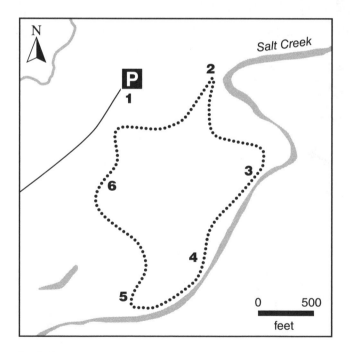

1. Lot
2. Junction
3. Junction
4. Bridge
5. Begin ascent
6. Junction

> Take a break from nearby congested Hocking Hills trails to enjoy an underused gem.
> View the largest of the 12 known natural bridges in Ohio.
> Enjoy the quiet alongside the peaceful Hocking River.
> See a variety of wildflowers in season.

Area Information

Natural bridges made out of rock formations have fascinated Americans since Thomas Jefferson described his favorite one near Lexington, Virginia. Twelve such bridges are known to be in Ohio. Although this phenomenon is commonly found in limestone, all of Ohio's natural bridges are not found in the limestone region of southwest Ohio; rather, all of them are located in the sandstone-dominated regions of south central and eastern Ohio.

These bridges were formed millions of years ago when much of the Midwest was under a warm inland sea. As the sea receded when the Appalachian Mountains were formed, the Blackhand sandstone left behind was left to the process of erosion that resulted in these few bridges remaining in the state. Of these, the Rockbridge is the largest at about 100 feet. The arch is between 10 and 20 feet in width and crosses a 5-foot ravine just a few hundred yards from the Hocking River.

The preserve is located in the heart of Ohio's Hocking Hills region, which is the best known—and therefore the most crowded—natural region in the state. But Rockbridge is a secluded enclave known to only the most devoted nature lovers. Located between U.S. Route 33 (the major highway of Hocking County) and the Hocking River, Rockbridge is equally accessible by land and by water. The small gravel parking lot is rarely crowded, and the site offers a landing spot where canoeists on the Hocking can leisurely get out and take a look around. The hiking trails in the preserve also offer a variety of hardwoods and seasonal wildflowers. The preserve contains two trails. The Natural Bridge Trail goes from the parking lot to the natural bridge, while the Beech Ridge Trail is a shorter loop trail that branches off from the Natural Bridge Trail.

Directions: From U.S. Route 33 at a point less than 2 miles southwest of the village of Rockbridge, turn east on Dalton Road. The turnoff spot is marked by a sign. Proceed for 0.75 mile, going parallel to Route 33, then veer north to the parking lot.

Hours open: The preserve is open year-round during daylight hours.

Facilities: The preserve has no facilities. A small gravel parking lot with a box containing brochures is located here.

Rules and permits: Rules for all state nature preserves apply—no pets, hunting, fishing, plant collecting, fires, camping, or rock climbing. No permit is necessary.

Contact information: The address for Rockbridge State Nature Preserve is 11475 Dalton Road, Rockbridge, Ohio 43149; the phone number is 614-265-6453.

Other Areas of Interest

Lake Logan State Park is located near the junction of U.S. Route 33 and State Route 664 (at 30443 Lake Logan Road, Logan, Ohio 43138; the phone number is 740-385-6842). This park is known for excellent fishing.

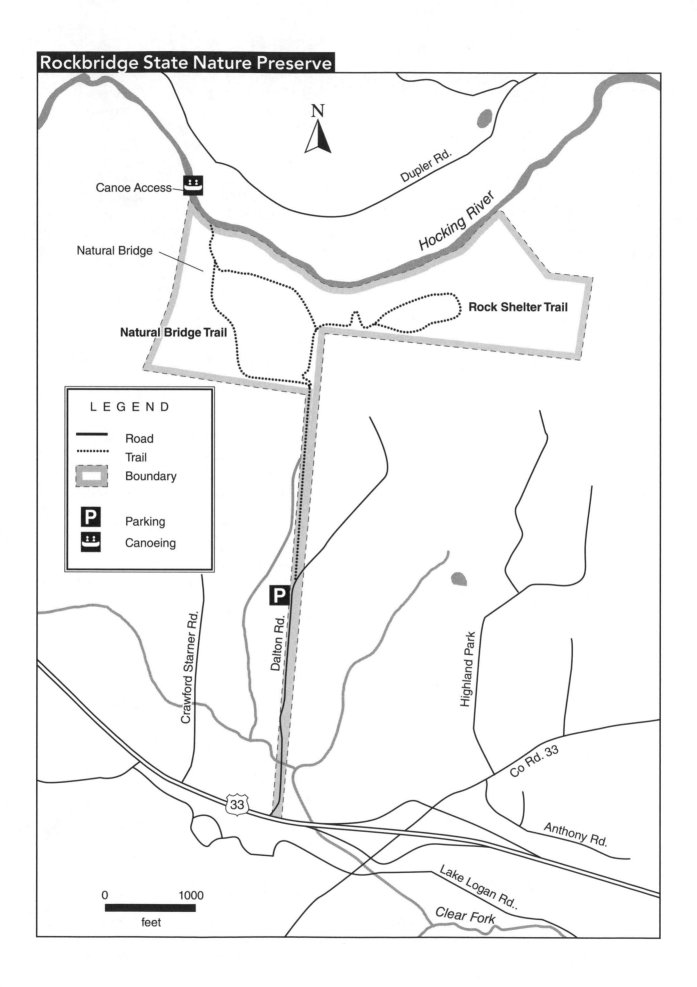

Rockbridge State Nature Preserve

N

Canoe Access

Natural Bridge

Natural Bridge Trail

Rock Shelter Trail

Dupler Rd.

Hocking River

LEGEND

Road
Trail
Boundary
P Parking
Canoeing

Crawford Starner Rd.

Dalton Rd.

Highland Park

Co Rd. 33

Anthony Rd.

Lake Logan Rd..

Clear Fork

33

0   1000

feet

Natural Bridge Trail

 Hiking distance: 1.6 miles round trip

Estimated hiking time: 1.25 hours

Hike in a secluded natural spot that features one of the most spectacular natural bridges in the state (and is not far from the crowded trails of the Hocking Hills).

Caution: The trail covers some steep hills that can be slippery when wet.

Trail directions: Leave your car in the small gravel parking lot at N 39° 33.979, W 82° 29.965 (1). The trail follows a narrow mowed path between a fence and a field for about 0.3 mile. After ascending a hill, you will enter a wooded area at N 39° 34.292, W 82° 29.934 (2). After entering the woods, the trail briefly continues a steep ascent before cresting. Just after beginning to descend, the trail splits into two routes—marked A and B—at N 39° 34.393, W 82° 29.922 (3). This split is located at about 0.5 mile from the parking lot.

Take the left fork and continue downhill through a deciduous forest. At about 0.6 mile, you will cross a small bridge at N 39° 34.478, W 82° 30.093 (4). About 0.1 mile later, the A and B trails are reunited. Just after this junction, the trail descends slightly and comes to a rare (for Ohio) natural bridge at N 39° 34.567, W 82° 30.111 (5). This bridge, which gives the preserve its name, is to the left of the trail and is unmistakable as you approach it. You are now on top of a 95-foot-long natural bridge that you can walk across. This is the longest of the 12 known natural bridges in Ohio. A side trail also goes down to the bottom of the natural bridge, so you can observe the phenomena from the underside as well.

After appreciating the natural bridge, continue to descend the trail for another 0.1 mile or so until you come to the end of the preserve at the banks of the Hocking River; this location is at N 39° 32.648, W 82° 30.090 (6). The Hocking is canoeable most of the year, but this location is upstream from the active liveries. This spot still looks seasonally navigable and

also offers a secluded spot to observe a peaceful river.

At your leisure, retrace your steps and return to the natural bridge (point 5) and the junction of trails A and B. This time, take the B trail (now on your left) to return by a different route. After continuing uphill on this path for about 0.15 mile, you will come to a trail junction at N 39° 34.481, W 82° 29.919 (7). At this point, a sign marks the departure of the rock shelter loop trail. If you pass up this option, continue for another 0.1 mile and return to where the A and B trails originally split off (point 3). Continue on the route you came in on for another half mile and return to the parking lot.

1. Lot
2. Enter woods
3. Junction
4. Bridge and junction
5. Natural bridge
6. Hocking River
7. Junction

> Hike the rugged terrain found at Ohio's largest state park.

> Sample the diversity of a park that offers camping, a lodge, golf, boating, swimming, and 14 hiking trails.

> View overhang ledge caves, such as Hosak's Cave, that result from the geology of the park.

Area Information

Covering a whopping 17,229 acres, Salt Fork is not only the largest of Ohio's 72 state parks, but it is also one of the most accessible. Located near the junction of Interstates 70 and 77, the park is an easy drive for anyone in the state. Although the name for the region comes from a salt well used by Native Americans, the park and man-made lake that dominate it are both relatively recent improvements.

The lake was supposed to serve as a reservoir, providing water to the nearby city of Cambridge. But in the 1960s, these plans were expanded to include recreational opportunities. The earthen dam for the lake was completed in 1967, and 5 years later the 148-room Salt Fork Lodge was added. Further lodging opportunities include 37 two-bedroom cottages, 17 chalet-style cottages, and a campground with 192 sites with electricity. The park also has group and equestrian camps. The nearly 3,000-acre Salt Fork Lake features a 2,500-foot beach, which makes it one of the state's largest inland beaches. Fishing is particularly popular on the lake; bluegill, bass, walleye, and muskellunge are all in abundance. To accommodate boaters, the park includes two marinas with a total of 469 rental docks, along with 10 boat launch ramps. There is no horsepower limit, so waterskiing is popular here.

Seasonal activities include public hunting for a variety of game. In winter, visitors can enjoy sledding, cross-country skiing, snowmobiling, ice skating, ice fishing, and ice boating. The park also has an 18-hole golf course with a driving range and putting green as well as a miniature golf course. Also, the park contains 19 miles of snowmobile trail and 12 miles of bridle trail.

In addition to these man-made amenities, Salt Fork contains a diversity of plant and animal life. The rugged hills and meadows house populations of deer, turkey, fox, and squirrels. Common birds seen here include cardinals, goldfinch, and barred owls. Among the wildflowers that can be found here are goldenrod, wild geranium, violets, asters, and trillium.

Park Trails

Archery Trail (an inland loop trail in the center of the park), 1 mile

Hosak's Cave Trail (a short, steep walk to a ledge cave that can be dangerous, so be sure to stay on the trail), 0.5 mile

Shadebush Trail, 2.0 miles

Gunn's Glen Trail, 2.0 miles

Deer Run Trail, 1.5 miles

Hillcrest Trail, 1 mile

Beach Point Trail, 1 mile

Pine Crest Loop Trail, 1 mile

Directions: From Interstate 77, get off at exit 47 and take U.S. Route 22 east for 6 miles. The main entrance to the park (Park Road 1) is on the left.

Hours open: The park is open year-round.

Facilities: Salt Fork offers the full range of recreational opportunities—hiking, camping, boating, hunting, fishing, picnicking, swimming, skiing, skating, golf, and horseback riding.

Rules and permits: Pets are permitted in designated sites only. Water ski and no-wake zones are posted. All statewide fishing and hunting regulations must be observed.

Contact information: The park address is 14755 Cadiz Road, Lore City, Ohio 43755. You can phone 740-439-3521 for the park office; 866-644-6727 for camping reservations; or 740-439-2751 for the lodge.

Other Areas of Interest

Deerassic Park is nearby on State Route 22. This park is an outdoor recreation education center with displays, special events, and programs. Several of the lakes in the Muskingum Watershed Conservancy District are also nearby, the closest being Seneca Lake in Noble County and Piedmont Lake on the Harrison and Belmont County border.

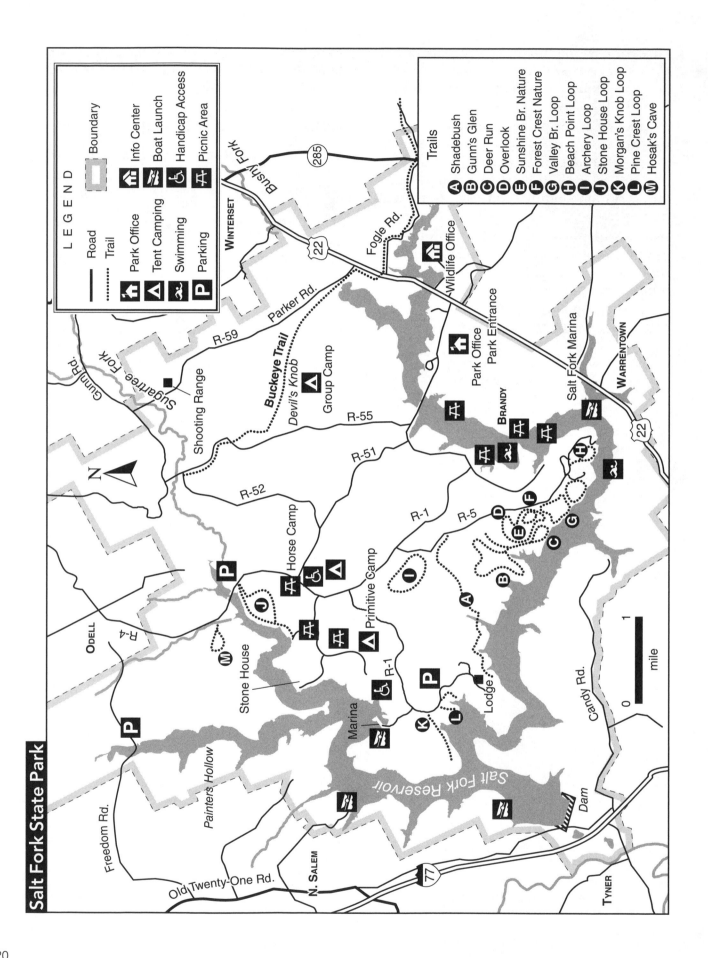

Salt Fork State Park

LEGEND

Road

Trail

Boundary

Park Office

Tent Camping

Swimming

Parking

Info Center

Boat Launch

Handicap Access

Picnic Area

Trails

Ⓐ Shadebush
Ⓑ Gunn's Glen
Ⓒ Deer Run
Ⓓ Overlook
Ⓔ Sunshine Br. Nature
Ⓕ Forest Crest Nature
Ⓖ Valley Br. Loop
Ⓗ Beach Point Loop
Ⓘ Archery Loop
Ⓙ Stone House Loop
Ⓚ Morgan's Knob Loop
Ⓛ Pine Crest Loop
Ⓜ Hosak's Cave

North Country Trail and Buckeye Trail

Hiking distance: 7.8 miles round trip

Estimated hiking time: 4 hours

Take a rugged hike on a trail with steep hills on the fringe of Ohio's largest state park.

Caution: The trail is steep and does not drain well. Mosquitoes and ticks can be bothersome in the summer.

Trail directions: From the junction of State Route 22 and Interstate 77 (exit 47), go east on 22 for just over 7 miles. Turn left on Parker Road and go 0.2 mile to the gate of a group camping area. If you have a second car, leave it here and proceed another 2 miles to the intersection with Gunn Road. Go left here on a gravel park road and continue for 1 mile. When you see a No Outlet sign, turn left, go 0.1 mile, and park at a bridge over a creek at N 40° 07.927, W 81° 27.730 (1).

From here, cross the stream and follow the state park road up a steady hill. The route is marked by the familiar blue 2-by-6-inch paint stripes of the Buckeye Trail, but this section is also concurrent with the 3,600-mile-long North Country Trail that runs from North Dakota to New York. At 0.7 mile, you will come to a turnoff to the left at N 40° 07.284, W 81° 27.706 (2). Follow the trail through a short corridor that leads to a broad meadow, and be sure to stay on the near (north) end, because the trail is unmarked until it reenters the woods at the northeast corner of the meadow.

Stay in the hilly hardwood forest for another mile until you come to a sharp left turn at N 40° 07.036, W 81° 27.307 (3). In another 0.8 mile—at N 40° 06.540, W 81° 27.409 (4)—you will arrive at a hilltop opening that offers a view of some distant hills, even in full foliage. Salt Fork Lake is on the right, but it is not visible unless the leaves are off. In another 0.5 mile, you'll come to a large dead tree—at N 40° 06.210, W 81° 27.371 (5)—that had to be cut through because it fell directly on the trail. Deer and wild turkey can be found anywhere along the route here. Proceed another 0.4 mile to where the trail turns sharply left at N 40° 05.894, W 81° 22.221 (6). The trail now enters a meadow that offers a broad view of hills off in the distance.

Here the trail begins to descend and follows the edge of the meadow until it reenters the woods. In another 0.3 to 0.4 mile, the trail levels out and turns left uphill at N 40° 05.800, W 81° 26.960 (7). From here, it is a short climb to the restrooms of the camp and only another 0.3 mile to the campground gate at N 40° 05.778, W 81° 26.722 (8). If you have a second car here, you won't need to make the 3.9-mile return hike on the route you took to get here.

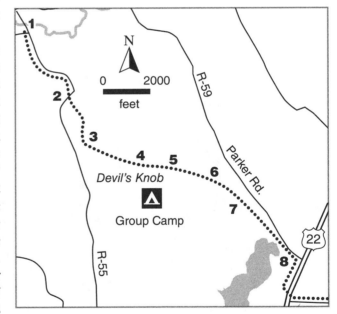

1. Park
2. Turn left
3. Turn left
4. Devil's Knob
5. Dead tree
6. Turn left
7. Climb
8. Campground

Kennedy Stone House Trail

Hiking distance: 1.6 miles round trip

Estimated hiking time: 1 hour

Take a lakeside walk in the woods, ending at a restored 1840s-era stone house.

Caution: The hillside along the lake can be slippery.

Trail directions: To get to the trail parking lot, get off Interstate 77 at exit 47 and go northeast on U.S. Route 22 for 6.5 miles. Turn left at the entrance to Salt Fork State Park and proceed on Park Road 1 for 5.6 miles. The parking lot is on the right—at N 40° 07.907, W 81° 29.183 (1)—just before the road crosses a leg of Salt Fork Lake. Park in the lot here, cross the road, and enter the woods.

The trail splits almost right away; take the right fork that follows the lake shoreline. At about 0.3 mile, you will cross a stream at N 40° 07.804, W 81° 29.671 (2). As you continue on, the main trail reunites with the uphill trail fork at around 0.4 mile at N 40° 07.714, W 81° 29.803 (3). Stay on the reunited route for another 0.4 mile until you arrive at the Kennedy Stone House at N 40° 07.672, W 81° 29.982 (4).

This house was built by Benjamin Kennedy around 1840. His descendants owned the property until Salt Fork State Park purchased it in 1966. The home originally overlooked a valley; however, when Salt Fork Lake was made, the surrounding valley went underwater, and today the home can be approached by both land and lake. In addition to the boat dock

Kennedy Stone House overlooked a valley when it was built around 1840, but today Salt Fork Lake sits in the front yard.

on the grounds, there is a road to the site that was built after the house was restored in 2003.

The house was purchased and restored by the Friends of Kennedy Stone House, and this organization now operates a museum on the site. Current hours are 1 to 5 p.m., Friday through Monday from May through October. The grounds also contains a pavilion, a docent's cabin, and a side trail that leads to a family cemetery.

For the return trip, begin on the route you came in on. Return to point 3, but this time, take the right (uphill) fork that veers away from the lake. After crossing a second streambed in about 0.5 mile, you will begin to turn downhill at N 40° 07.861, W 81° 29.266 (5). Soon you will meet the lakeside trail and return to the parking lot.

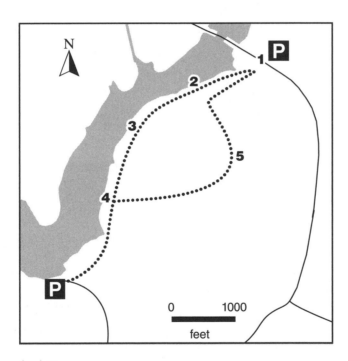

1. Lot
2. Cross stream
3. Junction
4. Stone House
5. Descend

> Find splendid isolation in one of the prettiest areas of the state.

> Tackle rugged topography in former coal-mining lands.

> Sample various types of trails as part of a national network.

Area Information

The 241,000-acre Wayne National Forest is administered by three offices in southeastern Ohio. The administrative and purchasing units are located in Ironton, Marietta, and Athens. The Athens unit includes 67,000 acres in Athens, Hocking, Morgan, Perry, and Vinton counties. Passing through this rugged topography are a variety of trails.

Probably the most widely used of these is a 75-mile All-Terrain Vehicle Trail at Dorr Run in Hocking County. Concentrating ATVs in this area does free up the rest of the forest for quiet introspection, but this popularity may lead to expansion. For horseback riders, there is the 19-mile Stone Church Horse Trail and Camp. And backpackers can be challenged by the 13-mile Wildcat Hollow loop, which also ties into a 29-mile backpack loop around Burr Oak State Park. The Buckeye Trail, North Country Trail, and American Discovery Trail all pass through the Athens Unit.

Almost every activity in the national forest is free, and nowhere are public lands less crowded. In addition to a variety of tree and wildflower vegetation, the area contains animals not usually found in Ohio. Black bears and bobcats have been sighted in these remote hollows because both species are making a comeback in Ohio. More common wildlife such as deer, wild turkey, and fox can also be found here.

Directions: The headquarters office of the Athens Ranger District is on U.S. Highway 33 between Nelsonville and Athens.

Facilities: Forest activities include hiking, mountain biking, horseback riding, and all-terrain vehicle riding. Most trailheads have primitive restrooms but not much else.

Hours open: The park office is open only from 8 a.m. to 4:30 p.m. Monday through Friday, but the forest is open year-round during daylight hours.

Rules and permits: Permits are required for ATVs, horses, and mountain bikes. Camping is permitted everywhere on Wildcat Hollow Backpack Trail.

Contact information: The park office is at 13700 U.S. Highway 33, Nelsonville, Ohio 45764; their phone number is 740-753-0101.

Other Areas of Interest

Many of the best parks in the state are just outside the area covered by the Athens unit. Some, such as Burr Oak and Hocking Hills state parks, are discussed elsewhere in this book.

Wayne National Forest, Athens Unit

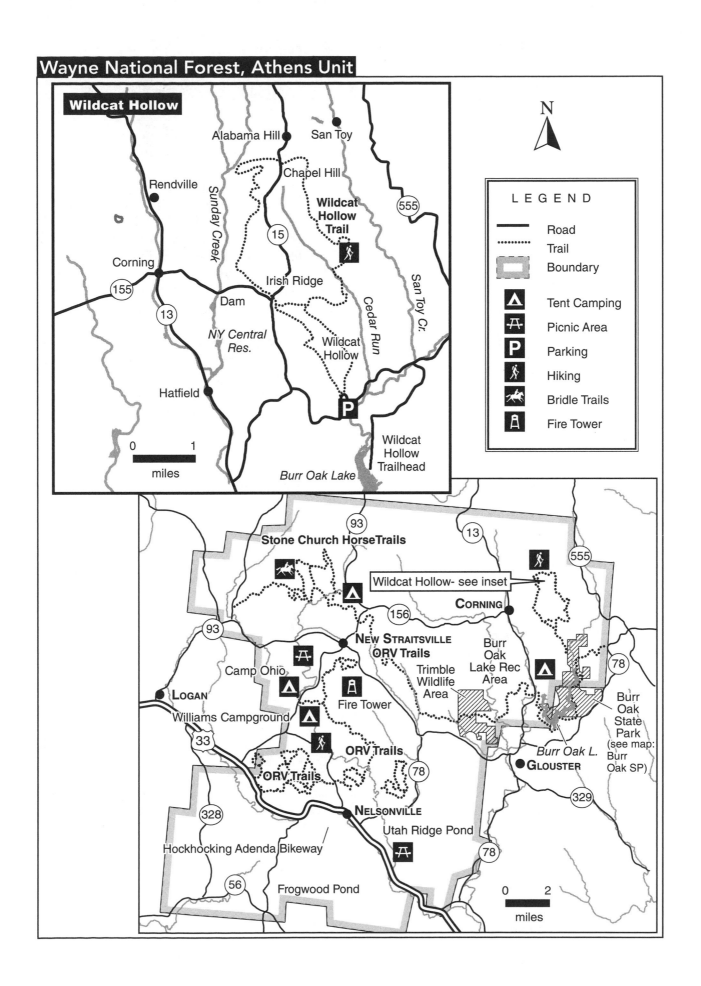

Wildcat Hollow

Rendville

Alabama Hill

San Toy

Chapel Hill

Wildcat Hollow Trail

Sunday Creek

15

555

Corning

155

13

Irish Ridge

Dam

NY Central Res.

Cedar Run

San Toy Cr.

Wildcat Hollow

Hatfield

0   1
miles

Wildcat Hollow Trailhead

Burr Oak Lake

N

LEGEND

—— Road

········ Trail

Boundary

Tent Camping

Picnic Area

P Parking

Hiking

Bridle Trails

Fire Tower

Stone Church Horse Trails

93

13

555

Wildcat Hollow- see inset

156

CORNING

93

NEW STRAITSVILLE

ORV Trails

Burr Oak Lake Rec Area

78

Camp Ohio

Trimble Wildlife Area

Burr Oak State Park (see map: Burr Oak SP)

LOGAN

Fire Tower

Williams Campground

33

ORV Trails

Burr Oak L.

ORV Trails

GLOUSTER

78

329

ORV Trails

NELSONVILLE

328

Utah Ridge Pond

Hockhocking Adenda Bikeway

78

56

Frogwood Pond

0   2
miles

Wildcat Hollow Backpack Trail, Day Hike

Hiking distance: 4.5 miles

Estimated hiking time: 3 hours

Hike a scenic and rugged trail in total solitude.

Caution: The trail does not drain well and can get very muddy after a rain.

Trail directions: To get to the trailhead, take State Route 13 between Corning and Glouster. About 4 miles south of Corning, turn east on Irish Ridge Road and follow the signs. The trailhead is at N 39° 34.219, W 82° 01.579 (1). Restrooms are here, but there's no water here or anywhere else. The small lot off of Sunday Creek Road is the only access point to the 13-mile Wildcat Hollow Backpack loop. This loop can also be combined with the 29-mile Burr Oak Backpack Trail that goes around Burr Oak Lake, which would make for a 42-mile stretch for backpacking.

For day hikers, there is a shorter option. A connector trail cuts through the center of the loop, making a 4.5-mile day hike. Enter the woods at the north end of the parking lot, going past an introductory sign that is the last official word hikers get from their hosts. Pass through a stand of pines, and in about 0.3 mile the trail splits at N 39° 34.361, W 82° 02.024 (2). Take the left fork, which goes along Eel's Run and crosses this stream several times.

The trail is marked by white diamond blazes posted on trees. The next 2 miles show a gradual rise, but the trail is designed to minimize the strain of climbing. Although the trail is well marked and carefully designed, it drains poorly and can become a sea of mud after a rain. The vegetation is also close, and some stream crossings can be difficult at high water. Another thing to keep in mind is that primitive-weapons hunting is permissible in the area, so dress accordingly.

After following the stream for a while, the trail turns away and continues to climb. In about 2 miles, the trail meets Irish Ridge Road at N 39° 35.449, W 82° 03.180 (3), where the Connector Trail branches off. Just ahead on the main route, the trail crosses the road and passes by an abandoned one-room schoolhouse at N 39° 35.476, W 82° 03.177 (4) before continuing on its 13-mile loop. If you make this side trip, return back to point 3 and turn away from the road on an abandoned haul road. This connector trail then returns to the wood for another 0.4 mile before meeting the return side of the loop at N 39° 35.416, W 82° 02.498 (5).

A sign here points that a right turn returns you to the trailhead. The return route is on higher ground, so it is drier and easier to walk on. The trees here tend to be more oak and hickory in contrast to the maple, ash, and beech found in the lower ravines. Camping with fires is permitted anywhere on the backpack trail, and there are many remains of elaborate campsites that can be reused.

After almost 2 miles the trail drops down to point 2, and from here retrace your route to the parking lot.

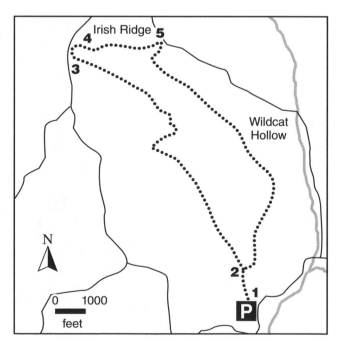

1. Lot
2. Junction
3. Irish Ridge Road
4. One-room schoolhouse
5. End of connector

> Combine trails to make your own route on rugged national forest land.

> Experience the diversity of wildlife found in the marsh, lake, and wood environment here.

> Give yourself a workout on strenuous and invigorating trails.

Area Information

The Wayne National Forest is the largest collection of public land in Ohio, comprising about 238,000 acres. This land is not contiguous; rather, it consists of smaller parcels spread out over southeastern Ohio. The national forest is divided into three separate units, and the Ironton Unit is the largest with just over 102,000 acres. This unit covers Gallia, Jackson, Lawrence, and Scioto Counties in southernmost Ohio.

While the Athens and Marietta Units are located in the coal region and the oil and gas region, respectively, the Ironton Unit is in an area known for its iron furnaces. Referred to as the Hanging Rock region, this area produced much of the nation's iron between 1833 and 1916. This was done by building sandstone blast furnaces that burned charcoal from trees. This industry not only provided employment for the region, but also produced much of the iron that the Union needed to win the Civil War.

The most developed and well-known site in the Ironton Unit is the Vesuvius Recreation Area. The name comes from the Vesuvius Iron Furnace, the remains of which are still on the grounds. This area is found in southernmost Ohio, just 7 miles from the Ohio River near the location where West Virginia and Kentucky meet. The main attraction here is Vesuvius Lake, which was built by the Civilian Conservation Corps in 1939. The rugged hills surrounding the lake are forested with mixed hardwoods, dominated by oaks and hemlocks.

▎A large rock formation near a swimming hole at Vesuvius Lake.

Unusual animals found here include black bear, bobcats, timber rattlesnakes, and the endangered Indiana bat. The area also contains a series of hiking trails; the most prominent are the 7.5-mile Lakeshore Trail and a 16-mile backpack loop that encircles the area.

Directions: Lake Vesuvius is off of State Route 93, just 6 miles north of Ironton. From 93, turn east on County Road 29 and go about 1 mile to the trailhead parking lot across from the remains of Vesuvius Furnace near the dam.

Hours open: The recreation area is open year-round.

Facilities: There is no drinking water, but restrooms are located in the parking lot and campgrounds. A small museum here is open during the summer months.

Rules and permits: Pets are permitted, but no bicycles are permitted on the trails. Swimming in the lake is only allowed in designated areas.

Contact information: The park office is located at 6518 State Route 93, Pedro, Ohio, 45659. The phone number is 740-534-6500.

Other Areas of Interest

Dean State Forest (also in Lawrence County) is located just a few miles north off of State Route 93.

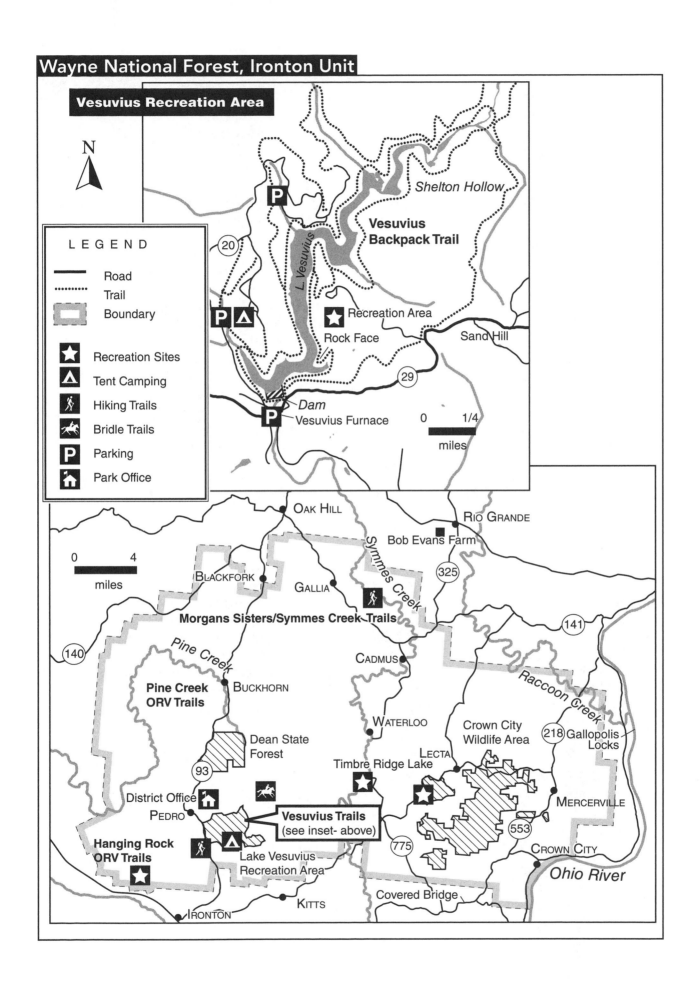

Wayne National Forest, Ironton Unit

Vesuvius Recreation Area

N

Shelton Hollow

Vesuvius Backpack Trail

L. Vesuvius

P

20

P △

P Recreation Area

Rock Face

Sand Hill

29

Dam
Vesuvius Furnace

0   1/4
miles

LEGEND

— Road
••••••• Trail
▢ Boundary

★ Recreation Sites
△ Tent Camping
🏃 Hiking Trails
🐎 Bridle Trails
P Parking
🏠 Park Office

Oak Hill

Rio Grande

Bob Evans Farm

325

Blackfork

Gallia

Symmes Creek

🏃 Morgans Sisters/Symmes Creek Trails

141

0   4
miles

Pine Creek

Cadmus

Raccoon Creek

140

Pine Creek ORV Trails

Buckhorn

Waterloo

Crown City Wildlife Area

218 Gallopolis Locks

Dean State Forest

93

Lecta

🐎

Timbre Ridge Lake ★

★

Mercerville

District Office 🏠

Pedro

★

Vesuvius Trails (see inset- above)

553

Hanging Rock ORV Trails

🏃 △

★

Lake Vesuvius Recreation Area

775

Crown City

Ohio River

Kitts

Ironton

Covered Bridge

Vesuvius Backpack and Lakeshore Trail

Hiking distance: 7.5 miles

Estimated hiking time: 5 hours

Take a rugged hike among the hills and shores of southernmost Ohio.

Caution: Blazing on the trails is spotty, and there is a lot of tree fall. The lowland portions can be muddy, and gnats and poison ivy are plentiful. On the day that I was at this park, a car was broken into, so crime can be a problem.

Trail directions: Park in the lot by the dam at N 38° 36.330, W 82° 37.824 (1). Across the road are the remains of Vesuvius Furnace, which employed 100 men between 1833 and 1906, burning 350 acres of timber annually to produce 8 to 12 tons of iron daily. Today, the man-made lake named for the furnace provides a variety of recreational experiences, including hiking on two long trails. The 8-mile Lakeshore Trail follows the shoreline, while the 16-mile Backpack Trail encircles the area. These trails come together at the far end of the park, so it is possible to arrange a hike using them in several combinations. This hike follows the eastern side of the lake by taking the Backpack Trail out and following the Lakeshore Trail back.

Go to the dam and follow the trail into the woods for about 0.2 mile. Take a right turn on the Backpack Trail, which is marked by white diamond blazes with a yellow circle. Climb a set of steps and come to some old chimneys at N 38° 36.431, W 82° 37.757 (2). Stay on this route for nearly a mile; you will come to the intersection with the campground road at N 38° 36.666, W 82° 37.025 (3). The trail goes up and down through a hickory and oak forest where many trees have fallen across the path. Proceed through several ravines for almost 3 miles until you gradually descend to a streambed at N 38° 37.563, W 82° 36.492 (4).

At this spot, the Backpack and Lakeshore Trails are connected by the Aldrich Cutoff at the head of the lake where Storms Creek widens to feed into the lake. But the trail can get very muddy here and is not well marked. Proceed cautiously along the streambed for 0.1 mile to the junction with the eastern half of the Lakeshore Trail, which is blazed with white diamonds and a blue circle, at N 38° 37.650, W 82° 37.519 (5). Bear left so the water is on your right, and continue as the stream widens into a lake.

You are at a lower altitude now, but the trail follows a convoluted path as it snakes around many inlets. This is the most secluded part of the route and offers many impressive views of the lake. Proceed on this route for over 2 miles until you arrive at the junction of the red-blazed Whiskey Run Trail at N 38° 37.092, W 82° 37.563 (6). This short side trail goes to the Iron Ridge Campground and rejoins the Lakeshore Trail just down the path. Not long after this, you will come to a side path that leads to a cave at N 38° 36.958, W 82° 37.622 (7). Take the brief detour before returning to the trail.

The lake has widened now and is completely visible. In another 0.5 mile, you will come to a prominent rock outcropping that marks a popular swimming hole at N 38° 36.547, W 82° 37.592 (8). The view here is spectacular, but because you are getting close to the main parking lot, this area is likely to be more crowded. Stay at this spot as long as you can before continuing on for another 0.5 mile to the dam and point 1.

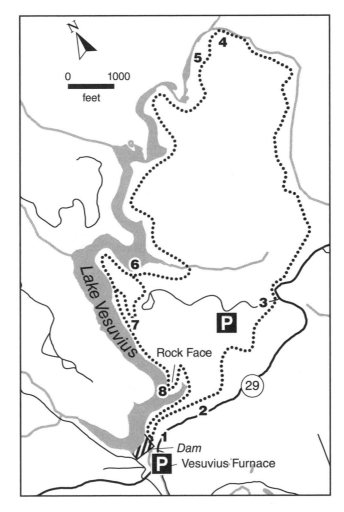

1. Lot
2. Chimneys
3. Cross campground road
4. Aldrich cutoff
5. Lakeshore Trail
6. Junction
7. Cave
8. Large rock

> Enjoy some of the most rugged terrain that Ohio has to offer.

> Hike over 90 miles of trails, many of which are part of a national trail network.

> Sample a wide variety of outdoor recreation experiences.

Area Information

As Ohio's only national forest, the Wayne National Forest is one of the largest pieces of publicly owned land in the state. But the Wayne is not contiguous; rather, it is a series of parcels within a purchase area that is scattered across several southeastern Ohio counties. The 238,000-acre forest is administered in three separate offices in Athens, Ironton, and Marietta.

The Marietta Unit encompasses 63,381 acres in Washington, Monroe, and Noble Counties. Over half of this total is in the rugged hills of eastern Washington County. The area contains nearly 90 miles of trails, including a 40-mile stretch of the North Country Trail (which extends from North Dakota to New York). The Marietta Unit is also host to the Covered Bridge Scenic Byway Auto Tour and offers opportunities for canoeing, backpacking, horseback riding, and mountain biking. Several campgrounds are found along the Little Muskingum River, and a full-service campground and boat launch are located at Leith Run on the Ohio River.

This isolated area of the state has always been underpopulated. The sandstone- and shale-based geology makes farming difficult on any scale, although the area leads the state in timber, coal, and natural gas production. Lamping Homestead is a loop trail that is located on the farm of an early family of homesteaders in Monroe County. In Washington County, the Scenic River Trail runs from some of the highest hills in the area to the shores of the Ohio River. Both offer the best in Ohio hill hiking.

Hours open: Trails in the Wayne National Forest are open year-round in daylight hours.

Facilities: Lamping Homestead has restrooms and picnic tables, as well as a campground. The Scenic River Trail has facilities at the Leith Run end, including restrooms and a full-service campground.

Rules and permits: No permits are needed for hiking or campfires.

Contact information: The Marietta Unit is headquartered at 27750 State Route 7, Marietta, Ohio 45750. The phone number is 740-373-9055.

Other Areas of Interest

Other trails in the Marietta Unit include the Ohio View Trail, Archer's Fork Loop, and the Covered Bridge Connector Trail. A 33-mile section of the North Country and Buckeye Trails runs from Ring Mill in Monroe County to Lane Farm near Marietta.

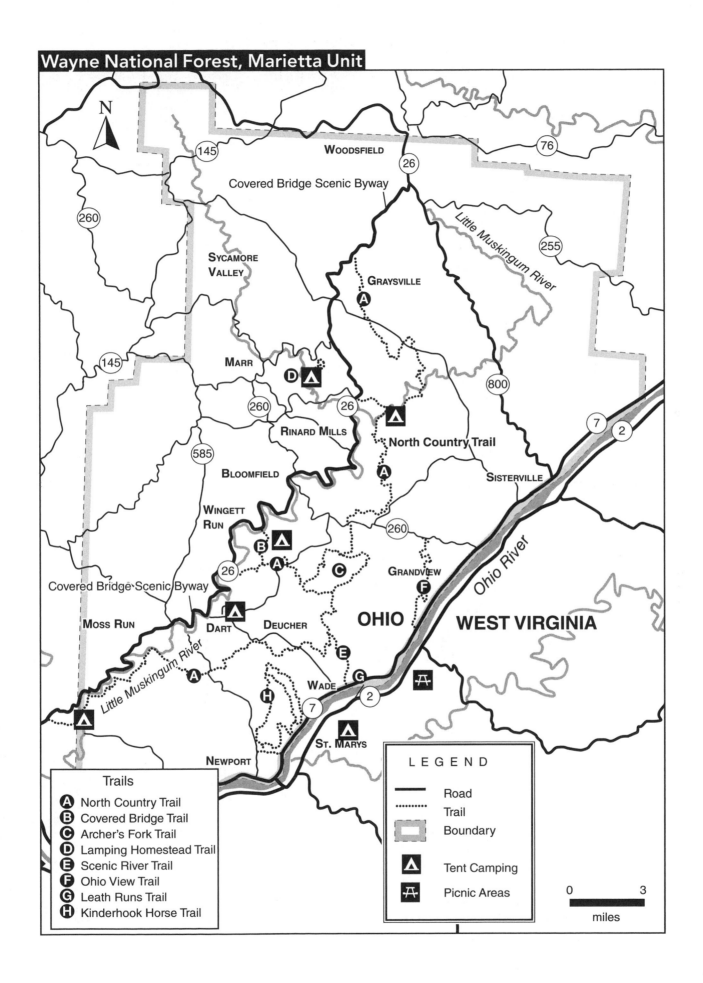

Wayne National Forest, Marietta Unit

N

(145) WOODSFIELD (26) (76)

Covered Bridge Scenic Byway

(260)

Little Muskingum River

(255)

SYCAMORE VALLEY

GRAYSVILLE

Ⓐ

(145) MARR

Ⓓ ▲

(260) (26)

RINARD MILLS

▲

(800)

North Country Trail

(585)

BLOOMFIELD

Ⓐ

SISTERVILLE

WINGETT RUN

Ⓑ ▲

Ⓐ

(26)

Ⓒ

(260)

GRANDVIEW

Ⓕ

Ohio River

(7) (2)

Covered Bridge Scenic Byway

MOSS RUN

Little Muskingum River

▲

DART

DEUCHER

Ⓐ

Ⓔ

Ⓖ

WADE

OHIO

WEST VIRGINIA

🛉

(7) (2)

Ⓗ

▲

▲

NEWPORT

ST. MARYS

Trails

Ⓐ North Country Trail
Ⓑ Covered Bridge Trail
Ⓒ Archer's Fork Trail
Ⓓ Lamping Homestead Trail
Ⓔ Scenic River Trail
Ⓕ Ohio View Trail
Ⓖ Leath Runs Trail
Ⓗ Kinderhook Horse Trail

LEGEND

—— Road

········· Trail

▢ Boundary

▲ Tent Camping

🛉 Picnic Areas

0   3

miles

Lamping Homestead

Hiking distance: 3.6 miles round trip

Estimated hiking time: 2.5 hours

Hike a rough-hewn trail that is an isolated delight—this trail is a true diamond in the rough.

Caution: Although fairly well blazed, this rough trail is not benched at all, which means it drains so poorly that you can slip in even the driest of seasons. In addition, numerous stumps and roots are under the leaves on the uneven surfaces of the trail.

Trail directions: Lamping Homestead is found on State Route 537, 2.6 miles from State Route 26. Turn off on Township Road 307 and immediately turn left into the parking lot at N 39° 37.848, W 81° 11.394 (1). From the small gravel lot, it is about 0.1 mile to a large pond. The trail begins to your left at N 39° 37.756, W 81° 11.370 (2); the trail follows the shore through a wooded picnic area. After another 0.1 mile, you will cross a wooden bridge and enter the woods at N 39° 37.896, W 81° 11.225 (3). After leaving the shoreline, follow a tributary for 0.3 mile until you arrive at N 39° 37.866, W 81° 10.944 (4). Cross the ravine here and begin a steady ascent in the deciduous hardwood forest that features mainly maples and beeches. Deer and wild turkey are common here, and on my first visit, our group spotted a fox.

After about 0.4 mile and an ascent of nearly 300 feet, the trail crests in a white pine plantation. Immediately afterward, at N 39° 37.611, W 81° 10.935 (5), you'll come to a turnoff for a shorter loop trail. If you choose to turn right and descend this way, you can return to the parking lot in less than a mile, completing a shorter 1.8-mile loop.

If you continue on through the clearing and back into the woods, the trail generally skirts the edge of the ridge just below the crest. The trail is marked with white plastic diamonds that have arrows on them; these are nailed to trees. These markings are frequent and generally work fine, but if one nail falls out, this can make for a turn blaze when none is intended.

Follow the trail for 0.9 mile to N 39° 37.028, W 81° 11.262 (6), where it makes a turn to the right. When the leaves are off, you can see the Clear Fork of the Little Muskingum River from here.

Continue on the trail over a series of hills. Though the trail is clearly marked, it is rough and not level; roots, rocks, and uneven surfaces are in abundance. Without proper drainage, the trail can be slippery even at dry times. Follow the route carefully, taking note of occasional views of the streambed in the valley below.

After about a mile and a quarter, the trail intersects with the shorter loop trail coming down from point 5 at N 39° 37.573, W 81° 12.249 (7). From here, proceed another half mile to the lake and parking lot. In the lot, you will see a plaque explaining that the Lamping family was a pioneer group of homesteaders who first settled in the area in the 1800s. Today, the isolated area is administered by the Wayne National Forest.

1. Lot
2. Lake
3. Enter woods
4. Cross ravine and climb
5. Crest turnoff
6. Right turn
7. Junction

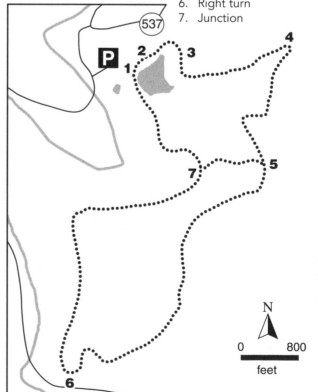

River Trail Loop

 Hiking distance: 6.5 miles round trip

Estimated hiking time: 5 hours

Take a hilltop hike in a national forest, exploring a trail that leads to a spectacular Ohio River overlook.

Caution: The trail is steep in spots with roots; the area is slippery if you get off the trail.

Trail directions: From exit 1 of Interstate 77, go upstream (northeast) on State Route 7 along the Ohio River for about 19 miles. Turn left on County Road 14 and start climbing immediately. Turn right on County Road 9 and follow the ridge past German Cemetery Road until you get to a labeled parking area on the right at N 39° 28.500, W 81° 10.631 (1). Park in the dirt area here where River View Trail meets the Buckeye and North Country Trail. Head into the all-hardwood forest at the River Trail sign and proceed on a fairly level path just below the ridge top. After about 0.9 mile, you will come to a sign marking a junction with the River Loop Trail on the right at N 39° 27.858, W 81° 10.320 (2). Stay on the main route and immediately begin a moderately steep climb. At the top of this hill—at about the mile point— you will cross a gravel haul road used by oil and coal companies at N 39° 27.822, W 81° 10.242 (3). You will travel roughly parallel with the road for about one third of a mile when you pass a gas storage tank at N 39° 27.744, W 81° 10.006 (4).

Continue on into the woods for another 1.1 miles (the route is fairly level). At this point— which is at N 39° 26.951, W 81° 09.835 (5)— you will be able to see the hills of West Virginia in the distance, provided the leaves are off. If not, proceed another 0.3 mile to N 39° 26.711, W 81° 09.828 (6), and you will be able to see the Ohio River below you. From here on, the river is in view in all seasons. Go another 0.16 mile and you will come to the other junction with the River Loop Trail at N 39° 26.686, W 81° 09.765 (7).

From this point, you have several options. You can continue on your route and begin a steep descent that has several switchbacks. After a quarter mile, you will come to a parking lot just off of State Route 7 at N 39° 26.633, W 81° 09.149 (8); if you have two cars, you can have one here waiting at the end of a 3.3-mile hike. But the trail goes on across Route 7, and if you follow it another 0.7 mile, you will be able to dip your feet in the Ohio River at the Leith Run Campground. This full-service camping area (closed in winter) is another good place to leave your second car. The elevation here is 601 feet above sea level, which is 528 feet lower than the Haul Road at point 3. That's about as much vertical relief as you will find on a day hike in Ohio.

However, if you just have a single vehicle and are looking for a loop hike, you can follow the River Loop Trail sign to make your return trip. Follow the circuitous, hilly route (which is not as well blazed) from point 6 for 2.7 miles until you reunite with the River View Trail at point 2. From here, it is less than a mile back to your starting point.

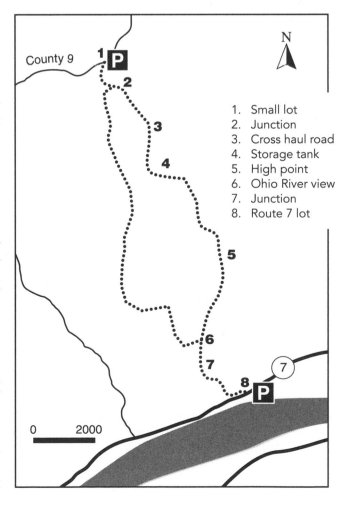

1. Small lot
2. Junction
3. Cross haul road
4. Storage tank
5. High point
6. Ohio River view
7. Junction
8. Route 7 lot

Archer's Fork Loop

Hiking distance: 9.3 miles

Estimated hiking time: 7 hours

Challenge yourself with one of the toughest day hikes in the state.

Caution: This is a difficult hike that should not be undertaken by novices. The hike includes at least seven climbs of over 250 feet spread out over 9 miles. Most hikes in this book can be done in tennis shoes, but for this one, boots and walking sticks are recommended.

Trail directions: From State Route 260 between Bloomfield (22 miles northeast of Marietta) and New Matamoras on the Ohio River, turn south on Shay Ridge Road (Township Road 34). Go 1.4 miles to a sign for the North Country Scenic Trail and turn left. Just up a hill is a cemetery with a parking lot at N 39° 31.416, W 81° 10.860 (1). Park here and head downhill on the rutted remains of a road. At about 0.2 mile, a sign marks the turnoff from the "road" to the loop at N 39° 31.324, W 81° 10.853 (2). Almost immediately after entering the woods, you can spot a recess ledge cave that marks the 12 o'clock spot on the loop.

Save the cave for later and turn to the right, following a ridge above the cave. In about 0.5 mile, you'll come to a turnoff for the Irish Run National Bridge at N 39° 30.878, W 81° 10.855 (3). Turn left and make a slight detour to view Ohio's most impressive natural bridge, which is 51 feet long, 16 feet thick, and 39 feet above ground. Then return to the main trail, crossing a road soon afterward, and proceed through the mixed hardwood forest. In about 1.1 mile, the trail descends and crosses Irish Run at N 39° 30.287, W 81° 11.234 (4). Try to stay dry while fording and follow alongside the stream for another 0.5 mile. A house is located near here, which is worthy of note because it's likely the only one you will see all day.

At N 39° 30.083, W 81° 11.738 (5), the Covered Bridge Connector Trail comes in on the right. This 2-mile trail connects to the Covered Bridge Trail described elsewhere in this chapter. Continue on the main trail, and within 0.1 mile, you should cross the stream, which may be deep at times, and then cross the road near it. Then you will begin one of many steep climbs. This one levels into a meadow and then reenters the woods in an abandoned roadbed. Follow this for over a mile until you come to a gate at N 39° 29.832, W 81° 10.772 (6). Continue on for another 0.3 mile, where you will come to a trail intersection at the 4-mile mark at N 39° 29.868, W 81° 10.416 (7).

This first part of the loop has been on the Buckeye and North Country Trails, but here these trails veer off into the woods on the right. To continue on the Archer's Fork Loop, follow the white diamond blazes that go to the left. Descend an extremely steep hill that offers views of many interesting rock formations made of Permian sandstone. You may also notice many abandoned oil and gas wells that were once a major part of the area economy.

About a mile past where the Buckeye and North Country Trails branch off, the trail crosses a stream at N 39° 30.302, W 81° 09.663 (8). A small parking lot is located at a nearby road here, and this is also a good area for a lunch break. Continue on for another 1.2 miles to another stream fording at N 39° 30.829, W 81° 08.997 (9). At this spot, the Ohio View Connector Trail goes off to the right toward a trail that leads to the Ohio River. Archer's Fork Loop Trail crosses regularly between the Little Muskingum and Ohio River watersheds, which explains a lot of the hill climbs. But by combining this trail with the Covered Bridge and Ohio View Connector Trails, it is possible to hike directly from the Little Muskingum to the Ohio, which offers lots of backpacking options.

Stay to the left on the loop trail for another 0.6 mile, where the trail crosses a road and there is a small parking lot at N 39° 31.058, W 91° 08.856 (10). Next, you will climb another steep hill. Note that the upland forest is dominated by oaks and hickory, while the stream valley has more sycamore, beech, and maples. At the highest point, the trail around here is about 1,200 feet above sea level, which is over 600 feet higher than the Ohio River just a few miles away.

After another 1.2 miles of rugged terrain, the trail comes alongside and then crosses a road along Irish Run at N 39° 31.109, W 81° 09.868 (11). Here the Buckeye and North Country Trails come in from the north, and you will remain on these trails for the remainder of the loop. Cross the stream, reenter the woods, and then climb yet another steep hill. Because

the Wayne National Forest is a checkerboard collection of property, hikers need to stay on the trail in order to avoid straying onto private property. Fortunately, this trail is generally well blazed.

In another 0.5 mile, the trail crosses another road at N 39° 31.308, W 81° 10.242 (12) and goes up for one last arduous climb. Around here, you can also see a lot of club moss and lichens. The trail then finally levels out, and the distance to point 2 is just 0.5 mile. Stop at the cave and celebrate your success before returning to point 1.

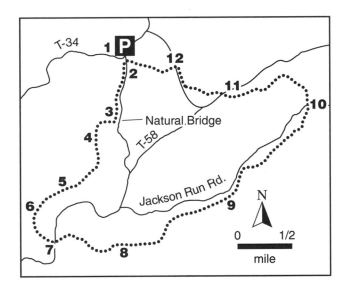

1. Lot
2. Cave at top of loop
3. Natural bridge
4. Cross Irish Run
5. Junction
6. Gate
7. Leave Buckeye Trail
8. Cross stream
9. Cross stream
10. Cross road
11. Cross road
12. Cross road

Covered Bridge Trail

Hiking distance: 4.5 miles

Estimated hiking time: 3 hours

Canoeing distance: 4.5 miles

Take an amphibious trip that is half hike and half canoe trip.

Caution: Because of low water levels, the canoe portion of this trip can be undertaken only in late spring, and even then the water could be too high.

Trail directions: Take State Route 26 out of Marietta and drive 22 miles northeast to the Rinard Covered Bridge. Leave a canoe under the bridge, using a bicycle chain lock to secure the canoe to a tree if you are worried that someone will walk off with it within the next few hours. Then turn around and drive 3.5 miles back toward Marietta to the Hune

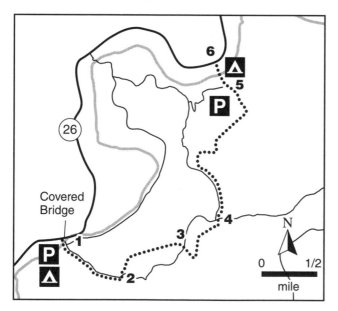

1. Campground lot
2. Cross road
3. Cross road
4. Cross road
5. Haught Run Campground
6. Rinard Covered Bridge

Covered Bridge, one of the five such bridges across the Little Muskingum River. Cross the bridge and enter the small campground. Park your car near the restrooms at N 39° 30.351, W 81° 15.032 (1).

Retrace your route to the campground entrance and follow the white diamond blazes that run parallel to the road. The trail soon crosses this road, enters the woods, and begins a steady climb. Remains of the oil industry can be seen in this area, and the campground also contains a plaque and old oil well. The mixed-hardwood forest yields an abundance of wildflowers, particularly in spring, which is also the best time to canoe the stream.

After going 1.1 miles, the trail crosses a dirt road at N 39° 30.351, W 81° 13.505 (2). The most difficult climbs are done now, and you may have some good views of the valley below. Reenter the woods, and in another 0.5 mile, the trail passes an old cemetery and comes to a road at N 39° 30.489, W 81° 13.390 (3). A sign here marks the junction with a connector trail to the Archer's Fork Loop. If you follow this path on the road past the Mt. Pleasant Church, it will reenter the woods and go 2 miles to the 9-mile Archer's Fork Loop Trail. From here, a hiker could continue east to the Ohio View Trail and complete a 20-mile trail connection between the Little Muskingum and Ohio Rivers. The Archer's Fork Loop is also in the center of a 30-mile north-south stretch of the North Country and Buckeye Trails that is all on national forest land, so hikers have many long-distance hiking options.

But to stay on the Covered Bridge Trail, you should cross the road and reenter the woods at the sign pointing the way. In another 0.8

| Rinard Covered Bridge is the transfer point for a combined hiking and canoe excursion.

mile, the trail crosses Township Road 35 at N 39° 31.127, W 81° 13.445 (4). Now begin descending through the woods toward stream level. One downside to this otherwise scenic hike is the muddy mess left by ATVs that are often used in this area. After about 1.4 miles, the trail crosses Haught Run and enters the Haught Run Campground, which also has restrooms.

After leaving the campground at N 39° 21.550, W 81° 13.317 (5), you should follow Haught Run Road along the banks of the Little Muskingum. In about 0.4 mile, you will arrive at the Rinard Covered Bridge at N 39° 32.123, W 81° 13.213 (6). There are fewer than 1,000 covered bridges left in the country, and only one state has more than Ohio. The Rinard Bridge has been flooded out several times, most recently in 2004, but the trusses are the same ones used since 1876.

To complete this rare amphibious operation, get in your canoe and paddle 4.5 miles downstream to your car at point 1. Be sure to scout water levels first, because the river dries up in summer and can run too high in spring. After passing the village of Wingett Run, the river route winds through isolated stretches that are far from any road, before coming out at another scenic covered bridge. Another advantage to this adventure is that you can take a combined hike and canoe trip without needing a second car.

> Visit the largest conservation center for endangered species in North America.

> Tour the 10,000-acre preserve and participate in a variety of activities.

> Take a free stroll through one of the largest butterfly transects in the state.

Area Information

Located in southeastern Ohio near the junction of Interstates 70 and 77, the Wilds is a unique place. Established in 1984, this 10,000-acre preserve is dedicated to the multiple goals of conservation and educational tourism. For visitors, the area offers a chance to view a wide variety of wildlife in a natural habitat. In addition, an increasing variety of recreational opportunities are available. Celebrity zookeeper Jack Hanna has referred to the Wilds as the "Garden of Eden of the animal world."

The Wilds is located on reclaimed strip mine land donated by American Electric Power (AEP). One original idea was to provide breeding grounds for 300 animals that normally don't breed in captivity, but this concept has been significantly expanded on. The original visitor center was dedicated in 1989, and the first animals arrived 2 years later. In 1994, the Wilds was opened to the public, and the place has been growing and evolving at a rapid pace ever since.

The Wilds is affiliated with the Columbus Zoo and has always maintained an educational and conservationist approach. Researchers on staff have closely monitored the breeding of all wildlife, including such exotic creatures as camels, rhinos, and giraffes. But the public is also welcome to take tour buses right through the newfound habitat of such species. Visitors park in the main lot along International Road and are taken by bus to the gift shop and visitor center where guided tours begin.

Activities have gradually expanded beyond the standard tours. Recent additions include fishing, horseback riding, camping, a mountain bike trail, and a zipline canopy tour that allows visitors to glide through the treetops above the preserve. The focus on the educational aspect has led to a group campsite for student groups who tour the area. A special Sunset and Safari tour also includes a dinner at the Overlook Cafe before the tour.

The Wilds is a private, nonprofit conservation center, but most activities come with a price. Exceptions to this are the Butterfly Habitat Trail just outside the main parking lot and the mountain bike trail along State Route 146.

Directions: The Wilds is in Muskingum County, southwest of State Route 146 and the village of Cumberland. Signs mark the way from the New Concord exit (exit 169) of Interstate 70 and the Belle Valley exit (exit 28) of Interstate 77.

Hours open: Tours leave hourly between 10 a.m. and 4 p.m., except during winter, but the Butterfly Trail is free and accessible anytime.

Facilities: The visitor center area includes a gift shop and snack bar, and a group campground is located on the grounds. For overnight guests, the Wilds also has a lodge, cabins, and the new Nomad Ridge collection of modern yurts. Reservations are required for overnight lodging.

Rules and permits: Pets are not permitted anywhere on the grounds. All guests must remain in vehicles or in designated areas.

Contact information: The Wilds is located at 14000 International Road, Cumberland, Ohio 43732. The phone number is 740-638-5030.

Other Areas of Interest

Two state parks are located in Muskingum County. Blue Rock State Park is just a few miles to the southwest; this park has a campground and a small lake. Dillon Lake State Park is located northwest of Zanesville; this park has a man-made lake and is better known for camping, fishing, and boating.

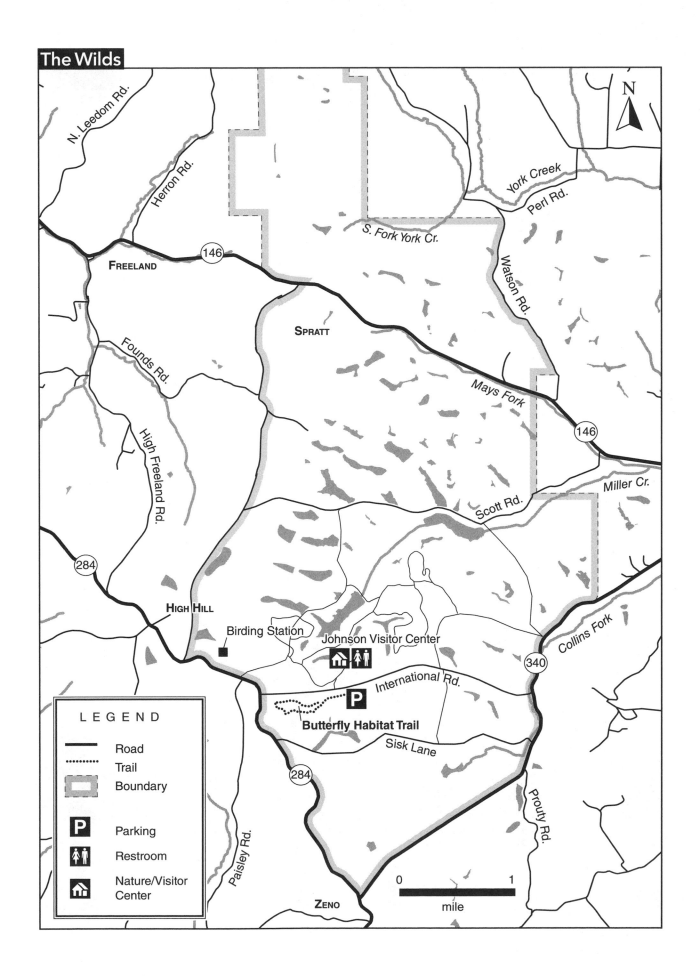

The Wilds

LEGEND

— Road

···· Trail

Boundary

P Parking

Restroom

Nature/Visitor Center

0 ————— 1
mile

N

141

Butterfly Habitat Trail

Hiking distance: 1 mile round trip

Estimated hiking time: 30 minutes

At a location known for large mammals, take a pleasant walk in a field devoted to butterflies.

Caution: The portion of the trail near the ponds can be wet at times.

Trail directions: The parking lot for the Butterfly Habitat Trail is the same as the main lot for the Wilds. To get there from the village of Cumberland, take State Route 340 south from the western edge of town and proceed 2.5 miles to International Road. Turn right here and go west for 2 miles to the main lot. Across the road, you'll find a kiosk and sign marking the trailhead at N 39° 49.530, W 81° 44.215 (1).

Follow the well-mowed path, moving parallel to the road, for 0.1 mile until it veers left at N 39° 49.514, W 81° 44.321 (2). In another 0.1 mile, the trail crosses a wooden bridge at N 39° 49.460, W 81° 44.398 (3). Cross here and continue to go straight. You will see numbered signs and a few side trails cut, but most of those detours reconnect to the main route, and the numbers do not match this guide. Proceed another 0.2 mile to where the trail leaves the meadow and enters a brief wooded area at about N 39° 49.443, W 81° 44.595 (4).

After leaving the woods, the trail skirts a marshy pond. After another 0.1 mile, you will return to the meadow and turn left at N 39° 49.446, W 81° 44.644 (5). In less than 0.1 mile, the trail turns around and heads back at N 39° 49.468, W 81° 44.713 (6). The return route stays in the meadow and is roughly parallel to International Road. A variety of wildflowers have been planted here for the specific purpose of attracting butterflies. The wildflowers offer

The Butterfly Trail at The Wilds offers a variety of both butterflies and wildflowers.

spectacular colors throughout the warmer months, and the best time to view butterflies is in the heat of late July and early August.

This hike passes through one of the largest butterfly transects in Ohio. The trail, which was developed in 2003, passes through fields containing 50 varieties of tall prairie grasses and wildflowers. This, in turn, attracts a wide variety of butterfly species. Among the 25 varieties that have been spotted here are the eastern tiger swallowtail, pearl crescent, red admiral, cabbage white, eastern tailed blue, red-spotted purple, viceroy, and, of course, monarch. The trail is walked weekly and is well maintained, so you should enjoy the stroll through this field. Continue on the route for another 0.4 mile until you return to point 3; then retrace the route back to the trailhead.

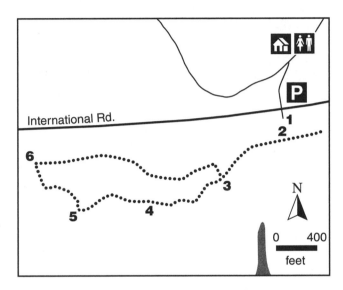

1. Kiosk and lot
2. Turn left
3. Bridge
4. Enter woods
5. Turn left
6. Turn back

> Hike the Buckeye Trail alongside peaceful waters of a quiet lake.

> Enjoy a secluded trip to a park that is both on the interstate and out of the way.

Area Information

Despite being right next to Interstate 77, Wolf Run State Park is a quiet park in a quiet part of the state. The 1,300-acre park is centered around a 220-acre lake that was made in 1968. Although the lake is well stocked with bass, bluegill, trout, and catfish, a 10-horsepower limit for boaters has kept things quiet. This quiet can sometimes be broken by the small Noble County Airport, whose single runway cause planes to fly directly over the center of the V shape formed by the lake. A nearby primitive group campground is the state's only fly-in camp.

Wolf Run lies in the unglaciated portion of Ohio, and the predominant bedrock here is sandstone, with alternating layers of coal. The forests that surround the lake are mixed second growth, which makes for good plant diversity, particularly among ferns. The park gets its name from the Wolf family, who were among the first to settle here. The state first acquired property here in 1963, and the dam and spillway made way for the lake and dedication as a state park in 1968.

The campground at Wolf Run has 71 electric and 67 nonelectric sites, although only a handful of them are on the lake. Showers and laundry facilities are available, and each campsite has a picnic table and fire ring. A camper cabin is also available for rental. In addition, a basketball hoop and playground are located in the park. The park contains 5 miles of trails, including a section of the Buckeye Trail on the western end of the lake and a trail from the campground to the free 200-foot public swimming beach. Multiple picnic areas are available, as well as a shelter that can be reserved.

Directions: Get off Interstate 77 at the Belle Valley exit and head south through town on State Route 821. Turn left at the edge of town on State Route 215; after going less than a mile, turn left and follow the signs.

Facilities: Restrooms are located at the campground, beach, and several picnic sites. Boats and games can be rented from the camp office. A boat launch ramp is located near the beach.

Hours open: The park is open year-round during daylight hours.

Rules and permits: Visitors swim at their own risk—there is no lifeguard. Also, pets are not permitted on the beach, although they are allowed in the campground.

Contact information: The park is located at 16170 Wolf Run Road, Caldwell, Ohio 43724; the phone number is 740-732-5035. However, the park mailing address is at Salt Fork State Park, 14755 Cadiz Road, Lore City, Ohio 43755; the Salt Fork phone number is 740-439-3521.

Other Areas of Interest

Seneca Lake is located a few miles to the northeast. This is a 3,500-acre lake in the Muskingum Watershed Conservancy District system. The AEP Recreation Land—which features camping, hunting, fishing, and a 20-mile off-road portion of the Buckeye Trail—is located just to the southwest.

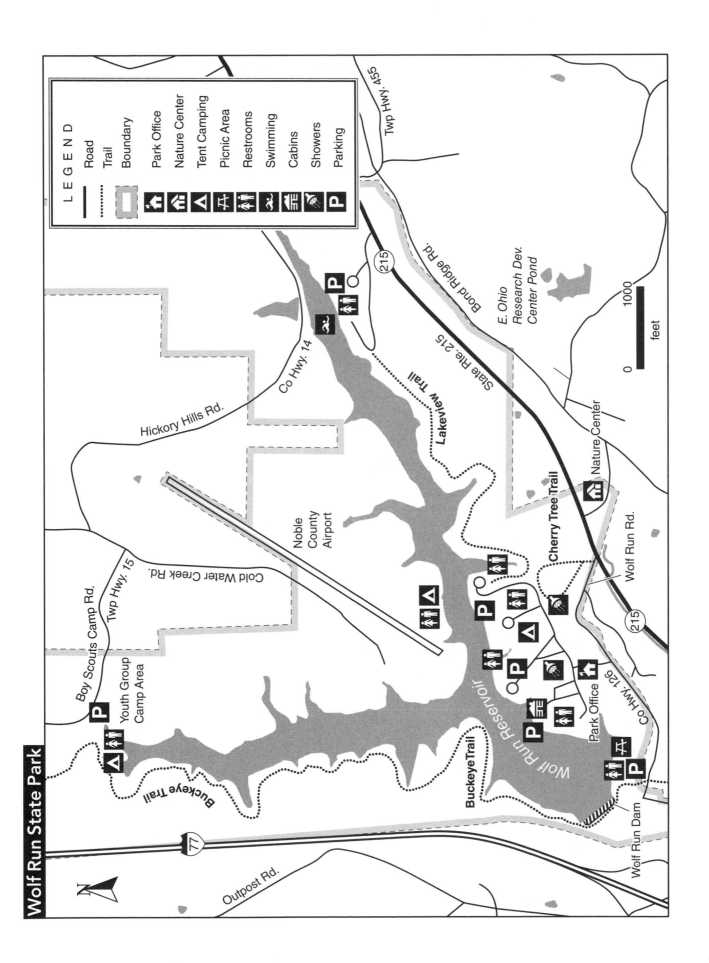

Wolf Run State Park

LEGEND

——	Road
⋯⋯	Trail
▢	Boundary
⛺	Park Office
🏛	Nature Center
△	Tent Camping
⛱	Picnic Area
🚻	Restrooms
🏊	Swimming
🏚	Cabins
🚿	Showers
P	Parking

Twp Hwy. 455

State Rte. 215

Bond Ridge Rd.

E. Ohio Research Dev. Center Pond

Co Hwy. 14

Hickory Hills Rd.

Lakeview Trail

Noble County Airport

Cherry Tree Trail

Nature Center

Wolf Run Rd.

Cold Water Creek Rd.

Twp Hwy. 15

Boy Scouts Camp Rd.

Youth Group Camp Area

Wolf Run Reservoir

Buckeye Trail

Park Office

Co Hwy. 126

Wolf Run Dam

Outpost Rd.

77

N

1000

0

feet

145

Wolf Run, Buckeye Trail

 **Hiking distance:** 4.6 miles round trip

Estimated hiking time: 3 hours

Follow the shoreline of a quiet lake in a secluded park.

Caution: Trails that cross streams near the lake can get muddy.

Trail directions: Park at the dam parking lot just outside of Belle Valley at N 39° 47.329, W 81° 32.813 (1). Proceed down to the dam, walk across it, and turn right to follow the shoreline. Almost immediately, the trail enters the woods and begins to climb at N 39° 47.497, W 81° 32.873 (2). Follow the familiar blue blazes of the Buckeye Trail through a forest filled with oaks, tulips, maples, beech, black cherry, and white ash.

After about 0.3 mile, the trail descends to cross a feeder stream at N 39° 47.725, W 81° 32.875 (3). Unfortunately, this part of the trail is too close to the interstate, but the sound of the freeway fades as the hike progresses. In another 0.2 mile, you'll come to a hilltop clearing—at N 39° 47.715, W 81° 32.636 (4)—that enables you to see the two legs of the lake as they meet and make a V shape. Descend through

1. Dam lot
2. Enter woods
3. Cross stream
4. Clearing
5. Pipeline and meadow
6. Bridge
7. Ascend
8. Primitive campground

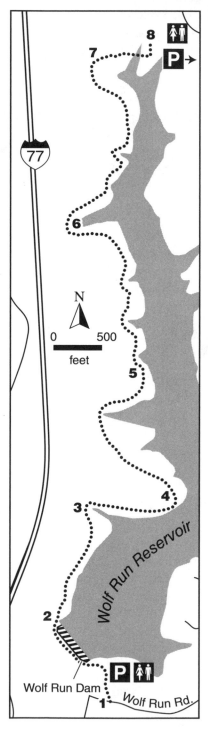

another stream crossing, and in 0.4 mile, the trail enters an open meadow at N 39° 47.911, W 81° 32.698 (5). This is a cleared path for a gas pipeline, but the meadow has a variety of wildflowers in spring.

Reenter the woods on the other side of the meadow. In this area farther from the dam, the trail is more likely to be overgrown and have fallen trees, but you are also more likely to see deer or wild turkey here. The trail continues to follow the shoreline, and after another 0.6 mile, it crosses a bridge over a feeder stream at N 39° 48.242, W 81° 32.863 (6). You'll encounter two more bridges in the next half mile; the second one precedes a steep climb at N 39° 47.612, W 81° 32.697 (7). Climb this last hill and arrive at a primitive camp overlooking the end of the lake at N 39° 47.705, W 81° 32.615 (8). The blazing on these last stretches is good, but the trail is often overgrown.

The primitive campground has outhouses, tables, and fire rings, but not much else. This spot is reachable by car, however, so parking one here would make for a 2.3-mile one-way hike. If not, you should turn around and retrace your route to point 1.

Southwest

The southwestern quadrant of Ohio offers quite a bit of geologic diversity. Most of the area is in the Till Plains region, which offers good soil for crops. But a tiny sliver of the Bluegrass region, or Low Interior Plateau, slips north of the Ohio River into an area sometimes called the Little Smokies. This small section near the Edge of Appalachia Preserve contains sharper hills that are not actually mountains but can at least be called *mountainesque*. This rugged, isolated region is like the rest of southwestern Ohio in its diversity of wildflowers.

Human habitation of this region goes back to the ancient mound builders, who were here 2,000 years ago. They left a trace at Fort Ancient and at Serpent Mound, one of only two effigy mounds found in Ohio. These ancient people headquartered a prosperous trading empire in southern Ohio, and they showed an advanced understanding of celestial physics. They may have been the ancestors of the Shawnee and Miami tribes who inhabited the area when European settlers arrived. Later on, when cities such as Cincinnati and Dayton were developed, the region hosted a network of canals and roads.

The Great Miami and Scioto rivers are the main streams that drain the region and flow into the Ohio. But the scenic Little Miami River may offer the most to hikers. At the headwaters, the Little Miami flows through Clifton Gorge, a spectacular canyon, before passing through John Bryan State Park and Glen Helen Nature Preserve. Farther downstream, the Little Miami (which is designated as a National Scenic River) runs alongside a 70-mile stretch of crushed asphalt that passes by many scenic and historic spots. The river empties into the Ohio near Cincinnati, which also offers a variety of scenic and historical hikes.

> Walk near routes that were used previously by Indian tribes and escaping slaves.

> Enjoy the scenic splendor of the Little Miami River watershed.

> Visit one of the best fishing and boating lakes in the state.

Area Information

Although Caesar Creek Lake has been in existence only since 1978, the history of the area goes back much further. Fossils found here indicate that the region was under a shallow sea hundreds of millions of years ago. The land that is here now plays host to 65 species of plants as well as forests filled with oak, hickory, beech, and maple trees. In 1978, the U.S. Army Corps of Engineers dammed the Caesar Creek valley and created a 2,800-acre lake. The State of Ohio leases the 7,200 acres around the lake (from the Corps of Engineers) for Caesar Creek State Park and Wildlife Area.

Human interaction with the region can be traced back to about 2,300 years ago when the mound-building Hopewell culture was here. Between 1000 and 1600 AD, the Fort Ancient Indians inhabited the valley, and they left some of their best work nearby. The Wyandot, Miami, and Shawnee tribes were living here when Europeans arrived in the late 1700s. But the creek and state park get their name from a slave named Caesar who was captured in an Indian raid in 1776. Caesar hunted and fished along the creek that was named for him. An Indian path along the banks of the Little Miami was called Bullskin Trail, and an Underground Railroad route later followed the path.

Today, the park offers a wide variety of options. Near the dam, the Corps of Engineers has a visitor center with exhibits and displays regarding the story of the area. Pioneer Vil-

The Dam at Caesar Creek State Park is a popular fishing spot.

lage, a collection of relocated log homes and shops around a village green, is located near the center of the southern edge of the lake. The campground contains 283 electric sites; it also has showers, flush toilets, and a playground. Four cabins are available for rental, and the park has four picnic areas with grills, drinking water, and three picnic shelters. The lake has four boat launch ramps and enough dry moorage rental for 64 boats. There is no horsepower limit on the lake. Fishing is especially good for bass and crappie, and the lake has a 1,300-foot public swimming beach. In addition to hiking trails that include a stretch of the Buckeye Trail, the park contains four bridle trails and two mountain bike trails. Visitors can explore over 50 total miles of trail in this park.

Directions: Caesar Creek is located along State Route 73 east of Waynesville and just west of Interstate 71. The dam is near the junction of Oregonia and Clarksville Roads.

Hours open: The park is open year-round.

Facilities: Restrooms are available at several locations.

Rules and permits: A free permit is required for fossil collecting.

Contact information: The park address is 8570 East State Route 73, Waynesville, Ohio 45068. The phone number of the visitor center is 513-897-1050. The campground phone number is 937-488-4595.

Other Areas of Interest

Caesar Creek Gorge State Nature Preserve, which offers a walk through a scenic gorge, is located just downstream from the dam. Caesar Lake State Park is located just to the west.

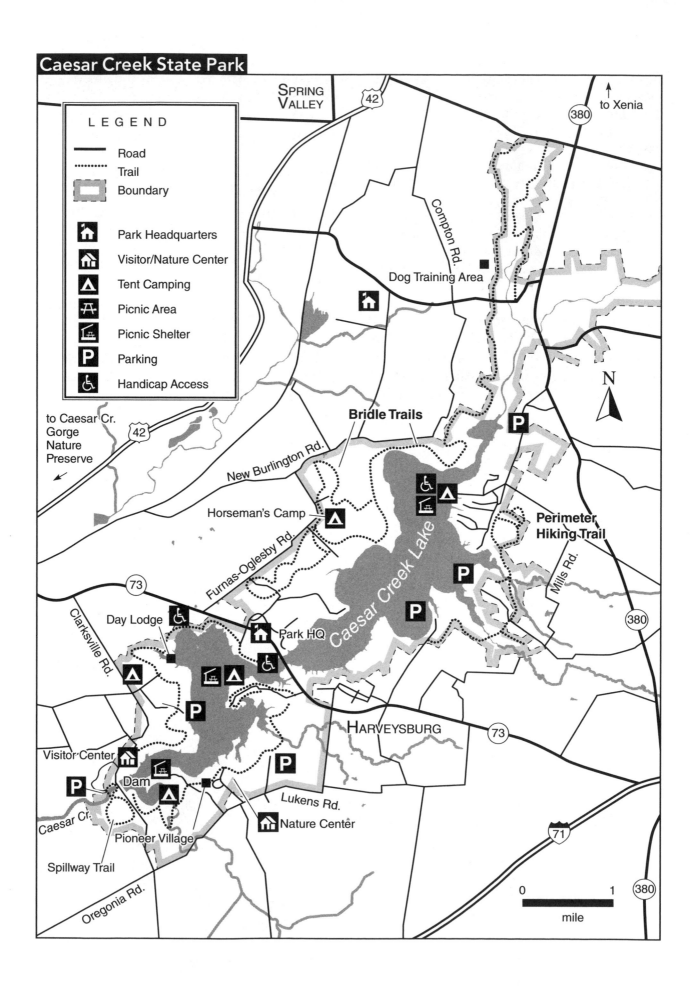

Caesar Creek State Park

LEGEND

— Road
..... Trail
Boundary

Park Headquarters
Visitor/Nature Center
Tent Camping
Picnic Area
Picnic Shelter
P Parking
Handicap Access

SPRING VALLEY

42

380

to Xenia

Compton Rd.

Dog Training Area

to Caesar Cr. Gorge Nature Preserve

42

Bridle Trails

P

N

New Burlington Rd.

Horseman's Camp

Furnas-Oglesby Rd.

Caesar Creek Lake

Perimeter Hiking Trail

Mills Rd.

P

P

P

380

73

Day Lodge

Park HQ

Clarksville Rd.

P

HARVEYSBURG

73

P

Visitor Center

Dam

P

Lukens Rd.

Nature Center

Pioneer Village

71

Spillway Trail

Caesar Cr.

Oregonia Rd.

0   1
mile

380

150

Spillway Trail

Hiking distance: 1.6 miles

Estimated hiking time: 1 hour

Walk alongside a scenic creek in the shadow of a great dam and spillway.

Caution: When walking along streams, hikers always have a risk of encountering wet terrain.

Trail directions: The dam is at the southwest corner of Caesar Creek Lake. Drive over the top of the dam and turn down the hill to the spillway. A parking lot is located here at N 39° 28.994, W 84° 03.873 (1). This location also has flush restrooms, a picnic shelter and tables, and a fishing platform that gets a lot of use. Cross a bridge over the creek near the restrooms, turn right, and walk for almost 0.3 mile. At this point, a side trail turns left and goes up a hill at N 39° 28.906, W 84° 03.873 (2). Leave the Buckeye Trail and go left into the woods.

In about 0.2 mile, you will come to a bench at N 39° 28.787, W 84° 03.980 (3). Just after this, you'll encounter a junction of trails. Turn right and go 0.1 mile to where the trail ends in a meadow at N 39° 28.779, W 84° 03.843 (4). This is a good place to observe wildflowers. Return to the trail junction and continue along the trail for another 0.3 mile. You will come to another trail junction at N 39° 28.931, W 84° 03.671 (5); go straight here and you'll almost immediately hit a paved surface. Follow this for another 0.2 mile until you return to the bridge near point 1.

But, rather than cross the bridge, you should turn right and follow Caesar Creek upstream toward the dam. You'll likely see several people fishing along the spillway. After about 0.2 mile, you will come to a set of steps that eventually cross over the top of the spillway at N 39° 29.085, W 84° 03.780 (6). This is the base of Caesar Creek Dam, which is 165 feet tall and 2,750 feet long; the dam drains a 237-square-mile watershed. After crossing the spillway, return to the parking lot on the other side.

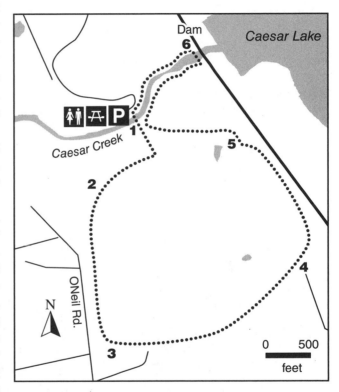

1. Lot
2. Turn left
3. Bench
4. Meadow
5. Junction
6. Dam

> Sample a wide range of recreational options near the nation's 15th largest city.
> Take advantage of well-groomed and well-maintained parks that are easy to get to.
> Experience a variety of both natural and human history.

Area Information

Metro Parks is a conglomeration of 15 diverse parks found in the Columbus area. Although most of these parks are near Columbus, they are actually scattered over seven central Ohio counties. The mission of Metro Parks is conservation as well as providing opportunities and places for people to discover and experience nature. Established in 1945, Metro Parks protects over 25,000 acres and provides a plethora of recreational and educational opportunities. Many of the parks have elaborate nature cen-

ters, and all have regularly scheduled activities throughout the year. All activities in the Metro Parks are free, thanks to support of a Metro Parks levy in 2009.

Highbanks is the northernmost of the Metro Parks. This park encompasses 1,158 acres between the Olentangy River and U.S. Route 23, and it includes woods, fields, and wetlands. The natural history of the area goes back 350 million years to when Ohio was under an inland ocean, but the human history also goes way back: A 2,000-year-old Adena Indian burial mound can be found on the grounds. Also, the park is bordered by the Edward F. Hutchins Nature Preserve, a 206-acre area that provides a habitat for rare vegetation and diverse wildlife.

Not far away is Blendon Woods Metro Park, which contains 653 acres. Most of this is rolling woodlands, but the park also features the 118-acre Walden Waterfowl Refuge nestled around 11-acre Thoreau Lake. This refuge contains two

The Lodge at Highbanks Metro Park features exhibits and displays of natural wonders.

elevated observation shelters equipped with spotting scopes to better enable viewing of the 226 species of birds that have been spotted on the grounds.

Directions: To get to Highbanks, take U.S. Route 23 north from the top of the Interstate 270 Outerbelt loop. Go 3 miles to the park entrance on the left, just before Powell Road. To find Blendon Woods, take Interstate 270 to the State Route 161 exit toward New Albany. Proceed 1.6 miles and take the Little Turtle Way exit. Turn right and go to Old State Route 161, turn right again, and then go a half mile to the park entrance on the left.

Hours open: Highbanks is open from 6:30 a.m. until 10:00 p.m. from April through September, and from 6:30 a.m. until 8:00 p.m. during the other months. The nature center opens at noon on weekdays and at 10:00 a.m. on weekends and stays open until about an hour before sunset. Hours are the same for the park and nature center at Blendon Woods; in addition, the waterfowl refuge is open the same hours as the park.

Facilities: In addition to the nature center, Highbanks offers restrooms, picnic facilities, a natural play area, sledding hills, and day camp facilities. At Blendon Woods, you can find restrooms, a nature center, picnic areas, cross-country ski trails, an ice skating pond, day camp facilities, and an 18-hole golf course.

Rules and permits: No permits are needed to enjoy the free activities at the Metro Parks. Check with the main office to find details on specific activities, restrictions, and events.

Contact information: Highbanks is located at 9466 Columbus Pike (U.S. Route 23 North), Lewis Center, Ohio 43035. Blendon Woods is located at 4265 East Dublin-Granville Road, Westerville, Ohio 43081. The Metro Parks headquarters is at 1069 West Main Street, Westerville, Ohio 43081; the phone number is 614-891-0700. The Metro Parks website is at www.metroparks.net.

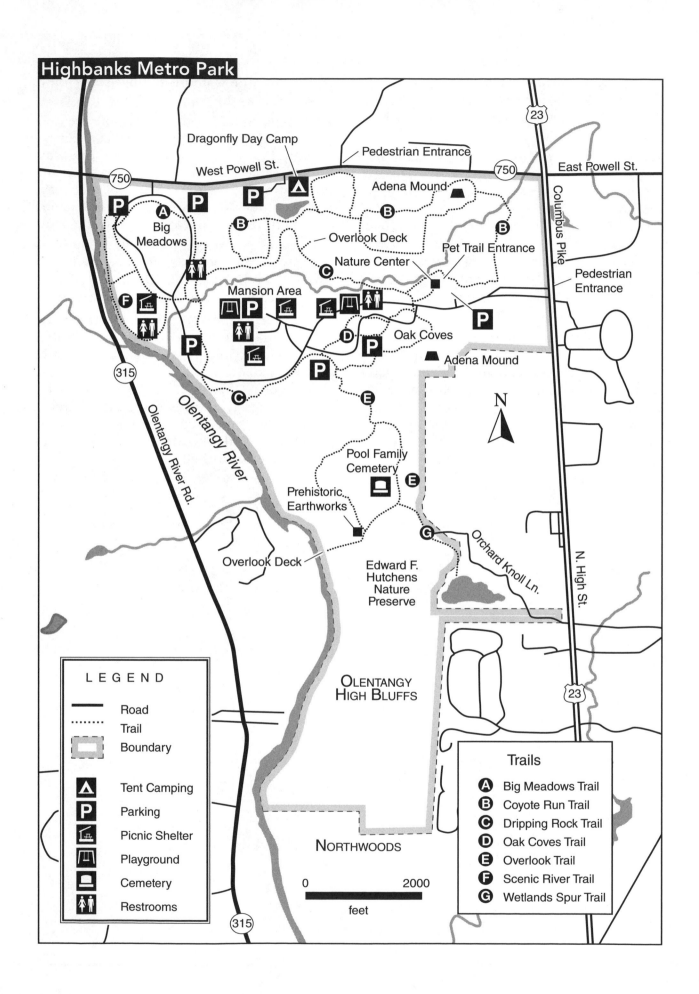

Highbanks Metro Park

Dragonfly Day Camp
Pedestrian Entrance
West Powell St.
Adena Mound
East Powell St.
Big Meadows
Overlook Deck
Pet Trail Entrance
Nature Center
Pedestrian Entrance
Mansion Area
Oak Coves
Adena Mound
Columbus Pike
Olentangy River Rd.
Olentangy River
Pool Family Cemetery
Prehistoric Earthworks
Edward F. Hutchens Nature Preserve
Orchard Knoll Ln.
N. High St.
Overlook Deck
OLENTANGY HIGH BLUFFS
NORTHWOODS

N

LEGEND

——	Road
····	Trail
▢	Boundary
▲	Tent Camping
P	Parking
🏕	Picnic Shelter
🛝	Playground
⬓	Cemetery
🚻	Restrooms

Trails

- Ⓐ Big Meadows Trail
- Ⓑ Coyote Run Trail
- Ⓒ Dripping Rock Trail
- Ⓓ Oak Coves Trail
- Ⓔ Overlook Trail
- Ⓕ Scenic River Trail
- Ⓖ Wetlands Spur Trail

0   2000
feet

Park Trails

Highbanks contains several interlocking trails:

Big Meadows Path,
1 mile

Coyote Run Trail,
3.5 miles

Dripping Rock Trail,
2.5 miles

Oak Coves Path,
0.4 mile

Overlook Trail,
2.3 miles

Scenic River Trail,
0.6 mile

Wetlands Spur Trail,
0.4 mile

Blendon Woods also has several interconnected trails:

Brookside Trail,
0.75 mile

Goldenrod Pet Trail,
1.25 miles

Hickory Ridge Trail,
0.25 mile

Overlook Trail,
0.6 mile

Pond Trail,
0.3 mile

Ripple Rock Trail,
0.4 mile

Sugarbush Trail,
2 miles

Other Areas of Interest

The Metro Park system also includes 13 other parks:

Battelle Darby Creek, 1775 Darby Creek Drive, Galloway, Ohio 43119

Blacklick Woods, 6975 and 7309 East Livingston Avenue, Reynoldsburg, Ohio 43068

Chestnut Ridge, 8445 Winchester Road Northwest, Carroll, Ohio 43112

Clear Creek, 185 Clear Creek Road, Rockbridge, Ohio 43149

Glacier Ridge, 9801 Hyland Croy Road, Plain City, Ohio 43064

Heritage Park and Trail, 7262 Hayden Run Road, Hilliard, Ohio 43026

Inniswood, 940 South Hampstead Road, Westerville, Ohio 43081

Pickerington Ponds, 7680 Wright Road, Canal Winchester, Ohio 43110

Prairie Oaks, 3225 Plain City-Georgesville Road, West Jefferson, Ohio 43162

Scioto Audubon, 395 West Whittier Street, Columbus, Ohio 43215

Sharon Woods, 6911 Cleveland Avenue, Westerville, Ohio 43081

Slate Run Farm and Park, 1375 State Route 674 North, Canal Winchester, Ohio 43110

Three Creeks, 3860 Bixby Road, Groveport, Ohio 43125

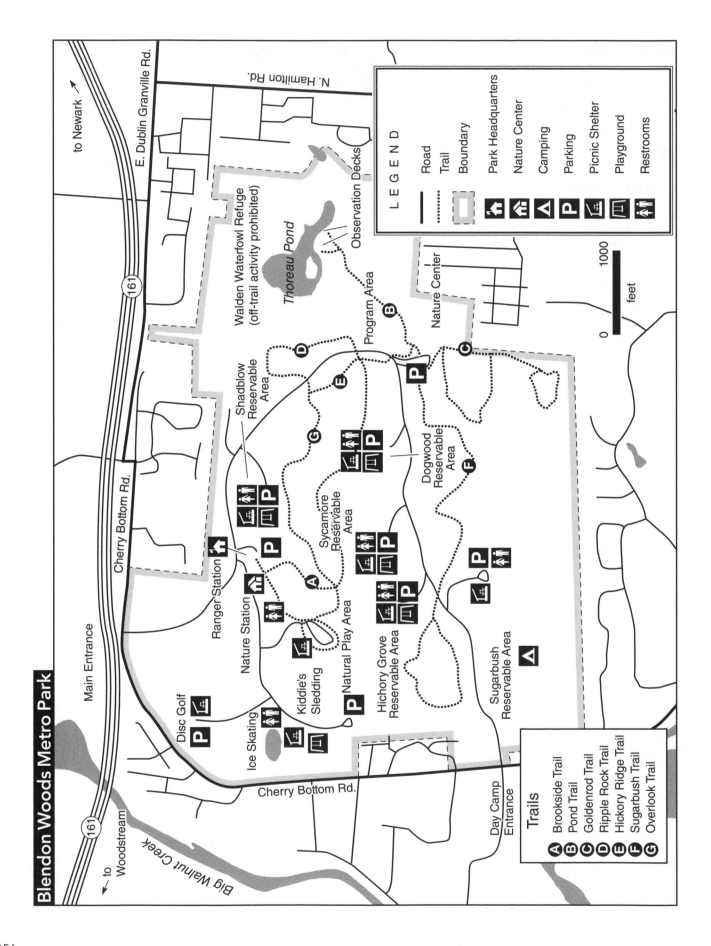

Blendon Woods Metro Park

to Newark

to Woodstream

161

Big Walnut Creek

Main Entrance

Cherry Bottom Rd.

E. Dublin Granville Rd.

N. Hamilton Rd.

Walden Waterfowl Refuge
(off-trail activity prohibited)

Thoreau Pond

Observation Decks

Program Area

Nature Center

Shadblow
Reservable
Area

Sycamore
Reservable
Area

Dogwood
Reservable
Area

Hickory Grove
Reservable Area

Sugarbush
Reservable Area

Ranger Station

Nature Station

Natural Play Area

Kiddie's Sledding

Ice Skating

Disc Golf

Cherry Bottom Rd.

Day Camp
Entrance

LEGEND

———	Road
....	Trail
⬚	Boundary
🏛	Park Headquarters
🏛	Nature Center
⛺	Camping
P	Parking
🏕	Picnic Shelter
🎠	Playground
🚻	Restrooms

0   1000
feet

Highbanks Metro Park Trail

Hiking distance: 3.4 miles round trip

Estimated hiking time: 2 hours

Hike a well maintained urban park that feature views of both skyscrapers and Indian mounds.

Caution: Many trails crisscross Highbanks Metro Park, so get a map from the nature center to make sure you are on the correct trail.

Trail directions: To get to Highbanks, take U.S. Route 23 north from the top of the Interstate 270 Outerbelt. Go north for 3 miles until you get to the park entrance on your left. At this point, you are on the Franklin-Delaware county line, and if you look back to the south on a clear day, you can see the Columbus skyline. Take the main park road for 0.4 mile until you arrive at the nature center at N 40° 09.095, W 83° 01.492 (1).

Pass in front of the nature center and cross the park road on the Dripping Rock Trail for 0.2 mile. At this spot—which is at N 40° 08.968, W 83° 01.473 (2)—you will see a trail that leads to the Adena Indian mound. Take this route another 0.2 mile to N 40° 08.887, W 83° 01.476 (3); you will now come to a low mound of dirt that is approximately 2,000 years old. The ancient Adena people populated Ohio a few millennia ago and used mounds like this for burying their dead and for other ceremonial purposes. They usually built these mounds along rivers but out of the floodplain, and this particular small mound is one of the northernmost that have been found.

Retrace your steps back to point 2 and go left, continuing on the Dripping Rock Trail

Ancient natives looked down on the Olentangy River from this spot in Highbanks Metro Park 2,000 years ago.

for another 0.3 mile. Here you will meet the Overlook Trail at N 40° 08.871, W 83° 01.809 (4). Turn left at this trail and go another quarter mile and across a bridge until the trail splits off at N 40° 09.843, W 87° 01.706 (5). Take the right fork and you will quickly come to a short path that goes to the small cemetery of the Pool family, a group of early homesteaders. Take a quick look and then go back on the Overlook Trail for another 0.6 mile until you meet up with the other end of the loop at N 40° 09.843, W 83° 01.706 (6).

Turn right here and almost immediately you will pass through earthworks built by the Cole people. This tribe of Indians was more recent than the Adena, so these earthworks were built a mere millennium ago. Proceed another 0.2 mile until you come to the overlook that the trail is named for. A large wooden deck here—at N 40° 09.375, W 83° 01.876 (7)—offers a view from the shale cliffs that give the park its name. Down below you can clearly see a long stretch of the Olentangy River.

To return, retrace your steps to point 6, but this time take the loop trail on the right. About 0.1 mile after this junction, you will come to a turnoff for the Wetland Spur Trail at N 40° 09.489, W 83° 01.628 (8). If you want to add another 0.8 mile to your hike, take this trail to a pond that has a wooden structure that offers excellent views of diverse waterfowl. If you choose to stay on the Overlook Trail, you will continue to walk through a forest of white ash, oak, and pawpaw trees until you return to point 5 and then retrace your steps back to point 4.

At the junction with the Dripping Rock Trail, go left this time and continue a short distance to where this trail meets the Oak Coves Path at N 40° 09.918, W 83° 01.918 (9). This trail on the right immediately crosses the park road

and goes through the Oak Coves Picnic Area for 0.4 mile until you return to the nature center.

Be sure to stop in at the center and view the displays on the flora, fauna, and geology of the park, as well as an excellent diorama explaining the practices of the Mound Builders. A platform behind the building offers an excellent spot for bird watching.

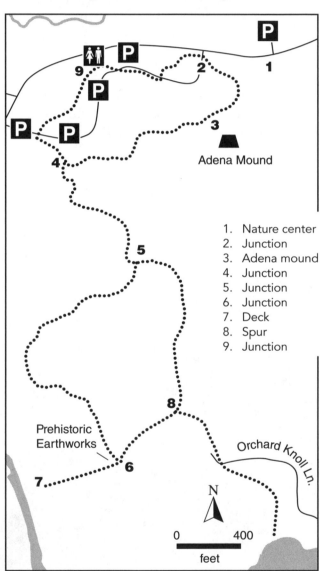

1. Nature center
2. Junction
3. Adena mound
4. Junction
5. Junction
6. Junction
7. Deck
8. Spur
9. Junction

Blendon Woods Metro Park Trail

 **Hiking distance:** 2.4 miles round trip

Estimated hiking time: 1 hour 15 minutes

Hike through a nice wooded refuge for the urban dweller, and be sure to stop and watch the waterfowl.

Caution: Because this is a well-maintained trail located in a congested area, you can expect the trail to be crowded at times.

Trail directions: From Interstate 270, take State Route 161 toward New Albany onto East Dublin-Granville Road. Go 1.6 miles, take the Little Turtle Way exit, and then turn right. Go to Old State Route 161 and turn right; the park entrance is 0.5 mile ahead on the left. Follow the main road to the parking lot for the nature center at N 40° 04.233, W 82° 52.426 (1). Go back across the road and take the Hickory Ridge Trail for about 0.1 mile to where it meets the Brookside Trail at N 40° 04.341, W 82° 52.409 (2). Turn left at the Brookside Trail and proceed into a forest that features over 40 native tree species. Among those that predominate here are beech, black walnut, and hickory. You will cross over a small stream.

Proceed another half mile or so until you come to the Overlook Trail at N 40° 04.382, W 82° 52.975 (3). Turn right on this trail and start the climb slightly uphill deeper into the forest. After about 0.3 mile, you will climb a set of stairs at N 40° 04.455, W 82° 52.654 (4). In another 0.15 mile, you will meet Ripple Rock Trail at N 40° 04.436, W 82° 52.997 (5). This trail immediately crosses the main park road and loops around for 0.4 mile, coming out at the nature center at point 1.

❚ Thoreau Pond in Blendon Woods Metro Park is a delight for waterfowl enthusiasts.

Blendon Woods Metro Park Trail   > continued

The nature center offers seasonable exhibits and presentations, and it is well worth a visit. However, you should first venture onto the Pond Trail immediately behind the nature center. A walk of about 0.4 mile takes you to Thoreau Lake and a diverse display of water-fowl; this is located at N 40° 04.415, W 82° 52.140 (6). Return to the nature center and take a close look around before leaving. Two structures provide protected close-up views of the ducks and Canada geese, and they offer telescopic views as well. This is an excellent spot for avian photography, and you are also likely to see blue heron and great horned owls.

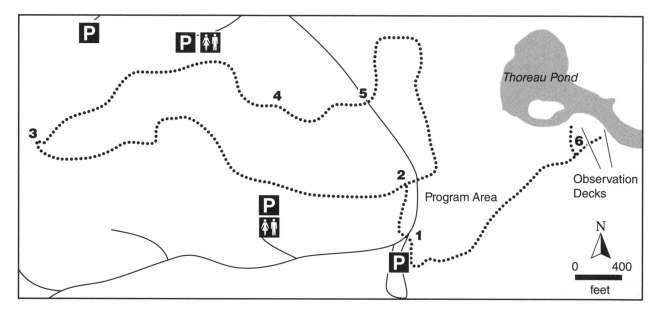

1. Nature center
2. Junction
3. Junction
4. Stairs
5. Cross road at junction
6. Thoreau Pond

> Enjoy a large lake and park that are less than 25 miles from downtown Cincinnati.

> Hike through a diverse hardwood forest.

> Take a hike on all or part of a 32-mile backpack trail that encircles the lake.

Area Information

East Fork State Park is where Cincinnati goes to enjoy outdoor recreation. Less than 25 miles from the city, this 8,000-acre park is centered around a 2,160-acre lake that was built by the U.S. Army Corps of Engineers in 1978. The lake is an angler's and boater's paradise, but the park also has numerous hiking opportunities. In addition to several shorter trails, two long trails wind near the shores of William Harsha Lake. A 12-mile Backpack Trail lies on the southern shore of the lake, while the 32-mile Steve Newman Worldwalker Perimeter Trail encircles the lake and features four primitive campsites. This trail is named for a native of nearby Bethel who circumnavigated the globe on foot between 1983 and 1987.

The East Fork area is in the watershed of the Little Miami River, which was first inhabited by the Adena culture who built mounds here over 2,000 years ago. Today the region is known for a diversity of wildlife that features woodland, swamp, and prairie species. East Fork is also one of the few places in Ohio where Illinoian glacial deposits can be found.

Although relatively new for a state park, East Fork offers a wide range of amenities. Harsha Lake has six boat launch ramps and no horsepower limit, so it has become a mecca for fishing and sport boaters. The lake also has a 1,200-foot swimming beach. Eight full-service picnic areas and two shelters are provided in the park. For campers, the park campground offers 384 electric sites and 8 rental cabins. The campground features playgrounds, a miniature golf course, basketball courts, and horseshoe courts. In winter, visitors can enjoy sledding, ice skating, ice fishing, and cross-country skiing. The park also contains four bridle trails and a mountain biking trail.

Directions: The main entrance to the park is off of State Route 125, just east of where State Route 222 turns off to the south. Turn north here on Bantam Road and follow the signs to the nature center on the fringe of the park. Just past this and on the other side of the road, you'll find a trailhead parking lot.

Hours open: The park is open year-round in daylight hours.

Facilities: Trails in the park offer limited campsites and numerous restrooms.

Rules and permits: Pets are permitted in all areas.

Contact information: The park office is located at 3294 Elklick Road, Bethel, Ohio 45103. The phone number is 513-734-4323.

Other Areas of Interest

Other attractions in Clermont County include Stonelick State Park and the Cincinnati Nature Center, both of which offer ample hiking opportunities.

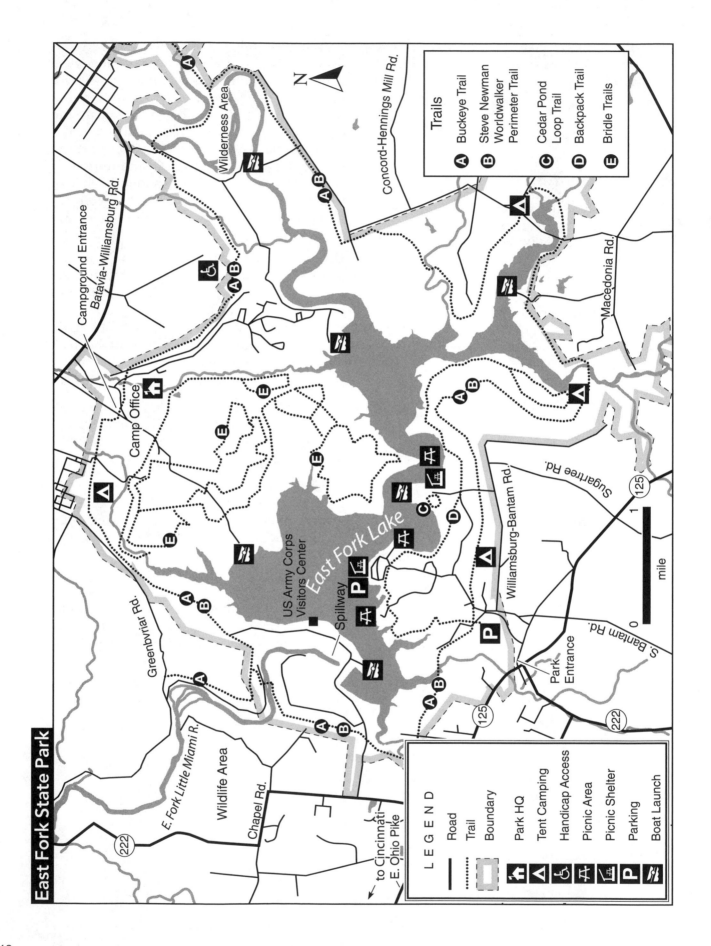

East Fork State Park

Trails

- Ⓐ Buckeye Trail
- Ⓑ Steve Newman Worldwalker Perimeter Trail
- Ⓒ Cedar Pond Loop Trail
- Ⓓ Backpack Trail
- Ⓔ Bridle Trails

LEGEND

- Road
- Trail
- Boundary
- Park HQ
- Tent Camping
- Handicap Access
- Picnic Area
- Picnic Shelter
- Parking
- Boat Launch

East Fork Lake

US Army Corps Visitors Center

Spillway

Campground Entrance

Wilderness Area

Camp Office

Greenbriar Rd.

Batavia-Williamsburg Rd.

Concord-Hennings Mill Rd.

Macedonia Rd.

Sugartree Rd.

Williamsburg-Bantam Rd.

Park Entrance

S. Bantam Rd.

Chapel Rd.

E. Fork Little Miami R.

Wildlife Area

to Cincinnati
E. Ohio Pike

125

222

0   1   mile

Backpack Trail and Backcountry Trail Loop

Hiking distance: 5 miles

Estimated hiking time: 3 hours

Enjoy a wooded hike with occasional views of a large lake.

Caution: The trail can be muddy and is steep in spots.

Trail directions: Park at the trailhead lot near the nature center at N 39° 00.408, W 84° 08.522 (1). This lot is at the convergence of several trails and also hosts a bird blind where hikers can observe indigenous waterfowl. Head north here, leaving the Newman Perimeter Trail behind, and follow the Backpack Trail, which is also concurrent with the Buckeye and North Country Trails.

The trail crosses ravines and streambeds, and it includes steep climbs and descents as it approaches the lakeshore. After hiking for over a mile, cross Park Road 3 at N 39° 01.034, W 84° 08.446 (2). The trail gradually veers toward the right, and the lake is sometimes now in sight, depending on the foliage and the time of year. After going almost another mile, cross Park Road 2 at N 39° 00.901, W 84° 08.050 (3). This is the road to the public beach area, which is just ahead on the left.

Reenter the woods on the other side of the road, and the trail gradually heads away from the lake. After about a mile, the Buckeye Trail leaves the route and veers off on the left. Just after this, you should cross Park Road 1 at N 39° 00.417, W 84° 07.720 (4). Follow the route into the woods for another half mile to a primitive campsite. Here the trail reunites with the 32-mile-long Newman Perimeter Trail that leads back to point 1.

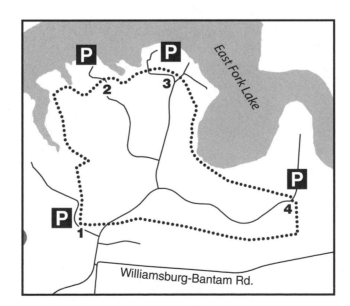

1. Trailhead lot
2. Cross road
3. Cross road
4. Cross road

> Sample a rare urban walk that features views of both the city and the Ohio River.

> Explore the end of the Buckeye Trail as well as a part of the coast-to-coast American Discovery Trail.

> Stop to visit the art museum and conservatory that you will be walking past.

Area Information

This book usually shuns urban hikes based on the belief that walking on sidewalks is not really hiking. However, Eden Park is an exception to this rule for a couple of reasons. For one thing, Eden Park is a city park on public land. And the park is also a part of two major trails. Eden Park is the southern terminus of the Buckeye Trail, as well as part of the American Discovery Trail, a California-to-Delaware trail that enters Ohio on the Roebling Bridge in downtown Cincinnati.

The 186-acre park was originally designated to hold the city's water supply. The land came from city patriarch Nicholas Longworth, who grew grapes for his vineyards on nearby hillsides in the Mount Adams neighborhood. Today, this well-known park is more famous for its cultural offerings than recreational ones, although walkers and joggers can always be found here.

The cultural attractions of the park include Krohn Conservatory, which features over 3,500 plant species from around the world. The conservatory also hosts a unique annual butterfly show. The park is also home to the Cincinnati Art Museum and the home theater for Playhouse in the Park. And, although walking may be done on pavement, visitors will see plants galore along the way, as well as lakes and scenic views of Mount Adams and the Ohio River.

Directions: Eden Park is located between Interstate 71 and U.S. Route 50 (Columbia Parkway). Take Columbia Parkway east from downtown to Kemper and turn left. Go uphill to Victoria Parkway and turn left. Follow the signs to the art museum for parking.

Hours open: The park is open year-round in daylight hours. Hours for the conservatory and art museum vary.

Facilities: Public restrooms are available at the intersection of Eden Park Drive and Art Museum Drive.

Rules and permits: Pets are permitted anywhere in the park, but they must be leashed.

Contact information: The park is located at 950 Eden Park Drive, Cincinnati, Ohio 45202. The phone number for Cincinnati Parks is 513-221-2610.

Other Areas of Interest

Other attractions in the Cincinnati area include the Cincinnati Zoo and Botanical Garden and the Mount Airy Arboretum.

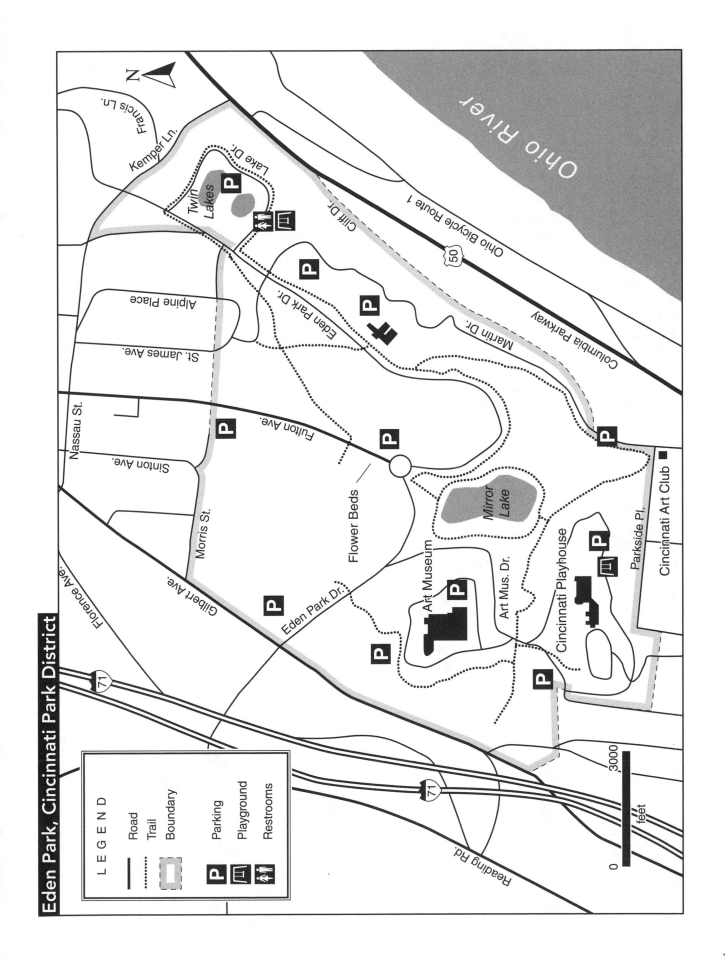

Eden Park, Cincinnati Park District

LEGEND

——	Road
········	Trail
▢	Boundary
P	Parking
🏛	Playground
🚻	Restrooms

Ohio River

165

Eden Park Trail

Hiking distance: 2 miles

Estimated hiking time: 1 hour, 15 minutes

Take a city stroll in an area that is part of a national trail network.

Caution: This hilly hike is along public streets, so watch out for traffic.

Trail directions: Park at the free public lot near the art museum at N 39° 06.773, W 84° 29.836 (1). Proceed for 0.2 mile to the intersection of Art Museum Drive and Eden Park Drive at N 39° 06.870, W 84° 29.726 (2). Turn right and go downhill for 0.1 mile to a traffic roundabout where Fulton Road comes in at N 39° 06.877, W 84° 29.622 (3). On one side of this traffic circle, you'll see public restrooms; on another side, you'll see the trademark gazebo whose image dominates the signage.

Walk to the gazebo and then take a lap around scenic Mirror Lake. This shallow pond has a fountain in the center and is usually hosting Canada geese and other waterfowl. After returning to the gazebo, walk along a path called the Hinkle Floral Trail that runs parallel to Eden Park Drive. After about 0.3 mile, the path comes to the intersection of Eden Park Drive and Martin Drive at N 39° 06.875, W 84° 29.471 (4). The Krohn Conservatory is located just across Martin Drive. This conservatory is home to thousands of plant species from around the world and is well worth an inside visit.

If you choose to remain outdoors, turn right and go downhill on Martin Drive past the red brick water tower building (which is 172 feet tall) that supplied the city in the 19th century. In 0.2 mile, you'll come to the intersection with Cliff Road at N 39° 06.742, W 84° 29.479 (5). Follow Martin Drive downhill for another 0.2 mile to the junction with Parkside Place at N 39° 06.626, W 84° 29.588 (6). Be sure to check out the view of the nearby Mount Adams neighborhood on the way. This is the corner of the park, so turn right here and begin climbing uphill.

In about 0.2 mile, Parkside Place is met by Loudon Street at N 39° 06.634, W 84° 29.828 (7). Cross Loudon here and climb up a set of steps that comes up around the rear of the art museum. Turn right on the first paved road and follow it for about 0.2 mile until you arrive at an opening that offers a vista of the Ohio River at N 39° 06.678, W 84° 29.670 (8). Sit on one of the benches here to soak up the views of the city and river below before continuing on for another 0.2 mile to the original parking lot.

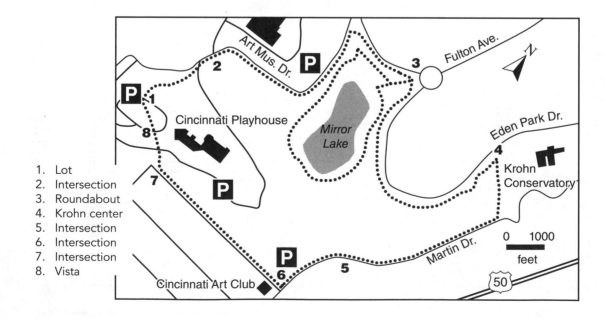

1. Lot
2. Intersection
3. Roundabout
4. Krohn center
5. Intersection
6. Intersection
7. Intersection
8. Vista

> Explore the geological anomaly of an area of Appalachia that extends north of the Ohio River.

> Take advantage of the opportunity to enjoy an abundance of wildflowers contained in a small area.

> Sample vistas that are more mountain-like than any others found in Ohio.

Area Information

The Edge of Appalachia Preserve is a unique part of Ohio's natural heritage. Located in the watershed of Ohio Brush Creek in Adams County, the area is a geological extension of Kentucky's Bluegrass Region. A sliver of this geologic region crosses the Ohio River and fits in between the Interior Low Plateau to the west and the unglaciated Appalachian Plateau to the east, making this Appalachian escarpment a wedge that seems out of place. In geological terms, this region is truly the edge of Appalachia, and being on the cusp of several regions guarantees a wide biodiversity. Over 1,200 species of vascular plants are found near the last 12 miles of Ohio Brush Creek before it empties into the Ohio River.

The administration of this preserve is as unique as its geology. The Richard and Lucile Durrell Edge of Appalachia Preserve is jointly run by the Cincinnati Museum Center and the Ohio Chapter of the Nature Conservancy. The Cincinnati Museum Center is an educational organization headquartered in the museum complex at Cincinnati's Union Terminal, while the Nature Conservancy is a global land preservation organization. The unusual nature of the landscape was noted as far back as 1839, when frontier geologist Dr. John Locke explored the area by wagon. But it wasn't until the 1950s that serious preservation efforts were launched. Dr. E. Lucy Braun, a professor of botany at the University of Cincinnati, was a guiding force behind these efforts. Dr. Braun

was fascinated by the region throughout her lengthy career, and she became increasingly concerned about its survival in the face of development. In 1959, she was able to link Cincinnati area garden clubs with the fledgling Nature Conservancy to purchase 42 acres of Lynx Prairie near Ohio Brush Creek. Today, the Edge of Appalachia Preserve is the largest private land preserve in the eastern United States with 11 parcels of land covering over 13,000 acres. Four of these spots—Lynx Prairie, Buzzardroost Rock, the Wilderness, and Red Rock—have been designated National Natural Landmarks by the National Park Service.

Directions: The local office for the Edge of Appalachia Preserve is located on Waggoner Riffle Road just south of State Route 125 between Lynx and West Union.

Hours open: Office hours are restricted, but the sites are open year-round during daylight hours.

Facilities: The preserve has no facilities—no toilets, drinking water, picnic tables, or campsites.

Rules and permits: Hunting, rock climbing, and plant collecting are forbidden, as are pets, horses, and vehicles. Hikers are asked to remain on the trails in order to minimize the damage of the human footprint. Most visitors explore at their own pace or come with an educational group. These group activities are listed in the newsletters of the Cincinnati Museum Center and the Nature Conservancy.

Contact information: For more information, contact Edge of Appalachia Preserve System, 3223 Waggoner Riffle Road, West Union, Ohio 45693; the phone number is 937-544-2880 or 937-544-2188. You may also contact the Cincinnati Museum Center at Union Terminal, 1301 Western Avenue, Cincinnati, Ohio 45203; the phone number is 513-287-7000 or 800-733-2077.

Other Areas of Interest

Shawnee State Forest offers a variety of day hike and backpacking opportunities in an area touted as the "Little Smokies" of Ohio. Containing over 60,000 acres, it is the largest single section of public land in the state. The forest offers trails that are rugged but well worth the effort. For more information, call Shawnee State Forest at 740-858-6685.

Serpent Mound State Memorial is just a few miles upstream on Ohio Brush Creek. This ancient Indian effigy mound is over a quarter mile long and was built over 1,000 years ago. Saved from development by scholars intrigued by the mysteries of Ohio's Stonehenge, the area is now state owned and features hiking trails and a 25-foot-high tower. For more information, call 937-587-2796 or 800-752-2787.

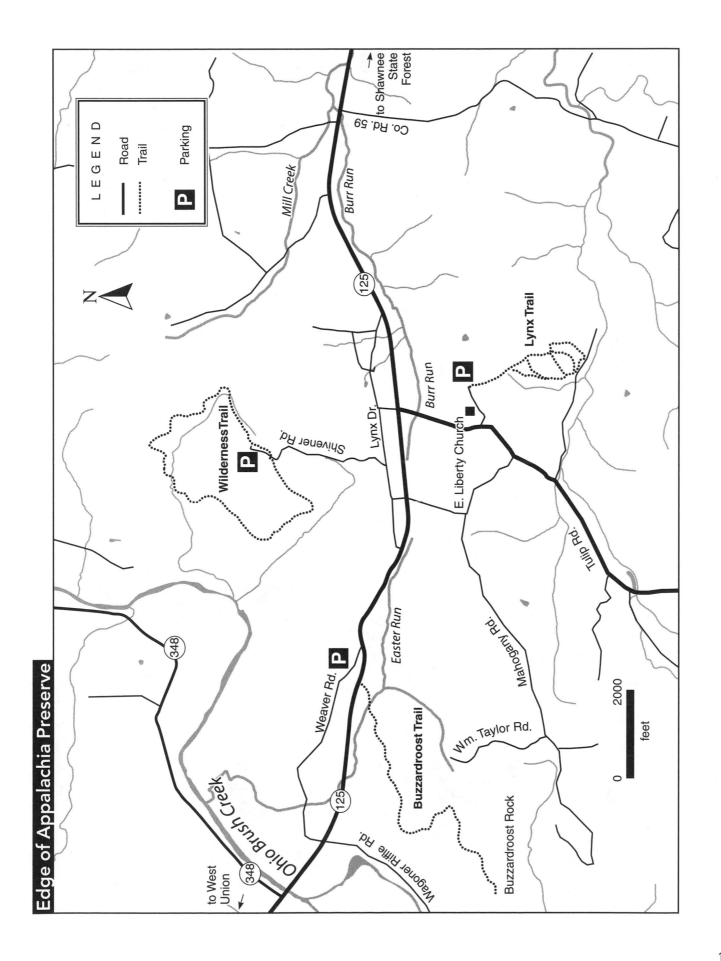

Edge of Appalachia Preserve

169

Buzzardroost Rock Trail

 **Hiking distance:** 3.5 miles round trip

Estimated hiking time: 2 hours

Take a rugged hike that culminates in one of the most spectacular vistas found in the state.

Caution: At one end of the trail, you must take care in crossing State Route 125, which is a heavily traveled thoroughfare. At the other end, you should be sure to stay on the trail and avoid climbing on the dangerous rock formations that are all around. The area in between can get muddy at times.

Trail directions: The parking lot N 38° 46.482, W 83° 26.088 (1) is located on Weaver Road, which turns north off of State Route 125 briefly before returning to the highway. Park in the small gravel lot and follow the trail downhill toward the highway. A crosswalk is provided on the road N 38° 46.464, W 83° 26.139 (2), but you should be careful and look for fast-moving traffic. After crossing the road, you will reenter the woods. At 0.3 mile, you will come to a footbridge across Easter Run N 38° 46.405, W 83° 26.218 (3), a westward flowing tributary of Ohio Brush Creek.

On the other side of the bridge, you'll find a guest registry, and afterward the trail begins to ascend gradually. The route goes through a cedar glade N 38° 46.404, W 83° 26.286 (4), and at about 0.9 mile, a large boulder is located on the left N 38° 46.314, W 26° 26.634 (5). The trail goes by several other large chunks of dolomite and soon begins a

If you enjoy climbs to mountain-like vistas, Buzzardroost Rock is well worth the effort.

series of switchbacks. Serious hikers know that switchbacks mean steep grade ahead, and the climb here can be taxing.

At about 1.1 miles, the trail ascends a steep hill and turns sharply to the right N 38° 46.102, W 83° 26.746 (6). The trail now covers a more gentle climb until it starts to level out on a ridgeline. From here, you can get a sense that a good view may be forthcoming, because you can start to see portions of the valley floor 500 feet below. You may also see some buzzards, or turkey vultures, heading for their roost, but both times that I hiked this trail I was more impressed by a large murder of crows patrolling the valley.

Finally, at about 1.7 miles, you will come to a footbridge over a rock chasm N 38° 45.920, W 83° 27.185 (7) that leads to a platform on the top of Buzzardroost Rock. This pinnacle is a 75-foot-high column of Peebles dolomite

that was originally referred to as Split Rock by frontier naturalist John Locke. The steel platform on top of the rock is 81 by 36 feet and was built by volunteers.

Buzzardroost Rock is impressive enough in its own right, but the view from the top is what makes this spot truly spectacular. The 2-hour hiking time for this hike refers to walking time only, and you should spend at least an hour savoring the view. Looking down at Ohio Brush Creek flowing south, you can see for miles and soak in a vista that is more mountainlike than any you might expect to see in Ohio. From the valley directly below to the steep hills in the distance, the view is well worth the arduous climb. Take all the photos you want, but be sure to stay within the fenced-in platform area.

Return by the same route, taking time to enjoy the abundance of wildflowers available in season.

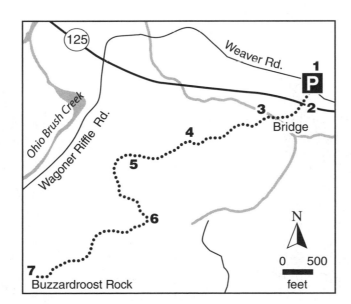

1. Lot
2. Cross road
3. Footbridge
4. Cedar glade
5. Large boulder
6. Steep hill and right turn
7. Platform

Lynx Prairie Trail

Hiking distance: 1.5 miles round trip

Estimated hiking time: 1 hour

Take a stroll in fields that offer the best in wildflowers.

Caution: The trailhead is difficult to find, but this hike is worth the effort. The hike itself is easy and flat and offers a good cool-down walk after the more strenuous Buzzardroost Rock Trail.

Trail directions: The village of Lynx is 7 to 8 miles east of West Union on State Route 125. Once you get there, go south on Tulip Road for 0.3 mile. Turn left into the parking lot of the East Liberty Church. Signage is sparse, so you must know that you need to go through the cemetery behind the church and park at the end of the lane N 38° 46.043, W 83° 24.697 (1). Across the cemetery and at the end of the woods, you'll see a sign marking the beginning of the preserve.

The Edge of Appalachia Preserve is the largest private nature preserve in the eastern United States. Of the 11 parcels that make up the preserve, the 53-acre Lynx Prairie tract was the first one purchased. This is not a traditional wide-open prairie, but rather a compact opening in the woods. But the thin soil on top of the dolomite bedrock offers a home to nearly 100 rare and endangered plant species and offers a glimpse of original growth.

From the trailhead, start out walking through the woods and proceed 0.2 mile to a bridge that precedes a sign post N 38° 45.907, W 83° 24.635 (2). Lynx Prairie is really several smaller prairies connected by three loop trails that are marked in green, white, and red. The green trail branches off first here, but for a better hike, stay on the main trail until it reaches the red trail loop N 38° 45.740, W 83° 24.539 (3) at about 0.6 mile. Take a right turn here and follow this loop trail until it returns to the same spot. On the return, go left here and follow the outer edge of the white and green loops to get back to the main trail at the entrance. Sign posts are provided at all trail loop junctions.

In the spring, the scenery is dominated by such wildflowers as Indian paintbrush and shooting star. But the period from late July through September is when Lynx Prairie offers its most spectacular panoply of wildflowers. The prairie also has an impressive array of prairie grasses, featuring prairie dock and big bluestem that grow as tall as 9 feet. And of course this diversity also attracts a wide variety of pollinators (butterflies and other insects). Birds such as the pileated woodpecker are often found nearby, but the lynx that gave its name to the nearby village is nowhere to be found.

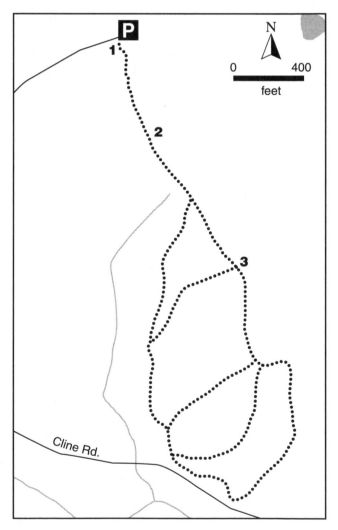

1. Lot
2. Bridge
3. Red trail loop

> Sample a park system that features everything from Indian mounds to tributes to aviation's pioneers.

> Enjoy hiking, canoeing, horseback riding, cycling, and other activities in 19 locations.

> Visit six different visitor centers throughout the Greater Dayton area.

Area Information

The Five Rivers Metroparks system is a regional park system that serves the Dayton metropolitan area. The "five rivers" referred to in the title are the Great Miami, Mad, and Stillwater Rivers and the Wolf and Twin Creeks. These five waterways converge near Dayton, and many of the system's 19 parks are located alongside them. The Metroparks system also contains eight conservation areas.

Created in 1963, the Five Rivers Metroparks encompass 15,400 acres of public land. The focus is on outdoor recreation and education, and park sites cover both human and natural history.

Here are the 19 facilities in the Metroparks system:

Aullwood House and Garden

Carriage Hill

Cox Arboretum and Gardens

Deeds Point

Eastwood

Englewood

Germantown

Hills and Dales

Huffman

Island

Possum Creek

RiverScape

PNC Second Street Market

Sugarcreek

Sunrise

Taylorsville

Twin Creek

Wegerzyn Gardens

Wesleyan

The Dayton area is rich in history, beginning with ancient Indian villages and the state's tallest Indian mound in Miamisburg. More recently, the Wright brothers gave wings to man while experimenting in their hometown of Dayton. Their work at Huffman Prairie provided some of the first public exhibitions of flight, and the famous Air Force Museum is near here. North of town, dams that were built for flood control after 1913 have created abundant opportunities for outdoor recreation. The Metroparks sites at or near these areas take full advantage of these unique features.

Directions: The 19 parks in the system are scattered throughout Montgomery County. Directions for specific parks are included in the hike section.

Facilities: The Five Rivers system offers a wide variety of educational and recreational opportunities. The system includes programs at several locations, a downtown farmers' market, and even a speakers' bureau. The system also offers reservable shelters as well as a wide array of trails for outdoor enthusiasts.

Hours open: All parks are open from 8 a.m. to 10 p.m. from April through October and from 8 a.m. to 8 p.m. from November through March.

Rules and permits: Fires and fossil collecting are permitted only in designated areas. Dogs are allowed only when on leashes that are no longer than 8 feet. Bicycles are not permitted on hiking trails.

Contact information: The Taylorsville Metropark is located at 2000 State Route 40, Vandalia, Ohio 45377. The Englewood Metropark is located at 4361 National Road, Vandalia, Ohio 45377. The phone number for the Five Rivers Metroparks system is 937-275-7275.

Other Areas of Interest

Sycamore State Park is nearby between Brookville and Trotwood. For history and aviation buffs, Dayton hosts the Air Force Museum and four separate sites that make up the Dayton Aviation Heritage National Historic Park.

Aullwood Audubon Nature Center and Farm is located right across the street from the north entrance to Englewood Metropark. This facility offers exhibits, programs, and hiking trails.

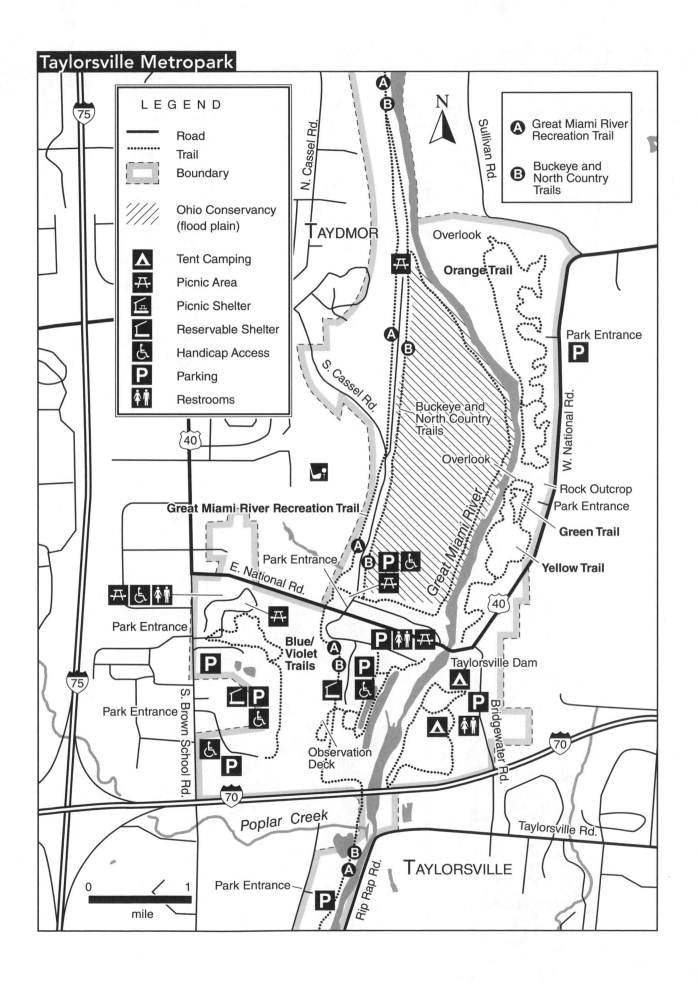

Taylorsville Metropark

LEGEND

——	Road
····	Trail
▭	Boundary
/////	Ohio Conservancy (flood plain)
⛺	Tent Camping
⛱	Picnic Area
🏠	Picnic Shelter
🏠	Reservable Shelter
♿	Handicap Access
🅿	Parking
🚻	Restrooms

A — Great Miami River Recreation Trail

B — Buckeye and North Country Trails

N

TAYDMOR

Sullivan Rd.

N. Cassel Rd.

S. Cassel Rd.

Overlook

Orange Trail

Buckeye and North Country Trails

Overlook

Great Miami River

Park Entrance

W. National Rd.

Rock Outcrop
Park Entrance

Green Trail

Yellow Trail

Great Miami River Recreation Trail

Park Entrance

E. National Rd.

Blue/ Violet Trails

Park Entrance

Park Entrance

S. Brown School Rd.

Taylorsville Dam

Observation Deck

Bridgewater Rd.

Poplar Creek

Taylorsville Rd.

TAYLORSVILLE

Rip Rap Rd.

Park Entrance

0   1
mile

75

40

70

175

Englewood Metropark

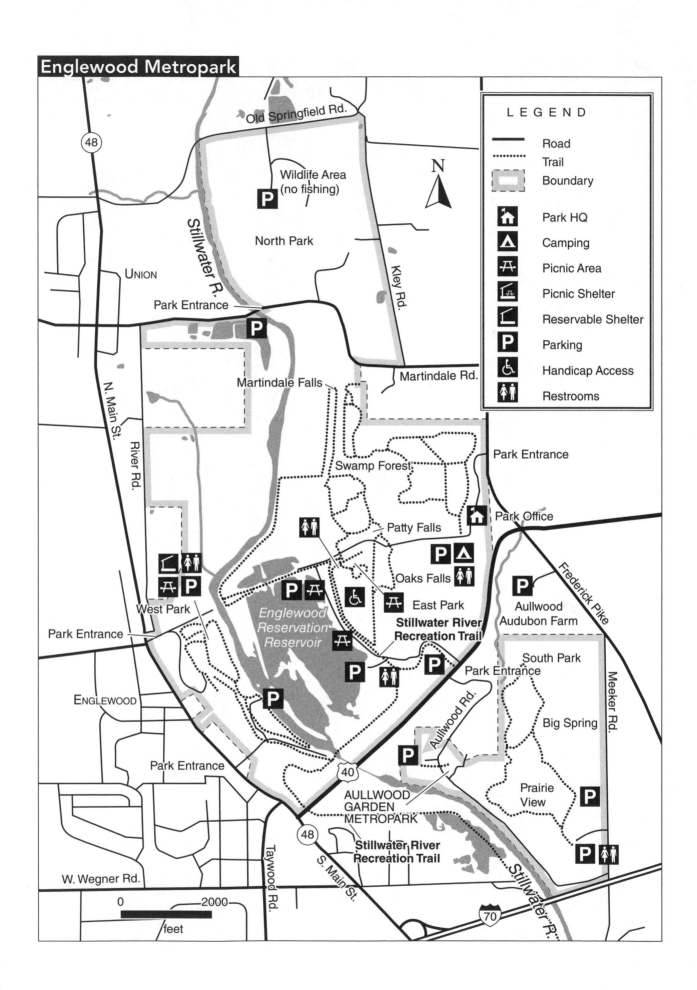

L E G E N D

——	Road
·····	Trail
▢	Boundary
🏠	Park HQ
⛺	Camping
🎪	Picnic Area
🏕	Picnic Shelter
◿	Reservable Shelter
P	Parking
♿	Handicap Access
🚻	Restrooms

Old Springfield Rd.

48

Wildlife Area
(no fishing)

North Park

Stillwater R.

UNION

Park Entrance

N. Main St.

River Rd.

Martindale Falls

Martindale Rd.

Swamp Forest

Park Entrance

Park Office

Patty Falls

Oaks Falls

East Park

Stillwater River
Recreation Trail

Aullwood
Audubon Farm

West Park

Englewood
Reservation
Reservoir

Frederick Pike

Park Entrance

ENGLEWOOD

Park Entrance

South Park

Big Spring

Meeker Rd.

Aullwood Rd.

Park Entrance

40

AULLWOOD
GARDEN
METROPARK

Prairie
View

48

Stillwater River
Recreation Trail

Stillwater R.

W. Wegner Rd.

0   2000

feet

Taywood Rd.

S. Main St.

70

Kley Rd.

Taylorsville Dam to Tadmor

Hiking distance: 2.6 miles round trip

Estimated hiking time: 1.5 hours

Take an easy walk while exploring the past along a scenic route.

Caution: The paved trail can get crowded.

Trail directions: Just after driving across the top of Taylorsville Dam from the east on U.S. Route 40, turn north, go past a canoe access road, and park in a small lot at N 39° 52.378, W 84° 10.083 (1). Follow the paved path north. The Buckeye Trail turns off on the right just after leaving the parking lot. The trail enters the woods and veers left at a sign marking the way to Tadmor at N 39° 52.404, W 84° 10.038 (2). The blue blazes through the woods follow the towpath of the Miami and Erie Canal, and the path runs parallel to the canal bed and the paved cycling and jogging path.

After 0.6 mile, the trail crosses a gravel road at N 39° 53.021, W 84° 09.578 (3). On the right, you can see fields showing the rich soil of the Great Miami River Valley. Reenter the mixed hardwood forest and gradually lose sight of the more crowded paved trail.

After another 0.7 mile of solitude, the trail crosses another gravel road and goes beneath a power line at N 39° 53.412, W 84° 09.533 (4). The Miami River is now visible on the right, and you have reached the outskirts of Tadmor. This town was once thought to have a bright future because it was located at the junction of the Miami River, the National Road, the Dayton and Michigan Railroad, and the Miami and Erie Canal. But much of the commerce was only temporary, and the building of Taylorsville Dam by the Miami Conservatory district after the flood of 1913 wiped out what was left of the town. If you reenter the woods on the Buckeye Trail here, the trail follows the river, and you'll pass signs that point out the former location of various town landmarks.

After exploring this sufficiently, return to point 4 and turn right on the road. At the top

of a short hill, the road meets the paved Great Miami River Recreational Trail at N 39° 53.428, W 84° 09.548 (5). Turn left here and follow the Great Miami River Recreational Trail back to point 1. Additional trails are located on the other side of the dam; this 13,000-acre park has 13 miles of trail.

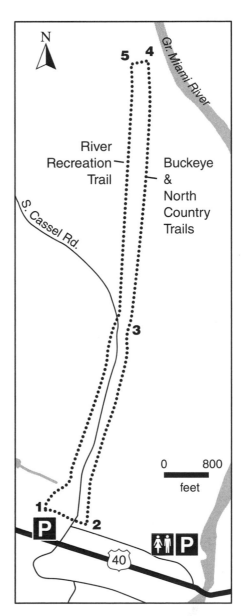

1. Lot
2. Buckeye Trail enters woods
3. Cross road
4. Tadmor
5. Return on Recreation trail

Englewood Metropark, White and Green Trails

Hiking distance: 2.4 miles

Estimated hiking time: 1.5 hours

Enjoy a hike that enables you to see three small waterfalls in a short span.

Caution: Be careful on precipices of the waterfalls.

Trail directions: Take State Route 48 north off Interstate 70 for 1 mile. Then turn right on U.S. Route 40 east and cross Englewood Dam. Just after crossing, turn right on the park road and bear right for 1 mile to the Patty Shelter. Park near the restrooms at N 39° 52.598, W 84° 17.103 (1). Cross the road at the junction of multiple trailheads and follow the white-blazed trail. This is just one of many trails; the 2,000-acre park has 12 miles of trail.

The white trail forks soon after entering the woods. Take the right fork, then veer left quickly when you see the sign marking the way to Martindale Falls. Follow the well-manicured trail through the mixed hardwood forest for 0.4 mile until the trail meets the green trail at N 39° 53.185, W 84° 17.156 (2). A sign here points out that the white trail now heads back toward the Stillwater River, so bear right on the green trail.

Follow the path uphill for about 0.5 mile until you arrive at Martindale Falls, which can be heard long before it is seen; this waterfall is located at N 39° 53.406, W 84° 17.101 (3). Enjoy the view from the bottom before turning and climbing a set of wooden stairs and a steep hill. Take a look at the falls from the top and then turn right to head back. After 0.5 mile, the green trail turns left as the yellow trail joins it at N 39° 53.178, W 84° 17.121 (4). On the right here, you will see some rare pumpkin ash trees. Cross a long boardwalk through a swamp forest and proceed for 0.4 mile until you arrive at Patty Falls at N 39° 53.053, W 84° 16.582 (5). The green trail turns left here, but first you should take a side trip to a platform below that offers a close-up view of the cascade.

Go another 0.1 mile and cross the main park road at N 39° 53.026, W 84° 16.532 (6). Reenter the woods and soon you'll come to Oaks Falls at N 39° 52.584, W 84° 16.505 (7). This is not as spectacular as the other two falls, but like the others, it can be heard before it's seen. Now, go downhill and veer right to a junction where the green trail turns right on a briefly paved surface at N 39° 52.561, W 84° 17.003 (8). Follow the green trail to the main park road at N 39° 53.031, W 84° 17.001 (9). Here the green trail turns left and returns to point 1, but before making this turn, you should check out the stone bridge on the right at this spot. This bridge was part of the original National Road that came through in the early 1800s. This road is now U.S. Route 40, but it had to be rerouted through here when the Englewood and Taylorsville Dams were built for flood control. The dams put parts of the original road under water, so Route 40 today goes around these parks and crosses over their dams.

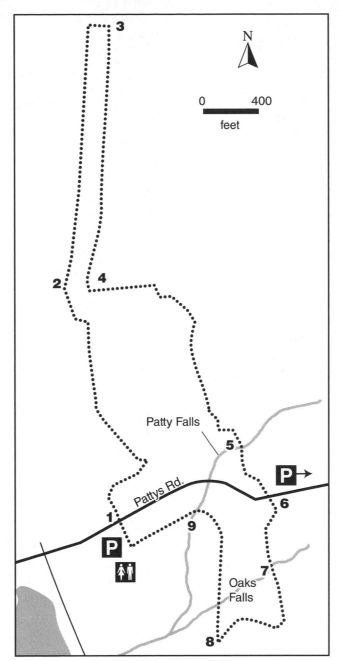

1. Lot
2. Junction
3. Martindale Falls
4. Junction
5. Patty Falls
6. Cross road
7. Oaks Falls
8. Paved section
9. Turn left at road

> Learn while you walk on the ceremonial grounds of an ancient people.

> Enjoy the views and wildlife high above the Little Miami floodplain.

> Take hikes on a series of interconnected trails that cover the region.

Area Information

Peaceful Fort Ancient is one of Ohio's best sites for mixing human and natural history. The park has an abundance of wildflowers and great views of the Little Miami Valley, and this area has been occupied for over 2,000 years. The "fort" is situated on a tree-covered ridge that rises 235 feet above the river, but it's not a military structure. It is an earthen embankment that snakes around for 3.5 miles and has hand-built walls that range from 4 to 23 feet in height. The nearly 70 openings in the fort walls indicate that earthworks had a ceremonial rather than military function. The fort was built by the Hopewell Indians, who moved to the area around 100 BC. Around 900 AD, the site was occupied by the Fort Ancient culture, who may have been the ancestors of the tribes who were here when European settlers established historic contact.

Today the site is a 768-acre state memorial with 126 acres within the perimeters of the original fort. The wooded area around the fort is thick with sugar maples, poplars, oaks, sassafras, and buckeyes. Several varieties of wildflowers are found in the meadow above the floodplain, including some rare species. And wildlife is abundant. Visitors may see deer (I saw three the afternoon I was there), foxes, raccoons, and large birds such as turkey vultures and red-tailed hawks.

A major attraction at Fort Ancient is the museum run by the Ohio Historical Society. With over 9,000 square feet of exhibits, the museum covers the 15,000 years of American Indian activity in the Mid-Ohio Valley. Nearby are gardens that display the kinds of crops grown by Ohio's original permanent settlers. The trails here are also part of a larger network. A steep side trail connects the fort to the Little Miami Scenic Trail, a 70-mile-long paved multipurpose path that is also a part of the Buckeye Trail. The Little Miami is also an ideal canoeing stream, and a livery is located nearby.

Directions: Take exit 36 off of Interstate 71. Follow the signs to State Route 350, which leads directly to the park entrance in 7 miles.

Hours open: Museum hours vary, but the park gates are unlocked only from 10 a.m. to 5 p.m. daily. However, trails can be accessed from the Little Miami Scenic Trail in all daylight hours.

Facilities: Restrooms and a gift shop are found in the museum. A picnic shelter is located near the Earthworks Trail. Group tours can be arranged.

Rules and permits: The museum charges admission, although it is free for members of the Ohio Historical Society. Pets on leashes are permitted.

Contact information: The address for Fort Ancient State Memorial is 6123 State Route 360, Oregonia, Ohio 45054. The phone number is 513-932-4421.

Other Areas of Interest

The Little Miami Scenic Trail, a 70-mile multiple-use path, is adjacent to Fort Ancient. A connector trail leads to it.

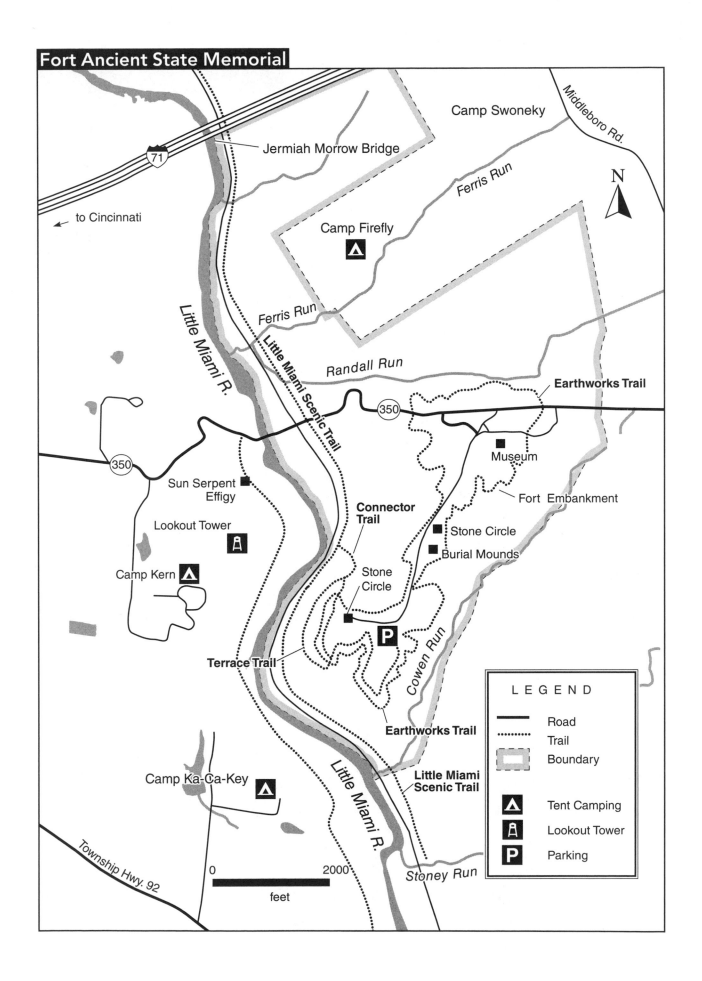

Fort Ancient State Memorial

to Cincinnati

Jermiah Morrow Bridge

Camp Swoneky

Middleboro Rd.

Ferris Run

Camp Firefly

Ferris Run

Randall Run

Earthworks Trail

Little Miami R.

Little Miami Scenic Trail

350

Museum

Sun Serpent Effigy

Fort Embankment

Lookout Tower

Connector Trail

Stone Circle

Burial Mounds

Camp Kern

Stone Circle

Terrace Trail

Cowen Run

Earthworks Trail

Little Miami Scenic Trail

Camp Ka-Ca-Key

Little Miami R.

Township Hwy. 92

0   2000

feet

Stoney Run

LEGEND

——	Road
····	Trail
▭	Boundary
⛺	Tent Camping
🗼	Lookout Tower
P	Parking

Earthworks Terrace and Connector Trails

Hiking distance: 1.5 miles

Estimated hiking time: 1 hour 15 minutes

Walk the perimeters of a "fort" that has been around for over 2,000 years.

Caution: The trail to the Little Miami River is very steep.

Trail directions: Take the main entrance off of State Route 350 and go past the museum on the main (paved) park road. Follow this until the road curves at a large parking lot at N 39° 23.984, W 84° 05.651 (1). This part of the earthworks is the South Fort, and the Earthworks Trail enters the woods across the road from the parking lot. Proceed about 0.3 mile along the side of the paved road to a platform at N 39° 24.032, W 84° 05.871 (2). This is the North Overlook, which offers a broad view of the Little Miami. From here, you can also see the Interstate 71 bridge across the river, which at 275 feet above water level is the highest bridge in Ohio.

From here, go right and head downhill. Almost immediately, you will come to the junction with the Little Miami Connector Trail at N 39° 24.079, W 84° 05.829 (3). Take a right on this trail—it is a drop of over 100 feet in 0.1 mile straight down to the river. Next to the river—at N 39° 23.143, W 84° 05.873 (4)—the trail meets the Little Miami Scenic Trail, a 70-mile paved stretch that runs from Milford to Springfield. This trail is part of the Buckeye and North Country Trails and is also widely used by joggers and cyclists. The river next to the trail is often crowded with canoes from nearby liveries.

The Little Miami River is often filled with canoeists as it flows past Fort Ancient.

Return back uphill to point 3 and turn right onto what is called the Terrace Trail. This trail follows beneath the ridgeline at the fort's openings and is still within earshot of river activity. Follow this path for 0.4 mile until the Terrace Trail reenters the fort at Pass Overlook at N 39° 23.860, W 84° 05.889 (5). Now you are back on the Earthworks Trail, which winds around the South Fort's perimeter. After

staying in the woods for almost 0.2 mile, the trail enters a meadow and turns to the right at N 39° 23.867, W 84° 05.771 (6). The South Overlook is just 0.1 mile away at N 39° 23.789, W 84° 05.780 (7). From here, you can enjoy another long-distance view, and sightings of larger birds are common. After enjoying the view, return to the trail for another 0.4 mile to point 1.

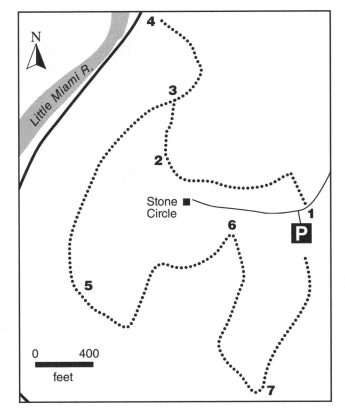

1. Lot
2. North Overlook
3. Junction
4. Little Miami Trail
5. Pass Overlook
6. Turn right
7. South Overlook

> View an unusually large biodiversity resulting from a geological oddity.

> Visit a 2,000-year-old Native American "fort."

> Get a good workout by hiking up to a spectacular view.

Area Information

Fort Hill has plenty to offer for naturalists, anthropologists, and recreational hikers. The area is situated at the junction of several geological regions, which has resulted in a wide diversity of flora and fauna. The location is at the edge of the Allegheny Plateau and just south of the glacial boundary; the Till Plains and Bluegrass Region are also nearby. This confluence has resulted in the flourishing of 675 different plant species in the 1,200-acre park, including 30 kinds of ferns. Some of these plants, such as the sullivantia and Canada yew, are rare and endangered species normally found far to the north. A wide array of birds visit the area, and in recent years, bobcats have also been seen here.

The human history of the park area is also intriguing. Fort Hill was constructed by natives of the Hopewell culture between 100 BC and 400 AD. The "fort" was most likely used for ceremonial rather than military purposes, even though its location on a hilltop some 400 feet above Baker Fork would seem to indicate a defensive purpose. Fort Hill is encircled by 1.5 miles of earthen walls that are 40 feet wide and range in height from 5 to 15 feet. The walls are considerably eroded now, but hikers can still find some of the 33 openings in the wall that are spread out among the 48-acre enclosure.

Modern-day hikers can get a good workout on Fort Hill's 11 miles of trail. The 400-foot climb from the parking lot to the fort entrance is a good start. And because Fort Hill is also along the Buckeye Trail, hikers can make this part of a long-distance experience. Three trails essentially form concentric rings around the hilltop enclosure. The Fort Trail is 2.3 miles long and goes straight to the top of Fort Hill right away. It is marked with red blazes. The yellow-blazed Gorge Trail is 4.1 miles long and follows along Baker Fork before going to the fort. The blue-blazed Deer Trail is 5.2 miles long and casts a wider net that includes Keystone Arch, a rare natural bridge. All three loop trails have a difficulty rating of three boots because of the steepness of the terrain.

Directions: To get to Fort Hill, take State Route 41 either 15 miles north from State Route 32 or 10 miles south from U.S. Route 50. Just south of the intersection of State Route 753, turn west on Fort Hill Road and go 0.5 mile to the parking lot.

Hours open: Fort Hill is open year-round in daylight hours.

Facilities: Restrooms and picnic shelters are located near the parking lot. In 1968, a museum was built to showcase the area's natural and human history (the hours vary).

Rules and permits: No permits are required for hiking.

Contact information: Fort Hill State Memorial is located at 13614 Fort HillRoad, Hillsboro, 45133; the phone number is 800-283-8905 or 937-588-3221.

Other Areas of Interest

Pike State Forest is a few miles east in Pike County. Paint Creek State Wildlife Area is 10 miles north, and Rocky Fork State Park is a similar distance to the northeast.

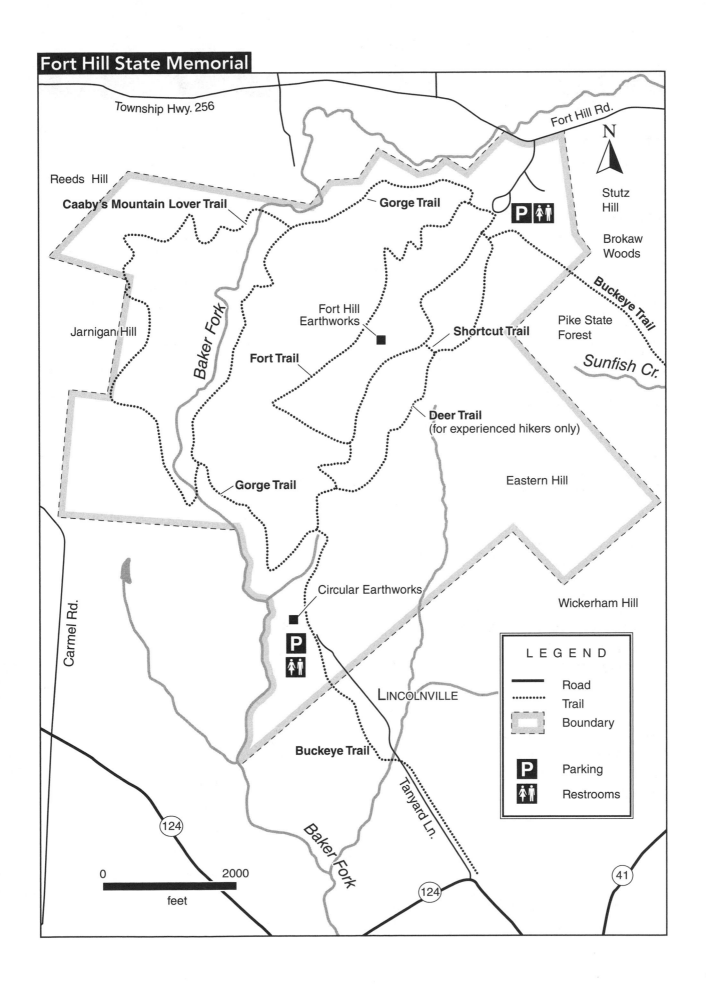

Fort Hill State Memorial

Township Hwy. 256

Fort Hill Rd.

Reeds Hill

Caaby's Mountain Lover Trail

Gorge Trail

Stutz Hill

Brokaw Woods

Jarnigan Hill

Baker Fork

Fort Hill Earthworks

Shortcut Trail

Fort Trail

Gorge Trail

Deer Trail
(for experienced hikers only)

Buckeye Trail

Pike State Forest

Sunfish Cr.

Eastern Hill

Circular Earthworks

Wickerham Hill

Carmel Rd.

LINCOLNVILLE

Buckeye Trail

Tanyard Ln.

Baker Fork

124

124

41

L E G E N D

— Road
······· Trail
Boundary
P Parking
Restrooms

0   2000
feet

Fort Trail

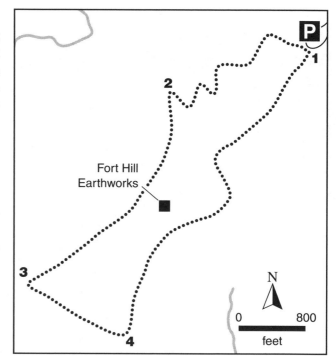 **Hiking distance:** 2.3 miles

Estimated hiking time: 1.5 hours

Take a strenuous hike on a beautiful ridge that was used by ancient peoples.

Caution: This trail is quite steep and starts out with a 400-foot climb in less than half a mile. Mosquitoes can also be a problem.

Trail directions: Go past the museum and park in the lot near the picnic shelters and restrooms at N 39° 07.298, W 83° 23.787 (1). At the southwest corner of the parking lot, you'll find a kiosk with trail information. Right behind this, the trail enters the woods and begins climbing immediately. The trail includes numerous switchbacks, and you will need to stop and rest frequently while climbing 400 feet in elevation.

Because of the strenuous nature of this climb, the heat of summer is not the best time to hike Fort Hill. A better time for this hike is in the winter (when the lack of leaves makes the ridge views more impressive), in the fall (when the foliage is spectacular), or in the spring (when a variety of wildflowers put on a stunning display).

After 0.5 mile of steady climbing, the trail levels out at N 39° 07.186, W 83° 24.112 (2). This is the entrance to the fort area, although the enclosure walls are barely visible. The trail now follows the ridge for another 0.5 mile before reaching the back end of the fort enclosure at N 39° 06.800, W 83° 24.479 (3). The valley below is sometimes visible from the mixed hardwood forest. The ancient Hopewell culture who built this enclosure left behind some barrow pits but few artifacts. It is believed that the Hopewell used their hilltop forts for ceremonial and religious purposes.

After lingering at the top for a suitable amount of time, you should begin the descent. The trail switches back and is not as steep as the ascent on the front end. In about 0.4 mile, the Fort Trail is joined by the Gorge Trail at N 39° 06.322, W 83° 24.230 (4). Turn left here; the two trails are concurrent for the 0.8 mile back to point 1.

1. Lot
2. End climb
3. Begin descent
4. Junction

> Explore a 1,000-acre private preserve that is unusually well developed.

> See abundant wildflowers, 400-year-old trees, limestone cliffs, and waterfalls.

> Visit the Yellow Springs that the local town is named after.

Area Information

Glen Helen Nature Preserve has been associated with Antioch University since 1929, when Antioch alumnus Hugh Taylor Birch donated the land in the name of his daughter Helen. And Antioch University, which is just across the street from Glen Helen, has been synonymous with its host village of Yellow Springs, a small town with a long history of progressivism.

The sites in Glen Helen go back much further than the ancient geological eras. The valleys found here were cut by glacial melt waters that also left behind limestone cliffs, dolomite columns, and granite boulders. The 1,000-acre preserve features 25 miles of hiking trails near the banks of Birch and Yellow Springs Creeks near the confluence with the scenic Little Miami River. In addition, the preserve includes the Yellow Springs that the village takes its name from. The orange and yellow color of this abundantly flowing spring comes from the iron found in the water.

Glen Helen has become inseparable from Antioch, and the school's most famous old building is across Corry Street from the Glen Helen parking lot. The school was established by forward thinkers who named innovative educator Horace Mann as the first president, and Antioch has been at the forefront of progressive politics ever since. In the 19th century, the college and community were a hotbed of abolitionist and Underground Railroad activity. This has resulted in Yellow Springs becoming a multicultural and avant-garde town located in a generally conservative part of the state. Noted children's author Virginia Hamilton and comedian Dave Chappelle are among those who once resided in Yellow Springs. After hiking the preserve, visitors can also find it entertaining to walk among the shops downtown.

Directions: Glen Helen is located off Corry Street in Yellow Springs. If you are entering the village from the north on State Route 68, turn left at the first light, and the Glen Helen lot will appear shortly on the left.

Facilities: At the northern end of the parking lot, visitors will find a nature center that includes a gallery. A museum is located near the trailhead; this museum offers interactive exhibits and also has restrooms and drinking water. A paved bicycle path also runs parallel to Corry Street.

Hours open: The preserve is open daily year-round from dawn to dusk. The museum and gallery hours vary according to season, so visitors should contact them ahead of time.

Rules and permits: Everything in the preserve is free. Pets must be leashed, and groups of more than 10 people are required to get permits.

Contact information: The preserve office is at 405 Corry Street, Yellow Springs, Ohio 45387. The phone number is 937-769-1902.

Other Areas of Interest

The Little Miami River Scenic Bikeway, an 85-mile-long route, passes nearby and has its northern terminus in the neighboring city of Springfield.

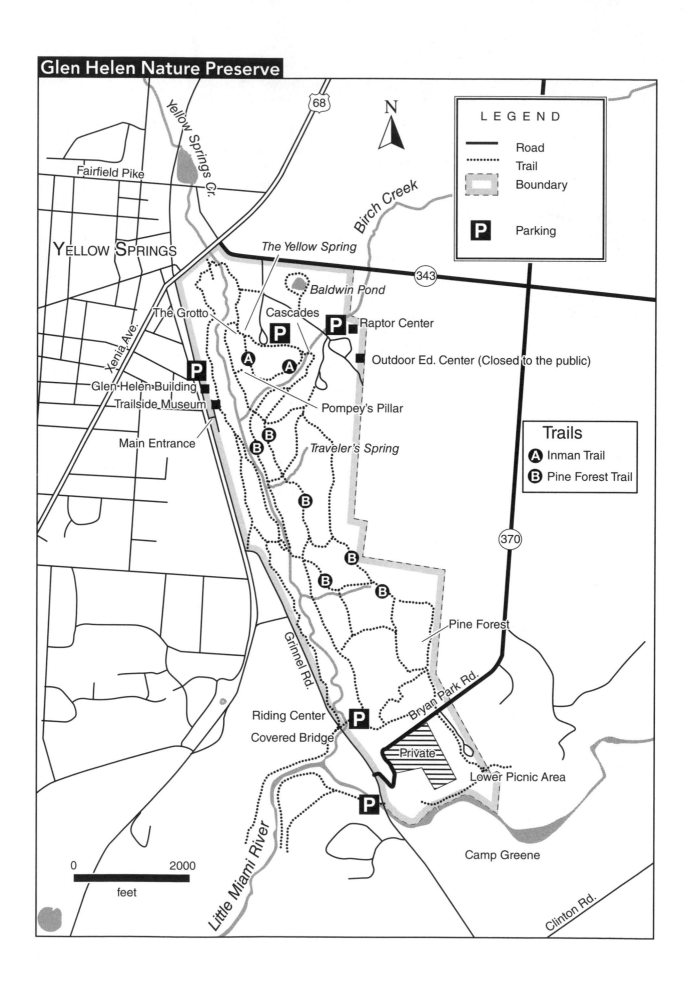

Glen Helen Nature Preserve

LEGEND

Road

Trail

Boundary

P Parking

Yellow Springs Cr.

US 68

N

Birch Creek

Fairfield Pike

YELLOW SPRINGS

The Yellow Spring

343

Baldwin Pond

The Grotto

Cascades

P

P Raptor Center

Xenia Ave.

Ⓐ

Ⓐ

Outdoor Ed. Center (Closed to the public)

P

Glen Helen Building

Trailside Museum

Pompey's Pillar

Main Entrance

Ⓑ

Traveler's Spring

Ⓑ

Trails

Ⓐ Inman Trail

Ⓑ Pine Forest Trail

Ⓑ

Ⓑ

370

Ⓑ

Ⓑ

Ⓑ

Pine Forest

Grinnel Rd.

Bryan Park Rd.

Riding Center

P

Covered Bridge

Private

Lower Picnic Area

0   2000

feet

Little Miami River

Camp Greene

Clinton Rd.

Glen Helen Natural Area

Hiking distance: 1.5 miles

Estimated hiking time: 1 hour

Hike to a spring and waterfall in one of Ohio's most interesting small towns.

Caution: The trail is rocky and can be slippery when wet.

Trail directions: Take State Route 68 south from Interstate 70 to the junction with State Route 343. Just south of this is the village of Yellow Springs. Cross the creek and turn left immediately at the first traffic light on Corry Street. You will soon spot the parking lot for Glen Helen on the left at N 39° 48.030, W 83° 53.078 (1). At the northern end of the lot, you will see a nature center and gallery. Enter the woods at the southern end of the lot and walk past the Trailside Museum, which features many interactive attractions.

After leaving the museum area, descend a stone staircase and cross Yellow Springs Creek on a wooden bridge. After 0.1 mile, the trail comes to a T intersection at N 39° 48.050, W 83° 53.003 (2). Take the left fork, and soon (on the right) you will see a unique dolomite column known as Pompey's Pillar. Continue on a clear path strewn with abundant wildflowers such as trillium, jack-in-the-pulpits, and Dutchman's breeches. The trail soon leaves the streambed and winds uphill. Just after a side trail comes in on the left, the trail comes to the Yellow Springs that give the town its name at N 39° 48.158, W 83° 53.023 (3). The yellowish rusty color comes from the high concentration of iron. The spring flows at a rate of 60 to 100 gallons per minute and was once believed to have healing powers.

Follow the wide path up past a kiosk that is devoted to the white oaks that are common here; in another 0.1 mile, you will pass a side road with a small parking lot. From here, it is just another 0.1 mile to the Cascades at N 39°

48.131, W 83° 52.475 (4). Cross the wooden bridge at the head of this scenic waterfall and start to loop back by taking a trail on the right. Follow along the other shore of Birch Creek and proceed downstream, taking time to note smaller cascades in the stream below. In 0.4 mile, you'll come to a four-way junction at N 39° 48.015, W 83° 52.567 (5). A right turn leads downhill to a stepping stone ford of the creek, and the path returns to the museum to complete a 1.5-mile hike. Continuing on straight leads to a covered bridge near where Yellow Springs Creek meets the Little Miami River, which makes for a nice 4.4-mile loop. On the return route to the museum, notice the large granite boulders strewn about by the glacier.

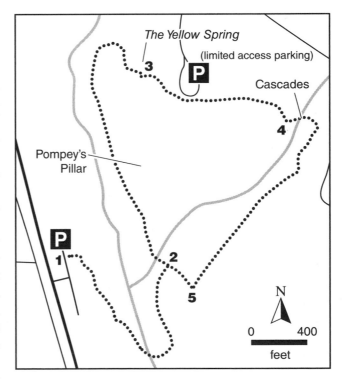

1. Lot
2. Junction
3. Yellow Spring
4. Cascades
5. Junction

> Walk where the ancients did through a prehistoric Native American fort.

> View two important rivers and their confluence from the hilltops.

> Interact with a wide variety of plant and bird life.

Area Information

This scenic ridge area near the confluence of the Great Miami and Ohio Rivers has been inhabited for over 15,000 years, going back to when nomadic Paleo-Indian hunters were here. More recently, Hopewell Indians built an earthen fort and burial mounds around 300 BC. And the Shawnee and Miami tribes were both living in the area when European settlers first arrived in the late 1700s. In modern times, Shawnee Lookout became one of the 21 parks in the Hamilton County Park District in 1967.

Shawnee Lookout occupies 1,515 acres and may be better known for its 18-hole golf course. The course clubhouse, known as Shawnee Centre, contains a pro shop, but it also contains a visitor center with archaeological exhibits pertaining to the original natives. The park also offers playgrounds, picnic areas, and a reservable shelter. Adjacent to the park, the Oxbow Wetlands is home to 270 bird species and also provides fishing opportunities and canoe access to the Great Miami River. In the park, visitors can also explore the Springhouse School and Log Cabin that show how the pioneers lived. Shawnee Lookout is host to a great variety of plant life. Among the common varieties found here are Virginia creeper, hawthorn, blue violet, wild grape, and pawpaw. Three good nature trails are located in the park, along with numerous interpretive signs explaining the natural and human history of the area.

Directions: Take U.S. Route 50 to the town of Cleves. Turn south on Nebo Road and turn right just afterward on Miami Street. This street becomes Lawrenceburg Road, which runs parallel to the Great Miami River. Follow this road for 4 miles to the park entrance on the left.

Hours open: The park is open daily from dawn to dusk.

Facilities: Numerous restrooms are provided throughout the park. The clubhouse for the golf course also has a snack bar.

Rules and permits: Pets are permitted in the park.

Contact information: The park is located at 2008 Lawrenceburg Road, North Bend, Ohio 45052. The phone number for the golf clubhouse is 513-941-0120. To contact the Hamilton County Park District, write to 10245 Winston Road, Cincinnati, Ohio 45231; you may also call 513-521-7275.

Park Trails

Blue Jacket Trail (offers views of the Great Miami River; named for Shawnee war chief Blue Jacket, who fought the Americans in the 1790s), 1.25 miles

Little Turtle Trail (offers views of the Ohio River; named for the Miamis' tribal war chief Little Turtle, who fought the Americans in the 1790s), 2.1 miles

Other Areas of Interest

Mitchell Memorial Forest is just a few miles away.

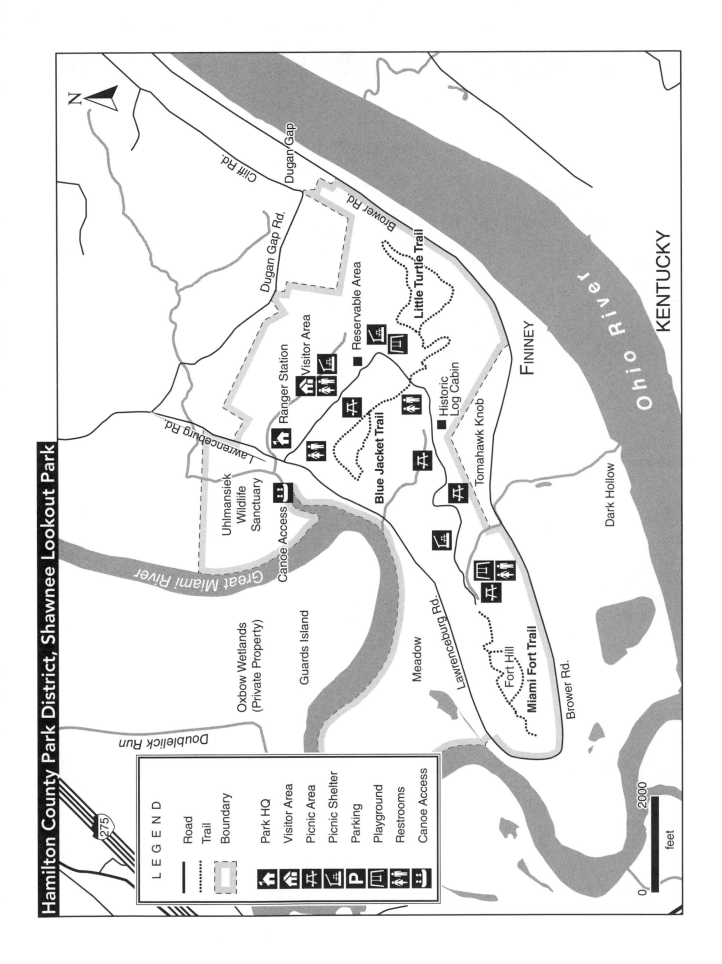

Hamilton County Park District, Shawnee Lookout Park

LEGEND

———	Road
....	Trail
☐	Boundary
	Park HQ
	Visitor Area
	Picnic Area
	Picnic Shelter
P	Parking
	Playground
	Restrooms
	Canoe Access

Oxbow Wetlands (Private Property)

Guards Island

Doubleick Run

Great Miami River

Uhlmansiek Wildlife Sanctuary

Canoe Access

Lawrenceburg Rd.

Ranger Station

Visitor Area

Reservable Area

Blue Jacket Trail

Little Turtle Trail

Historic Log Cabin

Tomahawk Knob

Meadow

Lawrenceburg Rd.

Fort Hill

Miami Fort Trail

Brower Rd.

Dark Hollow

FININEY

Dugan Gap

Dugan Gap Rd.

Cliff Rd.

Brower Rd.

Ohio River

KENTUCKY

N

0   2000

feet

Miami Fort Trail

Hiking distance: 1.5 miles

Estimated hiking time: 1 hour

Hike the same ridge that the ancients did and view a great river confluence.

Caution: The trail is hilly and can be wet.

Trail directions: The trailhead is found at the very end of the 2-mile-long road that runs the length of the park. A small lot is located in a cul-de-sac at N 39° 07.236, W 84° 48.520 (1). Enter the woods at the sign here and begin walking uphill. After about 0.1 mile, you'll see a sign marking the beginning of Fort Miami at N 39° 07.228, W 84° 48.673 (2). This "fort" is a clearing surrounded by low earthen walls that were built by the Hopewell Indians for ceremonial purposes around 300 BC.

Bear right along the ridge top, taking note of overlooks that offer a view of the Great Miami River to the west. After about 0.3 mile, the trail turns to the left at a barrow that the ancients used. Here you'll find a side trail at N 39° 07.145, W 84° 48.922 (3). The side trail leads directly to the Shawnee Lookout that gives the park its name. Follow this route for 0.2 mile until the trail ends at a bench at N 39° 07.048, W 84° 49.070 (4). Although the actual confluence of the Great Miami and Ohio is obscured, you can still get a clear view of Ohio, Indiana, and Kentucky from here. This is a spot that natives visited for centuries, although the Interstate,

railroad tracks, and power plants are new additions.

After soaking up the view, return to point 3 and continue on the loop trail. The forest growth is thick here and can be wet at times, but you will also see evidence (sometimes marked by signs) of ancient native activity. In a little over 0.2 mile—at N 39° 07.144, W 84° 48.719 (5)—you'll come to a memorial for David Carter Beard, the first national scout commissioner for the Boy Scouts of America. In another 0.1 mile, the trail completes its loop and returns to point 2. From here, you can retrace the route down to the parking lot.

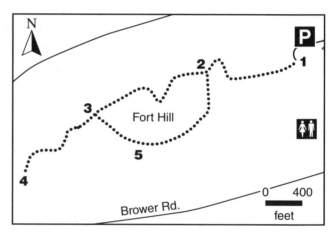

1. Lot
2. Sign
3. Junction
4. Lookout
5. Memorial

> Take a short pleasant walk at a secluded spot on the Ohio River.

> Learn about a number of interesting historical characters with a connection to this remote site.

> Pay respects to the first U.S. president to die in office.

Area Information

Harrison Tomb State Memorial is a remote, peaceful spot on a quiet stretch of the Ohio River west of Cincinnati. This area was supposed to have been the location of a great river city, but the town at the north bend of the river never developed. However, this is the site of the tomb of one American president and the birthplace of another.

William Henry Harrison is the president who's buried in the Harrison Tomb. The ninth U.S. president came to the Cincinnati area as a teenage soldier. After serving as General Anthony Wayne's aide in the Fallen Timbers campaign when the American army defeated the Indians in 1794—thereby making Ohio safe for settlement—Harrison married the daughter of a prominent landowner and began a political career. He served as governor of the Indiana

❙ North Bend is the grave site of one U.S. President and the birthplace of another.

Territory and a successful general in the War of 1812 before returning to his home here at North Bend. In 1840, he was elected to the presidency after a spirited campaign. However, while giving the longest inaugural address of any president, the 68-year-old Harrison caught cold and later died of pneumonia just one month into his term. He was the first president to die in office, and his body was interred here with great fanfare.

Harrison's home at North Bend is no longer standing, but this home was the birthplace of another U.S. president. Harrison's grandson Benjamin was born here in 1833. The connection between these generations is John Scott Harrison, the only man to be both the son and a father of a president. He is also buried here in the family vault, although his body was briefly stolen by grave robbers in 1878 before being recovered. And just across the road from the impressive 60-foot-high memorial, visitors will find Congress Green Cemetery, which contains the grave of Judge John Symmes, Harrison's father-in-law and the first owner of much of the land in southwest Ohio.

Today, this site is maintained by the Ohio Historical Society. Harrison's Tomb sits atop a hill that offers a view of a bend of the Ohio River that is opposite the northernmost point in Kentucky. A short nature trail goes into the woods behind the tomb and ends in a parking lot filled with kiosks explaining the history of the site. Across a side road is Congress Green Cemetery, which served as a family plot until 1861.

Directions: Harrison's Tomb is in North Bend, 20 miles west of Cincinnati, just off U.S. Route 50. You should exit Route 50 at Cliff Road and turn left on Brower Road, which crosses over the highway. The memorial is on the right just after you cross the highway.

Hours open: The memorial is open in daylight hours from March through December.

Facilities: The site has no public restrooms, but there is a drinking fountain. The tomb has steps and is not handicap accessible.

Rules and permits: The park closes at dusk. Pets are permitted.

Contact information: The address of Harrison's Tomb is William Henry Harrison Memorial, located at the intersection of Cliff Road and Brower Road, U.S. Highway 50, North Bend, Ohio 45052; however, no one is on site. For information, contact the Harrison Symmes Memorial Foundation, 110 Spring Street, Cleves, Ohio 45002; the phone number is 513-941-3744.

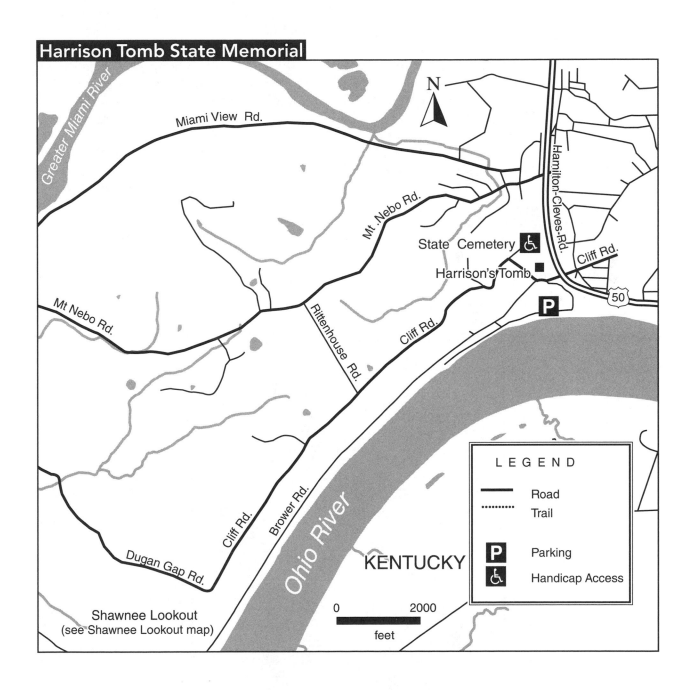

Harrison Tomb State Memorial

Greater Miami River

Miami View Rd.

Mt. Nebo Rd.

State Cemetery ♿

Harrison's Tomb ■

Mt Nebo Rd.

Rittenhouse Rd.

Cliff Rd.

Cliff Rd.

Hamilton-Cleves Rd.

50

Cliff Rd.

Brower Rd.

Dugan Gap Rd.

Ohio River

KENTUCKY

Shawnee Lookout
(see Shawnee Lookout map)

P

N

LEGEND

——	Road
••••••••	Trail
P	Parking
♿	Handicap Access

0   2000
feet

Harrison Tomb State Memorial Trail

Hiking distance: 0.6 mile

Estimated hiking time: 30 minutes

Take a short stroll through American history.

Trail directions: Park in the lot with the kiosk at N 39° 09.076, W 84° 45.139 (1). The nature trail enters the woods just behind the information kiosk. This trail goes into a woods of towering oaks for 0.1 mile before coming out at the base of the tomb at N 39° 09.048, W 84° 45.101 (2). This location includes a smaller parking lot with a handicap space and a drinking fountain. Climb the steps here to the tomb, which is located at N 39° 09.052, W 84° 45.062 (3). The remains interred inside the tomb include those of William Henry Harrison, his wife (Anna Symmes Harrison), and

several of their children, including John Scott Harrison, father of Benjamin Harrison. The front of the tomb also offers a good view of the Ohio River.

Return the way you came to point 1. Then cross the side street to Congress Green Cemetery at N 39° 09.075, W 84° 45.250 (4). Walk around the perimeter of the cemetery, which features the graves of veterans of both the Revolutionary and Civil Wars. In the center of the cemetery is the grave of Judge John Symmes, William Henry Harrison's father-in-law. Symmes was the original owner of the land between the Little and Great Miami Rivers. He anticipated that North Bend would be the site of the region's great city, but Cincinnati turned out to be the location of that city. Return from here to the parking lot.

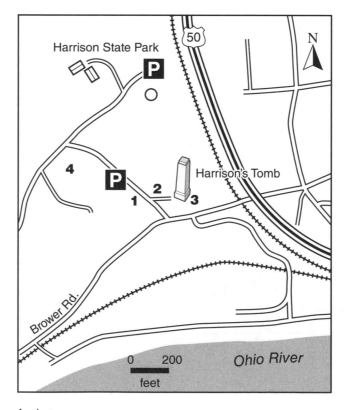

1. Lot
2. Base of tomb
3. Tomb
4. Cemetery

> Visit southeast Ohio's only remaining old-growth forest.

> Enjoy the waters of Lake Acton, along with its variety of bird and fish life.

> Sample both the solitude of a state nature preserve and the activity of a busy state park.

Area Information

In an area that is surprisingly hilly, it is even more surprising to know that Hueston Woods was once part of an ocean. Over 400 million years ago, this region was covered by a shallow sea that ran over the dolomite limestone bedrock. Today, fossil remnants of sea life are still found here. After the sea had eroded away and the glaciers had visited, a rich and fertile soil developed over the area.

It was this soil that attracted Matthew Hueston, a soldier who served in the Indian Wars of the 1790s that resulted in the Native Americans losing their homeland to the encroaching pioneers. Hueston was the original buyer of this land, which he and his descendants farmed until the 1930s. However, the family spared a grove of maple trees from the plow and used them for making syrup. After the last of the Huestons passed away, the State of Ohio purchased the land in 1941 and designated it as a state forest. Additional land nearby was later purchased, a man-made lake was created, and Hueston Woods was made a state park in 1957. In 1973, the original 200-acre parcel of virgin timber was separated with the designation of State Nature Preserve. This stand of original growth is unique in an area where 95 percent of the original forest has been replaced by farm fields or urban areas. In addition to maples, this parcel also contains an abundance of beech trees, which make up 44 percent of the canopy, as well as white ash trees. The area also features a wide array of ferns, fungi, and wildflowers. In terms of wildlife, Hueston Woods is best known for its diversity of birds. In addition to the larger varieties such as wild turkey, pheasant, and grouse, visitors can also see numerous woodpeckers, bobwhite, and assorted songbirds. A bird banding station is located along the shores of Acton Lake, and bird watchers can be found here throughout the year.

State nature preserves in Ohio usually contain few, if any, facilities or amenities, but the state park of the same name that surrounds this preserve more than makes up for this. The high point of this preserve is the 94-room Hueston Woods Lodge that overlooks Acton Lake. The lodge, which is open year-round, has a dining room, snack bar, gift shop, swimming pools, tennis courts, game room, and meeting rooms. The park also has nearly 40 cottages available for rental. For campers, Hueston Woods contains nearly 500 campsites; about half of them offer electricity. An equestrian camp and a group camp area are also included in the park.

The state park offers a great variety of outdoor recreation opportunities. In addition to a 1,500-foot swimming beach, the park has 132 boat docks available at the 625-acre Acton Lake, although there is a 10-horsepower limit. The park also has miniature, disc, and regular golf courses; volleyball; horseshoes; archery; basketball; and a variety of winter sports. A nature center that emphasizes local bird life and fossils is also located in the park. And the park contains 10 picnic areas with tables and grills as well as 11 short hiking trails.

Directions: Hueston Woods is located off of State Route 732 just 5 miles north of Oxford. From the main park entrance just west of State Route 177, proceed a half mile and then go left and follow the lake shoreline for 2 miles.

Hours open: Both the nature preserve and state park are open year-round.

Rules and permits: Pets are permitted in the state park but not in the state nature preserve.

Facilities: The preserve offers restrooms in the Sugar House area.

Contact information: The park office is located at 6301 Park Office Road, College Corner, Ohio 45003. The phone number is 513-523-6347.

Other Areas of Interest

Rush Run Wildlife Area is just a few miles to the east, and Pater Lake Wildlife Area is a few miles south.

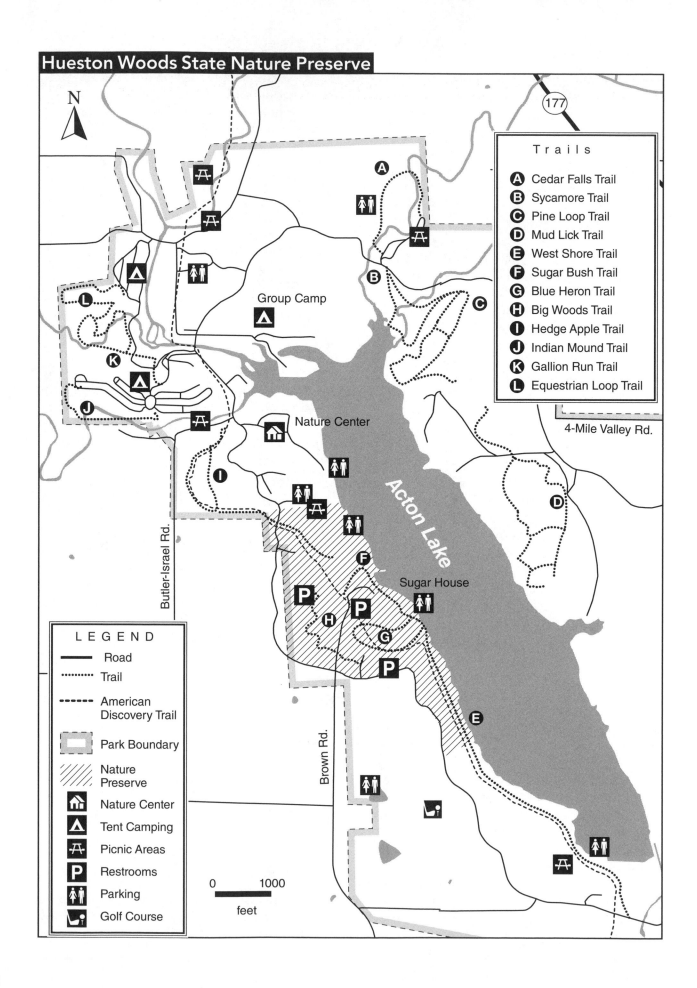

Hueston Woods State Nature Preserve

N

(177)

Trails

A Cedar Falls Trail
B Sycamore Trail
C Pine Loop Trail
D Mud Lick Trail
E West Shore Trail
F Sugar Bush Trail
G Blue Heron Trail
H Big Woods Trail
I Hedge Apple Trail
J Indian Mound Trail
K Gallion Run Trail
L Equestrian Loop Trail

Group Camp

Nature Center

Acton Lake

Sugar House

4-Mile Valley Rd.

Butler-Israel Rd.

Brown Rd.

LEGEND

—— Road
········· Trail
- - - - American Discovery Trail
Park Boundary
Nature Preserve
Nature Center
Tent Camping
Picnic Areas
P Restrooms
Parking
Golf Course

0   1000

feet

Big Woods and Sugar Bush Trails

 Hiking distance: 2.2 miles round trip

Estimated hiking time: 1.5 hours

Hike on a surprisingly hilly trail in an area of old-growth forest.

Caution: This trail runs along and through some streams and can get muddy.

Trail directions: Drive along the main loop road to the lot for the Big Woods Trail at N 39° 34.470, W 84° 45.680 (1). The trail heads into the woods on the right and begins to descend almost immediately. After the fourth bridge in a series of bridges at N 39° 34.258, W 84° 45.579 (2), the trail comes alongside a creek. It then follows this stream for 0.1 mile before fording at N 39° 34.168, W 84° 45.616 (3). Next, the trail climbs uphill for 0.1 mile before coming out on Brown Road at N 39° 34.162, W 84° 45.463 (4).

Go left along this paved road past a small parking lot with a kiosk. Bear to the right and in 0.1 mile you'll come to a sign on the right for the Sugar Bush Trail at N 39° 34.247, W 84° 45.418 (5). Head back into the forest; a turnoff for the Blue Heron Trail will appear in less than 0.1 mile at N 39° 34.217, W 84° 45.355 (6). Ignore this diversion and continue on in the woods. This portion of the trail is not far from a bird banding center, and you might see birders actively engaged in such activity.

Continue for another 0.3 mile past a pair of side trails until you arrive at a junction with the West Shore Trail at N 39° 34.209, W 84° 45.097 (7). Bear left and follow the shoreline of Acton Lake, the man-made lake at the center of the park and preserve. In less than 0.1 mile, you'll reach the Sugar House, where restrooms are located at N 39° 34.271, W 84° 45.121 (8). This location also includes a parking lot, picnic tables, and a side trail that leads to a peninsula with good views of the lake.

Now cross the end of Brown Road and follow the lakeshore for another 0.1 mile. At this point, the trail turns up the hill at N 39° 34.327, W 84° 45.210 (9). Leave the shore and start to climb uphill. In 0.1 mile, you'll come to a side trail that leads to the public beach at N 39° 34.327, W 84° 45.308 (10). Continue past this for another 0.1 mile until you arrive at Brown Road; you'll be on the other side of the road from point 5. From here, retrace your route 0.7 mile back to the Big Woods parking lot.

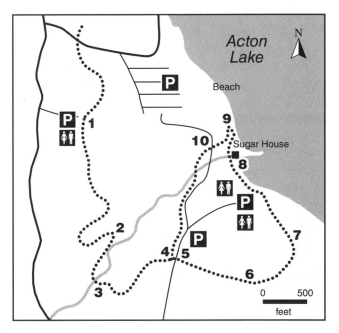

1. Lot
2. Bridge at creek
3. Ford creek
4. Cross road
5. Reenter woods
6. Junction
7. Lakeshore
8. Sugar House
9. Turn and ascend
10. Junction

> Hike above the spectacular gorge of the Little Miami River.

> Walk among the slump blocks and plant diversity along the shore of a designated scenic river.

> Wander through a region steeped in pioneer history.

Area Information

Clifton Gorge State Nature Preserve is a 268-acre parcel located on the canyon of the scenic Little Miami River. This small preserve is located between John Bryan State Park and the village of Clifton. The steep dolomite and limestone gorge was designated a National Natural Landmark in 1968. The preserve basically follows a 2-mile stretch of the Little Miami State and National Scenic River. Parking is at the eastern end of the preserve in the village of Clifton. Just a quarter mile away is the historic Clifton Mill, a water-powered grist mill known for its spectacular Christmas lights display.

The rest of this riverside tableau is located in adjacent John Bryan State Park, named for the man who bequeathed his farm to the state. This 752-acre park features some of the best plant diversity in Ohio—more than 341 species of wildflowers are found here. The Little Miami drops 130 feet through bedrock layers within the park boundaries, which makes for some unusual rock formations. Also, 90 varieties of birds are known to visit the park. In another time, the area was home to the Shawnee Indians and was part of the Pittsburgh-Cincinnati stagecoach line.

Today's park has a campsite with 10 electric and 50 nonelectric sites; all sites are equipped with picnic tables and fire rings. A group camp area for up to 100 people can be reserved, and a day use lodge can be rented. The park has four picnic areas, including one with a shelter house. Nine hiking trails—and two more that also permit bicycles—are located within the park. The Little Miami is an excellent stream for canoeing and fishing. Visitors will also find areas for sledding, cross-country skiing, and rock climbing and rappelling.

Directions: John Bryan State Park is on State Route 370 off of State Route 343 between the village of Clifton and Yellow Springs.

Facilities: Clifton Gorge has no facilities, but John Bryan has the full range available at most state parks.

Hours open: Both the park and the preserve are open year-round in daylight hours.

Rules and permits: Pets are permitted at any site in John Bryan, but they are forbidden in Clifton Gorge Nature Preserve. Fishing is also not permitted at Clifton.

Contact information: Clifton Gorge is located at 2331 State Route 343, Yellow Springs, Ohio 45387; however, for information you should contact the Division of Natural Areas and Preserves at 2045 Morse Road, Building C-3, Columbus, Ohio 43229. The phone number is 614-265-6561. John Bryan is located at 3790 State Route 370, Yellow Springs, Ohio 45387; but the park is administered from Buck Creek State Park, 1901 Buck Creek Lane, Springfield, Ohio 45507. The phone number is 937-767-1274 or 927-322-5284.

Other Areas of Interest

Buck Creek State Park is in nearby Springfield, and Little Miami State Park follows the banks of the river farther downstream.

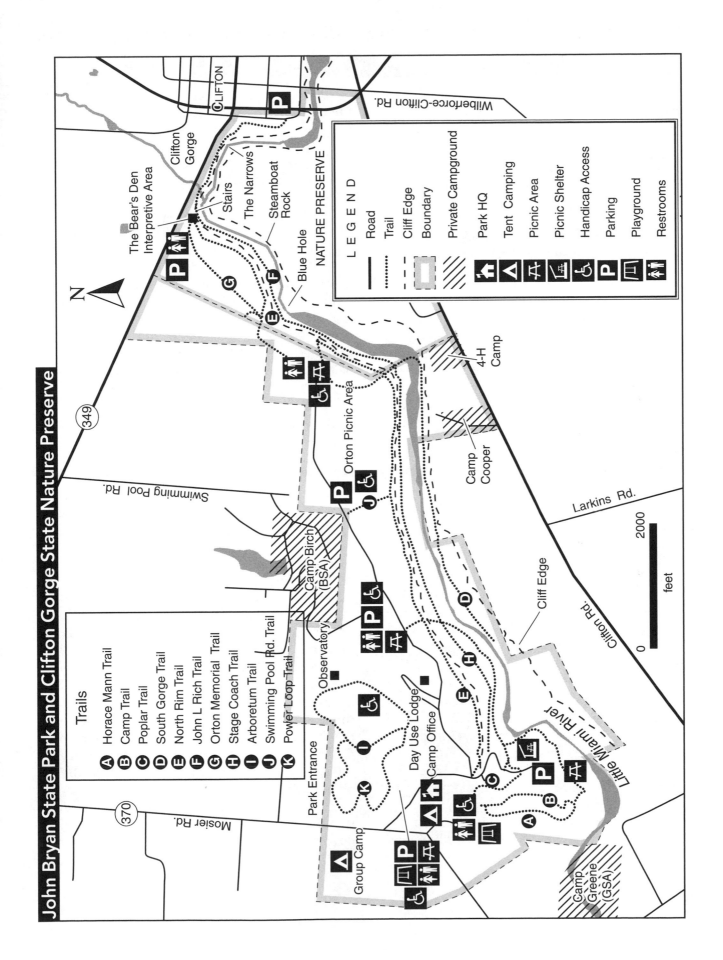

John Bryan State Park and Clifton Gorge State Nature Preserve

Trails

Ⓐ Horace Mann Trail
Ⓑ Camp Trail
Ⓒ Poplar Trail
Ⓓ South Gorge Trail
Ⓔ North Rim Trail
Ⓕ John L Rich Trail
Ⓖ Orton Memorial Trail
Ⓗ Stage Coach Trail
Ⓘ Arboretum Trail
Ⓙ Swimming Pool Rd. Trail
Ⓚ Power Loop Trail

LEGEND

—	Road
⋯	Trail
▦	Cliff Edge
⸺	Boundary
▨	Private Campground
🏠	Park HQ
⛺	Tent Camping
⛱	Picnic Area
🏕	Picnic Shelter
♿	Handicap Access
P	Parking
🎪	Playground
🚻	Restrooms

CLIFTON

Clifton Gorge

The Bear's Den Interpretive Area

Stairs

The Narrows

Steamboat Rock

Blue Hole

NATURE PRESERVE

Wilberforce-Clifton Rd.

Swimming Pool Rd.

Mosier Rd.

Park Entrance

Group Camp

Day Use Lodge

Camp Office

Observatory

Camp Birch (BSA)

Orton Picnic Area

4-H Camp

Camp Cooper

Cliff Edge

Larkins Rd.

Clifton Rd.

Little Miami River

Camp Greene (GSA)

370

349

2000

0

feet

201

John Bryan State Park Trail

Hiking distance: 5.1 miles round trip

Estimated hiking time: 3 hours

Hike past a canyon and stream that visitors have marveled at since before pioneer times.

Caution: A combination of slopes, rocks, and water makes this one trail where you need to tread carefully.

Trail directions: The town of Clifton, birthplace of Buckeye icon Woody Hayes, is located about 6.5 miles south of Springfield on State Route 72. The most notable site in town today is the huge red Clifton Mill, best known for the Christmas lights show that is put on there every year. In the past, several mills were located here at the headwaters of the Little Miami River, but this 1802 tourist attraction and restaurant is the only one standing today. Take a good look around before proceeding one block west to the Clifton Gorge parking lot at N 39° 47.698, W 83° 49.707 (1).

A kiosk is located at this spot; the kiosk gives some information about the human and natural history of the area. After entering the preserve, you'll encounter several overlook points where you can view the Little Miami running far below you. Although the chasm across the river seems pretty small, you wouldn't want to have to jump it. But that's what Cornelius Darnell had to do in 1778. Darnell was captured by Shawnee warriors in Kentucky that year and had been taken to the area. Among his fellow captives was Daniel Boone, who managed to escape and warn Boonesborough of impending attack. Darnell escaped separately, but he was discovered and chased to this spot where he made a 22-foot leap to safety. A plaque marks the spot.

Continue on in this area called the Narrows for 0.4 mile; you will then come to a highway bridge at N 39° 47.938, W 83° 49.928 (2). Keep on the route past another parking lot, and at 0.56 mile, you will reach a staircase at N 39° 47.948, W 82° 20.073 (3). Take these stairs for a 100-foot descent to the riverbank. The plant life changes in this area, and over 20 kinds of ferns are found here, along with 350 varieties of wildflowers and over 105 species of trees and shrubs.

As you follow along the riverbank, you will be on a stagecoach route that ran from Pittsburgh to Cincinnati in the 1800s. Along the dolomite columns around you, you will see a slump-block cave and several large rock formations in the river. The largest of these is Steamboat Rock at 0.7 mile into your hike—located at N 39° 47.820, W 83° 50.140 (4). This landmark and many others include explanatory plaques, as well as a wooden deck overlook. Continue another 0.2 mile to the scenic spot known as the Blue Hole at N 39° 47.719, W 82° 50.329 (5). This scene was the subject of a landscape painted in 1851 by Robert Duncanson, one of the first African-Americans to make a living as an artist. The painting is in the Cincinnati Museum of Art today.

At 1.15 miles, you will come to a bridge across the Little Miami at N 39° 47.498, W 87° 50.475 (6). This spot also marks the end of Clifton Gorge Nature Preserve and the beginning of John Bryan State Park. The only difference for hikers is that dogs are not permitted in Clifton Gorge. The trail here goes on both sides of the river, but for best results, you should cross over here to the southern shore. The trail on this side goes a little higher up on the hillside, but the river is usually still visible. Continue on this side for about 1.3 miles and then recross the river on a bridge at N 39° 47.143, W 82° 51.651 (7).

A variety of side trails are available in John Bryan, but for this hike, you should proceed downstream on the north bank for another quarter mile. Here you can get off the trail at N 39° 97.083, W 83° 51.830 (8); this is a spot that offers water, shelter, and restrooms. After taking a break, retrace your route to point 7, but this time continue on the north shore along the river. Continue on this route for another mile until you come to point 6 at the junction of Clifton Gorge and John Bryan. From here, you can retrace your route for another 1.25 miles back to Clifton Mill, where you can enjoy a well-earned meal.

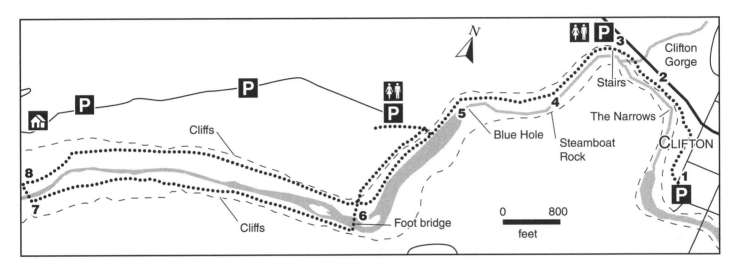

1. Lot
2. Highway bridge
3. Staircase
4. Steamboat Rock
5. Blue Hole
6. Cross bridge
7. Recross river
8. John Bryan

> Visit a dozen sites in a well-maintained smaller park system.
> View Charleston Falls, the tallest waterfall in southwestern Ohio.
> See rare plants, rock formations, and fossils in an undisturbed habitat.

Area Information

The Miami County Park District always tries to do things the right way. Established in 1967, the district maintains a dozen sites that total only about 2,000 acres, but these sites are all well maintained. The park district passed a levy in 2001 and has used this tax base to wisely develop its facilities. The trails are well cleared, and signs and maps are provided at major intersections. Boardwalks and platforms have been constructed to limit the human impact on natural habitat while still providing ample viewing opportunities. Even the split-rail fences at Charleston Falls are made from black locust trees that were found on the preserve.

Charleston Falls Preserve is the gem of the Miami County Park District. This 216-acre parcel is tucked away in a crowded area, but you won't be aware of development nearby. The highlight here is Charleston Falls, a 37-foot waterfall that flows over similar rock strata to Niagara Falls. Platforms above and below the falls offer ample opportunity to view the spectacle. These falls, just a mile east of the Great Miami River, have been well known for a long time, judging from the ancient Indian mounds, fire pits, and artifacts found nearby. The falls originate from small underground springs to the east, and the waters flow over fossilized sea creatures (such as trilobites) that are embedded in the limestone base.

An example of the many boardwalks found in Charleston Falls Preserve.

The Charleston Falls is not the only attraction found here, however. Many uncommon wildflowers—such as wild columbine, walking fern, purple cliff brake, and rock honeysuckle—can be seen here. The preserve also includes a planted tallgrass prairie and an observation tower that offers an excellent view. Near the falls is a small but deep circular cave in a limestone wall face. And visitors can also see Cedar Pond, a stocked lake that is so clear that the sign for it is written backward so it can only be read in the reflected water of the pond. All of these sites are connected by nearly 4 miles of clearly labeled trail. Other park activities include cross-country skiing, nature and campfire programs, hands-on environmental education, and picnicking.

Directions: From State Route 202, take Rose Road west and go for about a mile. You will see the signs that mark the parking lot for the preserve.

Facilities: Modern full-service restrooms are located at the parking lot, and picnic tables are nearby. The special structures at the preserve include an observation boardwalk at the falls, a wildlife observation deck at the pond, and a viewing platform at the prairie.

Hours open: The park is open from 8 a.m. to sunset every day of the year.

Rules and permits: To preserve the integrity of the natural habitat, visitors are asked to stay on the trails and to refrain from removing natural materials. Dogs must be on a leash.

Contact information: The Miami County Park District office is located at 2645 East State Route 41, Troy, Ohio 45373; the phone number is 937-335-6273. The address for Charleston Falls Preserve is 2535 Ross Road, Tipp City, Ohio 45371.

Other Areas of Interest

The Brukner Nature Center, a private preserve on the Stillwater River, is about 5 miles west of Troy.

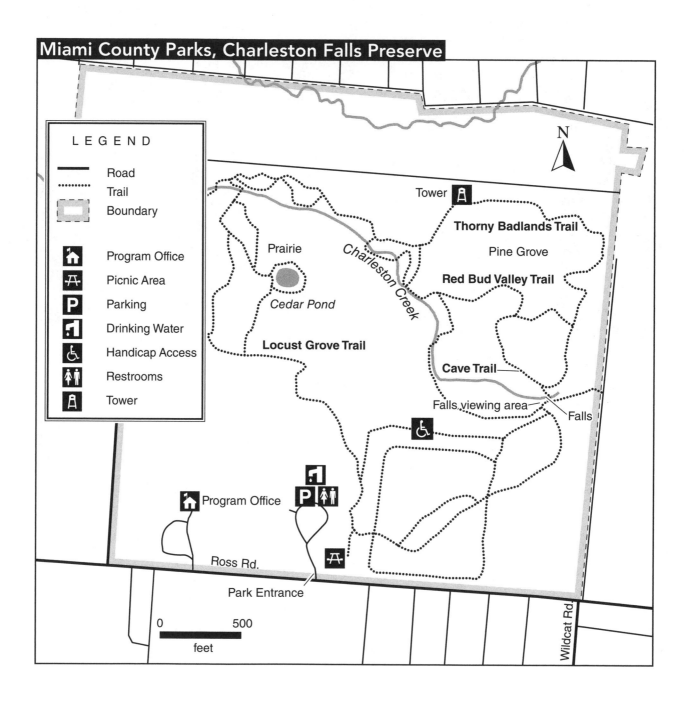

Miami County Parks, Charleston Falls Preserve

LEGEND

—— Road
·········· Trail
Boundary

Program Office
Picnic Area
Parking
Drinking Water
Handicap Access
Restrooms
Tower

N

Tower

Thorny Badlands Trail

Pine Grove

Prairie

Charleston Creek

Red Bud Valley Trail

Cedar Pond

Locust Grove Trail

Cave Trail

Falls viewing area

Falls

Program Office

Ross Rd.

Park Entrance

Wildcat Rd.

0   500

feet

Charleston Falls Preserve Trail

Hiking distance: 1.6 miles

Estimated hiking time: 1 hour

View waterfalls, rock formations, and a pristine pond in a well-maintained park.

Caution: Stay on trails around rock formations.

Trail directions: Take State Route 202 north from Interstate 70 for 4 miles to Ross Road. Turn left and go 1 mile; the preserve parking lot is on the right. Park near the full-service restrooms and go to the trailhead kiosk at N 39° 54.576, W 84° 08.530 (1). Go left at the sign pointing the way to the falls. A fork appears right away; take the right branch to go directly to the falls.

Follow the wide gravel Main Trail for 0.3 mile to where it crosses a short wooden bridge at N 39° 55.030, W 84° 08.387 (2). This is the top of 37-foot Charleston Falls, the highest waterfall in southwest Ohio. Just ahead is an overlook that offers a view from the top that is worth the side trip. Enjoy this view and then return to point 2 and take the wooden steps down to the falls.

The falls were created when Charleston Creek eroded the limestone down to the shale that was left over from when this area was under a shallow sea. Savor the view from the platform at the bottom and then continue on the trail; almost immediately, you'll come to a limestone cave at N 39° 55.055, W 84° 08.390 (3). The Cave Trail ends in less than 0.2 mile when it climbs and meets the Cliff and Redbud Valley Trails at N 39° 55.088, W 84° 08.400 (4). Turn left and follow the Redbud Valley Trail. Follow this route down a hill and over a boardwalk for 0.2 mile until it meets the Main Trail at N 39° 55.137, W 84° 08.480 (5). These trails are not blazed, but there

are signs and maps at all major intersections that make it difficult to get lost.

Turn left on the marked Main Trail and continue through a forest of oak, maple, and hickory. This area also contains many kinds of wildflowers, such as hepatica, wild columbine, and mayapple. After 0.3 mile, you will cross Charleston Creek on a wooden bridge and come to the junction with the Prairie Path at N 39° 55.159, W 84° 09.022 (6).

Turn left here and go 0.1 mile to a short path that leads right to Cedar Pond at N 39° 55.110, W 84° 08.592 (7). This small, cattail-ringed pond is so clear that a sign labeling it is written backward so it can only be read in the reflection in the water. But beneath the placid water, largemouth bass can be found.

Return to the Prairie Trail junction, but now turn left to continue back to the Main Trail, which appears in 0.1 mile at N 39° 55.068, W 84° 09.004 (8). Turn left here and follow the trail for 0.3 mile back to point 1.

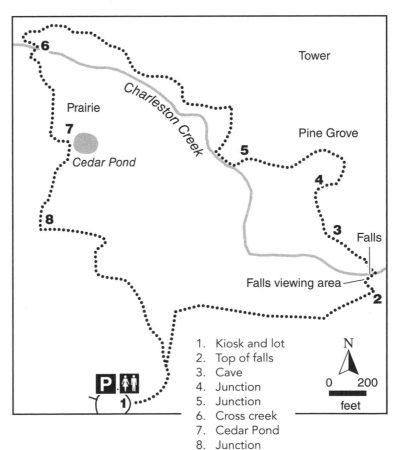

1. Kiosk and lot
2. Top of falls
3. Cave
4. Junction
5. Junction
6. Cross creek
7. Cedar Pond
8. Junction

> Follow the Buckeye Trail along the historic route of the Miami and Erie Canal.

> View the sites connected with the earliest conflict between natives and settlers.

> Visit an Indian museum and an early farmhouse, and ride on a canal boat.

Area Information

The route chosen for the Miami and Erie Canal was significant long before the canal was built. In 1752, a stockade near Piqua built by English fur traders was destroyed by French-led renegades in the first recorded battle on Ohio soil. During the American Revolution, Kentucky-bound Indian raiding parties would head upstream on the Maumee and Auglaize Rivers, then portage their supplies over the hump between the Lake Erie and Ohio River watersheds. Then they would stop at a trading post run by French trader Peter Loramie, then head downstream on Loramie Creek and the Great Miami.

Kentuckians on counterraids would run this route in reverse, and in 1782, troops under George Rogers Clark destroyed Loramie's store. During the Indian Wars of the 1790s, a new trading post was built by James Girty, a member of a notorious family of renegades, at the northern end of the portage in present-day St. Marys. Anthony Wayne's men destroyed this post in 1794, and Wayne subsequently built forts at Piqua, Fort Loramie, and St. Marys in order to supply his troops by a water route. When it came time to build canals, the same considerations of geography led to the canal following the same general route.

Today, the Ohio Historical Society's gateway site of Piqua encompasses this colorful early era. Visitors to this 250-acre site can visit a museum devoted to the Eastern Woodland Indians, ride on a 70-foot-long replica of a working canal boat, and tour the original 1820s brick farmhouse of Indian agent and canal commissioner John Johnston. An Indian mound earthwork is also on the site, as well as a marker for the original 1752 fort and battle site. Remnants of a canal lock can be found above the museum, and Lockington is located a few miles north. Lockington is another Ohio Historical Society site that shows the remains of a multiple-lock system at the highest elevation along the canal route. And, as so often is the case, these historical locations are connected by the Buckeye Trail that follows the route of the canal.

Directions: The Johnston Farm and Piqua Historical Area are located north of Piqua. Take State Route 66 northwest out of town and turn right on Hardin Road. The parking area will soon appear on the right.

Facilities: Restrooms and a gift shop are located at the museum.

Hours open: The trail and the Lockington Locks sites are always open. The museum is open only in summer from 10 a.m. to 5 p.m., Thursday through Sunday.

Rules and permits: Visitors are asked to stay on the trail and to stay off private property.

Contact information: The Johnston Farm and Indian Agency is located at 9845 North Hardin Road, Piqua, Ohio 45356. The phone number is 937-773-2522.

Other Areas of Interest

Lake Loramie State Park is just a few miles to the north, while the Stillwater Prairie Preserve (administered by the Miami County Park District) is 8 miles west of Piqua. Just above Lockington is the 200-acre Lockington Preserve, which has hiking trails and lock remains near a reservoir.

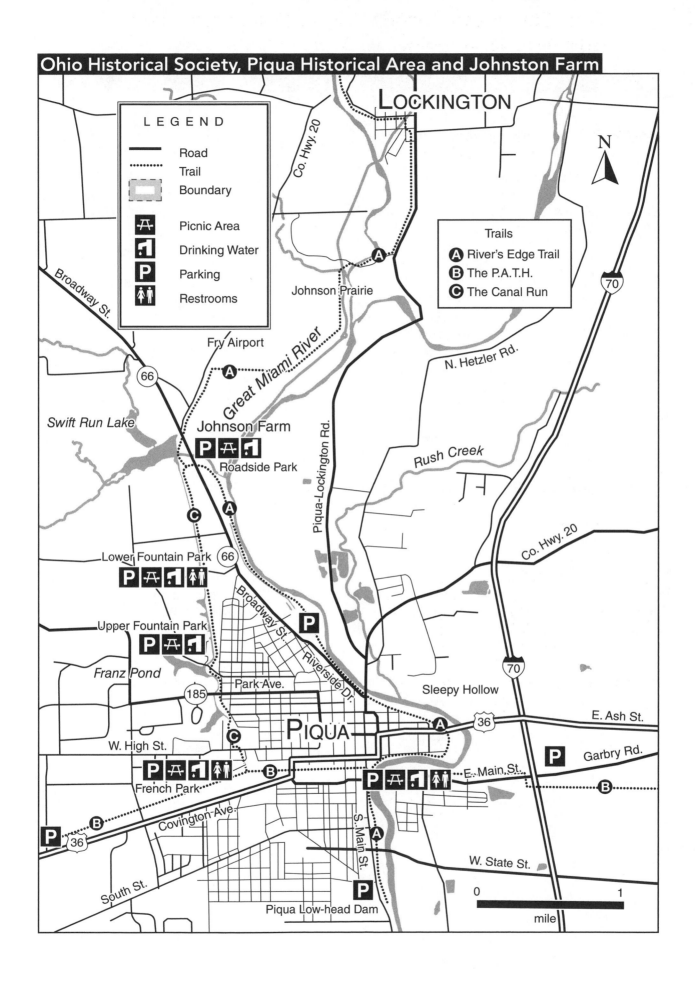

Ohio Historical Society, Piqua Historical Area and Johnston Farm

LEGEND

— Road
...... Trail
Boundary
🏕 Picnic Area
💧 Drinking Water
🅿 Parking
🚻 Restrooms

LOCKINGTON

Co. Hwy. 20

N

Trails
Ⓐ River's Edge Trail
Ⓑ The P.A.T.H.
Ⓒ The Canal Run

Johnson Prairie

Fry Airport

70

N. Hetzler Rd.

66

Great Miami River

Swift Run Lake

Johnson Farm

🅿🏕💧

Roadside Park

Rush Creek

Ⓐ

Ⓒ

Piqua-Lockington Rd.

Co. Hwy. 20

Lower Fountain Park

🅿🏕💧🚻

66

Broadway St.

🅿

70

Upper Fountain Park

🅿🏕💧

Riverside Dr.

Sleepy Hollow

Franz Pond

185

Park Ave.

Ⓐ

36

E. Ash St.

W. High St.

Ⓒ

PIQUA

🅿

Garbry Rd.

🅿🏕💧🚻

Ⓑ

🅿🏕💧🚻

E. Main St.

Ⓑ

French Park

Ⓑ

Covington Ave.

S. Main St.

Ⓐ

36

W. State St.

🅿

South St.

🅿

Piqua Low-head Dam

0   1

mile

Broadway St.

Piqua to Lockington on the Buckeye Trail

 Hiking distance: 7 miles round trip

Estimated hiking time: 3.5 hours

Hike along the waterways that spawned so much of early Ohio history.

Caution: The trail follows public highways, so be alert for traffic.

Trail directions: Take State Route 66 for 0.7 mile north of Piqua, turn right on Hardin Road, and go 0.3 mile to the Ohio Historical Society parking lot at N 40° 10.576, W 84° 15.371 (1). Near the lot, you'll see the original 1815 farmhouse of Indian agent John Johnston and an 1808 double-penned log barn that is still used. Johnston first saw this area as a teenage wagoner with Anthony Wayne's army, and he swore he would one day build a house at the site of an excellent spring he found here. As an Indian agent who was trusted by all natives, Johnston held a conference here that helped keep Ohio-based tribes neutral during the War of 1812. The farmhouse today is open for tours led by costumed docents.

Continue on to the museum, which is designed to resemble a blockhouse from Fort Piqua. The museum specializes in American Indian life and has restrooms and a gift shop. Next, find the blue blazes in the mowed area of the northwest corner of the historical area. Behind the museum, a 1-mile stretch of the Miami and Erie Canal has been rebuilt. These small waters are plied by the General Harrison, a 70-foot-long canal boat run by costumed crews.

When you get to the towpath, turn left and head upstream. In about 0.4 mile, the trail passes the remains of Lock 8, which is as far as the General Harrison goes. Just above this, you'll come to a dam on the Great Miami River that is just below where Loramie Creek joins the river. The trail turns north at this point. To the left, you'll see the original site of Fort Pickawillany, the first structure built in Ohio by English-speaking white men. Before 1750, the French enjoyed an exclusive trade relationship with the Native Americans of Ohio, but a chief known as Old Britain invited British traders to his village here. The British offered such competition that a French-led force of Indians attacked and burned the trading post in 1751. The traders escaped, but Old Britain was boiled and eaten.

The trail now runs parallel to a township road as well as the canal, and it eventually comes out at Landman Mill Road at N 40° 11.399, W 84° 14.295 (2). The trail then follows the road across Loramie Creek at the site of the old 1851 Loramie Mill. In 0.3 mile, the trail turns left on a paved county road at N 40° 11.429, W 84° 14.106 (3). It stays on the road for another 0.8 mile. The Buckeye Trail stays on public land whenever possible, but sometimes it is forced to follow public roads.

After entering the village of Lockington, the trail breaks off and winds up at a set of locks on Museum Street at N 40° 12.288, W 84° 14.056 (4). The Ohio Historical Society has a marker here, and the whole set of locks is on the National Register of Historic Places. This marks the beginning of the highest stretch along the canal, so many locks were needed here. The canal was not completed until 1845, and within 10 years it was threatened by railroads; the system was never used after the 1913 flood. But the efforts made on this massive undertaking are memorialized here. The Miami and Erie Canal ran for 249 miles and required 105 locks and 22 aqueducts between Toledo and Cincinnati. It was said that there was one dead worker for every 6 feet of canal.

After exploring the locks here, you can return via the same route for a 7-mile hike (unless you have a second car waiting here).

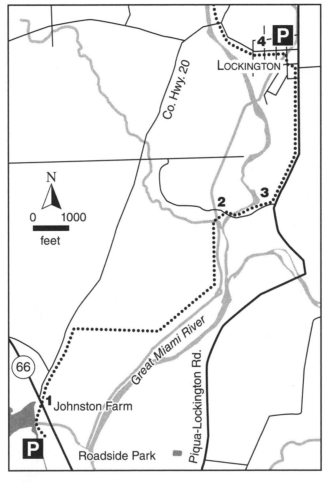

1. Lot at Johnston Farm
2. Meet road
3. Left on road
4. Lockington Locks

> Make one of the steepest climbs of any Ohio trail.

> Be rewarded with a spectacular view of a long stretch of the Ohio River.

> Visit a tiny preserve that contains three of only a handful of Ohio's natural bridges.

Area Information

Although not offering much of a hike in the traditional sense, Raven Rock is a climb that any outdoor-loving Buckeye should make. Located within sight of where the Scioto River enters the Ohio River, the top of this preserve offers a sweeping view of the Ohio River Valley nearly 500 feet below. This tiny preserve consists of only 95 acres and offers what may be the most challenging climb in the state—but the view makes it worth the effort.

Raven Rock was dedicated as a state nature preserve in 1994 by naturalist Charles Asa Brown, but the spot was well known long before that. It is said that the Shawnee tribe used this vantage point for planning assaults on boatloads of settlers coming down the Ohio during the late 18th century. The spot where they stood was Raven Rock Arch, one of a small number of natural arches found in Oho. There are two others in the cliff face below Raven Rock, which makes this preserve the most densely packed collection of natural bridges in the state.

Raven Rock State Nature Preserve offers a great view of the Ohio River 500 feet below.

Directions: Raven Rock is located just west of downtown Portsmouth. From where U.S. Routes 23 and 52 meet at the mouth of the Scioto River, take 52 West for less than a mile. A small parking lot is opposite West Portsmouth High School.

Hours open: The preserve is open year-round during daylight hours.

Facilities: None. There are plaques at the summit but no other markers or amenities of any kind.

Rules and permits: As with all state nature preserves, there is no camping, fires, or pets permitted. Removing any plants is forbidden. Obtain permission before hiking.

Contact information: There is no mailing address or phone number for Raven Rock. To discuss anything, contact the Ohio Department of Natural Resources Division of Natural Areas and Preserves at 2045 Morse Road, Building C-3, Columbus, Ohio 43229. The phone number is 614-265-6561.

Other Areas of Interest

There are several other nearby attractions also discussed in this book, such as Shawnee State Park and the Edge of Appalachia Preserve. Brush Creek State Forest is also nearby on the border of Scioto and Adams counties.

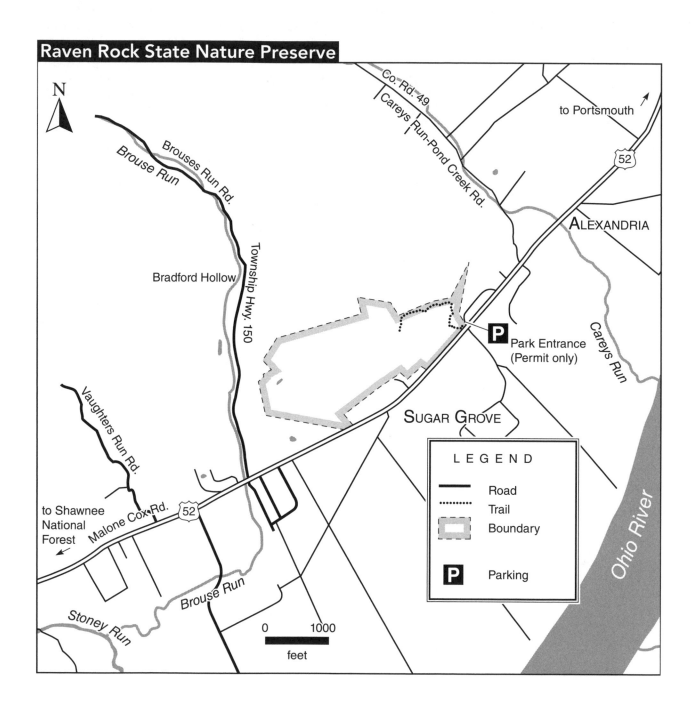

Raven Rock State Nature Preserve

N

Brouses Run Rd.
Brouse Run
Bradford Hollow
Township Hwy. 150
Vaughters Run Rd.
to Shawnee National Forest
Malone Cox Rd.
52
Stoney Run
Brouse Run

Co. Rd. 49
Careys Run-Pond Creek Rd.
to Portsmouth
52
ALEXANDRIA
P Park Entrance (Permit only)
Careys Run
SUGAR GROVE
Ohio River

LEGEND
———— Road
••••••• Trail
Boundary
P Parking

0   1000
feet

Raven Rock Arch

Hiking distance: 0.6 mile

Estimated hiking time: 1 hour

Make a short but rugged climb to one of the best vistas around.

Caution: This trail is extremely steep, so use caution in both ascending and descending.

Directions: Park by the sign in the small parking lot at N 38° 43.138, W 83° 00.057 (1). Enter the woods and begin climbing immediately on a series of switchbacks. After 0.2 mile is a rock where you can rest at N 38° 43.189, W 83° 00.183 (2). You have already climbed 170 feet in altitude, and this is a good spot to look out at the river valley below.

Here the switchbacks end and the trail heads straight up the cliff. You will need to stop and rest along the way, but in another 0.1 mile the trail levels out at N 38° 43.126, W 83° 00.280 (3). The altitude here is 980 feet, which represents a climb of nearly 500 feet in less than a third of a mile—a grade that is steeper than many mountain trails. There are some explanatory plaques here, but the main attraction is the view.

On the left you can see the confluence of the Scioto and Ohio rivers and downtown Portsmouth when the leaves are off. Across from the spot, West Portsmouth High School campus blends into the Ohio River, with the hills of Kentucky beyond. The spot commands an extensive view of the Ohio for miles, and it's easy to see how useful an observation point this once was. The natives who used this spot stood on Raven Rock Arch, a natural arch that is part of the rock formation that gives the preserve its name. It is only 15 feet long and is as narrow as 14 inches at one end. There are two other natural arches on this cliff face that can't be reached.

Take plenty of time to soak in this view before returning down the same route. Be particularly careful on the return trip. It took us 37 minutes to climb to the top but only 14 minutes to career back down the trail.

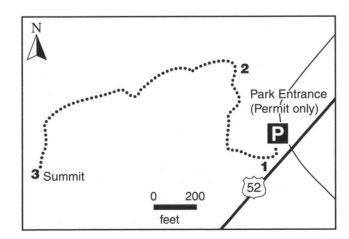

1. Lot
2. Resting place rock
3. Raven Rock

> Follow along near a route used by Native Americans and pioneers.

> Hike among steep hills and enjoy long-range views.

> See a variety of birds and other wildlife.

Area Information

Scioto Trail State Park gets its name from the path used by human navigation for hundreds of years. The route alongside the Scioto River has also been referred to as the Warrior's Path. In ancient times, the Adena and Hopewell cultures settled in this region, and they left their mounds throughout Ross County. More recently, native tribes such as the Shawnee used this route when white men arrived. The Shawnee traveled south along the river to their hunting grounds in Kentucky, and they could also follow the river north toward the headwaters of the Sandusky River and then on to Lake Erie. The white pioneers followed this path north from Kentucky when settling Ohio in the late 18th century.

This route was easy to follow because it was generally flat. One exception was right here, on the boundary between Mississippian and Devonian bedrock just south of where the glacier stopped. The countryside here is more rugged and typical of southern Ohio. The steep hillside features the usual oak and hickory forests. Common wildflowers found here include spring beauties, Dutchmen's breeches, blue phlox, and geranium. Many kinds of ferns, mosses, and lichens are among the sandstone, and the park is a great spot for morel mushrooms. The park is also ideal for birders, with wild turkeys, ruffled grouse, pileated woodpeckers, and even whippoorwills among the usual finds. Common woodland creatures like deer, raccoon, and fox mingle with the more exotic black bear and bobcat.

The first purchase for public land here was in 1922, but it was during the Depression that the Civilian Conservation Corps built the roads, lakes, and other recreational facilities. As is the case with many Ohio state parks, Scioto Trail is adjacent to a state forest of the same name. The Scioto Trail Park and forest combine to 9.616 acres, but it is the park that contains the amenities. Among these are two small lakes that allow electric motors only and have their own campgrounds. Stewart Lake has a primitive hike-in campground with 18 nonelectric sites, while Caldwell Lake has a boat ramp and a 55-site campground, 40 of which are equipped with electricity. Caldwell Lake also has a store with snacks and boat rentals that is open on summer weekends. All campsites have latrines, picnic tables, and fire rings. There is a small waking beach at Caldwell Lake. The park also has 17 miles of bridle trails and two camper cabins for rental.

Directions: Scioto Trail State Park is off U.S. Highway 23 between Chillicothe and Waverly. Take 23 to just north of the Ross and Pike County line and turn east on State Route 372, which becomes Stoney Creek Road. Go past Stewart Lake and turn left on Forest Road 3 to the park office.

Facilities: The park has three scenic picnic areas with tables and grills and two shelters that can be reserved. There are restrooms at both Caldwell and Stewart Lakes and a playground and courts at Caldwell Lake.

Hours open: The park is open year-round in daylight hours.

Rules and permits: Pets are permitted at all sites. Hunting is permitted in the state forest but not the state park.

Contact information: The park is located at 144 Lake Road, Chillicothe, Ohio 45601, but the administrative mailing address is Tar Hollow State Park, 16396 Tar Hollow road, Laurelville, Ohio 43135; the phone number is 740-887-4818.

Other Areas of Interest

Lake White State Park is to the south, just south of Waverly; to the west is Pike Lake State Park.

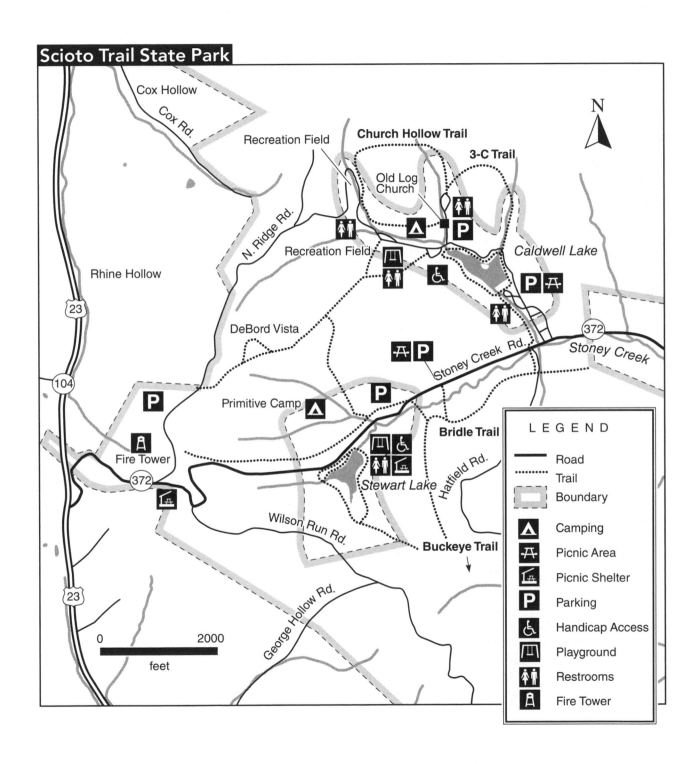

Scioto Trail State Park

Caldwell and Stewart Lake Loop

Hiking distance: 2.7 miles

Estimated hiking time: 1.5 hours

Take a strenuous but scenic hike in a secluded park.

Caution: This trail is very steep and has uneven surfaces.

Trail directions: Take Stoney Creek Road through the center of the park and turn north at the park office. Just ahead on the left is the parking lot for Caldwell Lake at N 39° 13.655, W 82° 57.009 (1). Park here at the dam where there are also restrooms and walk around the west side of this small lake. The gazebo on an island in the lake can be reserved for events.

After 0.3 mile, the trail comes to the main campground at N 39° 13.792, W 82° 57.302 (2). A sign here marks the trail route and there are restrooms. Also near here is a log replica of the Presbyterian Church that was the first church in the area. Follow the sign directions and begin climbing a steep grade. The trail is unblazed but easy to follow. After a climb of 0.4 mile and 300 feet in altitude is a trail junction at N 39° 13.617, W 82° 57.712 (3).

Veer to the left here and follow a ridge line for about 0.1 mile to another junction at N 39° 13.590, W 82° 57.783 (4). A sign here notes that a right turn leads to a fire tower that is part of a longer loop, so turn left and head toward Lake Stewart. Follow the ridge for another 0.3 mile and take time to appreciate the views. The trail then begins to drop off steeply, and the uneven footing as it drops straight down can be dangerous. I fell down here on a dry November day, and I can only imagine how treacherous this stretch can be when wet.

Once the trail levels off, it crosses a stream and twists around a meadow before crossing Stoney Creek Road at N 39° 13.200, W 82° 57.544 (5). This is the parking lot for Stewart Lake, and there are restrooms here. The lake is actually out of sight on your right, but a short walk will take you to its shores. Reenter the woods on the south side of the road and turn left, following Stoney Creek as it flows toward the Scioto River just a few miles to the east. In about 0.1 mile, the trail is joined by the Buckeye Trail at N 39° 13.180, W 82° 57.469 (6). The Buckeye Trail skirts the southern portion of the park, but for the next mile the blue blazes get interspersed with the white blazes of a bridle trail as the two routes cross.

After following the stream for about 0.6 mile, the trail comes to Forest Road 5 (Hatfield Road) at N 39° 13.389, W 82° 56.843 (7). From here it is easier to follow the road, particularly in wet weather. Turn left and follow Hatfield Road for a quarter mile to the junction with Stoney Creek Road at N 39° 13.493, W 82° 56.695 (8). Almost immediately is the park road turnoff at the park office that will take you back to point 1.

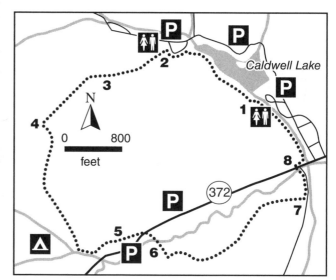

1. Caldwell Lake lot
2. Campground
3. Climb to junction
4. Veer left at junction
5. Cross road at Stewart Lake
6. Join Buckeye Trail
7. Meet road
8. Intersect main road

> Visit one of only two Indian effigy mounds within Ohio's borders and the longest effigy mound in North America.

> View a site used by natives over a thousand years ago.

> Appreciate the views of the hilly landscapes of southern Ohio.

Area Information

The site of Serpent Mound State Memorial is unique in many ways. For one thing, the view from the plateau overlooking Ohio Brush Creek is spectacular, offering a long-range view of an area affected by an underground gas explosion several thousand years ago, which resulted in types of rock not normally found in the area. But the Serpent Mound itself is the attraction that is most impressive—a low mound in the shape of a snake that is a quarter mile long and was apparently used by ancient natives for ceremonial purposes.

Serpent Mound was first thought to have been built by the ancient Adena culture approximately 2,000 years ago. Indeed, some conical Adena mounds are located at the site. However, recent evidence has indicated that the mound is "only" 1,000 years old and was built by the more recent Fort Ancient culture. The earthwork depicts a wriggling snake with an open mouth that is about to swallow a large oval. It was built by laying out stones in a pattern and then covering them, first with yellow clay, and then with soil. The mound is about 4 feet high and 20 feet across at the base. The purpose of the mound remains unknown; however, the fact that certain features align with celestial features, such as solstices, indicates that the illiterate culture had an extensive knowledge of astronomy.

The observation tower at Serpent Mound State Memorial offers an excellent overview of the effigy mound built by prehistoric tribes.

Many Indian mounds in Ohio were plowed over by early settlers, but fortunately, Serpent Mound avoided that fate. In 1887, Harvard archaeologist Frederick Ward Putnam excavated the site and realized its significance. Putnam displayed artifacts from the mound and raised funds for Harvard to purchase the site. Harvard deeded the property to the State of Ohio in 1900 with the stipulation that public access must be allowed. Today, Serpent Mound is operated by the Ohio Historical Society and the Arc of Appalachia Preserve System. A World Heritage site, the mound is visited by people from all over the globe. On the grounds today, visitors will find a museum and gift shop that stresses the Native American culture. The site also includes a 25-foot-high tower that offers a good view of the layout of the mound.

Directions: Serpent Mound is located on State Route 73, just 4 miles west of its junction with State Route 41 in Locust Groves. Abundant signage is provided in the area.

Hours open: The park is open year-round in daylight hours. The museum is open from 10 a.m. to 5 p.m. seasonally; the museum charges a parking fee, although it is free for members of the Ohio Historical Society.

Facilities: Public restrooms and a picnic shelter are located near the parking lot. The museum offers a gift shop as well as displays and artifacts, and numerous special events are held on the grounds. A 25-foot-high tower offers a unique view.

Rules and permits: Visitors are asked to keep off the mound and to stay on the paved path that encircles it. Pets are permitted.

Contact information: The park office is at 3850 State Route 73, Peebles, Ohio 45660. The phone number is 937-587-2796.

Other Areas of Interest

Brush Creek State Forest is located to the southeast on State Route 73, just across the Scioto County line. Adams Lake State Park and Adams Lake Prairie are located to the south on State Route 41, just outside the Adams County seat of West Union.

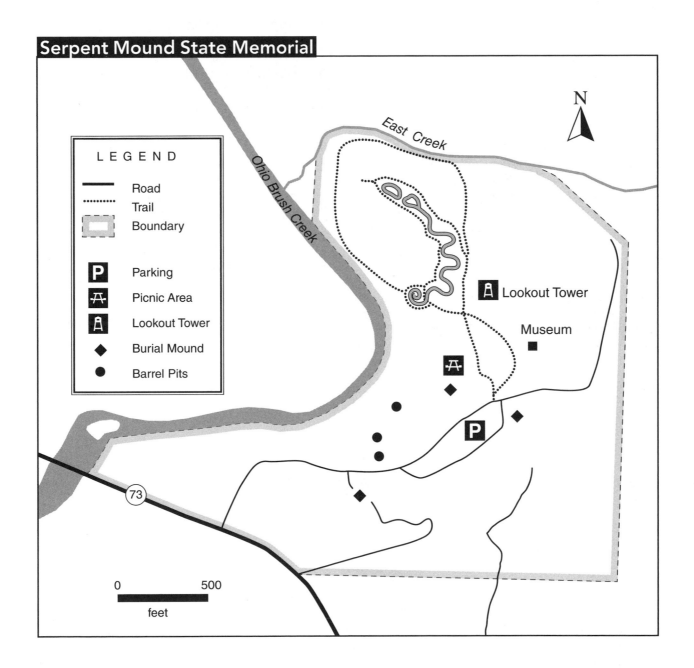

Serpent Mound State Memorial

LEGEND

— Road
······ Trail
▢ Boundary

P Parking
⊼ Picnic Area
♙ Lookout Tower
◆ Burial Mound
● Barrel Pits

East Creek

Ohio Brush Creek

♙ Lookout Tower

Museum ▪

⊼

P

73

0   500
feet

N

Ohio Brush Creek Trail

Hiking distance: 1 mile round trip

Estimated hiking time: 45 minutes

Take a hike along a route that has been traveled for over 1,000 years.

Caution: The hike includes a steep descent to creek level, and the bottom lands can be muddy.

Trail directions: Park in the lot and proceed to the museum, which is located at N 39° 01.443, W 83° 25.771 (1). From here, it is just 0.1 mile to the trail junction that leads to the tower at N 39° 01.517, W 83° 25.800 (2). You can climb this tower now or on the return trip, but be sure to make the 25-foot climb to survey the entire serpent—from the coiled tail to the open mouth.

Proceed past the tower on the paved path for another 0.1 mile. At that point, a sign marks the turnoff for the Ohio Brush Creek Trail at N 39° 01.572, W 83° 25.805 (3). The trail goes into a wooded area that features sycamores and red cedars. Begin descending immediately for

another 0.1 mile until you arrive at the level of the creek at N 39° 01.591, W 83° 25.906 (4). From here, veer left and follow the base of the plateau where the mound is located.

Ohio Brush Creek will soon appear on the right. Ancient native peoples always built their ceremonial sites along streams, but they had the foresight to place them well above the floodplain. In about 0.2 mile, you will be directly below the mouth of the serpent at N 39° 01.592, W 83° 25.887 (5). From here, you can see rock outcroppings and long dolomite columns rising up 100 feet to the mound site.

Continue on briefly before beginning the ascent back to the mound; in about 0.2 mile, you will return to point 2. From here, take a brief side trip along the paved path to the serpent's tail. At this spot, an overlook offers a great view of the broad expanse of farmland in the Brush Creek Valley. You can return to the museum from here or continue to follow the paved path around the entire mound until you arrive back at the tower. Just make sure that you allow time to properly appreciate the ambience of the unique location.

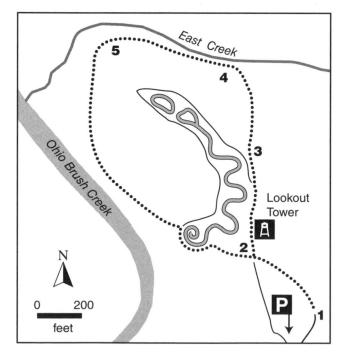

1. Museum
2. Tower
3. Brush Creek Trail turnoff
4. Creek level
5. Below serpent mound

> Take a rugged day hike in Ohio's largest state forest.

> Patrol the hunting grounds of the state's original tribal residents.

> Look for rare wildlife that may include bobcat, black bears, and timber rattlesnakes.

Area Information

At over 63,000 acres, Shawnee is by far the largest of Ohio's state forests. It is also one of the most impressive. The region is referred to as the Little Smokies. This region is part of the Allegheny Plateau, an ancient uplift that created the rugged hills that are foothills of the Appalachian Mountains. The Shawnee tribe was using the area as hunting grounds when white men arrived, and their name is all that has remained.

However, many of the natural features remain intact. In the area today, visitors may see not only such common game as raccoon, deer, and wild turkey, but also more rare (for Ohio) species such as black bear and bobcat. The area is also known for snakes, such as the timber rattler and the dangerous copperhead. The oak and hickory that dominate the ridge tops—and the beech and maples in the hollows—also yield an abundance of wildflowers. A few species of rare orchids, most notably the tiny whorled pogonia and the snowy orchid, can be found here.

Land was first acquired for the forest in 1922, when 5,000 acres were purchased for the Theodore Roosevelt State Game Preserve. In the 1930s, the Civilian Conservation Corps built camps and lakes in the area. Shawnee became a state forest in 1951, and a 1,165-acre sliver (mainly along State Route 125 in the center of the forest) is now designated as Shawnee State Park. The state park includes man-made Turkey Creek and Roosevelt Lakes, and it has a 50-room lodge with dining and

Timber rattlers are common in Shawnee State Forest.

game rooms, indoor and outdoor pools, and meeting rooms. The park also contains 25 rental cottages and a campground with 107 sites. The lakes are stocked with fish and also feature public swimming and boat rentals. An excellent nature center is located at Roosevelt Lake.

Facilities in Shawnee State Forest are more Spartan, which is part of their charm. The forest has several bridle trails, and a 58-site equestrian camp is located at Bear Lake. For serious hikers, the main attraction is a 40-mile backpack loop that encircles the forest. Portions of this trail are part of the Buckeye Trail and North Country Trail system, and they offer some of the best hiking on this route. Six campsites are interspersed along this route, most of which offer drinking water. For day hikers, there is a 7.2-mile day hike loop just north of State Route 125. By using parts of this loop with a connecting trail, hikers can divide the backpack loop into two halves—one north of Route 125 and the other south of it.

Directions: From the junction of U.S. Routes 23 and 52 in Portsmouth, take 52 west along the Ohio River for 6.6 miles. Turn right on State Route 125 and go 6 miles to the trailhead near Turkey Creek Lake at the lodge road turnoff.

Hours open: The forest is open year-round.

Facilities: Forest campgrounds provide drinking water. More advanced amenities are available in Shawnee State Park.

Rules and permits: Camping is permitted only in designated areas, and backpackers are required to register for a free permit. Fires are permitted only in designated rings, but pets are permitted.

Contact information: The Division of Forestry office for Shawnee State Forest is located at 13291 U.S. Highway 52, West Portsmouth, Ohio 45663. The telephone number is 740-858-6685.

Other Areas of Interest

Shawnee State Forest surrounds Shawnee State Park, which offers numerous outdoor opportunities as well as a resort and conference center. Contact the park at 4404 State Route 125, West Portsmouth, Ohio 45663; the phone number is 740-858-6652.

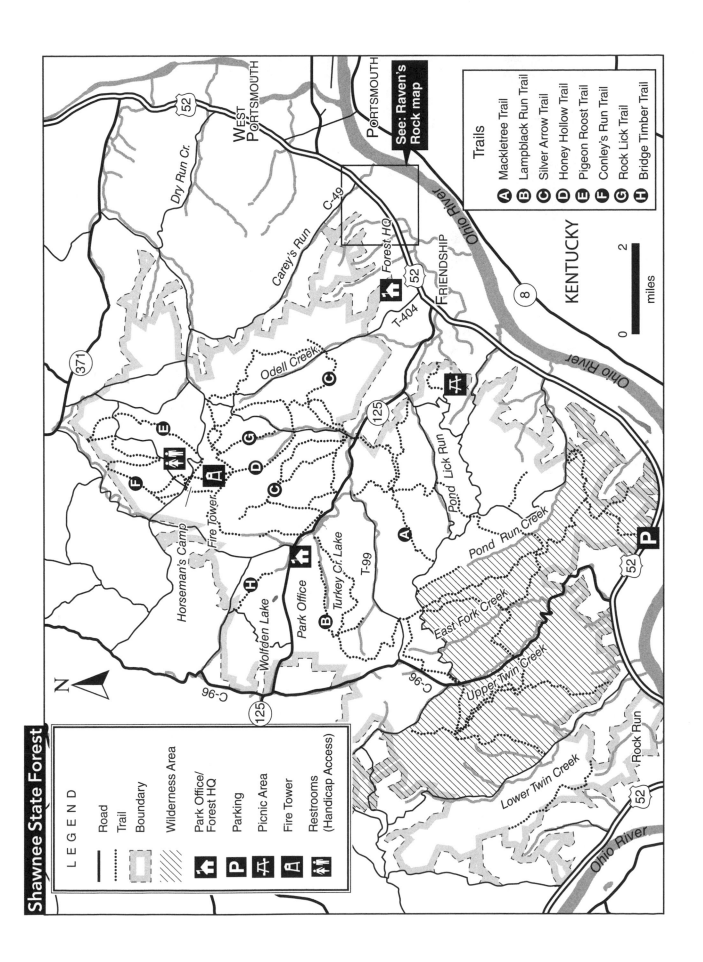

Shawnee State Forest

L E G E N D

Road	——
Trail	··········
Boundary	☐
Wilderness Area	▨

Park Office/ Forest HQ 🏛
Parking 🅿
Picnic Area ⛻
Fire Tower ⛺
Restrooms (Handicap Access) 🚹

Trails

Ⓐ Mackletree Trail
Ⓑ Lampblack Run Trail
Ⓒ Silver Arrow Trail
Ⓓ Honey Hollow Trail
Ⓔ Pigeon Roost Trail
Ⓕ Conley's Run Trail
Ⓖ Rock Lick Trail
Ⓗ Bridge Timber Trail

See: Raven's Rock map

KENTUCKY

0 2 miles

Day Hike and Connector Trail

Hiking distance: 5.2 miles
one way

Estimated hiking time: 3.5 hours

Connect two ends of a 40-mile backpack loop that is part of a national and statewide trail network.

Caution: This is a difficult hike filled with climbs and descents and the possibility of encountering poisonous snakes.

Trail directions: Park at the lot just past Turkey Creek Lake where the road to the lodge branches off at State Route 125; this lot is located at N 38° 44.508, W 83° 11.840 (1). A kiosk here reminds hikers that this is the trailhead for the 40-mile-long Shawnee Backpack Loop. Backpackers are required to self-register here, but this is not necessary for day hikers. This portion of the trail is also part of the Buckeye Trail and North Country Trail, but you will not be on it for long.

Follow the route across State Route 125 and almost immediately turn right on a connector trail that runs parallel to Route 125. Follow this trail for about 1.4 miles to an intersection at N 38° 44.281, W 83° 11.180 (2). To the right, it is 0.4 mile to the Day Hike Trail parking lot, where there is also a nature center. The hours are irregular, but the center is worth a visit; on the day we were there, we got to see a timber rattler get taken for a slither.

Stay on the trail veering left until it branches off soon afterward. Stay to the right and continue on southeast. This is the 7.2-mile Day Hike Loop, which is a circle within the northern half of the Backpack Loop. Continue on for another 1.5 miles until you reach a spot

opposite the Shawnee State Park campground at N 38° 44.772, W 83° 10.716 (3). The trail runs close to the highway here just opposite Roosevelt Lake, but most of the time there will be no reminders of civilization.

Continue up and down several hills for another 1.6 miles to a rocky streambed at N 38° 43.980, W 83° 09.669 (4). At this point, leave the blue blazes of the Day Hike Trail and veer to the right on a connector trail. Begin a steep climb that leads to a turnoff to Camp 3 at N 38° 43.573, W 83° 09.383 (5). This is the third of seven campsites spread around the Backpack Trail at 3- to 6-mile intervals. These primitive campsites are the only places to get fresh water along the Backpack Trail. The connector trail ends here.

A left turn would lead the hiker on an 18-mile counterclockwise loop back to point 1. A right turn leads back to State Route 125 at Camp Oyo at N 38° 43.631, W 83° 09.254 (6). Proceeding on the Backpack Trail would require a 22-mile clockwise loop back to point 1. So, as a day hiker, you should either have a second car here or be prepared to return via the same route, which would make for a 10.4-mile hike (with a difficulty rating of 5 boots).

1. Lot
2. Junction
3. Opposite campground
4. Rocky streambed
5. Camp 3
6. Camp Oyo

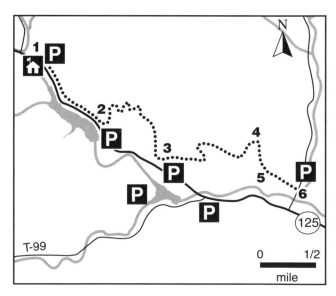

> Enjoy the solitude of an out-of-the-way state park.

> Hike rugged sandstone hills with beautiful views in all seasons.

> Sample a variety of plants, trees, and animal life.

Area Information

Tar Hollow State Park gets its name from the pitch pine trees found in the area. Early settlers extracted pine tar from the knots and heartwood of this tree and used it for salves and lubricants. These pioneers had to be resourceful because the rugged hillsides they were trying to farm didn't give them much to work with. Like their predecessors, the ancient Hopewell culture from 2,000 years ago and the Shawnee and Mingo tribes who used to hunt here, the pioneers lived a hardscrabble life in these rugged hills.

It's hard to believe that the region was once covered by a warm, shallow sea. As it receded, sand and gravel were washed in and sandstone was formed from the sediment. Today, the rugged Appalachian foothills are filled with a variety of wildlife that includes wild turkey, timber rattlesnake, and the elusive bobcat. Oak and hickory trees join the pitch pines along the ridgetops, while the stream valleys are filled with maple, black willow, sycamore, and buckeye. Among the wildflowers found here are bloodroot, wild geranium, cardinal flower, and Solomon's seal.

Public acquisition of the land in the area began in the 1930s. The 15-acre Pine Lake was built as a WPA project, and in 1939 the Tar Hollow Forest was created. Ten years later, a state park was cut out of this, but the state forest that surrounds it is still the third-largest Ohio state forest at 16,000 acres. Tar Hollow State Park has nearly 100 campsites, most of which offer electricity. The campgrounds have showers and pit latrines and are near the swimming beach at Pine Lake. For fishermen, there is a boat launch near the beach, but in line with the peace and quiet of the region, only electric motors are permitted. A unique feature is a general store that offers supplies and souvenirs as well as boat rentals, a game room, and an 18-hole miniature golf course.

For trail enthusiasts, there are 25 miles of bridle trail and a 2.4-mile mountain bike trail. The best known hiking trail is the 21-mile Logan Trail, which is divided into northern and southern loops. This trail, named for a prominent Mingo chief, was built by the Boy Scouts. And, yes, the Buckeye Trail also passes through the park.

Directions: Tar Hollow is located where Ross, Vinton, and Hocking counties meet. It is off of State Route 327 about halfway between Laurelville (State Route 56) and Londonderry (U.S. 50). A sign marks the main entrance at Park Road 10.

Facilities: The park contains four picnic areas and seven regular houses and one large shelter house that can be reserved. Playgrounds and a basketball court are near the main campground as well as a primitive backpack camp at the fire tower.

Hours open: The park is open year-round during daylight hours.

Rules and permits: Hunting is permitted in the surrounding state forest but not in the state park. Pets are permitted at all campsites.

Contact information: The park office is at 16396 Tar Hollow Road, Laurelville, Ohio 43135; the phone number is 740-887-4818.

Other Areas of Interest

Near Chillicothe is Great Seal State Park, which offers some of the most mountainesque hiking in the state.

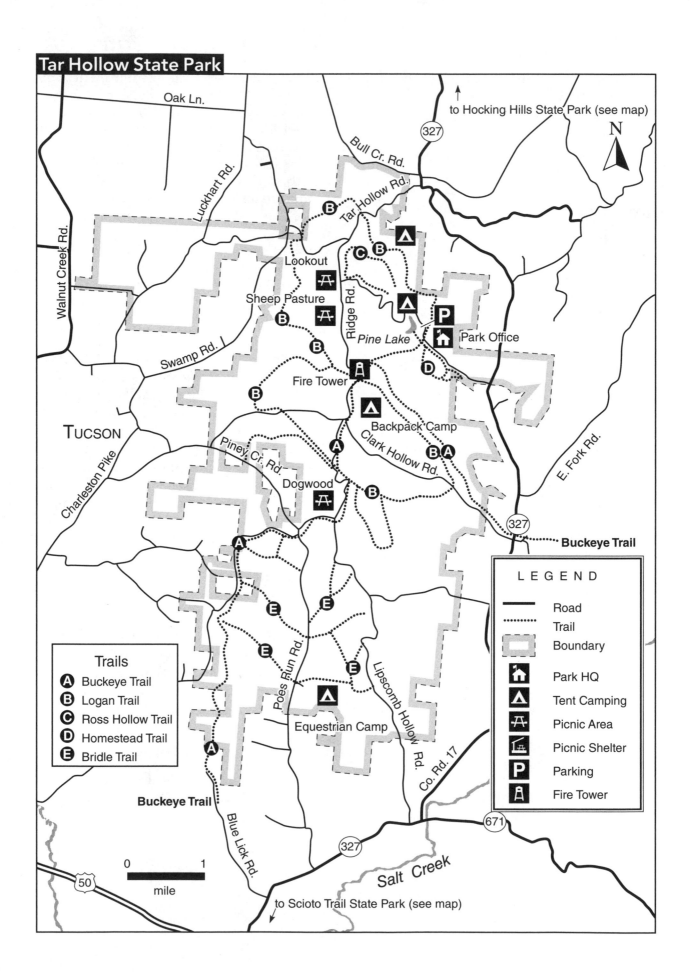

Tar Hollow State Park

LEGEND

— Road
.... Trail
Boundary
Park HQ
Tent Camping
Picnic Area
Picnic Shelter
Parking
Fire Tower

Trails

Ⓐ Buckeye Trail
Ⓑ Logan Trail
Ⓒ Ross Hollow Trail
Ⓓ Homestead Trail
Ⓔ Bridle Trail

to Hocking Hills State Park (see map)

N

Oak Ln.

Luckhart Rd.

Walnut Creek Rd.

Bull Cr. Rd.

Tar Hollow Rd.

Lookout

Sheep Pasture

Swamp Rd.

Ridge Rd.

Pine Lake

Park Office

Fire Tower

TUCSON

Piney Cr. Rd.

Charleston Pike

Dogwood

Backpack Camp

Clark Hollow Rd.

E. Fork Rd.

Buckeye Trail

Poes Run Rd.

Lipscomb Hollow Rd.

Co. Rd. 17

Equestrian Camp

Buckeye Trail

Blue Lick Rd.

0   1
mile

Salt Creek

to Scioto Trail State Park (see map)

Brush Ridge Trail

 Hiking distance: 3 miles round trip

Estimated hiking time: 2 hours

Hike some scenic ridgetops between two park landmarks.

Caution: Watch your footing on narrow, steep ridge trails.

Trail directions: Take the main Forest Road 10 past the office, lake, and campgrounds until it ends, then turn left on Forest Road 3 and go south to the Brush Ridge Firetower. Park in the lot here at N 39° 22.490, W 82° 45.760 (1). Climb the tower for a good overview before entering the woods at the northeast corner of the lot. The Brush Ridge Trail connects the Fire Tower to the other major park landmark, Pine Lake. This trail also serves as a cutoff between the northern and southern loops of the Logan Trail, and it is where the Buckeye Trail passes through the park.

| The fire tower at Tar Hollow State Park is also along a backpack trail.

Enter the woods and follow a dirt road for 0.1 mile until the trail leaves the road at N 39° 22.601, W 82° 45.667 (2). The trail rejoins the road a bit later as it skirts a ridgetop with a broad view. After about 0.6 mile, the blue blazes of the Buckeye Trail veer off to the right at N 39° 22.796, W 82° 45.279 (3). Stay on the main route following the red blazes of the Logan Trail through an oak and hickory forest. As the trail winds around just below the ridgetop, watch your step on the narrow path.

Continue as the trail starts to descend via a series of switchbacks. You will be able to see the area around Pine Lake long before you actually get there. In about 0.7 mile, the trail passes a sign for the Logan Trail at N 39° 23.003, W 82° 45.911 (4). Just after this, the trail crosses the spillway for Pine Lake at N 39° 23.038, W 82° 45.924 (5). Climb the spillway to view the 15-acre lake, or just walk across to the parking lot at the other side. Here, at N 39° 23.036, W 82° 44.898 (6), are restrooms, a shelter house, and other amenities not available at the fire tower. Spot a second car here if you have one, or turn around and retrace the route to point 1.

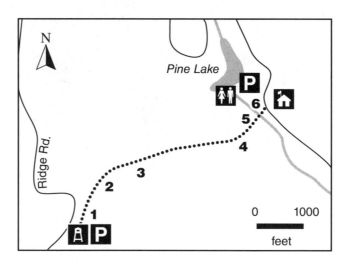

1. Fire tower lot
2. Trail leaves road
3. Buckeye Trail branches off
4. Sign
5. Spillway
6. Restrooms

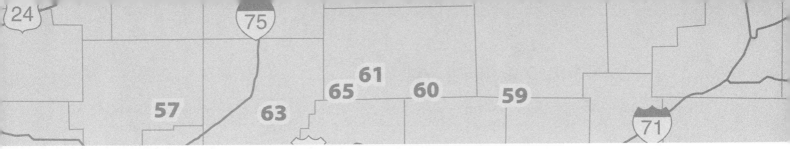

Northwest

The topography of the northwestern quadrant of Ohio is dominated by the western basin of Lake Erie. Though it's the shallowest of the Great Lakes, with an average depth of 216 feet, Lake Erie was once part of a vast shallow sea that covered the state. The receding of that sea some 350 million years ago left behind many interesting features. For example, sand dunes can be found today at Oak Openings, a Toledo Metropark.

The area that is today classified as part of the Lake Erie Plains once contained a 100-by-30-mile strip known as the Great Black Swamp. Once the area was drained and settled, it became one of the state's most fertile farm areas. Today, much of the region's land is still used for agricultural purposes, which means that less public land is available here for hikers than in other parts of the state.

The region today is noted for oak trees, marshes, and mosquitoes. The southern shores of Lake Erie are a paradise for birders; hundreds of migratory species stop seasonally along the shore. Parks at Magee Marsh and Maumee Bay offer ample opportunities and facilities for bird watching. And people don't normally think of island living when thinking of Ohio, but offshore islands in Lake Erie are another attraction. The 350-foot Perry's Victory Monument, which commemorates a naval victory in the War of 1812, offers a splendid view from South Bass Island. And nearby Kelley's Island is great for hikers and includes spectacular glacial grooves left in the bedrock by the last glacier some 14,000 years ago.

The region is drained by the Maumee and Sandusky Rivers, which are near the Wabash and Scioto watersheds. This made possible a water route connecting the Great Lakes to the Mississippi with only a small portage here and around Niagara Falls. Because of this water route, the area was important in pioneer times. Tribal conferences were held in the area in the 1790s. These involved tribes ranging from the Chippewa of the Northwest to the Iroquois of New York meeting with local tribes such as the Miami, Delaware, Shawnee, and Wyandot. France, England, and the United States all built several forts protecting these watersheds between 1750 and the War of 1812. Later on, the Miami and Erie Canal was built, which followed the path of the Miami and Maumee Rivers, connecting Cincinnati to the Great Lakes. Trails that follow this route are some of the best hiking routes in the region today, offering a glimpse of both human and natural history.

55 Delaware State Park

> Hike alongside a large lake named for an Ohio tribe of Native Americans.

> Walk among mixed hardwoods at a large campground.

Area Information

Delaware State Park is located along the shores of Delaware Reservoir in Delaware County just north of the city of Delaware. The ubiquitous name comes from the Delaware tribe, the natives who lived in the area around 1800. White settlers began appearing in the area not long afterward, arriving on the route that is now U.S. Route 23. During the War of 1812, a brick tavern just north of the park boundaries was enclosed by a wooden stockade and christened Fort Morrow. In 1951, the 1,300-acre lake was created by a flood control dam, and the area was designated as a state park.

Today, park activities are centered on Delaware Lake. There is no horsepower limit for boats, and three launching ramps are scattered around the shore. Boats and dock space can be rented, and the park has a fully equipped marina with fuel and boating supplies. A small pond near the marina offers fishing for youths aged 15 and under. The main lake is stocked with crappie, muskie, and bass; and swimmers can enjoy the 800-foot public beach.

The large campground at the park features 211 sites with electrical hookups, and it offers such amenities as flush toilets, showers, and laundry facilities. The campground has playgrounds and courts for volleyball, basketball, tetherball, and horseshoes. Bike rentals and disc golf are also offered. A group camp can be reserved, and the park has three fully stocked yurts that can be rented during warmer months. Eight picnic areas are provided in scenic spots overlooking the lake, and a large shelter house can be reserved. Hunting and winter recreational activities are abundant in season. Bird watching is a popular pastime, and the park contains five short hiking trails.

The park is situated in the midst of a fertile agricultural region that is on the top of a bed of limestone. A beech and maple forest once dominated the landscape, but the forest's second growth is more mixed. The result is a diversity that offers wildflowers such as trillium, phlox, and asters. Mammals such as fox, squirrel, and deer can also be seen in the area. Birders have ample opportunities to observe waterfowl and ring-necked pheasant.

Directions: Delaware State Park is on U.S. Route 23 almost exactly 20 miles north of the Interstate 270 Columbus Outerbelt. The entrance is well marked.

Facilities: The park offers a full panoply of services for outdoor enthusiasts.

Hours open: The park is open year-round in daylight hours.

Rules and permits: Pets are permitted at designated sites.

Contact information: The park is located at 5202 U.S. Route 23 North, Delaware, Ohio 43015. However, the park is administered from Alum Creek State Park, which has a mailing address of 3615 South Old State Road, Delaware, Ohio 43015-9773. The campground phone number is 740-363-4561, and the number at Alum Creek is 740-548-4631.

Other Areas of Interest

Adjacent to the park is the 4,670-acre Delaware Wildlife Area, which offers lake access and also contains 55 smaller stocked ponds for fishermen. Alum Creek State Park is southwest of the city of Delaware.

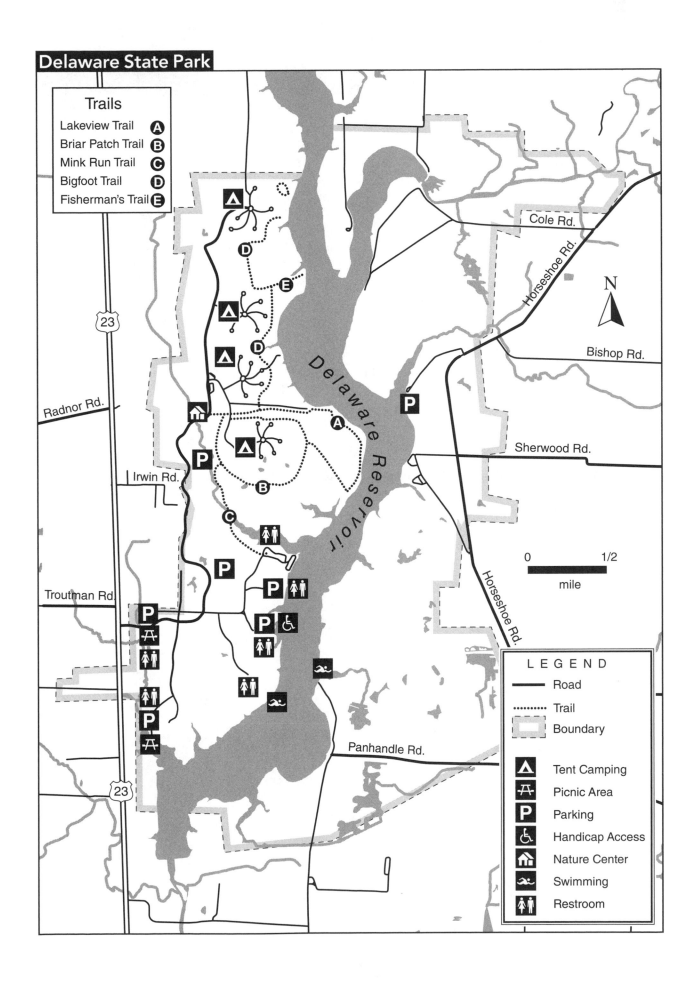

Lakeview Trail

Hiking distance: 1.6 miles

Estimated hiking time: 1 hour

Hike around the campgrounds and through the woods to the lakeshore.

Caution: The trail can get muddy near the lakeshore.

Trail directions: Take the main park entrance off of U.S. Route 23 and then make two quick left turns, following signs to the main campground. In about 1.5 miles, you'll come to the nature center at the campground entrance. Park in the lot on the right at N 40° 32.481, W 83° 03.479 (1). Go back up along the road you came in on for a few yards to the sign marking the Lakeview Trail. Turn left and enter the woods here; almost immediately, the Briar Patch Trail turns off to the right at N 40° 23.477, W 83° 03.452 (2). Proceed past this sign, and you will soon come to a paved camp road at N 40° 27.437, W 83° 03.416 (3).

On the other side of the road, you'll see two parallel trails labeled Lakeview and Briar Patch. Take the Lakeview Trail on the left and proceed into the woods. In about 0.2 mile, the Big Foot Trail branches off on the left at N 40° 23.431, W 83° 03.295 (4). Stay on the Lakeview Trail, and in another 0.3 mile, the lake becomes visible to the left at N 40° 23.416, W 83° 03.124 (5). This is the northern third of the lake, which is a no-wake zone. Below this point, the lake is a speed zone used by water-skiers taking advantage of the fact that there is no horsepower limit for boats.

After this, the trail veers to the right and roughly follows the shore. In about 0.5 mile, the trail turns away from the lake at N 40° 23.161, W 83° 03.498 (6). Turn right here and reenter a woods filled with poplar, oaks, and maples. In about 0.3 mile, the trail meets the Briar Patch Trail at N 40° 23.309, W 83° 03.179 (7). This trail encircles Camp Area 4, so turn right and follow the route back to point 3.

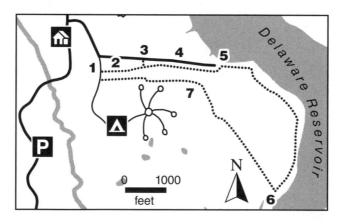

1. Lot
2. Junction
3. Cross road
4. Junction
5. Lake view
6. Leave shore and turn right
7. Junction

> See the last original-growth forest left in northwest Ohio.

> Walk in solitary splendor among trees that are over 120 feet tall.

> Stop at the family cemetery of the only private owners that the property has had.

Area Information

Goll Woods is an isolated spot that is well worth the drive off the beaten path. This 371-acre preserve is as pristine as it was some 400 years ago when many of the trees on the grounds got their start. No Europeans saw the preserve until French immigrant Peter Goll purchased 80 acres here in 1836. The Golls respected the tall trees on the property and let many of them stand as they farmed the property for four generations. The family sold the land to the state in 1966, and it became a state nature preserve in 1975. The Goll family cemetery is still on the grounds.

Goll Woods is a part of the Great Black Swamp, the region at the western end of Lake Erie that was originally part of the lake. The "black" in the title comes from the color of the soil that was filled with decayed vegetation from the shallow lake. It turns out that the soil was conducive to growing both crops and large trees. In addition to pines, the trees found here include maple, ash, elm, oak, hickory, tulip, and beech. Some trees may be as old as 500 years, and some of the older burr oaks are over 4 feet in diameter and over 120 feet tall. The largest black ash and rock elm trees in Ohio are here. Visitors should take the time to note not only that some of these trees have been here since before the Pilgrims, but also that the entire state was once covered by forest like this. This virgin timber has earned Goll Woods the designation as a National Natural Landmark. The preserve is also home to a variety of deer, owl, fox, squirrels, and frogs. Wildflowers are abundant, particularly in the spring. Some of the common wildflowers found here are green trillium (toadshade), bloodroot, columbine, toothwort, phlox, Dutchman's breeches,

thistle, jewelweed, and black-eyed Susan. A large variety of lichens can also be found here. Unfortunately, visitors may also encounter an abundant crop of mosquitoes once it gets warm.

Directions: Take U.S. Route 20A from the village of Burlington, which is just off of exit 25 of the Ohio Turnpike. Go south 1 mile on State Route 66. Then go west for 3 miles on Fulton County Road F. Turn south on Township Road 26 to find the parking lot.

Hours open: The preserve is open year-round in daylight hours.

Facilities: A kiosk with maps is located at the main parking lot, and an office building is nearby, but there is no running water or restrooms at the preserve.

Rules and permits: Pets are not permitted. Also, because this is a nature preserve with a focus on low-impact contact, picking of plants and wildflowers is forbidden.

Contact information: The mailing address of the preserve is Goll Woods Nature Preserve, 2045 Morse Road, Columbus, 43229; for information, you can call 419-445-1775.

Park Trails

Four trails come together at the kiosk in the preserve parking lot. In addition to the Toadshade Trail (which is used in the hike described here), this includes the following trails:

Tuliptree Trail, 1.5 miles

Cottonwood Trail, 1.75 miles

Burr Oak Trail, 1 mile

Other Areas of Interest

Harrison Lake State Park is 6 miles to the north, and Beaver Creek Wildlife Area is 6 miles to the west. For history and craft fans, Sauder Museum Farm and Village is 3 miles away in Archbold. This complex stresses historical crafts from farm life, and it also has an inn and campground.

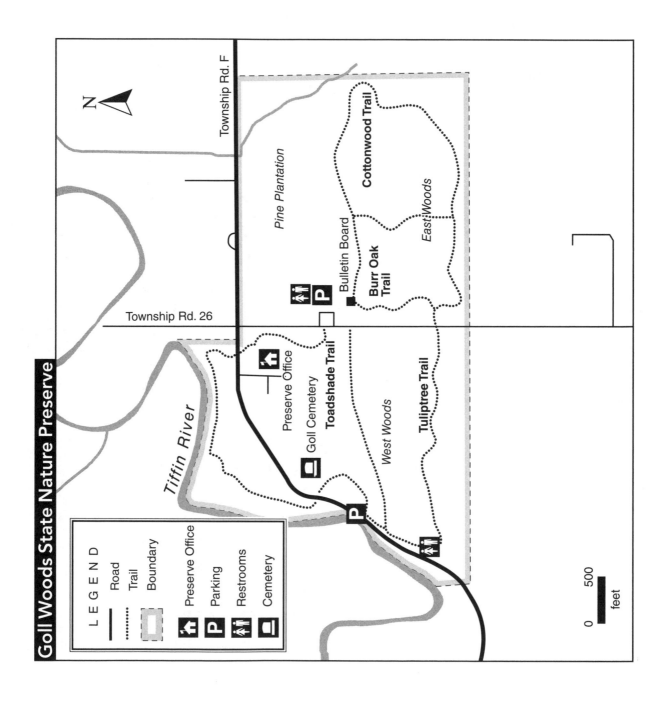

Goll Woods State Nature Preserve

LEGEND
Road
Trail
Boundary
Preserve Office
Parking
Restrooms
Cemetery

Tiffin River

Township Rd. 26

Township Rd. F

Pine Plantation

Preserve Office

Goll Cemetery

Toadshade Trail

West Woods

Tuliptree Trail

Bulletin Board

Burr Oak Trail

Cottonwood Trail

East Woods

N

0   500
feet

Toadshade Trail

 Hiking distance: 1.6 miles round trip

Estimated hiking time: 1 hour

Tour the last old-growth forest in northwest Ohio in solitude.

Caution: This isolated area has no facilities but plenty of mosquitoes.

Trail directions: Park in the main lot off of Township Road 26, the main north-south road that bisects the preserve. A kiosk with information is located here at N 41° 33.263, W 84° 21.690 (1). All four preserve trails can be accessed from here, but the Toadshade Trail begins on the other side of the road. Enter into the pine tree plantation where many of the trees are storm damaged. After 0.3 mile, you will cross a paved county road at N 41° 33.455, W 84° 21.797 (2); this is near the driveway to the park office.

Reenter the woods, and in 0.1 mile, you'll come to a wooden deck overlooking the Tiffin River at N 41° 33.525, W 84° 21.805 (3). The trail follows the river briefly before trailing off into the woods; after 0.3 mile, the trail crosses the county road at N 41° 33.359, W 84° 22.086 (4). Just across the road is the Goll Cemetery, named for the family of French immigrants who first purchased the land (for $1.25 an acre) in 1836. Turn right here and follow the road briefly before crossing and reentering the woods at N 41° 33.314, W 84° 22.102 (5).

Although most of the 500-year-old trees are on other trails in the preserve, you will see some large ones here in this mixed hardwood forest. The area also has an abundance of bird life: I encountered a pileated woodpecker and a red-tailed hawk when I was here. After 0.2 mile, the trail becomes concurrent with the Tuliptree Trail at N 41° 33.184, W 84° 22.151 (6). At this spot, a side trail leads to a parking lot on the nearby road. The lot overlooks a scenic spot on the Tiffin River, and walking the extra 0.1 mile to enjoy this view is worth it. Return to the trail and stay on the Toadshade Trail after a part of the Tuliptree Trail branches off immediately afterward. The Toadshade is concurrent with the other branch of the Tuliptree for the 0.5 mile back to the main parking lot. The trail comes out onto the road just below the kiosk and lot.

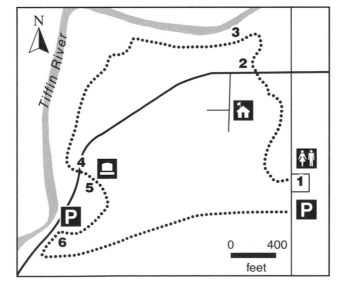

1. Kiosk and lot
2. Cross road
3. Deck on Tiffin River
4. Cemetery at crossroad
5. Reenter woods
6. Junction

> Enjoy a riverfront park that features diverse activities such as bird watching, fishing, and waterskiing.

> Hike the Miami and Erie Canal towpath and get a historical tour in the process.

> Sample the serenity of the Maumee River.

Area Information

Independence Dam is a small state park located next to the Maumee River. The 591-acre park is focused around Independence Dam, a cement dam that was built in 1924 to replace the original wooden dam whose purpose was to provide water for the Miami and Erie Canal that passed through here. The area around the dam became a state park in 1949.

Before that, the area was in the center of the Great Black Swamp, a leftover remnant from a shallow sea that covered Ohio some 350 million years ago. This area in northwestern Ohio—about 40 miles wide and 120 miles long—was not drained for settlement until after much of the rest of the state was already occupied. But the rivers that ran through the region hosted a coalition of Indian tribes that was clustered around the area where the Auglaize River meets the Maumee in present-day Defiance. In the 1790s, a pan-tribal conference involving over 3,000 members was held here, which was one of the largest concentrations of Native Americans up to that time.

The building of Independence Dam created a pool of deep water on the broad Maumee that is ideal for recreational boaters. There is no horsepower limit for boats, and just above the dam, a 4-mile area is open to waterskiing. For fishermen, the river is home to northern pike, crappie, smallmouth bass, catfish, and even walleye. A boat launch is located just above the dam. Below the dam, the shallow water is more suitable for canoes. It is also an ideal spot for bird watchers to view unusual species such as ospreys and eagles as they search for fish between the islands that dot the shallow water. The banks of the river are lined with beech, maple, black locust, and majestic sycamore trees. The park road between the riverbank and the towpath is also ideal for bicyclists.

Directions: Independence Dam State Park is on the northern shore of the Maumee River. The park is just off State Route 424, 2 miles east of the State Route 281 bridge and about 6 miles east of Pontiac Park in Defiance.

Facilities: The park has a primitive campground, a boat launch and marina, a playground, and two reservable shelters. Numerous grills, picnic tables, restrooms, and sources of drinking water are provided.

Hours open: The park is open year-round in daylight hours.

Rules and permits: All state boating and fishing regulations are enforced.

Contact information: The park is located at 27722 State Route 424, Defiance, Ohio 43512. However, it is administered through Harrison Lake State Park, which has a mailing address of 26246 Harrison Lake Road, Fayette, Ohio 43521; the phone number is 419-237-2593.

Other Areas of Interest

Mary Jane Thurston State Park, which has a marina on the south side of the Maumee, is located to the east in neighboring Henry County.

Independence Dam State Park

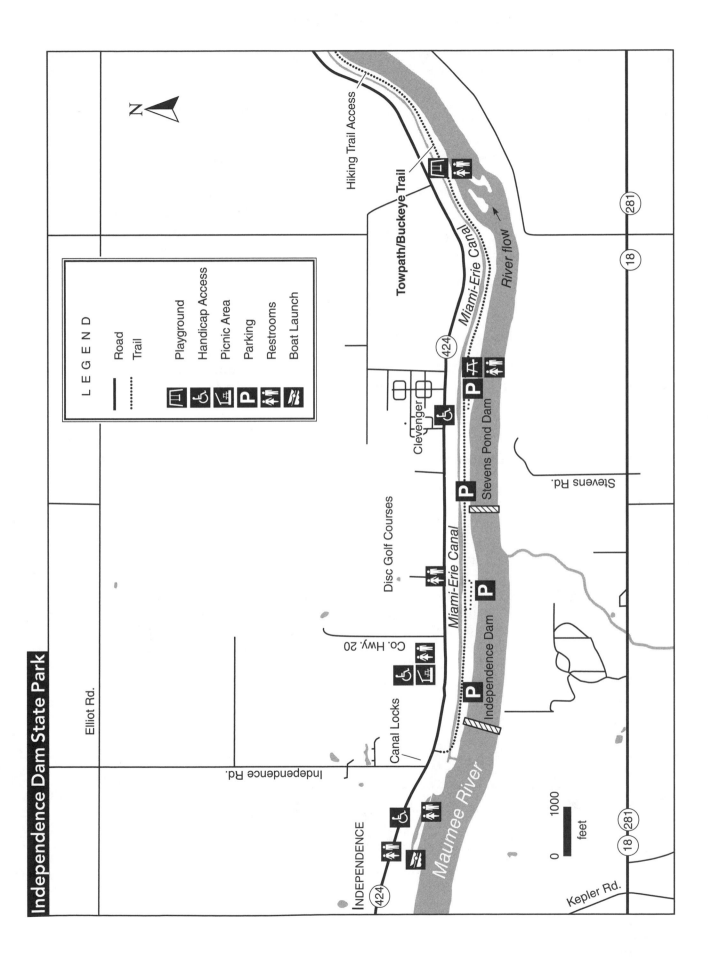

Towpath and Buckeye Trail

 **Hiking distance:** 4.8 miles round trip

Estimated hiking time: 2.5 hours

Look for all kinds of birds while walking along the scenic Maumee River.

Caution: This level trail is above the river, but it is alongside a park road, so watch for traffic.

Trail directions: Independence Dam State Park is on the north shore of the Maumee River on State Route 424; it is located 2 miles east of the Route 281 bridge across the river. Park in the marina lot near the restrooms at the boat launch at N 41° 17.422, W 84° 17.275 (1). The ubiquitous Buckeye Trail is also here as it follows the river and canal. Just 4 miles upstream (west), the Buckeye Trail is at Pontiac Park in downtown Defiance overlooking the confluence of the Auglaize and Maumee Rivers.

This spot has historically been linked to events involving Indian tribal unity. A marker notes that this is the purported birthplace of the famous chief Pontiac, the first chief to form a tribal coalition (which he did in 1763). In the 1790s, a large village here was the center of a multitribal group that defeated two U.S. armies until Anthony Wayne's army drove them out. Wayne then built Fort Defiance on the spot and defied the Indians to take it back.

Park at the marina and follow the familiar blue blazes downstream (east). In about 0.4 mile, the trail crosses the park entrance road off of State Route 424 at N 41° 17.350, W 84°

17.022 (2). Follow along between the park road and the river bank past the remains of Lock 13 on the Miami and Erie Canal. After 0.3 mile, the trail arrives at Independence Dam at N 41° 17.313, W 84° 16.471 (3). This cement dam was built in 1924 to replace a wooden dam, although state park status was not granted until 1949. The Maumee is as broad as ever here, but the dam makes for shallow water right below it. The many riffles and some smaller islands make this an excellent spot for bird watching. Common great blue herons fish here, and so do rare bald eagles.

Continue on below the dam, passing a playground area and more restrooms. After about 0.8 mile, you'll come to a small parking lot at N 41° 17.316, W 84° 15.451 (4). At this spot, a marker notes the site of Fort Starvation. In the War of 1812, American troops stationed in the Defiance area were poorly equipped, and over 100 of them died from exposure, illness, and lack of rations at a camp here in November and December of 1812. The bones of Kentucky militia members were discovered years later when workers were digging the canals.

Follow the blazes farther down past more shelters, restrooms, and a volleyball court. After about a mile, you will come to a small lot and the entrance to the camping area at N 41° 17.288, W 84° 14.462 (5). The Buckeye Trail continues on past the campground along the canal towpath toward the town of Florida. This small lot is a good place to leave a second car; otherwise, you can turn around and head back to the marina for a 4.8-mile hike.

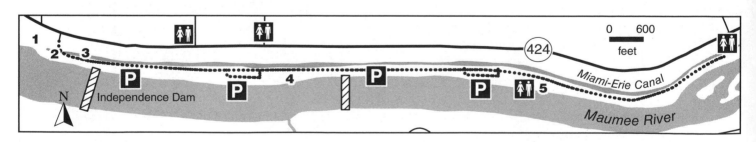

1. Lot
2. Cross road
3. Dam
4. Fort Starvation
5. Camping area lot

> Enjoy island life—Ohio style—at a park reached only by air or water.

> View the rocky north coast and catch a glimpse of the southern tip of Canada.

> See the fantastic glacial grooves left in the bedrock over 10,000 years ago.

Area Information

Kelley's Island is such a unique place that you will find it difficult to believe that you're in Ohio. And you're not physically connected to the rest of the state, because this tourist spot can only be reached by airplane or boat (except for snowmobiles in winter). The 2-by-4-mile island is one of the few inhabited islands in Lake Erie, and it is a popular destination in the summer months.

Kelley's Island State Park is a 677-acre park located mainly at the northern tip of the island.

As one would expect on an island, park activities are focused on the water. A public beach runs along the lake, and a double-lane boat launch ramp is available for boaters who are eager to tour or to fish for the famous Lake Erie walleye, perch, and bass. Kayaks can be rented at the beach in the summer. Stone pier or shoreline fishing is available, as is a fish cleaning house. In winter, the options include ice skating, ice fishing, and cross-country skiing. The park campground features 82 electric sites, 45 nonelectric ones, and a handful of rent-a-camp units and yurts. The campground has showers and flush toilets, as well as a picnic shelter, volleyball court, and playground. A youth group camp for up to 50 people is also on the site. Kelley's Island has been a state park since 1956.

Glacial Grooves State Memorial is located right across Division Street from the main

The north shore of Kelley's Island looks as rugged as any sea coast.

entrance to the park. Here the visitor can view grooves in the bedrock limestone left by the glacier some 13,000 years ago. These grooves, some of which are 15 feet deep and 35 feet wide, are considered the world's largest example of glacial striations. Just above this is a hiking trail that offers views of a rocky rugged coastline more reminiscent of Maine than of the Midwest. The plants found on this rocky island include varieties of both bog and coastal life. The area is known not only for fantastic birding, but also a wide variety of snakes, turtles, and salamanders.

Human history on Kelley's Island also goes back a relatively long way. At the southern end of the island, visitors can see Inscription Rock, where Native Americans carved petroglyphs on a limestone rock 400 to 500 years ago. More recently, the island became developed after Commodore Perry sailed from nearby South Bass Island to defeat the British fleet in 1813. Brothers Datus and Irad Kelley began purchasing land here in the 1830s. They eventually controlled all property and ran successful wine-making and limestone-quarrying operations. Today, a more sedate tourism has become the main industry on this quiet island.

Directions: Kelley's Island can be reached by ferry from Sandusky, Marblehead, or Port Clinton. Ferries deposit passengers near the southern end of Division Street, the main north-south artery. The park is 1.5 miles away at the northern end of Division Street.

Hours open: The park is open year-round, but it is difficult to get to in the winter.

Facilities: Restrooms are located at the beach and the campground.

Rules and permits: Pets are permitted at designated campsites. All state fishing and hunting regulations apply.

Contact information: The park is located at 920 Division Street, Kelley's Island, Ohio 43438; the phone number is 419-746-2546. However, the park is administrated through East Harbor State Park, 1169 North Buck Road, Lakeside-Marblehead, Ohio 43440-9610; the phone number is 419-734-4424.

Park Trails

In addition to the trail used for the hike described here, two other hiking trails can be found on Kelley's Island:

North Pond Trail (which has a boardwalk through wetlands), 1.1 miles

East Quarry Trail (which goes around the inland Horseshoe Lake, made by rainwater filling up a limestone quarry), 2.5 miles

Other Areas of Interest

East Harbor State Park is a few miles away on the mainland. This Marblehead Peninsula park has trails right along the lakeshore. South Bass Island next door also has a state park with a campground, as does Middle Bass Island to the north. Catawba Island also has a state park, but it is not really an island but rather the northern tip of Marblehead Peninsula. To the north is Pelee Island, the southernmost point in Canada.

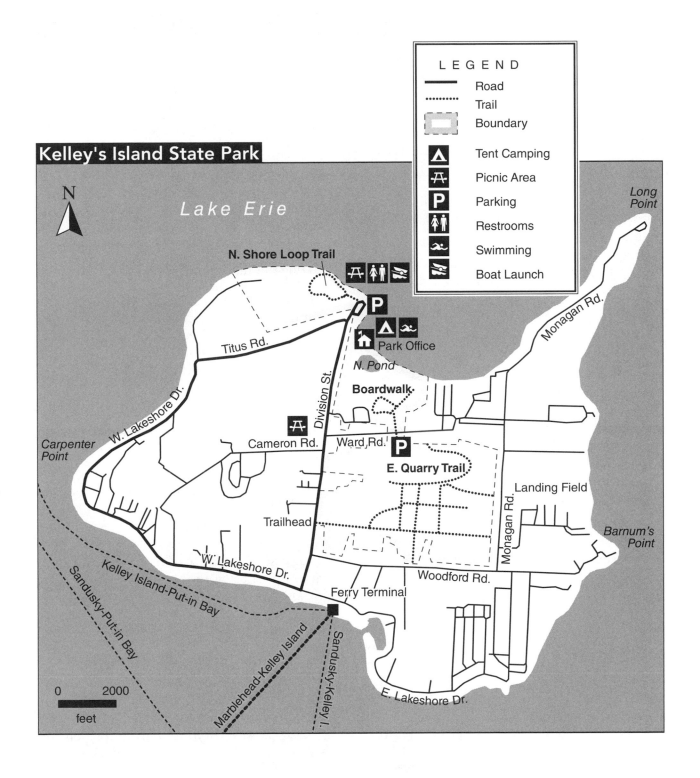

Kelley's Island State Park

Lake Erie

N

N. Shore Loop Trail

LEGEND
- Road
- Trail
- Boundary
- Tent Camping
- Picnic Area
- Parking
- Restrooms
- Swimming
- Boat Launch

Long Point

Titus Rd.

P

Park Office

N. Pond

Boardwalk

W. Lakeshore Dr.

Monagan Rd.

Carpenter Point

Cameron Rd.

Ward Rd.

P

E. Quarry Trail

Landing Field

Trailhead

Monagan Rd.

Barnum's Point

W. Lakeshore Dr.

Ferry Terminal

Woodford Rd.

Kelley Island-Put-in Bay

Sandusky-Put-in Bay

Marblehead-Kelley Island

Sandusky-Kelley I.

E. Lakeshore Dr.

0   2000
feet

Kelley's Island North Shore Loop Trail

 **Hiking distance:** 4.6 miles round trip

Estimated hiking time: 2.5 hours

Spend the day on Ohio's north coast, on an idyllic island with several outstanding natural features.

Caution: The trail is flat, and traffic in town is light, but the length of the hike can be tiring on a hot day.

Trail directions: Unless you have your own airplane, Kelley's Island can be reached only by boat. Ferry service originates in Sandusky, Marblehead, and Port Clinton; the ferries from all three locations deposit passengers and cars at the southern shore of the island. Begin your hike at the southern tip of Division Street in the downtown area at N 41° 35.636, W 82° 42.657 (1). This guide doesn't usually send hikers through urban areas, but Kelley's Island is more of a resort. So ignore the multiple offers to rent bicycles and golf carts and walk 1.5 miles up Division Street to the northern shore of the island.

Walk north through the mostly quiet downtown area for about 0.4 mile to the old stone church that serves as the local historical society museum at N 41° 35.921, W 82° 42.587 (2). Stop here or continue on in sparse traffic for 0.8 mile until a cemetery appears on the right. Members of the Kelley family are buried here, including such notables as Datus Kelley, who with his brother purchased the island in the 1830s and became involved in limestone quarrying and wine making—the two industries that the island was best known for before tourism came along.

In another 0.3 mile, you'll come to the entrance and campground for Kelley's Island State Park at N 41° 36.875, W 82° 42.396 (3). This location also contains a public beach and the northern terminus of State Route 575—the only state road on the island and likely the only Ohio state highway that never intersects with any other state routes. In another 0.2 mile,

you will come to the parking lot for Glacial Grooves State Memorial at N 41° 36.967, W 82° 42.374 (4).

This 400-foot-long site is the most famous example of glacial grooves in the world. These grooves were created when a glacier advanced into limestone bedrock some 25,000 years ago. Take the time to walk the 0.2-mile loop to marvel at the deep grooves. Then head on past an abandoned quarry to where the road ends at N 41° 37.056, W 82° 42.350 (5). This is where the North Loop Trail begins. Go through the woods for 0.2 mile until the trail forks at N 41° 37.061, W 82° 42.612 (6). Take the fork to the right. Then go for another 0.2 mile to where a small side trail branches off on the right at N 41° 37.172, W 82° 43.511 (7). Turn off here and almost immediately you'll be rewarded by the sight of the north coast.

In contrast with the tourist-dominated south end of Kelley's Island, the northern end is deserted and dominated by waves crashing over a rocky shore. To the west, you can see South Bass Island, dominated by the 350-foot-high monument commemorating Commodore Perry's naval victory on Lake Erie in 1813. To the north is Pelee Island, the southernmost point of Canada. On the day I was here, there was also an abundance of the sweetest tasting black raspberries, although the splendor of the tableau may have influenced the taste.

Return to the trail and proceed another 0.1 mile to another lakeshore turnoff at N 41° 37.195, W 82° 42.835 (8); this turnoff leads to an abandoned building. Stay on the trail and go another 0.3 mile to where the trail meets a dirt road at N 41° 37.047, W 82° 42.481 (9). Bear left and you will almost immediately return to point 7. Retrace your steps and smell the cedars as you return to the trailhead. On the ferry back to the mainland, be sure to notice the skyline (filled with roller coasters) of Cedar Point Amusement Park in Sandusky, as well as the 1822 Marblehead Lighthouse at the tip of the peninsula of the same name.

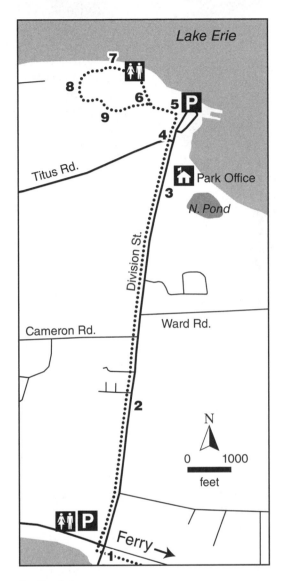

1. Dock
2. Museum
3. State Park entrance
4. Glacial Grooves
5. Trailhead
6. Fork right
7. Coast view
8. Junction
9. Dirt road

> Visit the Sportsmen's Migratory Bird Center to learn about Lake Erie's avian diversity.

> Try to see as many of the 300 bird species in the area as you can.

> Climb a 40-foot observation tower for a better view of marsh wildlife.

Area Information

While many Ohio locations specialize in certain types of flora and fauna, Magee Marsh is the best spot for bird watching. In this area on the shores of Lake Erie, over 300 species of birds of all kinds—but specifically waterfowl—can be found. On the grounds, visitors will also find the Sportsmen's Migratory Bird Center, which offers displays and programs connected with marsh wildlife. The 2,200-acre wildlife area has been named one of the top 10 bird watching sites in the country.

Since the 1800s, the marshes of Lake Erie have been known for excellent waterfowl hunting. As marshland increasingly came into the private hands of hunters, it became necessary to preserve some land for nonconsumptive use for waterfowl. The Ohio Division of Wildlife purchased the Magee Marsh Wildlife Area in 1951, with the goal of developing and maintaining high-quality wetland habitat. In the 1960s, a geese nesting program was begun in conjunction with other wildlife areas that today produces 10,000 goslings annually. Then, in 1970, the Bird Center was added.

The Bird Center building contains displays about marsh life and includes a display pond filled with indigenous fish, frogs, turtles, and snakes. A walking trail connects to a 42-foot observation deck. The center also houses the Crane Creek Wildlife Research Station, which is the headquarters for the Ohio Division of Wildlife's wetland wildlife research operations. The center is open from 8:00 to 5:00 Mondays through Fridays, and on weekends from 11:00 to 5:00, from March through November.

Magee Marsh is a great place to visit any time of year, but duck populations usually peak around mid-November. The marshes around here freeze later than the surrounding area, which keeps waterfowl here longer and also guarantees an earlier return in spring. Among the waterfowl that can be seen here are all sorts of ducks, geese, mallards, and teal. Large flocks of tundra swan also appear in spring. Many other species of birds can also be found here, such as eagles, falcons, hawks, osprey, and about 150 species of migrating songbirds, including 36 varieties of warblers.

Directions: Magee Marsh is between Lake Erie and State Route 2; it is located 11 miles east of Maumee Bay State Park and 17 miles west of Port Clinton. Turn north off of Route 2 at Denis Franklin Parkway at the site of the Black Swamp Bird Observatory. Then go about 0.7 mile to the trailhead and the Bird Center parking lot.

Hours open: The wildlife area is open during daylight hours. The area beyond the Bird Center is closed from mid-October through December for controlled waterfowl hunting, but the center and walking trail are open year-round.

Facilities: Restrooms are available in the Bird Center.

Rules and permits: Waterfowl and deer hunting are permitted but tightly controlled. Trapping is also permissible by permit.

Contact information: The wildlife area is located at 13229 West State Route 2, Oak Harbor, Ohio 43449; the phone number is 419-898-0960.

Other Areas of Interest

Ottawa National Wildlife Refuge—a federal preserve that is home to over 265 bird species—is right next door to Magee Marsh. The area also features hiking trails and an observation platform. Another area attraction that features bird watching is Crane Creek State Park.

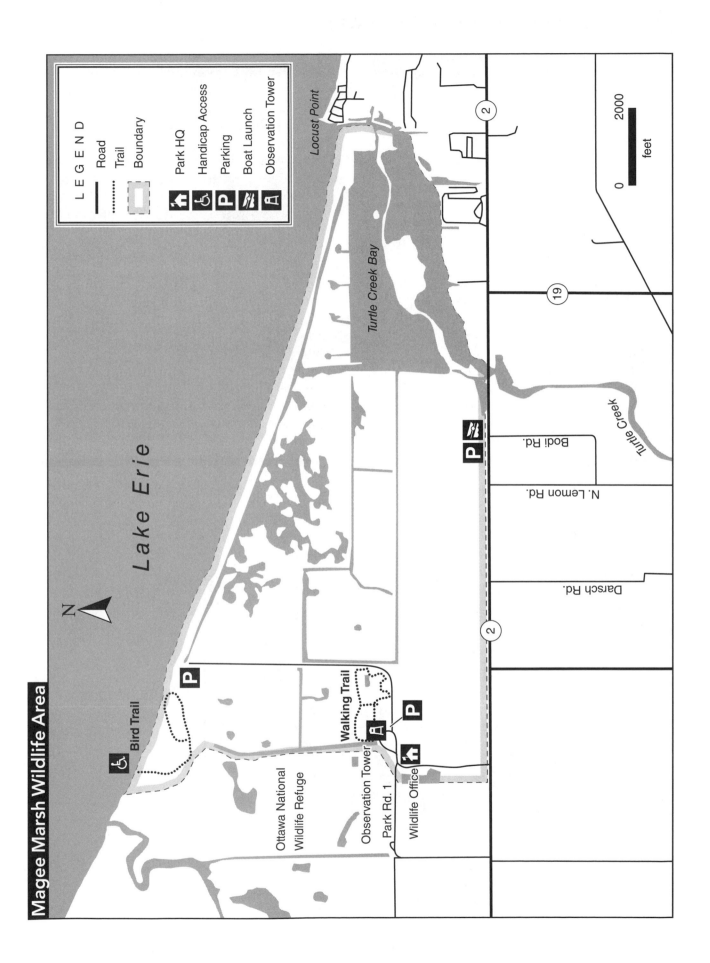

Magee Marsh Wildlife Area

Lake Erie

N

Bird Trail

Locust Point

Turtle Creek Bay

Ottawa National
Wildlife Refuge

Observation Tower

Park Rd. 1

Walking Trail

Wildlife Office

Darsch Rd.

N. Lemon Rd.

Bodi Rd.

Turtle Creek

2

19

2

L E G E N D

Road
Trail
Boundary

Park HQ
Handicap Access
Parking
Boat Launch
Observation Tower

0   2000

feet

Magee Marsh Walking Trail

Hiking distance: 1 mile

Estimated hiking time: 30 minutes

Take a walk on a flat trail in a classic Lake Erie marsh.

Caution: Though this is an easy walk on a flat path, the mosquitoes and deer flies are about as bad as anyplace in the state.

Trail directions: Park in the northeast corner of the lot at the Magee Marsh Migratory Bird Center. A sign for the Magee Marsh Walking Trail is located at N 41° 36.707, W 83° 11.227 (1). Follow the unmarked but easily discernible trail for 0.2 mile until it comes to a pond at N 41° 36.730, W 83° 11.088 (2). Here, and at all other major junctions, you will see signage explaining what sorts of wildlife can be found in the marsh. Continue on for another 0.1 mile to a bench at N 41° 36.772, W 83° 41.015 (3). In another 0.1 mile, you will come to a bridge over a stream at N 41° 36.825, W 83° 10.971 (4).

Cross this bridge and proceed for 0.2 mile to where a bench is positioned at N 41° 36.822, W 83° 11.202 (5). Here the trail turns and begins to head back. Follow along a sort of towpath between wet areas for another 0.2 mile until you come to another bench at N 41° 36.817, W 83° 11.355 (6). Stay on the main trail as it passes between ponds and wetlands. These waters may appear desolate or even fetid, but they are teeming with wildlife that is discussed in signage at various stops along the way.

Continue for another 0.1 mile past a boat dock; you will then come to the Magee Marsh Migratory Bird Center at N 41° 36.736, W 83° 11.334 (7). This facility has limited hours but offers a lot of information on the many migratory birds that pass by here. Follow behind the building for another 0.1 mile until you arrive at a two-story observation tower that overlooks the entire marsh area at N 41° 36.717, W 83° 11.220 (8). The parking lot is just a few feet away.

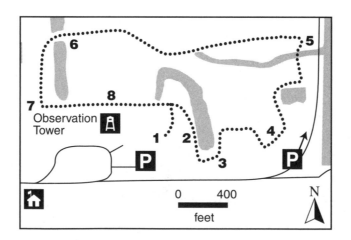

1. Lot
2. Pond
3. Bench
4. Bridge
5. Bench
6. Bench
7. Bird center
8. Observation tower

> Stay at an upscale lodge right on the shores of Lake Erie.

> Take a walk on a wooden boardwalk through a classic marsh.

> View a wide variety of birds, trees, and plants.

Area Information

Maumee Bay State Park offers all the best of what Lake Erie has to offer. This park has as much to offer as any in the state, which may explain why it is one of the most popular state parks. Established as a park in 1975, Maumee Bay added a 120-room lodge in 1991. Each room has a balcony, and the lodge features dining, a game room, racquetball courts, indoor and outdoor pools, and meeting and conference rooms. The park also has 24 cottages and a campground with 252 electric sites.

Picnic areas with grills are located near the public beaches—the park includes two beaches, one along Lake Erie and one on an inland lake. Six shelters that can be reserved are contained in the park. For boaters, a 32-slip marina is located on Lake Erie, where fishing enthusiasts can go after walleye and perch. Also, a 57-acre inland lake offers sailing, canoeing, and fishing (for smaller fish). Boats can be rented in summer from the Lake Erie beach. For summer sports, the park has bike rental, basketball and volleyball courts, and an 18-hole golf course. For winter sport buffs, offerings include sledding, ice skating, and cross-country skiing.

This platform in the marshes of Maumee Bay overlooks Lake Erie.

A unique feature of Maumee Bay is the Trautman Nature Center near the marsh boardwalk. This center contains interactive displays and exhibits, and it is located right in the center of the area that it explains. Lake Erie was much larger 13,000 years ago when it covered much of northwestern Ohio. When the lake receded, it left behind the flat, marshy region that came to be known as the Great Black Swamp. At Maumee Bay, these conditions have been preserved, and the wetlands here contain more species of wildlife than any other type of habitat. Snakes, turtles, frogs, and salamanders thrive here, as do over 300 species of birds, both songbirds and shorebirds. Nesting pairs of bald eagles are also found here. Among the plants commonly found here are cattails, buttonbush, cottonwood, and black willow.

Directions: From State Route 2 east of Interstate 280 in Toledo, take Curtice Road for 3 miles to the main parking lot.

Hours open: The park is open year-round. The Trautman Nature Center is open 10:00 to 5:00 on Monday through Friday and 10:00 to 6:00 on weekends.

Facilities: The lodge provides just about every amenity that a traveler could ask for. The campground has flush toilets, electricity, and playground equipment. Restrooms are also available at the nature center. Wheelchair accessible fishing piers are provided at the lake.

Rules and permits: Pets are permitted at the campgrounds. Hunting is permissible at the adjacent Mallard Club Marsh Wildlife Area.

Contact information: The address of the park is 1400 State Park Road, Oregon, Ohio 43616; the main phone number is 419-836-7758. The phone number for the camp office is 419-836-8828; the number for the nature center is 419-836-9117.

Park Trails

In addition to the trail used for the hike described here, the park also contains the following trails:

Bicycle and jogging trail, 6 miles

Mouse Trail, 3 miles

Other Areas of Interest

Cedar Point National Wildlife Refuge is just a few miles away, and Metzger Marsh Wildlife Area is a little farther east. Both are right on the shores of Lake Erie and feature the same sort of wildlife found at Maumee Bay.

▌Birdhouses are often occupied at Maumee Bay State Park.

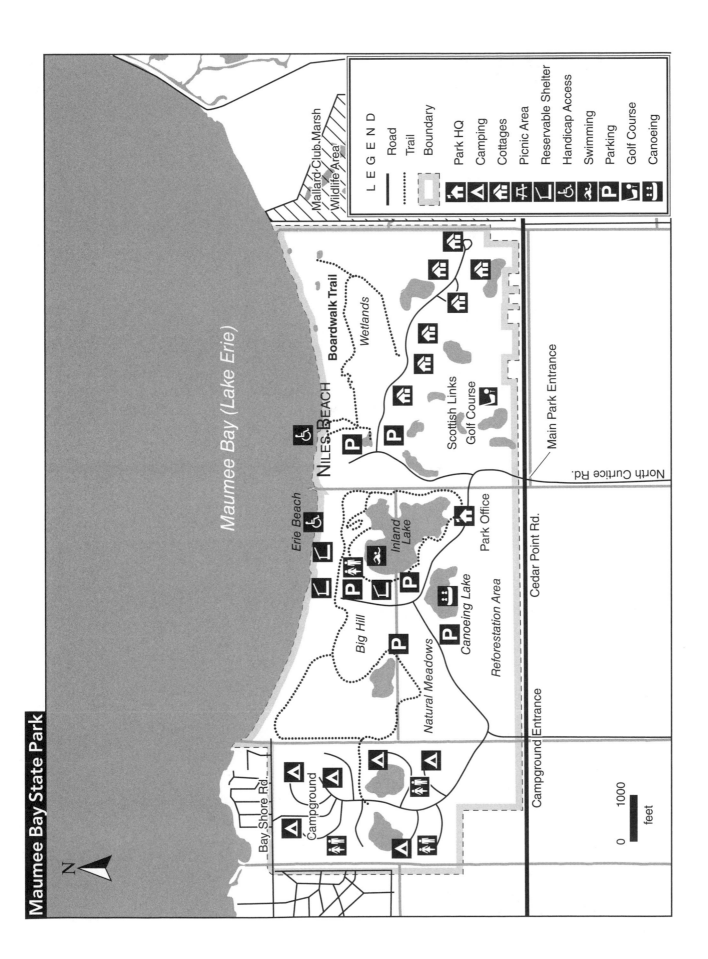

Maumee Bay State Park

Maumee Bay (Lake Erie)

Mallard-Club.Marsh
Wildlife Area

LEGEND

Road
Trail
Boundary

Park HQ
Camping
Cottages
Picnic Area
Reservable Shelter
Handicap Access
Swimming
Parking
Golf Course
Canoeing

Boardwalk Trail

Wetlands

NILES BEACH

Erie Beach

Scottish Links
Golf Course

Main Park Entrance

North Curtice Rd.

Inland
Lake

Park Office

Big Hill

Natural Meadows

Canoeing Lake

Reforestation Area

Cedar Point Rd.

Campground Entrance

Bay-Shore Rd.

Campground

0   1000

feet

N

Boardwalk Trail

Hiking distance: 2.2 miles

Estimated hiking time: 1 hour 15 minutes

Walk above the ground on a 2-mile boardwalk that provides a birding tour of the shores of Lake Erie.

Caution: Stay on the boardwalk to avoid marshy soil.

Trail directions: Park in the southeast corner of the parking lot near the Trautman Nature Center at N 41° 41.020, W 83° 22.052 (1). Visit the nature center to learn more about the 36 species of migrating warblers that frequent the park and the 1,500 square miles of the Great Black Swamp that once dominated the area. Over 90 percent of the wetlands of Ohio are now gone, and this site preserves what they were like. The nature center also offers restrooms and drinking water.

The boardwalk begins just on the other side of the nature center, and this impressive wooden structure proceeds above ground for the next 2 miles. The boardwalk is 6 feet wide and several feet above ground. It was constructed by the Ohio Civilian Conservation Corps in 1992. In about 0.1 mile, a trail turns off to the left and goes toward Maumee Bay Lodge at N 41° 41.042, W 83° 21.986 (2). Another part of this loop appears shortly afterward, but you should stay on the main boardwalk for another 0.2 mile to where the main loop begins at N 41° 41.078, W 83° 21.758 (3). At all boardwalk junctions, directions are painted on the walk to guide visitors.

Take the right fork and proceed another 0.2 mile until a route leads off to the right to another parking lot at N 41° 40.936, W 83° 21.567 (4). Continue on for another 0.2 mile to a turnoff that leads to an observation blind at N 41° 40.985, W 83° 21.370 (5). Turn right and go another 0.1 mile to N 41° 40.938, W 83° 21.315 (6), where the boardwalk ends at a bench. At first, the sound of boats from nearby Lake Erie is clearly audible, but by now the dominant sound is the variety of birds that can be found at the observation blind.

After enjoying the spot, return to point 5 and go right for another 0.1 mile to where a trail heads off toward an observation deck at N 41° 41.067, W 83° 21.307 (7). The boardwalk here passes through a tall cattail marsh, and signs point out that in terms of species variety, this type of marsh is roughly equivalent to a tropical rain forest. Take the route to the right and go for another 0.2 mile to a two-story observation deck at N 41° 41.175, W 83° 21.225 (8). From the top of this deck, Lake Erie is clearly visible, as are several varieties of marsh birds.

Enjoy this isolated view for a while and then return through the cattails to point 7. Then turn right and follow the boardwalk through more marshland. In addition to the sights of various warblers, you can enjoy the varied smells such as cedar trees. Proceed for another 0.4 mile until you arrive back at the beginning of the loop at point 3. From here, retrace your steps for another 0.3 mile until you return to the nature center.

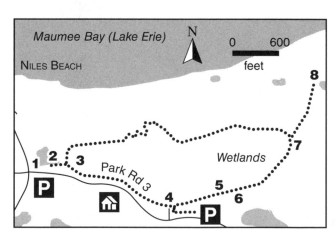

1. Lot
2. Junction
3. Take right fork
4. Junction
5. Turnoff to blind
6. Blind
7. Turnoff to deck
8. Deck

> Follow the same route used by Indian war parties and canal boats.

> Explore 40 miles of towpath from Lake Loramie to Delphos.

> Hike out in the open on a prairie along a waterway.

Area Information

The Miami and Erie Trail was the first trail created under the Ohio Trails Act. This 40-mile stretch of trail runs from Fort Loramie to Delphos and follows the water route used by Indian war parties during the American Revolution. Counterraids from Kentucky brought the rich fertile soil to the attention of white pioneers who began to settle here after the Greenville Treaty of 1795. The route followed by Anthony Wayne's supply posts became the route followed by the canal. Today, State Route 66 follows most of the canal route, but the Ohio Department of Natural Resources is taking steps to maintain the historical appearance of the canal route.

It took 20 years to build the canal; the project was not completed until 1845. For boats using the canal, it would take 5 days to travel the 250 miles between Toledo and Cincinnati at a pace of 4 to 5 miles per hour. And the canal era didn't last long, because it was soon replaced by railroads. But during its brief heyday, the canal thrived and was responsible for a lot of regional development. The Loramie Summit—a 21-mile stretch between Fort Loramie and St. Marys—was the high-altitude point on this route. Lake Loramie as well as Grand Lake at St. Marys were built as feeder lakes to keep the canal water flowing.

Today, the hiking trail roughly follows the 10-foot-wide towpath of the canal. The route is generally out in the open on flat ground alongside still streams. Hikers will see abundant wildflowers in spring and several noteworthy sites along the route. A 10-mile portion north of St. Marys has been maintained so that it is canoeable. In the canal-friendly town of St. Marys, a water route goes through a city park, the site of several locks, and the location of forts from the Indian Wars and the War of 1812. The trail runs through the charming towns of Minster and New Bremen—both of which were able to thrive because of the canal—before ending in Fort Loramie. Different parts of this route are maintained by different authorities, but the entire trail is uniformly easy to follow, especially because it is concurrent with the Buckeye Trail. This trail could be hiked all at once or broken up into sections; there are numerous convenient access points.

Directions: The towpath trail can be accessed from several points along State Route 66 between its northern terminus at the Jennings Creek aqueduct in Delphos and the southern end at the Loramie Creek aqueduct north of Fort Loramie.

Facilities: While trail access is easy, facilities are rare. Many parking lots and abundant signage can be found along the trail, but there is a lack of public restrooms and drinking water.

Hours open: This trail is always open.

Rules and permits: Hikers need to stay on the trail, because it borders private property.

Contact information: The Miami-Erie Canal Corridor Association is a nonprofit organization created in 1996 to champion the trail. The organization hopes to expand the trail south toward Piqua. The address for this organization is P.O. Box 722, St. Marys, Ohio 45885.

Other Areas of Interest

Lake Loramie State Park and Grand Lake St. Marys State Park are located on the two main feeder lakes at opposite ends of the Loramie Summit.

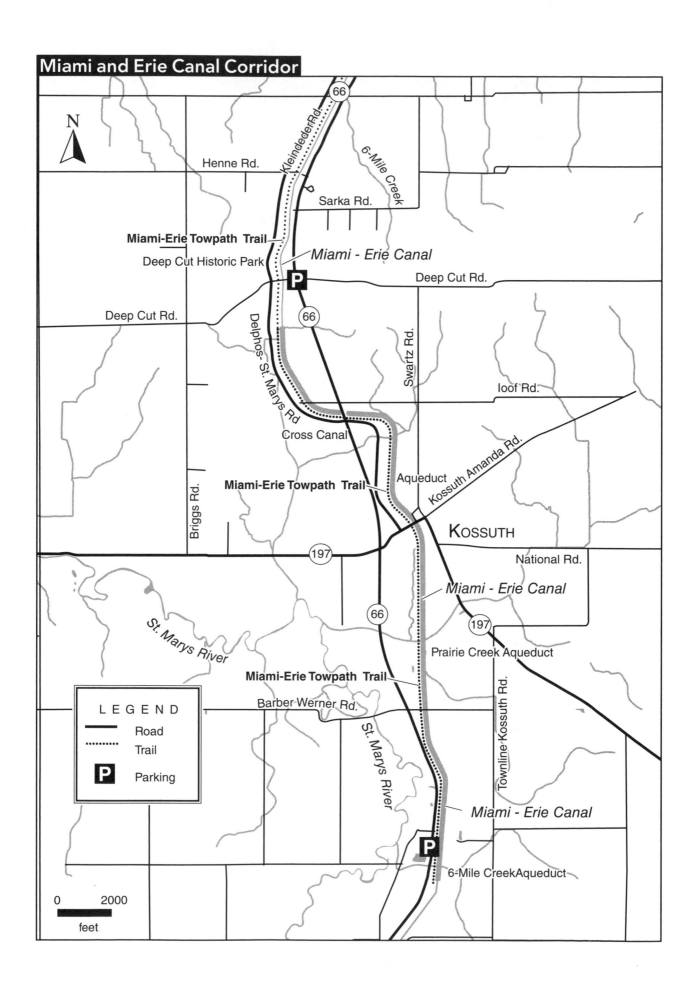

Miami and Erie Canal Corridor

N

Henne Rd.

Kleindederr Rd.

6-Mile Creek

Sarka Rd.

Miami-Erie Towpath Trail

Miami - Erie Canal

Deep Cut Historic Park

P

Deep Cut Rd.

66

Deep Cut Rd.

Delphos- St. Marys Rd

66

Swartz Rd.

Ioof Rd.

Cross Canal

Miami-Erie Towpath Trail

Aqueduct

Kossuth Amanda Rd.

Briggs Rd.

KOSSUTH

197

National Rd.

Miami - Erie Canal

66

197

Prairie Creek Aqueduct

St. Marys River

LEGEND

—— Road

········· Trail

P Parking

Miami-Erie Towpath Trail

Barber Werner Rd.

St. Marys River

Townline-Kossuth Rd.

Miami - Erie Canal

P

6-Mile Creek Aqueduct

0   2000

feet

Miami and Erie Towpath Trail, Deep Cut to Bloody Bridge

Hiking distance: 5.3 miles one way

Estimated hiking time: 2.5 hours

Follow a scenic and historic route along an old canal towpath.

Caution: The trail is out in the open, so wear sun protection in the summer.

Trail directions: Park in the Deep Cut Historical Park at N 40° 41.042, W 84° 21.559 (1). This park is on State Route 66 below Spencerville on the Auglaize-Allen county line. The park is a former roadside rest stop that is now administered by the Johnny Appleseed Metropark system in Lima. The park has informational plaques, picnic tables, and a shelter, but no water or restrooms are available here. The park gets its name from the 6,600-foot-long excavation made here when building the canal. This trench ranged from 5 to 52 feet in depth and cut through a ridge separating the Auglaize and St. Marys River watersheds.

Walk south on the edge of the park overlooking the water for 0.3 mile and cross a bridge over the canal at N 40° 40.558, W 84° 21.582 (2). Meet the towpath here and turn left to the south. This route is also part of the Buckeye and North Country Trails, but you will hardly need the blazing in order to follow the well-defined towpath. Cross the canal again after about a mile, and after 2.2 miles, you'll come to the village of Kossuth. The trail crosses State Route 197 at the Zion Methodist Church at N 40° 39.315, W 84° 21.003 (3). Below here, the canal is kept watered and is canoeable.

After another 1.5 miles of level towpath, the trail crosses the Six Mile Creek aqueduct at N 40° 37.349, W 84° 20.501 (4). This well-preserved aqueduct right next to State Route

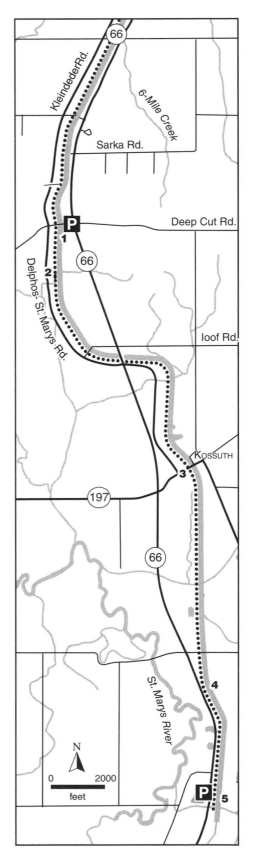

1. Deep Cut lot
2. Cross bridge
3. Cross SR 197 in Kossuth
4. Six-mile aqueduct
5. Bloody Bridge lot

66 was built to drain excess canal water into Six Mile Creek below. A newer bridge takes you across the aqueduct. After going another 0.7 mile below the aqueduct, you'll come to Bloody Bridge at N 40° 37.048, W 84° 21.096 (5). A small parking lot is located at the bridge, along with a plaque explaining how the bridge got its name. According to this plaque, during the canal's busiest era in 1854, a woman named Minnie Warren had to choose between two suitors. After she had made her choice, the loser confronted the couple on this bridge and decapitated his rival; then Minnie fell off the bridge and drowned.

Hikers can leave a second car here or return to Deep Cut for a 10.6-mile round trip hike. Other attractions to the south also offer various hiking options. Just below Bloody Bridge, the towpath crosses Route 66 again and goes on to Lock 14 and Forty Acre Pond before reaching St. Marys. Although the Ohio Department of Natural Resources has responsibility for all former canal lands, many other local agencies have cooperated in enhancing this trail.

> Enjoy a secluded hike in an uncrowded part of the state.

> Stroll along a couple of pristine smaller lakes.

Area Information

Mt. Gilead State Park is a quiet gem that is easy to get to. This tiny 181-acre park is centered around a 32-acre man-made lake that permits electric motors only. The park, located just outside the tiny county seat of Morrow County, lies between Routes 42 and 95.

This area north of central Ohio is where three glacial moraines converged and created some pretty rolling hills. The forest in the park today is second-growth beech and maple. Among the wildflowers found here are geranium, hepatica, trillium, and bloodroot. And the trees are filled with songbirds. Other wildlife includes skunks, raccoon, and white-tailed deer.

The first section of the two-part lake was made when a dam was built in 1930, and the larger lower lake was created when the tributary of Whetstone Creek was dammed further. This new lake area was turned over to the state in 1949 for use as a state park. The lakes occupy 32 acres and are stocked with bass and bluegill. Canoes, rowboats, and electric motors are the only boats permitted. There is no swimming allowed.

The campground at Mt. Gilead contains 59 electric sites that include fire rings, picnic tables, and latrines. It also contains a playground, a 200-seat amphitheater, and a camp store stocked with amenities and conveniences. A group camp on the site can serve up to 50 people, and two deluxe camper cabins are available in the warmer months. Volleyball, horseshoes, shuffleboard, disc golf, and basketball facilities are available. All forms of winter recreation are also available when weather permits. The park offers nature programs and special events as well as five picnic areas and three picnic shelters. The park's seven marked hiking trails range from 0.3 to 1.7 miles in length.

Directions: Mt. Gilead State Park is located less than a mile from the junction of State Routes 42 and 95 in downtown Mt. Gilead. Take Route 95 east and watch for signs.

Facilities: For such a small park, Mt. Gilead offers a surprisingly full range of options.

Hours open: The park is open year-round in daylight hours.

Rules and permits: Hunting and swimming are not permitted. Pets are allowed at designated sites.

Contact information: The park is located at 4119 State Route 95, Mt. Gilead, Ohio 43338; however, it is administered from Alum Creek State Park, whose mailing address is 3615 South Old State Road, Delaware, Ohio 43015. The phone number is 419-946-1961.

Other Areas of Interest

Kokosing Lake and Knox Lake Wildlife Area are located to the east in Knox County.

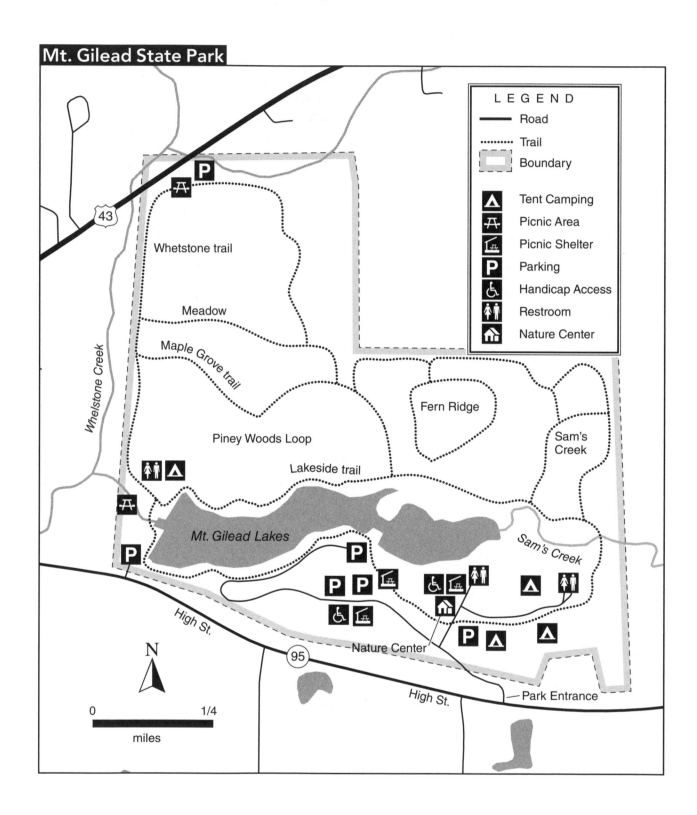

Mt. Gilead State Park

LEGEND

——	Road
········	Trail
⬚	Boundary
⛺	Tent Camping
🪑	Picnic Area
🏚	Picnic Shelter
P	Parking
♿	Handicap Access
🚻	Restroom
🏠	Nature Center

Whetstone trail

Meadow

Maple Grove trail

Piney Woods Loop

Fern Ridge

Sam's Creek

Lakeside trail

Mt. Gilead Lakes

Whelstone Creek

Sam's Creek

High St.

95

High St.

Nature Center

Park Entrance

43

N

0   1/4

miles

Lakeside Trail

Hiking distance: 1.7 miles

Estimated hiking time: 1 hour 15 minutes

Take a hike around a lake in a smaller, quieter, and more secluded state park.

Caution: Hikers may encounter some muddy hillsides in wet weather.

Trail directions: From the junction of State Routes 42 and 95 in Mt. Gilead, take 95 east for a half mile to the first (and lesser used) park entrance. Park in the small lot near the lower lake dam at N 40° 32.542, W 82° 49.071 (1). Go down a hill through a meadow to the spot below the dam where a bridge crosses Whetstone Creek at N 40° 32.599, W 82° 48.478 (2). On the other side, you'll come to a turnoff for the Maple Grove Trail, but you should veer right and continue to follow the shoreline.

Just past the end of the dam, you will come to a turnoff for the Piney Woods Loop Trail at N 40° 32.590, W 92° 48.584 (3). Ignore those blue blazes and stay to the right on the white-blazed Lakeside Trail, which soon climbs steadily. The lake remains in view, and soon you can see the dam that separates the lower and upper lakes. In about 0.4 mile, the trail passes the other end of the Piney Woods Loop Trail at N 40° 32.598, W 82° 48.414 (4). Stay on the Lakeside Trail past the red-blazed turnoff for the Fern Ridge Trail and keep going toward the end of the lake.

After nearly 0.5 mile, the trail is following a feeder stream. After a turnoff for the Sam's Creek Trail, the Lakeside Trail turns right and crosses a wooden footbridge at N 40° 32.535, W 83° 48.210 (5). Enjoy the streamside views here and then climb a steep hill that ends at the campground restrooms at N 40° 32.521, W 82° 48.260 (6). From here, follow the main campground road back to the main camp store at N 40° 32.500, W 82° 48.368 (7). Turn right here and follow the road past the amphitheater and nature center lot, where the trail leaves the road and descends into the woods.

In about 0.3 mile, the trail comes out at the parking lot for the upper lake dam at N 40° 32.558, W 82° 48.465 (8). Enjoy this quiet spot and walk out onto the dam, noting the contrast between the two small lakes. From here, continue to follow the shoreline, which is paralleled by a park road. Continue along the shores of the lower lake until you return to point 1.

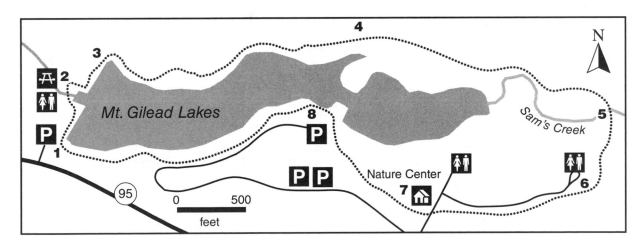

1. Lower-dam lot
2. Bridge
3. Junction
4. Junction
5. Footbridge
6. Climb to campground
7. Camp store and nature center
8. Upper-dam lot

> See sand dunes in the middle of Ohio farm country.

> Visit a preserve that is home to more endangered plant species than any other place in the state.

> Walk along the ancient shores of Lake Erie.

Area Information

Oak Openings Preserve is easily the most impressive of the 12 parks in the Toledo Metroparks system. Not only does this preserve include 4,000 of the 10,000 total acres of the system, but it is also home to more than 1,000 plant species. And not only does it host more endangered plant species than any other place in Ohio, but it is also a paradise for birders.

This diversity is the result of a unique set of circumstances. The Oak Openings is actually the name for a narrow 25-mile-long region of Lucas, Fulton, and Henry Counties. This region formed the western shore of Lake Warren, the ancient precursor to Lake Erie. Beneath this layer of soil, which ranges in depth from a few inches to 20 feet, is a clay that water cannot penetrate. This has resulted in a locale that is friendly to both sand dunes and swamps—along with the diversity of wildlife that they both attract. Oak Openings is also where the western prairie meets the eastern forest, which further contributes to this diversity.

The name Oak Openings comes from the open spaces beneath the broad oak trees that now dominate the landscape. The current preserve covers only a portion of the original area, but it has much to offer the outdoors enthusiast. For one thing, hikers can enjoy the 17-mile backpack loop that encircles the preserve. Several other shorter trails—often meeting at the Buehner Nature Center—are located in the center of the park. And the Wabash Cannonball and North Country Trails also run through the park.

Directions: From the west side of Toledo, take State Route 2 from exit 8 of Interstate 475. Go west 8 miles and turn left onto State Route 295; in 0.4 mile, bear right on Wilkins Road. Continue south for 2.4 miles to Oak Openings Parkway, then go right for about 0.3 mile to the Buehner Nature Center.

Hours open: The park is open daily during daylight hours.

Facilities: There is no camping in the park, but two private campgrounds are nearby. Water is available at the Springbrook and White Oak picnic areas on the backpack trail. The Buehner Nature Center offers interactive displays and events as well as public restrooms.

Rules and permits: Pets must be on a leash.

Contact information: The address for Oak Openings Preserve Metropark is 4139 Birdhorn Road, Swanton, Ohio, 43558; the phone number is 419-826-6463. You can also find information online at www.metroparkstoledo.com.

Park Trails

In addition to the trail used for the hike described here, the preserve also contains the following trails:

Ridge Trail
(silver blazes), 3.1 miles

Horseshoe Lake Trail
(yellow blazes), 1.5 miles

Ferns and Lakes Trail
(blue blazes), 2.9 miles

Evergreen Trail
(orange blazes), 1.9 miles

Springbrook Lake Trail
(teal blazes), 1.0 mile

Evergreen Trail
(green blazes), 1.4 miles

Mallard Lake Loop
(aqua blazes), 0.6 mile

Other Areas of Interest

Maumee State Forest is just to the southwest. The other Toledo Metroparks are Bend View, Blue Creek Conservation Area, Fallen Timbers Battlefield, Farnsworth, Providence, Secor, Side Cut, Swan Creek Preserve, Wildwood Preserve, and the Toledo Botanical Garden.

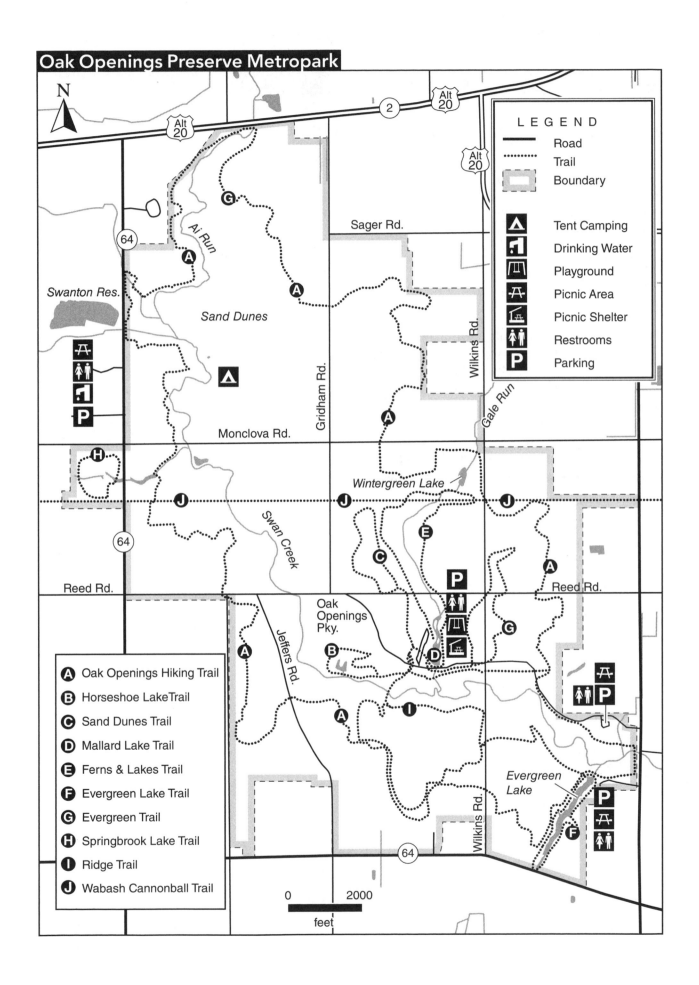

Oak Openings Preserve Metropark

LEGEND

——	Road
····	Trail
▭	Boundary
▲	Tent Camping
🚰	Drinking Water
🛝	Playground
🪑	Picnic Area
🏠	Picnic Shelter
🚻	Restrooms
P	Parking

Ⓐ Oak Openings Hiking Trail

Ⓑ Horseshoe Lake Trail

Ⓒ Sand Dunes Trail

Ⓓ Mallard Lake Trail

Ⓔ Ferns & Lakes Trail

Ⓕ Evergreen Lake Trail

Ⓖ Evergreen Trail

Ⓗ Springbrook Lake Trail

Ⓘ Ridge Trail

Ⓙ Wabash Cannonball Trail

Swanton Res.

Sand Dunes

Sager Rd.

Gridham Rd.

Monclova Rd.

Wilkins Rd.

Gale Run

Wintergreen Lake

Ai Run

Swan Creek

Reed Rd.

Reed Rd.

Oak Openings Pky.

Jeffers Rd.

Wilkins Rd.

Evergreen Lake

0   2000

feet

Sand Dunes Trail

Hiking distance: 1.9 miles round trip

Estimated hiking time: 1 hour

Hike where the western prairie meets the eastern forest and view Ohio's only inland sand dunes.

Caution: Being an urban park, Oak Openings can be crowded. Also, because the park is located so close to the Toledo Airport, the noise can be disruptive.

Trail directions: Park at the Buehner Nature Center at N 41° 32.706, W 83° 50.716 (1). This nature center has exhibits and displays about the wildlife in the park, and it is the trailhead for several of the shorter hikes in the park. The Sand Dunes Trail is marked by red signs and begins just west of the center. Go into a white pine forest and proceed 0.3 mile. At this point, the trail crosses a paved road at N 41° 32.956, W 83° 50.716 (2). Cross this all-purpose road and go another 0.2 mile to where the trail is briefly concurrent with the paved route at N 41° 32.978, W 83° 50.940 (3). The trail often crosses this bike path and other trails, but red signs and arrows always mark the Sand Dunes Trail.

Proceed another 0.3 mile; sand dunes begin to appear right before you cross the paved road at N 41° 33.196, W 83° 51.055 (4). Over the next 0.2 mile, you'll encounter short side trails that lead to Ohio's only inland sand dunes. During the glacial epoch, Lake Erie was much larger than it is now, and these dunes mark the western shore of that era. At 1.0 mile, the trail crosses the all-purpose paved road and begins to loop back at N 41° 33.341, W 83° 51.057 (5). Proceed on the sandy and mowed path through the woods for 0.5 mile; the trail then reconnects with the outgoing loop at N 41° 32.993, W 83° 50.829 (6). Just afterward, you'll cross the road at point 2, and it is then 0.4 mile back to the Buehner Center at point 1.

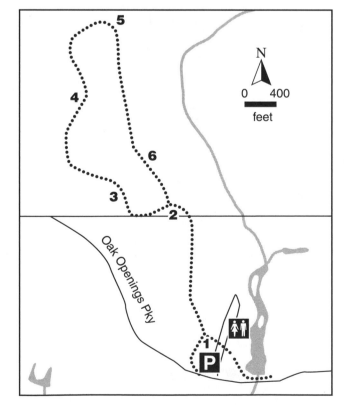

1. Nature center lot
2. Cross road
3. Meet paved route
4. Dune area
5. Turn back
6. Junction

> Hike along a scenic and canoeable river.

> View a wide variety of trees and wildflowers.

> Follow the same route used by messengers and troops during the War of 1812.

Area Information

The Sandusky County Park District maintains 11 facilities that cover 2,245 acres. Created in 1973, the park district is funded by a one mill property tax passed in 2007; additional funding comes from user fees, grants, and donations. Total park attendance is over 150,000 visitors per year.

One of the best attractions in the system is Wolf Creek Park along the shores of the Sandusky River. The park district leases this 93-acre site from the state, and the Buckeye Trail runs through it. This park includes two parking areas. The northern lot features a picnic area and canoe launch, while the southern lot has a primitive campground and a labeled nature trail. Wolf Creek Park also offers grills, water, a play area, and pit toilets—as well as a shelter that can be reserved.

The campground is open from April through December, and it contains 24 primitive sites with no water or electricity. Each site has a table and fire ring, but no firewood. Self-registration is at the campground entrance. Activities in the park and at the camp include hiking, fishing, canoeing, picnicking, birding, and cross-country skiing.

Directions: Both parking locations for Wolf Creek Park are just off of State Route 53 in southern Sandusky County.

Facilities: Wolf Creek Park has restrooms, picnic tables, picnic shelters, a campground, and a canoe launch.

Hours open: The park is open daily from 8 a.m. until dark.

Rules and permits: Campsites and shelters are available on a first come, first served basis.

Contact information: The address for the canoe launch is 2409 South Route 53, Fremont, Ohio 43420; and the campground is located at 2701 South Route 53 in Fremont. However, no one is on duty here. The park headquarters is located at 1970 Countryside Place, Fremont, Ohio 43420; the phone number is 419-334-4495.

Other Areas of Interest

Mull Covered Bridge, which is another Sandusky County Park location, is just across Route 53 from the southern entrance to the park.

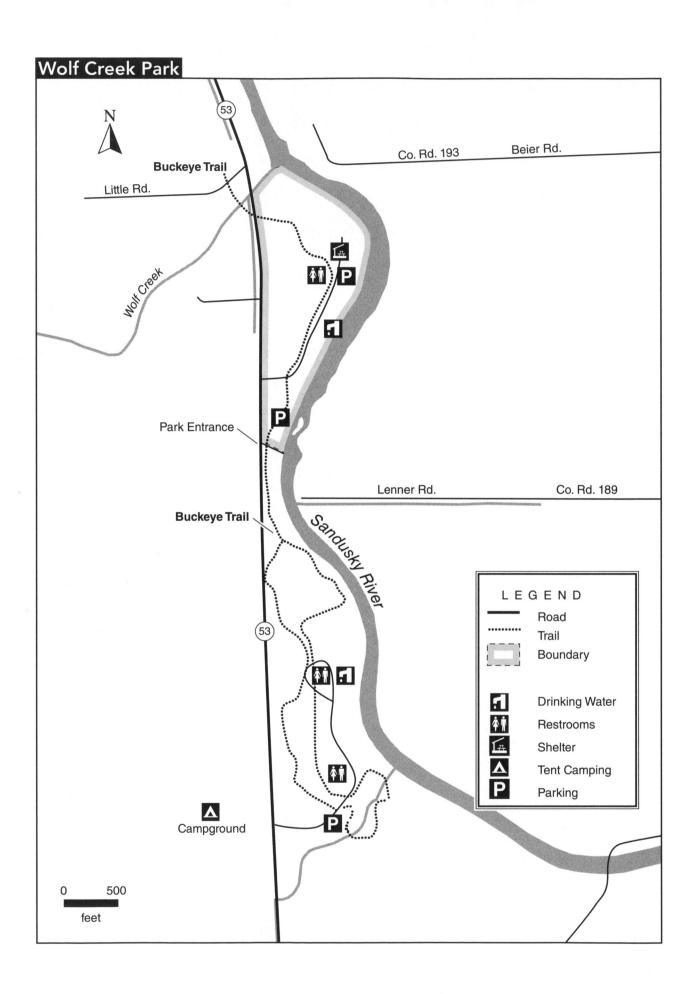

Wolf Creek Park

N

53

Buckeye Trail

Little Rd.

Co. Rd. 193   Beier Rd.

Wolf Creek

P

Park Entrance

Lenner Rd.   Co. Rd. 189

Buckeye Trail

Sandusky River

53

LEGEND

——— Road
.... Trail
Boundary

Drinking Water
Restrooms
Shelter
Tent Camping
Parking

Campground

0   500

feet

Wolf Creek Park, Buckeye Trail

Hiking distance: 3 miles round trip

Estimated hiking time: 1.5 hours

Take a walk in a park along a scenic river with historical overtones.

Caution: As is often the case along waterways, this trail can get muddy.

Trail directions: Wolf Creek Park is just off of State Route 53, 5 miles above the town of Fort Seneca and 5 miles south of the junction with State Route 6. Turn east into the northernmost of the two parking lots and veer left toward the restrooms at the end of the park road at N 41° 16.428, W 83° 09.574 (1). The Buckeye Trail enters the park here just after crossing Wolf Creek, and you will be on this trail for the entire hike.

Park in the lot here near the restrooms and follow the blue blazes back along the park road, passing several picnic areas and a kiosk. After 0.3 mile, you will come to the park entrance sign, and a canoe launch area is on the left at N 41° 16.288, W 83° 10.047 (2). The Sandusky is a wide but shallow river at this point, and this is a good spot to launch a canoe. The trail leaves the lot here on a mowed path in the narrow strip between the highway and the river.

Follow the marked route south along the Sandusky River. This is a good time to note some of the vagaries of Ohio geography—such as the fact that Upper Sandusky is south of Sandusky, and neither town is in Sandusky County. But this river did serve an important role as a supply route between American forts during the War of 1812. When troops at Fort Stephenson, just 10 miles north of here in Fremont, were turning back an attack despite being outnumbered by 20 to 1, General William Henry Harrison's headquarters was just below here at Fort Seneca. Fort Seneca is where Commodore Oliver Hazard Perry—after defeating the British fleet on Lake Erie—sent his famous message, "We have met the enemy and they are ours."

After about 0.4 mile, the trail splits at the beginning of a nature trail at N 41° 16.168, W 83° 10.044 (3). The left fork follows nearer to the river, but the right path is dryer and follows the Buckeye Trail. Both trails reconnect near the campground, so either is acceptable. Along both routes are signs that mark the trees found in the park, such as mulberry, hackberry, oak, tulip poplar, walnut, and box elder. Many wildflowers are also found here, including trout lily, bloodroot, toothwort, wingstem, and jewelweed.

After another 0.4 mile, the trails reunite briefly and come to the edge of a campground at N 41° 16.049, W 83° 10.019 (4). At this spot, you'll find restrooms and a park road that leads back to the highway. The Buckeye Trail forks off to the right and reenters the woods. In another 0.4 mile, the trail crosses the main park road at N 41° 15.512, W 83° 09.588 (5). The Buckeye Trail continues south into Seneca County, but here at the southern end of Wolf Creek Park, you will come to a parking lot and restrooms. You should leave a second car here if you have one, or you can turn around and retrace the route back to point 1.

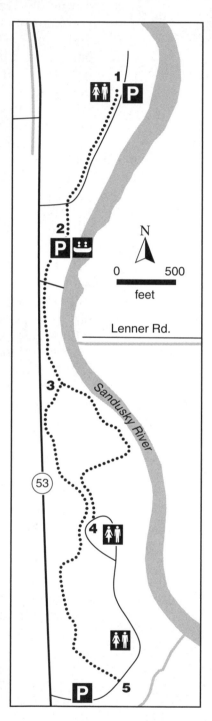

1. Lot
2. Canoe launch
3. Trail split
4. Campground
5. Road

> Visit a variety of parks that include riverfront parks, preserves, and even a battlefield.
> See the variety of wildlife found in swamps, prairies, rivers, and Great Lakes.
> View rare natural sights near a major metropolitan area.

Area Information

The 12 parks that make up the Metroparks of the Toledo area are a diverse lot. Five of these parks are right along the mighty Maumee River, three are labeled preserves, and one is a battlefield site. The parks contain over 10,000 acres, but 4,000 of that total is in the Oak Openings Region, a park so large and diverse that it is covered separately in this section. A visitor center is located in the Wildwood Preserve near the park system headquarters. Within the system, nearly a third of the rare plant species in Ohio can be found, and the park system also contains one of the few places in the state where you will find sand dunes.

Among the riverfront parks, Bend View is unique because this small area can be accessed only by human power. This park is located on a broad bend of the Maumee and offers sweeping views of both upstream and downstream from the shelter. Located along the Towpath Trail between the Farnsworth and Providence Metroparks, this park—and the view it provides—can be reached only by walking or bicycling at least 3 miles round trip from any parking lot. The Providence Metropark also offers tours of an 1846 mill and a canal boat ride that passes through a working lock.

Another unique park in the system is Fallen Timbers, the site of an important battle in 1794. A coalition of several tribes headquartered in northwest Ohio stymied American plans to settle Ohio in the 1790s. They defeated armies near Fort Wayne in 1790 and Fort Recovery

View of the Maumee River from Farnsworth Metropark.

(in Darke County) in 1791. Anthony Wayne was named commander of the American army, and after extensive training, his army advanced on Indian territory and proceeded up the Maumee, where they defeated an Indian attack on August 20, 1794. The battle showed for the first time that the new country could forge an army to be reckoned with, and it made Ohio safe for settlement. For the Native Americans, this battle marked the beginning of nearly a century of steady defeats at the hands of the army. A park and a statue mark the spot of this important battle.

Directions: The Metroparks system includes a dozen parks all over Lucas County.

Facilities: Many special programs and events are provided at various locations in the system. All parks have restrooms, and several have unique features such as a visitor center or boat rides.

Rules and permits: Individual regulations are posted at most parks.

Contact information: The park administrative offices are in the Manor House at Wildwood Preserve. The mailing address is 5100 West Central Avenue, Toledo, Ohio 43615; the phone number is 419-407-9700.

Other Areas of Interest

Crane Creek State Park is located at the eastern tip of Lucas County on the shores of Lake Erie. Maumee State Forest and Mary Jane Thurston State Park are located to the west, just outside the county borders. For history buffs, Fort Meigs, a rebuilt War of 1812 fort and battle site, sits at the head of the Maumee Rapids on the south shore of the Maumee in Perrysburg.

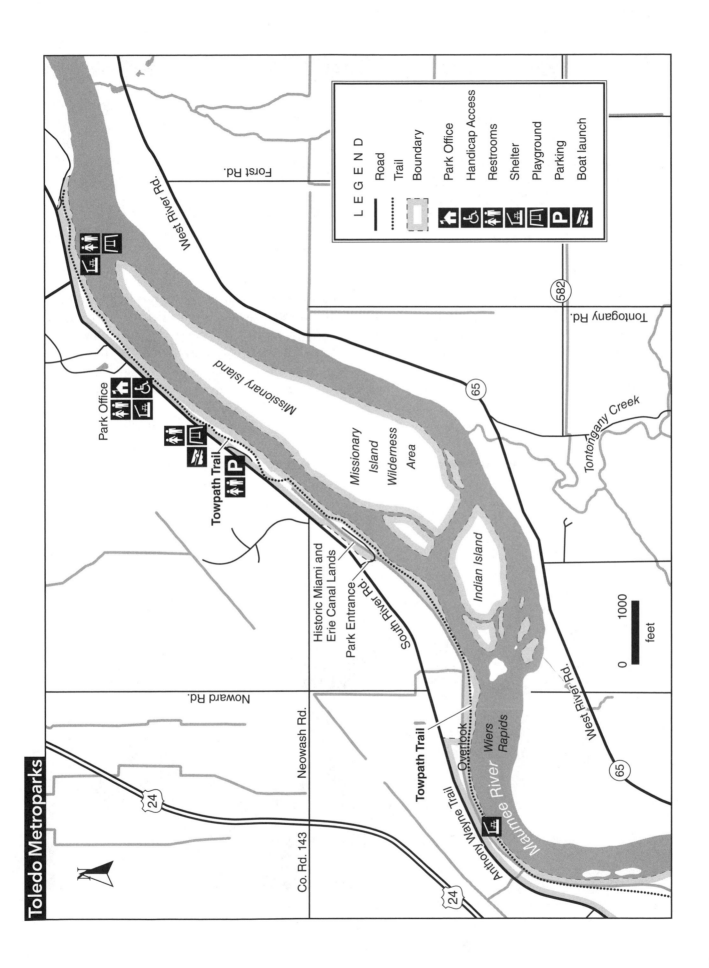

Toledo Metroparks

Farnsworth to Bend View Metroparks

 Hiking distance: 6.8 miles round trip

Estimated hiking time: 3 hours

Hike a historic stretch of a scenic river to a beautiful spot that is accessible only by foot or by bicycle.

Caution: Watch out for bicyclists.

Trail directions: Farnsworth Metropark is on the northern shore of the Maumee River near the town of Waterville. From the Route 24 exit of Interstate 475, take 24 west for 5 miles, turn left at the park sign, and park at the Roche de Bout shelter at N 41° 29.127, W 83° 44.071 (1). Roche de Bout is a large limestone outcropping in the Maumee that has been a known landmark since French fur traders began naming things here in the early 1700s. The spot was used as an Indian meeting location, and in 1908, the rock became part of the foundation for the Waterville Electric Bridge on the interurban line. A trail leads 0.3 mile to a platform offering a close-up overlook of the now abandoned bridge.

Restrooms are provided at the shelter here, and there is a platform overlooking the river. A plaque also notes that this was the location of Fort Deposit, an armed camp built by Anthony Wayne's army to store supplies on the eve of the Battle of Fallen Timbers in 1794. Two previous American armies had been defeated by a tribal coalition headquartered near here, and Wayne wanted his army to travel light. The successful battle the next day lasted less than one hour but had international ramifications, because it showed that the army of the new nation could protect and expand its borders.

▌ Roche de Bout in Farnsworth Metropark is a spot with a rich history.

Within a year after Fallen Timbers, separate U.S. treaties resulted in the British abandoning Detroit and other Great Lakes forts, the Spanish at New Orleans allowing Americans to use the Mississippi for shipping, and the tribal coalition permitting most of Ohio to be open for settlement. None of this would have been possible without the military victory on the Maumee.

From this shelter, go 0.6 mile and you'll come to the Indianola Shelter at N 41° 28.573, W 83° 44.372 (2). Opposite the trail here, you can see several large islands that are part of the Missionary Island Wildlife Area, which includes some prehistoric Indian sites. Restrooms and a separate parking lot are located at the shelter. Another 0.5 mile upstream, you'll come to the boat launch and towpath trailhead lot at N 41° 28.380, W 83° 44.558 (3). The restrooms here are at the beginning of an 8-mile towpath trail that runs to Providence Metropark. This route is also part of the Buckeye Trail.

Follow the well-marked towpath trail for 0.3 mile and you'll come to a bat box on a high pole at N 41° 28.275, W 83° 45.075 (4). This spot also has a shelter overlooking the river, one of three along the route. For the next 0.3 mile, the trail is bordered by private property on both sides, until it crosses a road at N 41° 28.119, W 83° 45.248 (5). Now the trail follows along the river through a forest of maple, sycamore, basswood, hackberry, and cottonwood. Benches overlooking the river along the way make it easier to observe the shorebirds, herons, osprey, and even eagles that fish these waters. The shallow river here makes for good fishing and also offers the soothing sound of rapids.

In 1.3 miles, the trail leaves Farnsworth Metropark and enters Bend View Metropark at N 41° 27.533, W 83° 46.265 (6). In another 0.3 mile, you'll reach the Bend View Shelter at N 41° 27.468, W 83° 46.429 (7). Here, at a remote spot accessible only to the nonmotorized, you can enjoy a broad view overlooking a sharp bend in the Maumee. Visitors can see for a long way both upstream and downstream from here, and the reservable shelter at this spot also has restrooms. Even though Route 24 may be heard in the background, this is a serene spot.

The towpath trail continues on to Providence Metropark. Highlights of this park include Ludwig Mill, dating from 1846, and a canal boat that takes visitors through a working lock. The Buckeye Trail crosses the river here and passes through the charmingly restored canal town of Grand Rapids before heading on to Mary Jane Thurston State Park. Hikers can continue on to these spots if they have a second car to spot there, or they can turn back and retrace the route back to point 1.

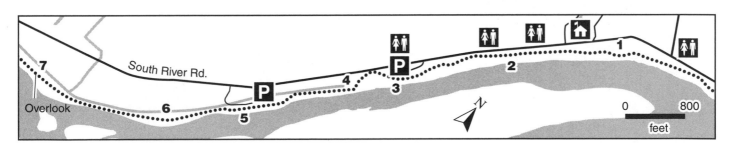

1. Roche de Bout shelter
2. Shelter
3. Trailhead/boat launch
4. Bat box
5. Cross road
6. Enter Bend View Metropark
7. Bend View shelter

Appendix

Ohio's Best Hikes by Category

For those hikers with special interests, here is a list of some hikes by category. Many hikers seek particular pleasures or challenges, and this guide addresses many of these interests. These are not ranked top ten lists, as they are not in order, although the first in each list is a personal favorite.

10 Hikes That Lead to Waterfalls

Three Waterfalls Hike, Cuyahoga Valley National Park

Glen Helen Nature Preserve

Charleston Falls Preserve, Miami County Parks

Mohican State Park

Grandma Gatewood Trail, Hocking Hills State Park

Tinker's Creek Gorge, Cleveland Metroparks

Englewood Preserve Metropark, Five Rivers Metroparks

Lake Katherine State Nature Preserve

Ash Cave, Hocking Hills State Park

Boord State Nature Preserve

10 Hikes With the Best Views

Rim Trail, Conkle's Hollow State Nature Preserve

Kelley's Island State Park

Shawnee Lookout Park, Hamilton County Park District

Raven Rock State Nature Preserve

Buzzardroost Rock Trail, Edge of Appalachia Preserve

Ledges Trail, Cuyahoga Valley National Park

Chapin Forest, Buckeye Trail—Lake County Metroparks

Malabar Farm State Park (Mt. Jeez)

Burr Oak State Park

Bend View Metropark, Toledo Metroparks

10 Most Difficult Hikes

Archer's Fork Loop, Wayne National Forest (Marietta Unit)

Shawnee State Forest

Buzzardroost Rock Trail, Edge of Appalachia Preserve

Vesuvius Backpack and Lakeshore Trail, Wayne National Forest (Ironton Unit)

Hocking State Forest

Three Waterfalls Hike, Cuyahoga Valley National Park

West Branch State Park

Salt Fork State Park

Covered Bridge Trail, Wayne National Forest (Marietta Unit)

Wildcat Hollow Backpack Trail, Wayne National Forest (Athens Unit)

10 Hikes With Handicap Access

Gorge Trail, Conkle's Hollow State Nature Preserve

Ash Cave, Hocking Hills State Park

Interpretive Trail, Flint Ridge State Memorial

Boardwalk Trail, Maumee Bay State Park

Serpent Mound State Memorial

Little Miami Scenic Trail, Fort Ancient State Memorial

Blackhand Gorge State Nature Preserve

Ohio and Erie Canal Corridor

Miami and Erie Canal Corridor

Farnsworth to Bend View Metroparks, Toledo Metroparks

10 Hikes With Unique Natural Features

Dysart Woods Outdoor Laboratory

Dunes Trail, Oak Openings Preserve Metropark (Toledo Metroparks)

Lynx Prairie Trail, Edge of Appalachia Preserve

Clifton Gorge State Nature Preserve—John Bryan State Park

Three Waterfalls Hike, Cuyahoga Valley National Park

Butterfly Habitat Trail, the Wilds

Rockbridge State Nature Preserve

Archer's Fork Loop, Wayne National Forest (Marietta Unit)

Glacial Grooves State Memorial, Kelley's Island State Park

Grandma Gatewood Trail, Hocking Hills State Park

10 Hikes With Connections to Native Americans and Mound Builders

Serpent Mound State Memorial

Fort Hill State Memorial

Fort Ancient State Memorial

Miami Fort Trail, Shawnee Lookout Park (Hamilton County Park District)

Highbanks Metro Park, Columbus Metro Parks

Flint Ridge State Memorial

Blackhand Gorge State Nature Preserve

Raven Rock State Nature Preserve

Piqua Historical Area

Farnsworth Metropark, Toledo Metroparks

10 Hikes That Connect With Backpacking Trails

Brush Ridge Trail, Tar Hollow State Park

Olds Hollow Trail, Lake Hope State Park

Wildcat Hollow and Burr Oak State Park

Vesuvius Backpack and Lakeshore Trail, Wayne National Forest (Ironton Unit)

Shawnee State Forest

East Fork State Park

Archer's Fork Loop, Wayne National Forest (Marietta Unit)

Oak Openings Preserve Metropark, Toledo Metroparks

Miami and Erie Canal Corridor

Ohio and Erie Canal Corridor

10 Streams With Hiking Trails Alongside Them

Maumee River

Auglaize River

Sandusky River

Tuscarawas River

Mohican River

Cuyahoga River

Beaver Creek

Licking River

Miami River

Little Miami River

10 Parks That Feature Nature Centers

Magee Marsh Wildlife Area

Maumee Bay State Park

Oak Openings Preserve Metropark, Toledo Metroparks

East Fork State Park

Caesar Creek State Park

Shawnee State Forest

Glen Helen Nature Preserve

Englewood Metropark, Five Rivers Metroparks

Highbanks Metro Park, Columbus Metro Parks

Hocking Hills State Park

10 Hikes With Historical and Other Museums

Eden Park, Cincinnati Parks

Serpent Mound State Memorial

Kelley's Island State Park

Fort Ancient State Memorial

Fort Hill State Memorial

Piqua Historical Area

Malabar Farm State Park

Fort Laurens State Memorial

Kennedy Stone House Trail, Salt Fork State Park

Flint Ridge State Memorial

About the Author

Gary S. Williams is a lifelong Ohioan and hiker. Since 1987, he has been actively involved with the Buckeye Trail Association, an all-volunteer group that builds, maintains, and promotes a 1,444 mile hiking trail that loops around Ohio. Within the association, he has served on the board of trustees, as columnist and editor of the organization's *Trailblazer* newsletter, as head of publicity, and as a member of the Trail Crew and a section supervisor for a 50 mile section of the Buckeye Trail.

You'll find other outstanding outdoor sports resources at

www.HumanKinetics.com/outdoorsports

In the U.S. call 1-800-747-4457

Australia 08 8372 0999 • Canada 1-800-465-7301
Europe +44 (0) 113 255 5665 • New Zealand 0800 222 062

 HUMAN KINETICS
The Premier Publisher for Sports & Fitness
P.O. Box 5076 • Champaign, IL 61825-5076 USA

 eBook
available at
HumanKinetics.com